W9-DDT-842

DISCARD

ILLUSTRIOUS AMERICANS:

JANE ADDAMS

One of a series of books
about great men and women,
each studied in three ways

BIOGRAPHY
PICTURE PORTFOLIO
HER OWN WORDS

ILLUSTRIOUS AMERICANS:

JANE ADDAMS

By Marshall W. Fishwick
and the Editors of Silver Burdett

Editor in Charge: Sam Welles

SILVER BURDETT COMPANY
A Division of General Learning Corporation
Morristown, New Jersey • Park Ridge, Ill. • Palo Alto • Dallas • Atlanta

CONTENTS

BIOGRAPHY 7

1 American Roots 8

2 The Start of a Midwestern Flowering 21

3 Woman Caught Between Two Worlds 31

4 From Dreams to Inhabiting Reality 41

5 Old Battles in a New Century 55

6 Great Stresses of War and Peace 66

7 Perseverance and Final Victory 79

LIBRARY OF CONGRESS CATALOG CARD NUMBER: 67-15875

PRINTED IN THE UNITED STATES OF AMERICA

PUBLISHED SIMULTANEOUSLY IN CANADA

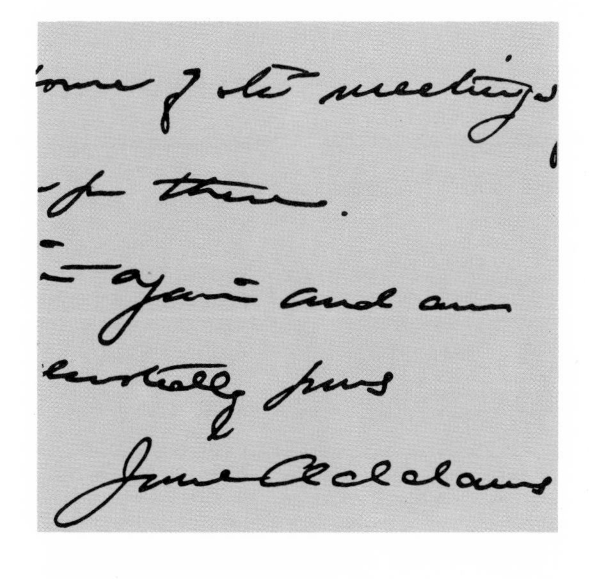

PICTURE PORTFOLIO 89

Child of a Victorian Midwest 90

Woman Adrift in Europe 92

From Riches to the Ragged 98

The Urban Poor 106

Social and Political Reforms 108

A Pragmatic Pacifist 110

Concerns for All Humanity 114

Her Legacy to the World 116

Her Legacy to Hull-House 118

HER OWN WORDS 121

A Model Father 122

From the Idea to the Deed 136

Chicago's King Lear 157

The Influence of Tolstoy 164

Her Political Role 185

Crusading for Peace 198

The Summing Up 221

Chronology 230

Annotated Bibliography 232

Index 235

Picture Credits 240

ACKNOWLEDGMENTS

The biography section of this book was written by Marshall W. Fishwick, Director of the Wemyss Foundation and of the American Studies Institute at Lincoln University, where he teaches. Dr. Fishwick took his Ph.D. at Yale, has lectured at many universities at home and abroad, and is a specialist in the history and culture of the United States. He edited *American Studies in Transition,* and has written eight books, including *American Heroes: Myth and Reality* and *Clara Barton* (an earlier volume in this series). His articles have appeared in various magazines and learned journals.

The editors have prepared the boxed observations on Jane Addams, selected the illustrations, and excerpted about 60,000 words that Miss Addams herself wrote, with a commentary placing each passage in a meaningful context.

Permission to quote from the unpublished Jane Addams Papers was granted by Swarthmore College. Excerpts from the following published sources have also been used with permission: *Twenty Years at Hull-House,* by Jane Addams. Reprinted with permission of The Macmillan Company. Copyright 1910 by The Macmillan Company, renewed 1938 by James W. Linn. *The Second Twenty Years at Hull-House,* by Jane Addams. Reprinted with permission of The Macmillan Company. Copyright 1930 by The Macmillan Company, renewed 1958 by John A. Brittain. *Peace and Bread in Time of War,* by Jane Addams, reprinted with permission of The Women's International League for Peace and Freedom. "The Social Deterrent of Our National Self-Righteousness, with Correctives Suggested by the Courageous Life of William Penn," by Jane Addams, reprinted with permission of *Survey Graphic.* "A Modern Lear," "Aspects of the Women's Movement," "A Toast to John Dewey," "Has the Emancipation Proclamation Been Nullified by National Indifference?"–all by Jane Addams, reprinted with permission of *The Survey.* "Why I shall Vote for La Follette," by Jane Addams, from *The New Republic,* September 10, 1924. "Tolstoy and Gandhi," by Jane Addams, copyright 1931 Christian Century Foundation. Reprinted by permission from November 25, 1931, issue of *The Christian Century.* From *Jane Addams: A Biography,* by James Weber Linn, by permission of Appleton-Century, affiliate of Meredith Press. Copyright, 1935, by D. Appleton-Century Company. *Exploring the Dangerous Trades: The Autobiography of Alice Hamilton,* reprinted with permission of Alice Hamilton. *And Crown Thy Good,* by Philip Davis, Philosophical Library, Inc., copyright 1952. *Counter-Currents,* by Agnes Repplier. Reprinted by permission of the publisher, Houghton Mifflin Company. *Beatrice Webb's American Diary: 1898,* David A. Shannon (ed.), 1963, the University of Wisconsin Press, reprinted with permission of the copyright owners, The Regents of the University of Wisconsin. "Grace Abbott of Hull-House, 1908-1921," by Edith Abbott, reprinted from *Social Service Review* by permission of the University of Chicago Press. Copyright 1950 by the University of Chicago.

Vincent Buranelli was senior editor for the volume. Henry Moscow wrote the text accompanying the Picture Portfolio. The picture research was done by Elizabeth Evans, and the text research by Denise Farrell and Judith Leavitt. Elizabeth Roberts and Mara Jayne Klein did the copy editing, and Louella Still Culligan prepared the index.

Designer: Wayne Young

Wisdom and experience shine through this portrait of Jane Addams, who was in her sixties when Lydia Lowry painted it.

BIOGRAPHY

Chapter 1 **AMERICAN ROOTS**

JANE ADDAMS was a country girl who reformed the big city. A native of rural Illinois in nineteenth-century mid-America, she went to booming, roaring Chicago, forged her lifework amid teeming streets and squalid tenements, and permanently changed the metropolis of her state. Only a genius could have done this. Jane Addams was a genius who, luckily, arrived on the scene at just the right moment to play her role in history. Between her birth in 1860 and her establishment of Hull-House in 1889, the United States, rising from the disaster of the Civil War, became a nation less and less agrarian, more and more urban. And Jane Addams imaginatively and energetically utilized the new urban environment, with its unsolved problems, to carry out the mission to which she dedicated herself.

That mission, based on individual effort, mutual help, peaceful reform, and faith in progress, placed her squarely in the American tradition—appropriately, for she had deep American roots. Her parents, John Huy Addams and Sarah (Weber) Addams, were originally from Pennsylvania, where their ancestors had lived since Colonial times. In 1681, William Penn had granted a tract of land in his new colony to an Englishman named Robert Adams, who crossed the Atlantic and became one of the earliest Pennsylvanians. He was joined by his brother Walter, progenitor of the line that produced Jane Addams. Walter's son Isaac (Jane's great-grandfather) seems to have been the first "Addams," adding the extra "d" apparently to avoid confusion with a relative of the same name. Isaac's son was Samuel Addams, and *his* son was John Huy Addams, the father of Jane Addams.

Born in 1822, John grew up in the rich farmlands close to the Pennsylvania Dutch country. Pious and hardworking, much concerned with personal salvation, John apprenticed himself to the owner of a flour mill on the Wissahickon Creek, soon developed the calloused and flattened "miller's-thumb," formed diligent habits that shaped his entire life, and developed a taste for books and ideas that he later passed on to his famous daughter. He also fell in love with Sarah Weber, a belle of Kreidersville, Pennsylvania, who had received a polished education in Philadelphia. Sarah, a keen-witted, personable girl "accomplished in music and drawing," reciprocated John's feelings. They were married in 1844.

Sarah's father, Colonel George Weber, an enterprising flour-mill owner, was descended from German immigrants who came to Philadelphia in 1727. Some of Colonel Weber's friends and relatives had migrated to Illinois; their reports of boundless opportunity in that rapidly growing region made him feel that young John Addams might make a success if he too headed west after his marriage to Sarah. In fact, the Colonel offered to travel with the newlyweds, evidently so that his expertise might be of assistance in the setting up of a new mill in the wilderness. John's father, Samuel Addams, was prosperous enough to provide four thousand dollars for the expedition, quite a handsome sum of money at a time when the average wage was only a few dollars a week—and one dollar went a long way.

"A two-wheeled conveyance"

So it happened that John Addams married Sarah Weber, and, as his diary puts it: "July 29, 1844. Myself and wife left Kreidersville at four a.m. in a two-wheeled conveyance." They would pick up Colonel Weber in New York City, and be on their way to Illinois. Following the frontier was nothing new for an Addams. John's great-grandfather had made the trip from England when "the frontier" was wherever Europeans could get a foothold on the Atlantic coast. His descendants took the rivers and Indian trails west, forgetting Old World customs and cottages, adapting to buckskin and log cabins. Like so many others, they pushed into the interior, mastering nature as they went but also being mastered by it.

This Chicago Historical Society print shows Indiana Quakers gathering for a meeting the year the Addamses moved west.

After the Revolution, the Northwest Territory—that broad basin between the Ohio River and the Mississippi—was the giant magnet luring men westward. Formerly it had been a domain of darkness, blocked off by the French, but known to have northern lakes spreading vast as a sea. Out beyond Pennsylvania, explorers said, were huge tracts, covered like a green rug by the great forest, pierced occasionally by deer or buffalo trails. Oak and maple, tulip and sycamore, beech and hickory covered the land. Then the woods ended. After that came two hundred and fifty miles of gently rolling plains, through which flowed rivers called Kaskaskia, Sangamon, and Illinois. The grass was so tall it bent and swayed like waves.

Studying the area on his maps, land-minded Thomas Jefferson drew tentative boundaries for fourteen new states. His suggested names—such as Cherronesus, Pelisipia, Sylvania, Assenisipia, and Polypotamia—combined native Indian words with classical Greek. Most of the names were far too complicated and soon forgotten; others, such as Illinoia and Michigania, were adapted with slight changes—but in any case the land was taken and loved. The pattern of immigration was set under the Jefferson, Madison, and Monroe administrations. Family farms, which these agrarian-minded Presidents insisted were the backbone of democracy, flourished.

Whooping and hollering men, who adopted nicknames like Buckeyes, Hoosiers, Badgers, Suckers, and Wolverines, poured into the region that was larger than all France, richer than fabled Cathay. In the fertile green fields they planted corn, wheat—and democracy. This land would feed their children's children, and people in far-off places. Here men of the new republic could stretch their muscles and imaginations, now that title to the rich farmlands had been cleared by a series of Indian treaties. The soil was waiting for the plow. Literature of the period reflected the spirit of the venture: "If you are willing to work at any honest business, for which your previous training has fitted you—if willing to join the great army, which, with the axe, the plough, and the steam engine, is striking out into the desert, and conquering an empire greater than was ever ruled by a Tamerlane or a Bonaparte—*come on!*"

In 1849, some doggerel in the Boston *Post* proclaimed:

"Come leave the fields of childhood
Worn out by long employ
And travel west and settle
In the state of Illinois."

Thousands of Easterners accepted this challenge to adventure, hardship, opportunity, and self-betterment. One man, especially, made the trek into the Midwest a national epic—Abraham Lincoln. Born in Kentucky in 1809, Lincoln was thirteen years older than John Addams. His parents took him to the Indiana woods when he was seven, and in 1830 the Lincolns continued farther west into Illinois, settling near the Sangamon River. Tall, gangling Abe eventually established himself in New Salem, where for six years he made a scanty living by managing a mill, keeping a store, and doing odd jobs. His skill in wrestling made him something of a frontier hero even before he took to law and politics. He was elected to the Illinois legislature in 1834 and married Mary Todd in 1842. Two years later, John Addams also wed and started west.

To northern Illinois

John, Sarah, and her father chose to go (via Albany and Buffalo) to the city named Chicago, from the Indian word meaning "wild onion." The Indians had roamed the area from time immemorial. Then Father Jacques Marquette and Louis Joliet arrived in 1673; these French explorers were the first white men to see the site on Lake Michigan that became Chicago. Pioneers, trappers, and traders came and went for another century, and, after the American Revolution, a permanent trading post arose. The United States formally took possession of Chicago with the erection of Fort Dearborn in 1803, but the garrison was massacred and the

Fort Dearborn symbolized American authority in the Chicago area after the Black Hawk War, but Indians still camped nearby.

fort burned during the War of 1812. Not until 1816 did more troops arrive to rebuild it. The area remained quiescent until the Black Hawk War of 1832, the result of which triggered a period of expansion. Twelve years after this war, the population numbered some eight thousand, the harbor had been deepened, the Illinois and Michigan Canal had been started, and Chicago had become a thriving emporium for traffic on the Great Lakes.

Such was the Chicago that greeted John Addams in 1844. He was not very impressed. Deep in mud, the business district, he noted in his diary, was "located entirely too low" for so sodden an area. The inhabitants appeared to be engaged mainly in mercantile business, and there were "in my opinion too many for the place." So the next day he bought a bay mare for $41, a "tolerably good" buggy and harness for $28, and kept moving west.

The road led into Stephenson county, one of the northern tiers in the state that had been established in 1818 as Illinois, and that still had to negotiate with the Indians for some of the territory within its boundaries. The new constitution placed major authority with the state legislature, leaving the judiciary and the governor somewhat at its mercy. There had been many financial and political problems, but Thomas Ford, elected governor in 1842, was a vigorous man who would, in his four-year term, reduce the state debt from $313,000 to $31,000. A census in 1845 placed Illinois's population at 662,150. The rich black soil, untouched for centuries, was ready for plow and seed. The rolling terrain—a mixture of prairie, forests, and lake bottom—seemed endless. Wheat, hay, oats, and corn would do wonderfully well here; it was a young miller's paradise.

So John Addams must have thought as he drove through the tall beardgrass spotted with such wild flowers as oxeyes, blazing stars, and purple patches of ironweed. In addition to the groves of oak and maple he observed pawpaw, wild plum, and crab apple. This was good country. It would become the heartland of a democracy stretching from one ocean to another. For three months John and Sarah Addams explored northern Illinois. Six miles north of Freeport, on the banks of the Cedar River, they found just what they wanted: a six-year-old sawmill and gristmill for sale with eighty acres of adjoining woodland. This was the place. John's first act after purchase was to plant Norway

LIKE FATHER, LIKE DAUGHTER

Miss Addams left all her papers to her nephew, James Weber Linn, who, in his perceptive biography of his aunt, observes that Jane and her father can be compared through the respective diaries that they kept at the age of twenty-two:

"The diary of this journey from Pennsylvania to Illinois, which John Addams kept for six months without the break of a day, many of the entries being made at considerable length, is of . . . historical interest. . . . The young Pennsylvanian was a shrewd observer of material things. But the personal interest of the diary is much more considerable than the historical. The record was intended for his own eyes only; indeed, until the little leather-bound volumes turned up in a 'secret drawer' of an old desk in the attic of the Addams homestead, full eighty-five years after they had been written, that record was probably seen by no other eye than his. And it is with himself, his own ambitions, uncertainties, exaltations and depressions of spirit, that he is . . . concerned.

"He reveals his eagerness for exact information, his caution as a bargainer, his determination not to be 'over-reached' as he determined never to over-reach; his industry, his endurance, his physical equability in temperament. It is curious to note how many of the entries conclude with an estimate of the day's feelings. Here are successive final lines from one week's entries in September, while he was waiting . . . in the hope that the owners of the mill he desired to buy might come to terms. 'So ended this day in tolerable spirits.' 'My spirits were however good to-day.' 'Upon the whole I was very much discouraged to-day.' 'This day spirits good.' 'I will endeavor to pray for better spirits.' 'Spirits to-day good while at work (he was helping to pick potatoes that day) but otherwise discouraged.' There is nothing precocious, or even mature, in such entries. Indeed when Jane Addams read them, for the first time, in her own old age, she was amazed. She had had no conception of her quiet father as qualmish in youth. The simplicity of the father's self-analyses is the more striking when they are compared to the similar diarial 'searchings after self-understandings' of the daughter at the same time of life—twenty-two. In a 'common-place book' dated 1882, the year after John Addams' death, and a gloomy year for Jane, she writes: 'The difficulty is not in bearing our ills, but in knowing what ills are necessary, not in doing what is right but in knowing what is right to do. I suppose to say that I do not know just what I believe is a form of cowardice, just going on trying to think things out instead of making up my mind, but then why am I happier when I am learning than when I am trying to decide? For I do not think there could be any happiness in being a coward.' The longing for self-understanding is the same, the souls of father and daughter dwelt in intimacy, but how different the approaches to self-knowledge! The difference is partly in the forms of their education, partly in the generations; the daughter was spiritually an inquirer, the father in many ways conventional; their wish however was the same, to possess and recognize the 'inner light.'"

pine trees on his new domain. He got to work, led the movement to construct a railroad through northern Illinois, and won a reputation as "the best-known man in the district." In 1854, he built a two-story gray brick house for his family. In this sturdy home, on September 6, 1860, his eighth child, Laura Jane, was born. She would carry the Addams name to every corner of the nation, and around the world.

A frail and sensitive child, Jane later described herself as "ugly," and placed the blame on the curvature of the spine from which she suffered. That description was scarcely justified. Early photographs show Jane as a dainty, winsome child with large, soft eyes, a meditative expression, and hair neatly parted in the middle—altogether an attractive figure. Her spinal condition obviously made her more withdrawn than she might otherwise have been, for, with the poignant intensity of the young, she exaggerated its effect on her appearance.

Absolute adoration

Jane had a happy childhood. She lived in a fine house over which presided a loving father who could afford to give his family the comforts of their period. John Addams worked, saved, profited from his integrity as a businessman, and acquired a bank in Freeport. Entering politics in 1854, he won eight successive elections to the Illinois legislature. He hated slavery, venerated Lincoln, and, although a Quaker, supported the Civil War, during which he encouraged enlistments so successfully that one company called itself the "Addams Guard." His interest in freedom was not restricted to

American Negroes. The events then convulsing Europe aroused in him a passionate desire for the destruction of the tyrannies to which so many nations were subjected. He took for his European hero Giuseppe Mazzini, the eloquent spokesman of the Italian *Risorgimento,* whose libertarian writings, widely admired outside his country, inspired his fellow Italians to struggle against Austrian and papal domination. Jane Addams never forgot the sorrow with which her father read of Mazzini's death in 1872.

Jane's older sisters, Alice and Mary, described their mother as an indomitable woman of realistic and pioneering spirit who had a strong influence on the family. Life had taught Mrs. Addams many hard lessons, and she passed some of them on. Jane barely remembered her, but what Alice, especially, related about their mother made a deep impression on the younger girl. Thus, Alice told Jane how she and her brother Weber had continued to play by the millrace—a dangerous thing to do—despite their mother's warning. Suddenly Mrs. Addams appeared and pushed the little lad into the water. Alice gazed in horror as her brother struggled helplessly. Mrs. Addams ran to a curve in the stream and fished him out as he was borne by the current to that spot. "There was no more careless playing by the millrace," Alice reported. Jane herself learned from her mother only at second hand, for she was but two years and four months old when Sarah Addams died only two weeks after the birth of a stillborn child, in the winter of 1863. This tragedy was a terrible blow to the family, especially to John Addams, bereft of the wife who had accompanied him west in 1844 and borne him nine children. The widower realized that he would have to have another woman in the house, yet he did not remarry for five years.

Meanwhile, during his daughter's formative years, he became for Jane the supreme inspiration for her life. In her own phrasing, her father was the "single cord" on which her memories of early life were strung—the cord that "not only held fast my supreme affection, but also first drew me into the moral concerns of life." She would never again meet a man who could arouse her utter and unalloyed admiration. Her memory as an adult validated her childhood conviction that he embodied everything good—love, kindness, wisdom, rectitude—and nothing bad. She responded to his affection with absolute adoration. Her greatest joy was to be with him, whether in the privacy of their home or on a stroll through the streets of Cedarville. Taking him as a model, she got up before dawn to read books because he had done so as a boy in Pennsylvania. She even rubbed her forefinger against her thumb in the hope that she would develop a miller's-thumb like his.

Yet it was his influence on her thinking, rather than on her daily schedule, that was pivotal. To him life was not a series of propositions to be debated, but an ideal of personal conduct to be followed. Although he contributed to every church in town, he joined none;

Mazzini (right) greets Garibaldi during the Italian revolt. The sign says "Young Italy," Mazzini's rallying cry.

he confessed to being a "Hicksite Quaker," and left it at that. Perhaps he considered the phrase self-explanatory, for the beliefs of the Hicksites were well known. The sect derived its name from Elias Hicks, a Long Islander who seceded from the main body of Friends because of a disagreement about theological principles. George Fox, the English founder of the Society, had preached both the Bible as a guide for all to follow and also the "inner light" as an individual guide. But subsequent Quaker leaders tended to stress one or the other of these two sources of religious truth. There were evangelical Quakers who relied principally on Scripture, and mystical Quakers for whom the "inner light" seemed sufficient. Both groups were represented among American Quakers, and they managed to maintain the unity of the movement until Elias Hicks began to preach the doctrine of the "inner light" so emphatically that he appeared to some Friends to be denying the authority of the Bible. The elders in Philadelphia tried to silence him. He in turn led his followers out of the orthodox fold in 1827.

The Hicksite Quakers developed their concept of the "inner light" into a creed that committed them to personal integrity, charity toward others, religious toleration, and democracy in church and state. This, then, was the religion to which John Addams subscribed. He set great store by the Bible, which he taught to the local children who came to Sunday School, but he was above all a man of the "inner light." Stoic in his insistence on self-dependence, he drummed this idea into Jane's head: "You must always be honest with yourself inside, whatever happens." In her fifties she referred to her father's counsel about truth and morality as "perhaps on the whole as valuable a lesson as the shorter catechism itself contains."

A favorite childhood haunt of Jane's was the flour mill, full of dusty, dusky corners and

A Quaker meeting waits silently for some "sign" from the "inner light." Members of the Society of Friends wore plain garb, used "thee" and "thou" for "you," and were active in most of the nineteenth century's humanitarian movements.

empty bins in which to romp. The piles of bran and shorts were as good as sand to play in—especially when the miller let her wet the edges of the pile with water carried in from the mill-race. A meditative child, she was given to dreams by night and reveries by day, and they often reflected a precocious sense of personal responsibility. She dreamed, at the age of six, that "everyone in the world was dead excepting myself, and that upon me rested the responsibility of making a wagon wheel."

In 1868 John Addams married Mrs. Anna Haldeman, a rich, handsome, talented, gregarious widow with two sons. The Addams and Haldeman families united, apparently with little friction, and life went on for all of them. The children were educated in a generation that depended on McGuffey's *Readers* as the staple of the curriculum. Schools being ungraded, classroom procedure was whatever the teacher wanted it to be. Administrations of the switch were as traditional as those of sulphur and molasses in the spring. The general emphasis in the schools of the Middle West was on the concrete and the practical. "Men are not educated to be mere walking abstractions," a group of western teachers had stated in 1835, "but active, useful men," adding that the job of the West was "to improve the organization of human society." Such mental training was the beginning of Jane's commitment to the socially useful.

Jane was an excellent student, fascinated from the start with the printed page. Among the books at home, she looked into translations of Homer and Virgil, but found herself more at ease with historical works—Plutarch, Washington Irving's *Life of Washington*, and John Clark Ridpath's formidable history of the world. Her father, to sweeten these large doses of heavy reading, offered her small monetary rewards, payable after cross-questioning on what she had read.

"Mr. Lincoln's Letters"

Carefully preserved in John Addams' desk reposed a small packet of papers that he considered priceless. It was marked simply: "Mr. Lincoln's Letters." Jane Addams could not finger these letters without emotion, for to her, as to her adored father, the Great Emancipator was a martyr, a hero, almost a demigod. The fact that Lincoln had known John Addams well for ten years—well enough to send him informal letters that began "My dear Double-D'ed Addams"—made the association even more vivid. Serving in the Illinois legislature during the days of Civil War contracts and Reconstruction opportunism, John Addams maintained his integrity. He acted strictly according to his "inner light," and so sterling was his reputation that he not only never accepted a bribe, but was never even *offered* one.

Jane Addams gazes reflectively into the middle distance in this revealing portrait from life, now hanging in Hull-House.

Lincoln understood this stern uprightness, like everyone else. "You will of course," the President said to Addams in one letter, "vote according to your conscience, only it is a matter of considerable importance to me to know how that conscience is pointing." No wonder John

Addams was considered, by all acquainted with him, as a "king of gentlemen." No wonder he kept several pictures of Lincoln in his Cedarville home, including two in his bedroom. Although Jane was not yet five at the time of Lincoln's assassination, the dreadful day of his death remained engraved on her memory. She was not in the house when the news arrived, but as soon as she entered it, she found her father weeping—openly, unashamedly. His habitual calm reserve, which she thought unshakable, had cracked. "The greatest man in the world" was dead, he told her. Despite her tender years, she comprehended something of the tragedy that came to her household from an event so far away, so removed from her experience. Looking back later, she saw that this was "my initiation, my baptism" into the harsh reality of the grown-up world.

Life went on, leaving "Mr. Lincoln's Letters" to be treasured and read. Fascinated with

"Old Abe," the bald eagle mentioned opposite, poses regally in 1863. At one inspection, General Grant saluted the bird.

books, Jane nevertheless spent many of her days out of doors, developing a romantic attachment to nature that never diminished afterward. When she settled in Chicago and began her social work, she felt sorry for the children of the slums because, among their other deprivations, they had never known the delights of the open country—the fresh air in the meadow, the bright sun on the tall corn, the autumn frost glistening on the pumpkins. She wished that these youngsters could have been transported from the city streets to the banks of the millstream rising into high bluffs near Cedarville, the bluffs pitted by mysterious caves that she and her stepbrother George had explored in the best Tom Sawyer-Becky Sharp tradition.

The abandoned limekiln was the arena where the two staged their mock combats, with George as "The Knight of the Green Plume," ready to tilt at all enemies, imaginary and real, from knights in armor to the snakes and muskrats that infested the underbrush. If nature was beautiful, it was also grim. The struggle for survival was brought home to Jane when she spotted hawks circling overhead and weasels prowling for rabbits, or when a muskrat turned at bay and bit George severely on the hand. Playing with George helped Jane to escape from her childish introversion.

George's mother, Jane's strong-willed stepmother, also left an indelible impression—though not all to the good. Mrs. Addams played the guitar, conducted play-readings, read the latest novels, and sought social advantages for herself and her relatives. Determined to impose on her new family more sophisticated manners and tastes, she added a bay window to the downstairs living room, moved her piano to the most prominent spot, and insisted on more formal meals in the dining room. The Addams girls were instructed to wear frocks "more tasteful in line and color." All this was quite different from the sterner, simpler life to which the Addams family was accustomed. But John did not object to the transformation.

The new Mrs. Addams was also determined to enjoy more gaiety and glamour than the ham-

In 1876, *Harper's Weekly* depicted the Bessemer method (page 18) of making steel by forcing air through molten pig iron.

let of Cedarville provided. The state capital at Springfield suited her better. Hence John's 1870 decision not to seek another term in the legislature, which met in Springfield, dismayed her. At this point she discovered that on such basic decisions, her husband did not need her advice. If Anna Haldeman Addams was ambitious, her husband was adamant. The political career of the man who had helped found the Republican party in Illinois and served his state well for sixteen years—who had even refused the nomination as governor of Illinois at a time when his election was all but assured—now came quietly but firmly to an end. Not outer acclaim but John Addams' "inner light" was his guide. There was nothing his new wife could do about it.

The riddle of life and death

Sometimes the elder Addams would take the family on excursions. A most memorable one was the sixty-five-mile trip to Madison, Wisconsin, to visit not only the state capitol building, but also its illustrious inmate—"Old Abe," war-eagle of the Eighth Wisconsin. This ride in the family buggy went north through the rolling countryside. Stops at country towns were spaced so as to provide excitement and variety: Beloit, Janesville, Milton Junction, Edgerton, Albion, Stoughton; then beautiful lakes Kegonsa, Waubesa, and Monona. "We were driven northward hour after hour," Miss Addams wrote, "past harvest fields in which the stubble glinted from bronze to gold and the heavy-headed grain rested luxuriously in rounded shocks, until we reached that beautiful region of hills and lakes which surrounds the capital city of Wisconsin."

The grand climax of the trip was in the capitol; she noted that "Old Abe" looked like the proud eagle on a Roman standard. His keeper, a veteran of the Civil War, ostentatiously in uniform, enthralled them with tales of the battles "Old Abe" had survived. For many visitors the pilgrimage to see the bird that symbolized the United States was unforgettable. Standing under the great classic dome, hearing the solemn roll call of bloody engagements, they recalled another Old Abe who had been the standard-bearer of his country's conscience. To the Addams family of Illinois, Lincoln gave patriotism, in Shakespeare's phrase, "a local habitation and a name." They lived in his aura and venerated his memory.

The Union, preserved by the martyred President, grew at a remarkable rate during Jane's childhood. Not quite five when the war ended, and sixteen when the Yankee troops finally withdrew from the South, she herself saw little of that dramatic growth. Later on she would understand the full significance of the radical changes that took place as the triumphant North concentrated its huge power to bolster industrial progress. Advances in agriculture, mining, and manufacturing were phenomenal. Introduction of the Bessemer smelting process turned this period into the Age of Steel and covered vast areas with smoke and soot. Robber barons came into their own—powerful businessmen, industrialists, and bankers who fought their way to the top in the fierce competition of the marketplace. Many Americans felt that Horatio Alger, with his "rags to riches" stories, reflected the essential mood of the nation in the post-Civil War period. Truth was indeed stranger than fiction in a land that placed no barriers before the aspirations and ambitions of the rugged individualist. Everyone craved success, and some achieved it.

But only some—there lay the root of a growing evil. The weak, the ineffectual, and the luckless could not hope to compete. They often fell far behind in the race for the good things of American life, their hopes blighted by a wretchedness from which they could not extricate themselves. Nor could they look to the government for assistance. This was the heyday of laissez-faire, which meant that the government had no right to interfere with the individual as long as he stayed within the law—no matter what the social consequences might be. As a result, the American dream for the captains of industry had become a nightmare for the common man.

In fact, the spirit epitomized by the nation's capital appeared to be one that favored the rich rather than the poor. In the 1870's, Washington was a city where corrupt practices flourished; speculators, lobbyists, and representatives of high finance made an art of wangling decisions in their favor from the President and Congress.

JANE AND HER STEPMOTHER

James Linn, as the son of Jane's older sister Mary, knew his aunt for nearly sixty years, her stepmother for several decades, and the whole Addams family situation with the intimacy of a close relative. Hence he is both authoritative and informative in telling how Jane's father came to choose his second wife, and to what extent his choice influenced Jane's own life:

"Prosperous, distinguished John Addams needed a wife. One day in 1867, as he was driving in to Freeport to the bank, as he did every day, the thought came into his mind, 'What a good wife for me Mrs. William Haldeman would make!' Now William Haldeman was a citizen of Freeport, with whom John Addams was well acquainted, and his wife was a handsome, able woman. Suddenly John Addams realized that he was considering marriage with another man's wife. He was amazed and displeased with himself. But when he reached town, he was informed at the bank that 'William Haldeman had died in the night.' What if the thought of Mrs. Haldeman had been sent him for guidance? A year later he offered her marriage, and his offer was promptly accepted.

"The second Mrs. John Addams was beyond any doubt a remarkable person. She lived to be ninety-three years of age, and was still handsome . . . when she died. She awed her neighbors, though she never allured them. . . . She was a skilled musician, giving lessons to Freeport aspirants. She was a constant reader, even of novels, which in her day and neighborhood were thought by most good people to be dangerous. But she did not confine her reading to novels; she was fond of reading plays aloud to her family, and as her son George and her stepdaughter Jane grew a little older she would gather them both round the livingroom table on many an evening, and read Shakespeare, taking the characters turn about. Once in a while even John Addams was induced to join in this reading-circle, but usually it was confined to Mrs. Addams, Jane, and George. Later at Hull-House it was the memory of these many evenings of reading aloud that led Jane Addams to put such emphasis on similar 'reading-clubs' for the neighbors. The stepmother played the guitar too, and sang endless songs from Tom Moore, whose lyrics she knew by heart, as well as many others. She was what in those days was called 'accomplished.'

"Mrs. Addams was fond of society; even at ninety an amusing talker when she chose to be; and in the early days after her second marriage she was determined to have more society than Cedarville afforded. She was not only as Mrs. John H. Addams a personage in that section of Illinois, but she knew herself to be a personage in her own right: well educated, witty, high-spirited, and rich. She meant not to remain in Cedarville. But she encountered a quiet will even stronger than her own. Not only did the family remain in Cedarville, but in 1870, two years after his second marriage, John H. Addams declined further renomination to the state senate. In the preceding session his new wife had gone with him to Springfield as a matter of

Anna Haldeman Addams

course, and there had been social wars and rumors of wars, of course in a mild way, but disturbing to the senator's mind. He never gave this as his reason for refusing further renomination, but his wife never had any doubt that it was his reason, and nagged him about it in consequence for years.

"In all minor matters Mrs. Addams had her own way. Mary, the oldest sister, who had managed the household since she was seventeen, quietly withdrew to Rockford Seminary, where she took lessons on the piano and in china-painting for a while, and then married [a] Presbyterian minister. . . . Alice, too, after a year or so, was sent to Rockford to school. Jane only remained at home, under her stepmother's domination.

"It was not a harsh domination, in itself. The little girl and her stepmother were fond of one another, and allowing for their difference in ages, had many of the same tastes. . . . The second Mrs. Addams brought with her to Cedarville her two sons, Harry and George Haldeman. Harry was eighteen, but George was only seven, six months younger than Jane. Eight years later Harry Haldeman married Alice Addams, after a tempestuous season in which the stepbrother and stepsister, violently in love, were vigorously opposed by the parents of both. Strong-willed Alice carried it through, though not until the very last moment was she sure that her father would attend the wedding. . . . Harry Haldeman did not much affect Jane's life. He was as cynical as she was the reverse. . . .

"But the younger brother, George, was, after her father, the devotion of Jane's girlhood, as they grew up together. Later he wished to marry her, although he resented her social ideals, which he regarded as vague, and he laughed at her sociological inquiries. In time, from concentration on study, particularly biological research at Johns Hopkins, he had a nervous breakdown from which he never fully recovered. But for nine years, from the time they were eight years old until they were seventeen, when she went away to Rockford Seminary and he to Beloit College, they were inseparable. . . . Whenever Jane Addams wrote or spoke of those nine years, she used always the pronoun 'we,' and it meant always 'Jennie and George.' "

The second Mrs. Addams persistently urged Jane to marry George, and Jane just as persistently refused: "Many years afterward, when both George and his mother were dead, one summer on the coast of Maine, Jane Addams used to sit occasionally in those circles which, with their hands resting on the table, await the rappings that follow, if any of the company are 'psychic,' and a believer in the 'spirits' once informed Jane Addams that she was psychic to a high degree. At any rate, after a moment or two of silence the table would begin to rap; invariably the first raps would indicate that Jane Addams was being addressed; and she would remark, half whimsically and half in boredom, 'Oh, it's my stepmother, of course, it always is. Now she will be reproaching me again for not having married George.' And the table would inquire with some petulance, 'How long are you going to keep on with that philanthropic nonsense?' "

Gould and Drew, left to right in this cartoon, were once partners—but Gould kept his money, while Drew went broke.

The scandals of the Grant Administration became so notorious that reformers began to demand a change in the system.

Jane Addams was nine when Jay Gould shook the nation by almost cornering gold on "Black Friday" of 1869. Gould and his piratical cronies, Daniel Drew and James Fisk, bought large amounts of gold at a low figure, took what they acquired out of circulation, and created a shortage that pushed the price up. The conspirators then provoked a panic on the stock exchange by spreading the false rumor that President Grant had decided to keep federal supplies of gold off the market, which meant that the shortage would continue, and that the price would keep climbing. This conspiracy might have reduced the nation's financial system to chaos if Grant, finally alerted to the peril, had not released four million dollars' worth of gold, a move that ruined many speculators as the price tumbled back.

Jane was thirteen when Mark Twain published *The Gilded Age,* a biting satire on the money-grubbing, sordid politics and blatant chicanery that permitted scoundrels like Gould to operate so flagrantly. A character in this novel describes one road to success in Washington: "A Congressional appropriation costs money. Just reflect, for instance. A majority of the House committee, say $10,000 apiece—$40,000; a majority of the Senate committee, the same each—say $40,000; a little extra to one or two chairmen of one or two such committees, say $10,000 each—$20,000; and there's $100,000 of the money gone, to begin with."

Misdeeds such as these abounded in America, but so did protests. Jane would find reformist ideas gathering strength when she stepped out of her secluded Cedarville home into the swirling, muddied currents of public life. Meanwhile, she had some growing up to do.

Not all of her buggy rides were as pleasant as the one to Madison. On a winter trip in 1875, when she was fifteen, she came to a turning-point in her life. Word arrived that Polly, the old family nurse, was dying in a lonely farmhouse about four miles away, and Jane was the only one who at that moment could go to her. Struggling through a snowstorm, Jane reached the farmhouse just before Polly succumbed. Alone by the bedside, transfixed with horror, the teenage girl saw the eyes of the stricken woman staring at her, heard the harsh rattle in the throat, watched death triumphant. Jane Addams felt fearfully alone in a bleak universe that seemed heedless of the sorrows of mankind. On the return to Cedarville, she trembled as the cold wind cut her tear-stained face. She was beginning to understand the human dimensions of the profound mystery that she termed "the riddle of life and death." She was beginning to realize how complicated the world is—and how complicated she herself was. Later, in recalling the episode of old Polly's death, Jane Addams summed up its meaning for herself: "Once to be young, to grow old and to die, everything came to that, and then a mysterious journey out into the Unknown."

Chapter 2
THE START OF A MIDWESTERN FLOWERING

IN 1877 a shy self-contained young girl aged seventeen left her home in Cedarville to get a college education and prepare herself for her lifework. Jane Addams would have preferred to go to far-off Massachusetts to attend Smith College, where she had been accepted, but her father decided she should follow in the footsteps of three older sisters who had gone to Rockford Female Seminary, thirty miles to the southeast in neighboring Winnebago County. John Addams was now on this institution's governing board; he liked the idea of Jane's being close by where he could "keep an eye on her." Later on, he promised, she could go to Europe, see the things deemed proper for ladies in Victorian days, and widen her experiences. But the diversity that Jane had read about she would not yet know personally. Instead, hers would be the tight little world of a strongly religious boarding school. Showing some of her father's stoicism, Jane appraised the situation, accepted the decision, and packed her bags.

Even in the last quarter of the nineteenth century it was unusual for girls to go on to higher education. A woman's place was in the home, so far as most middle-class Americans were concerned. Cooking, sewing, weaving, and child-rearing were their proper areas of interest. That John Addams had both the desire and the means to educate four daughters made his a truly exceptional family. He sensed, quite accurately, that education was becoming a critical factor in post-Civil War America. Between 1860 and 1880 over five hundred high schools were established in the United States, thereby creating thousands of teaching jobs for college graduates. The "schoolmarm" was already a stereotype in American society, but an increasing number of young men now joined her in the classroom. The development of a better psychology of education, with new methods, new subjects, and new textbooks, made teaching an intellectual challenge and a personal fulfillment. By 1870, male teachers were prominent in the school system.

An 1873 ruling handed down by the Michigan Supreme Court in the Kalamazoo case gave communities the right to tax themselves for the maintenance of secondary schools, thus starting a new era in the Midwest. That same year, St. Louis opened the first public-school kindergarten; the experiment proved so successful that it spread across the country. Higher education also underwent a transformation during Jane Addams' youth. Older universities were reorganized by famous educators like Harvard's Charles W. Eliot, who introduced electives, allowing undergraduates wide freedom to choose the subjects they preferred instead of being compelled to take rigidly prescribed courses. New institutions sprang up, the most celebrated being Johns Hopkins, a purely graduate school based on ideas imported from Germany. (Woodrow Wilson took his Ph.D. at

Two Harvard undergraduates, lounging in their fashionably cluttered room, pose for their 1870 class album.

Johns Hopkins in 1885.) Booker T. Washington founded Tuskegee Institute, providing Negro students with more opportunities to acquire learning. Rockford Female Seminary was only one of the many women's colleges that flourished across the land.

The federal government provided assistance. The United States Office of Education served as a clearinghouse for educational problems of cities and states. Land-grant colleges had already been established under the Morrill Act of 1862. They expanded their agricultural research and experiment stations with federal money appropriated under the Hatch Act of 1887—a boon to the Middle West from which Jane Addams came. Meanwhile, many private citizens were taking an interest in one major field with which Jane would have much to do later on—adult education. Lecturers addressed adult audiences at Chautauqua, New York, for the first time in 1874, and the word "Chautauqua" soon entered the language as a synonym for this type of lyceum.

Three years after Jane received her diploma at Rockford, John Dewey took his Ph.D. at Johns Hopkins. He would go on to champion a pragmatic philosophy called "instrumentalism" in which ideas are treated as instruments for probing and changing reality, and are retained, revised, or discarded according to whether they work or not. He would revolutionize education by insisting that the classroom must be integrated into the social background, so that American children may learn at school how to be worthy citizens of their democratic society. The importance of John Dewey for Jane was this: His philosophy influenced her practice more than any other.

Change was in the air in the 1870's and 1880's. This was an extremely creative and expansive period for American education.

The Rockford Female Seminary

Leaving home with her father one sunny September morning, Jane went due south to Freeport, then took the main road east to

Rockford. The ripened grain was golden in the fields; she felt close to this land that she would always think of as her own. Groves of fine elms and oaks could be seen on either side, surrounded by beds of colorful prairie flowers. That night they reached Rockford, founded in 1834 mainly by New Englanders. Named for the shallow rock-bottomed ford used by the Galena-Chicago stagecoach line before any settlement existed there, Rockford was known as "The Forest City."

John Addams pointed out the local landmarks, such as the railroad station. In 1852 the Chicago and Galena Union Railroad had reached Rockford, and the town had been growing ever since. John H. Manny's reaper factory, founded in 1853, was considered a rival of Cyrus McCormick's in Chicago. Rockford's hosiery business, begun in 1870, was booming. The Winnebago Court House, built on the public square facing West State Street, had provided one of Illinois's tragic news events of the previous spring. On May 11, 1877, the partly constructed dome collapsed, killing nine workmen and fatally injuring two others. The main part of the building, in yellow limestone of French rococo design, was finished in 1878.

But the place that interested Jane most was the Rockford Female Seminary on College Avenue. It had been chartered in 1847, making this one of the earliest institutions for female education in the Mississippi Valley; by 1851, the women of Rockford had contributed $1,000 for the land, and the men $3,500 for a building. The cornerstone of Colonial-style Middle Hall was laid in 1852, the same year Miss Anna P. Sill was elected principal, and the first seven graduates received their certificates in 1854.

Conscious of the heroic sacrifices that made the school possible, the students applied themselves with a seriousness and intensity that blanketed the campus. Rockford's chief purpose, as stated in the catalogue, was "to develop moral and religious character in accordance with right principles, that it may send out cultivated Christian women in the various fields of usefulness." Spearheading this passionate campaign was Miss Sill, who dominated the seminary and stayed at Rockford as principal for thirty-two years. Tenacious as a bulldog, she did not give up an idea once she had got her teeth into it. From the day of her arrival, she interpreted "various fields of usefulness" to mean service to God, particularly in the field of missions. Jane clashed with this stern mentor on more than one occasion. "She does everything for love of God *alone*," Jane wrote of Miss Sill in her diary, "and I do not like that."

For her part, Jane defined the phrase "various fields of usefulness" in a broader sense, groping toward the principle that service to man, whether religious or not, must enter into any sound criterion of right action as far as she was concerned. Her father had taught her to think for herself, and she did so—respecting the opinions of others, but not accepting them unless she felt personally committed. In a real sense, Jane differed not only with Miss Sill but also with the original purposes of Rockford Seminary. Jane always felt that her moral

"ALWAYS SOMETHING 'DOING'"

Corinne Williams Douglas, who, after Rockford, became an educator in Atlanta, reminisced thus of the undergraduate she remembered best: "My first memory of Jane Addams brings back to me a Sunday evening in . . . our freshman year. It was then the custom on Sunday evenings, after a supper of Puritan austerity, for all those who were sitting with their backs towards the center of the room, to rise solemnly and replace their chairs, facing inward. When this evolution had been completed on this particular September night, I found . . . just opposite me, Jane Addams. . . . The brown hair [was] drawn plainly back, with a decided inclination, never encouraged, to fall apart on the side, the chin raised, the head slightly bent to one side, the face turned at an angle to me as she gave her attention to the speaker. . . . School girls are not psychologists, and we never speculated as to why we liked to go to her room so that it was always crowded when the sacred 'engaged' sign was not hung out. We just knew there was always something 'doing' where she was, and that however mopey it might be elsewhere there was intellectual ozone in her vicinity."

A nineteenth-century missionary addresses converts in Ceylon. Many Rockford graduates went to such missions.

development during her school years was significant precisely because she had the moral stamina to stand up to her strong-minded superiors there. Her efforts helped to transform Rockford from a seminary to a college.

This side of her character, of course, did not reveal itself on the day of her arrival. Diminutive in size, and away from home for the first time, she suffered the qualms of most freshmen settling into college life. A classmate, Eleanor Frothingham Haworth, remembered that "on September 23, 1877 . . . I met a little girl with very pretty light-brown hair, pushed back, and particularly direct, earnest eyes; but she looked as I know I was feeling, very trembly inside. She said her name was Laura Jane Addams, and she had just come from Cedarville. . . . I have always wondered if I looked as young and worried as Jane did that day."

Even a careful observer would not have known during Jane's first weeks at Rockford that so small and timid a girl had such a bold mind and spirit of her own. Only five feet three inches tall, and weighing a mere ninety-five pounds, Jane no longer carried her head on one side, though her spine still gave her trouble. She had large blue eyes, well-defined thin features, and a light complexion. Even though she was enjoying better health than she had previously known, she seemed nothing more than an attractive but not outstanding newcomer. Before long, the picture changed. The rest of the undergraduates learned that Jane Addams was a very special person who generated her own type of electricity. She would never lose the meditative expression of her childhood, but a decided tilt of her chin showed a new firmness—and she was always ready for a debate or for a frolic. Since she had been accustomed to serious and amusing talks with her father for so long, she could meet her classmates on more than even terms.

Plain food, simple living, and hard work prevailed at Rockford. All of the girls made their own fires, and kept their rooms in order. When their daily lessons were done, they talked endlessly in the evenings about philosophies of life, social problems, and the question of whether women ought to have the vote (which they answered with a resounding affirmative). The lively, consuming interest that Jane and her close friends had in ideas was mirrored in the motto from Aristotle they put up on the wall of the chess-club room: "There is the same difference between the learned and the unlearned as there is between the living and the dead."

Piety, labor, reason

Tiny, independent Jane Addams read the prescribed books avidly, not just to obtain passing grades from her instructors, but because she wanted to understand literature, philosophy, and science. Her deep concern for religion, however, did not include a missionary vocation, and she refused to pretend otherwise. She dryly noted in her diary: "The desirability of Turkey as a field for missionary labor was enticingly put before me." Members of the student body and the faculty, and even the zealous Miss Sill, argued with her unavailingly. She was caught by the ideal of "mingled learning, piety, and physical labor," but "much given to a sort of rationalism." In short, she was determined to find her own way. Close by was one who would mean more to her than any sermon, book, or teacher at Rockford: another freshman who arrived in the fall of 1877, Ellen Gates Starr from Durand, Illinois. Ellen's consuming interest in the arts and the beauty of form set her off from most of the other students; it also struck a responsive chord in Jane Addams that made them friends not only for the year but for life. This was the same Ellen Starr who would become the co-founder, with Jane, of Hull-House more than a decade later.

Where Ellen found her natural outlet in art, and wrote more about medieval and Renaissance Florence than about biblical times in the city of Jerusalem, Jane seemed to be most stimulated by science. She joined the school's newly formed science club and set out to prove several theories by tests of her own. She placed glasses of water containing wheat and corn grains near the stove in her room and kept careful records of their germination. Biology, the favorite subject of her stepbrother George (now studying at nearby Beloit College), introduced her to the theory of evolution, set forth in Charles Darwin's *Origin of Species* in 1859.

Darwinism, Jane learned, involved two major points, the first of which concerned organic development. Darwin held that new forms of animal life develop out of old ones by a slow, gradual process over an immense span of time. Therefore, the species we know have not always existed—for example, the horse is descended from a dog-sized creature that lived eons ago.

Since Darwin applied his theory to man no less than to the lower orders, and said that human beings are descended from nonhuman ancestors, he provoked a heated controversy between scientists, who accepted evolution, and theologians, who felt that he was impugning the biblical account of Adam and Eve. Echoes of this controversy reached Rockford Female Seminary, where Jane Addams found that it could be exciting to speculate about evolution in a school where the prevailing sentiment of most teachers was all in favor of a fundamentalist theology, which held that the world was quite literally created in seven days and that Jonah quite literally survived in the belly of a whale. She accepted evolution because she believed the theory to be true. Besides, she derived consolation from the interrelation of all living things, with man as nature's crowning achievement.

An early American diagram of evolution traces it from tiny primordial sea creatures through fish, lizards, and mammals to man. The apparent resemblance of men and apes led to a search for the elusive "missing link" between the two.

Middle Hall, where Jane took her entrance examinations, is the central building in this picture of Rockford Seminary in 1878.

But she rejected Darwin's second point, at least in the form put forward by some Darwinians with regard to society and the state. Trying to explain the driving force behind evolution, Darwin argued that since all creatures have to struggle with their enemies and their environment, those born with helpful variations tend to survive. Thus, white foxes survive in the snowy Arctic because they are nearly invisible to their prey; black ones, on the contrary, die out for want of this protective coloring. In short, life develops through natural selection. The English philosopher Herbert Spencer coined the phrase "survival of the fittest," and used it as an excuse for denouncing social-welfare legislation, which he considered a violation of the natural law governing the universe. While Jane Addams was at Rockford, William Graham Sumner of Yale University was teaching his students Social Darwinism of an uncompromising kind and ridiculing the idea that any government has a right to mitigate the struggle for advancement, in which some people succeed and others fail. On the basis of what he took to be hard evolutionary science, Sumner defended laissez-faire to the hilt. He persuaded many Americans—but not Jane Addams—to accept Social Darwinism. The principle of allowing the fittest to survive, and the rest to go under, contradicted her whole approach to social, political, and economic problems.

Jane read widely in the sciences during her undergraduate days at Rockford, supplementing what was available in the meager school library with volumes borrowed from her brother-in-law Harry Haldeman on her visits home. (Harry, stepbrother of Jane and Alice before he married the latter, was to become "a clever and daring surgeon.") She was attracted to the scientific method: verification of facts by using laboratory techniques. Although not a researcher by temperament or inclination, she "pressed plants, stuffed birds, and pounded rocks" during summer vacations, "in some vague belief that I was approximating the new method." She was already concerned about the place of women in American life, a concern that would later carry her into the suffragette movement. In an essay she wrote in 1879, she asserted that a woman could grow accurate and intelligent only "through the thorough study of at least one branch of physical science, for only with eyes thus accustomed to the search for truth can she detect all self-deceit and dogmatism." So she urged girls to take up science for its training in hard, precise, objective thought. So that others might have access to more source material than she had had, Jane later presented to the Rockford Seminary library, in the first gift she made after coming into her share of her father's estate, a thousand dollars to be spent for books on the sciences. As an undergraduate, her vocational goal was to study medicine, take her M.D., and devote her life to the treatment of pain and disease.

As her years at Rockford passed, Jane Addams gained in confidence, authority, and influence—and caused her fellow classmate Eleanor Haworth to form a new opinion: "I do remember that whenever difficulties with Miss Sill came up for settlement, most of us 'let Jane do it' in presenting them. Miss Sill . . . tried regimentation, and there was opposition to it. We were quite willing to work hard, but we were sometimes on tiptoe with the desire to work in our own way. In our class in Moral Philosophy, Jane insisted on giving the name 'Don Quixote' the Spanish pronunciation. We backed her up with laughter at Miss Sill's 'Don Quix-ott.' Miss Sill suspended the whole class for two days, then took us back without comment. At chapel exercises that day Jane took my hymnal and wrote on the fly-leaf:

'Life's a burden, bear it.
Life's a duty, dare it.
Life's a thorn-crown? Wear it.
And spurn to be a coward.'

She was a rebel but she 'spurned to be a coward.' "

Such leadership brought Jane a whole series of honors—class president, editor of the college's magazine, and its leading public speaker. A marriage proposal came from Rollin Salis-

NO TIME TO MARRY

Jane once referred to love and marriage as perhaps the "highest gift which life can offer to a woman." Yet she never married. No doubt her physical condition had something to do with it. Moreover, the bright image of her father lived in her memory, an ideal that no other man could measure up to, making her unable to extend to a husband the full devotion that she believed to be the basis of a happy marriage. Also, she grew to maturity in an era that frowned upon working wives. The prim Victorians of her class held that a woman could have a marriage or a career, but not both. These being the alternatives, Jane chose a career, and to it she consecrated her entire being. As one admirer remarked: "She never had time to marry."

It was no lack of human sympathy that kept her single. She valued masculine acquaintances like Graham Taylor, Henry Demarest Lloyd, and John Dewey, whose daughter says that the philosopher "formed warm personal friendships with [Hull-House] residents, especially with Jane Addams." The ladies of Hull-House were her good friends, and one was her best friend—Mary Rozet Smith, a winning personality of whom glowing eulogies were written by many men and women. James Linn noted: "The friendship of Mary Smith soon became and always remained the highest and clearest note in the music of Jane Addams' personal life. . . . The illumination of Jane Addams' spirit dimmed when Mary Smith died; she walked as steadily as ever, but in the twilight. Mary Rozet Smith . . . was a member of many national and civic organizations [but] people interested her more than causes or schemes, and children perhaps more than any other sort of people. . . . No little child and no timidest of aliens or gawkiest of adolescents, ever knew Mary Smith without falling in love with her. . . . It is possible to believe that she was as tolerant as Jane Addams herself, and was unquestionably gentler. She lived and died serene."

Alice Hamilton, herself one of the most distinguished of all Hull-House residents, described her thus: "There is one supremely lovely figure which rises to one's mind whenever one thinks of Hull-House . . . and that is . . . Mary Rozet Smith, Jane Addams' closest friend and the most universally beloved person I have ever known. She left no mark on history but she left a deep mark on all who knew her. . . . She was one of those persons whose biographies are never written but who have a deep and abiding influence on their time. Her large, gracious home on Walton Place was a refuge for Miss Addams, who could hardly have carried on had she not been able to slip away to it from the West Side now and then."

bury, senior class president of Beloit College. Jane said "No." Salisbury took the rejection very personally; he remained a bachelor, and years later, while teaching at the University of Chicago, he never called on Jane Addams at nearby Hull-House.

"Be sincere and don't fuss"

Nothing shows her earnest and agonizing efforts to "find her way," especially in religious matters, so clearly as the letters she wrote to her intimate chum, Ellen Gates Starr. "Every time I talk about religion, I vow a great vow never to do it again," Jane confessed after struggling with theological abstractions. "My creed is ever be sincere and don't fuss." But fuss she did, for months on end, in a vain effort to come to terms with her inner doubts. "If I could fix myself with my relations to God and the universe, and so be in perfect harmony with nature and deity, I could use my faculties and energy so much better and could do almost anything." If, if, if—what a big little word that can be!

So Jane Addams kept searching, questioning, wondering. She tried "an awful experiment"—giving up all prayer for three months, and—to her great surprise—"feeling no worse for it." Ellen implored her to go back to her old ways, "for no good can come of such experiments, and harm *might.*" Jane could not turn from her doubting. For Ellen's benefit, she ended up quoting not the Bible, but a favorite quatrain from Matthew Arnold:

"Unaffrighted by the silence round them
Undistracted by the sights they see
These demand not that the things without them
Yield them love, amusement, sympathy."

Jane was trying to place the more speculative religious questions on the foundation of rationalism and thus somehow manage to root their abstractions in reality. Such an intellectual effort in her college days indicated that she could not rest content with her father's individualistic conception of the "inner light," and would continue to seek a corporate religion—a church—that united its adherents through a believable theology and realistic principles of moral conduct. If the "inner light" of John Addams led him unswervingly into righteous social action, Jane Addams felt the need of a more definite guide to keep her on the straight and narrow amid the ethical dilemmas of the daily round.

Ranging freely through the world of ideas during her Rockford period, Jane took delight in the masters of English literature who had something to say about the individual confronting the universe. The poetry of Robert Browning reinforced her natural optimism when she came across lines like this: "God's in His heaven/All's right with the world." Thomas Carlyle inspired her with the thought that men

These five British writers, all still living when Jane was at Rockford and being influenced by them, appear here in characteristic moods. Intense John Ruskin taught his Oxford students that art and ethics are closely related. Cultivated Matthew Arnold, also of Oxford, assailed the "philistines" for their insensitivity to the higher life of the mind. Philosophical Herbert Spencer took the cosmos for his province, and gave it an evolutionary interpretation. Brooding Thomas Carlyle seemed to the Victorians a Scottish seer thundering moralities like an Old Testament prophet. Mystical Robert Browning wrote some poems so obscure that "only God" understood them; he also defended his wife, Elizabeth Barrett Browning, against derogatory criticism.

John Ruskin

Matthew Arnold

A SIGNIFICANT FRIENDSHIP

While still in their teens, Jane Addams and Ellen Gates Starr began a friendship that would last the rest of their lives. But the co-founders of Hull-House always had basic differences in their personalities. In a letter to Ellen dated June 7, 1889, just before starting their joint settlement project, Jane wrote: "Dearest: I think I owe you an apology. . . . I gave $25.00 yesterday to Beloit College. I must stop doing things of that kind and save for our affair. I don't know why I am so weak and need you to keep me from my weakness. My greatest self-denial will come in my refusing to give to other things, and you must make yourself my bugbear for that. I need you, dear one, more than you can realize."

Linn's biography of Jane does much to explain the dissimilar, yet complementary, talents of the two: "Ellen Gates Starr and Jane Addams were freshmen together in Rockford. [Then Ellen] left college to teach . . . in Chicago, at the famous old Kirkland School for Girls, fashionable but strenuously educational too. . . . Ellen Starr taught English and 'art'—not drawing and painting, but appreciation. . . . [When] Jane confided to Ellen Starr her scheme for a house among the poor people somewhere in Chicago, Ellen embraced it at once, with that vivacity, sincerity and confidence . . . always characteristic of her. . . .

"A strange thing about Ellen Starr was that as she grew older she grew more, not less, intense. Her major interests at Hull-House at first were what they had been at the Kirkland School—in teaching. She organized reading classes and clubs; drew the young people by scores into the studio of the Butler Gallery for the study of painting; began at the grammar-school nearest to Hull-House that scheme for giving the public-schoolchildren of Chicago a chance to see good pictures every day, which has since developed so splendidly into the Public School Art Society; and finally studied and taught bookbinding as a fine art in a way that made it literally fashionable. It was partly through Ellen Starr's connection with the Kirkland School too that in the early 'nineties so many young women of social prominence came to Hull-House. . . . She was aspirational, shining, and serene. But as time went on . . . her interest in the unionization of women became intense. She concerned herself directly with strikes. . . . She picketed. She harangued. . . . She became a member in good standing of the Socialist Party, and argued for its tenets with a sort of charming fierceness. Her quest for beauty, her dream of bringing beauty into even the ugliest and most miserable of the lives about her, did not cease, but it was accompanied by a more passionate quest, a more partisan longing, for social justice. She remained an artist, but she became a combatant. . . . She crusaded down dirty streets, and frail and gentle as she was in appearance, was no more daunted by policemen than she would have been by Saracens. . . .

"No one ever forgot that she was a co-founder of Hull-House. On the other hand . . . the House . . . stood for tolerance, for opportunity, not for combat. . . . It was a City of Refuge, to whom might come all who . . . were oppressed by riches and responsibilities, as well as those who were oppressed by misery and by social theory. The only word upon the mat was 'Welcome,' the only motto over the entrance, 'May you find hope who enter here.' Miss Starr never doubted that tolerance was good, but was it not a good that interfered with the Best? There arose a militancy in her that found tolerance difficult. . . . In the end she satisfied that militancy, that desire for self-discipline, in the Church. She became a Roman Catholic. And with that submission of herself to authority, her old serenity returned."

Miss Starr left Hull-House after over forty years of residence and entered a Benedictine convent. She died in 1940.

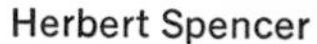
Herbert Spencer

Thomas Carlyle

Robert Browning

A strong family likeness emerges when these two photographs are placed side by side. At twenty-one, Jane has her father's physiognomy right down to the dimple in her chin.

should accept stern reality as essentially good despite its attendant evils, that they should utter the "Everlasting Yea" to life. John Ruskin taught her that optimism did not imply satisfaction with, or acceptance of, the human condition in its institutional manifestations. Ruskin set his face against the iniquities of the British industrial system, denounced progress for the few at the expense of the many, laid bare the fallacies of laissez-faire competition, and demanded that economic values be subordinated to human values. Matthew Arnold gave her the ideal of culture—"sweetness and light"—as something to help raise the masses.

Jane was so intrigued with Thomas De Quincey's *Confessions of an English Opium Eater* that she and four classmates slipped off to swallow doses of the drug—which was much easier to obtain without a doctor's prescription in that period than it is nowadays. They expected to enjoy the wonderful experiences described by De Quincey, "but," Jane recalled, "no mental reorientation took place, and the suspense and excitement did not even permit us to grow sleepy." The young teacher whom they had taken into their confidence was alarmed; she removed their De Quincey and the remaining opium, administered an emetic to each of the five girls, and ordered them to appear at worship after supper "whether you are able to or not!" Thus ended one adventurous nineteenth-century student's scheme of using a drug to create an artificial dreamworld.

Liking to be a winner

Another outlet for Jane's considerable energy was debating. In her last spring at Rockford she was chosen to represent the school at the Interstate Oratorical Contest. A young man from Illinois College, William Jennings Bryan (born, like Jane, in the year 1860), was there too. He would go on to become one of the golden voices of his generation. But on this occasion, he did not win the contest. Neither did Jane Addams, who ended up "exactly in the dreary middle." Throughout her life, she liked to be a winner. But she had the courage to know when she had lost, and the humor to allow her to see even a loss in perspective.

On a bright June morning in 1881, buggies, wagons, and saddle horses converged on Rockford Seminary. It was commencement time, and the three brick buildings were crowded with students and visitors. As the local newspaper chose to express it: "Seventeen Buds of Blooming Promise make their bow to Alma Mater and their debut before the world." Parents and friends of the graduates thronged East Hall for the commencement exercises at which the undisputed star was Jane Addams, class president and, as valedictorian, spokesman for the other girls who had gone through Rockford with her. She was an engaging figure as she stood at the rostrum discoursing on the rights and obligations of women in human affairs. Her address reflected high idealism, moral fervor, undeviating optimism, and faith in the future—and she would never contradict what she said that day.

The applause died away, the ceremonies ended, carriages wheeled out of the seminary grounds bearing the girls back to their homes, and Jane Addams knew that she had reached a peak of achievement and acclaim. She did not know that a dark valley of frustration and doubt lay just over the horizon.

Chapter 3
WOMAN CAUGHT BETWEEN TWO WORLDS

FOR JANE ADDAMS the spring of 1881 was bright and golden, a time for dreaming. But the summer that followed was a nightmare. With June came the thrill of graduation, the flurry of farewells, the pledges to "remember you always." Then back to Cedarville, snug and secure, where her idolized father and the others sustained her. Like her stepbrother George, Jane talked of going east in September to further her education by graduate study, he in biology and she in medicine. Whenever there was a dull moment, Mrs. Addams arranged a gay party and played on the guitar to add to the merriment. Life seemed to be singing.

Suddenly the singing stopped. On July 2, 1881, the telegraph lines crackled with news from Washington: President James A. Garfield had been shot, and mortally wounded, by a deranged, disappointed office-seeker. Jane gasped: The assassin, Charles J. Guiteau, was the son of a man who worked in her father's bank in Freeport. His half-sister, Flora, was a frequent family guest in Cedarville. Angry, venomous charges swept the country, centering on the Guiteaus. Jane, needless to say, had no thought of abandoning her friends because of public opinion; this was their hour of greatest need, and she did what she could to strengthen the Guiteaus to meet an ordeal rendered all the more pathetic by the insanity of the assassin. When he went to the gallows for the crime, she was with Flora, trying to take her friend's mind off the terrible events that would place a stigma on the name Guiteau forever.

Partly to get his family away for a vacation, partly to inspect mining properties in Michigan and Wisconsin, John Addams planned a trip that August. As always, Jane was glad to be at his side. The brisk northern air and the spicy pine trees of Michigan delighted her. She leaned out of the carriage to buy blood-red raspberries, the sweetest she had ever tasted. A few days later she watched boats, laden with silver cargoes of fish, skimming over blue Lake Superior. Her father's enthusiasm for the copper mines he had come to see delighted her, too. Suddenly one day, Mr. Addams doubled up with pain. "We must take him home at once," his wife said. They got as far as Green Bay, Wisconsin. There, in a hotel, his inflamed appendix ruptured and John Addams died. Vigorous and capable as ever at fifty-nine, he had been struck down in a few hours. The silent, stunned family brought the body home for burial. There, in the family cemetery near the creek in Cedarville, they laid him to rest next to his first wife Sarah and the four children who had died in infancy.

Pain like a knife

John Addams left behind an estate valued at $350,000—quite a fortune for his time and place. Neither his widow nor his children would have to worry about maintaining the station in

A contemporary news drawing shows Guiteau shooting Garfield (page 31) as the President is about to board a train.

life to which he had accustomed them. The most prominent family in Cedarville, they could live at their ease if they wanted to, or indulge their taste for travel without worrying about the cost. No matter. It was all dust and ashes as far as Jane was concerned. Her whole existence had been shaken by the loss of her father, the center of her thoughts for so many years. There was a vacuum, a void in her life that no other interest, for the time being at least, could fill. To her friend Ellen Starr she wrote shortly after the funeral: "The greatest sorrow that can ever come to me has passed, and I hope it is only a question of time until I get my moral purposes straightened." Actually, it took years rather than months before she regained her equilibrium.

Meanwhile, she often seemed hardly to know what was said or done around her. John Addams, the father-god, was dead, and Tennyson's term for one type of male-female relationship—"he for God only, she for God in him"—had some application here, as it may have had for an even higher percentage of men and women in that Victorian era than in most other periods of human history. No child is ever fully prepared for the effects of a beloved parent's death—but the growing independence Jane had shown in her Rockford days must have made at least some of her family and friends wonder why she did not demonstrate a greater strength and resilience in coping with this crisis. Still, life goes on, and Jane knew she must come to terms with it. She had already been accepted by the Women's Medical College in Philadelphia. Since George was going east for his graduate studies at Johns Hopkins, she would have to pull herself together and go east with him. Because they too felt cut off from what had been their life in Cedarville, Mrs. Addams and Jane's older sister Alice also decided to visit Philadelphia. The shutters of the Addams house were closed. The piano was covered. The fires were put out for the first time since John and Sarah Addams had moved in a generation earlier. Somehow the very heart of the family had stopped beating when the patriarch was buried six feet under the black soil across the creek.

The only solution, Jane sensed, was constant work, which would wipe out the memory of that dark, silent house. Her studies went well enough, but her health began to fail. In the spring she passed her examinations; but pain cut into her back like a knife, and her nerves seemed close to breaking. For tortured days and nights she lay pale and helpless in a Philadelphia hospital. Her brother-in-law, Dr. Harry Haldeman now, visited her and called in a noted back specialist. "She'll not live a year," this doctor concluded. "You don't know her," Dr. Haldeman replied. "She'll outlive us all."

Jane improved enough to make the journey home, in great pain, and even to return to Rockford. The seminary had been transformed into a college, and could in June 1882 grant her the B.A. degree she had actually earned a year earlier. Back home, she collapsed. Now she moved west, to Mitchelville, Iowa, where Dr. Haldeman was practicing. He decided that she had an abscess on her spine that only surgery would relieve. The operation was successful, although it was so extensive that it left Jane incapable of bearing children. After the operation she had to lie on a board for six months, then wear a heavy steel and whalebone brace. Fitting down to her hips, it acted as a crutch under her arms and took the pressure off her spine. No one can say what pain and despair the gallant young girl of twenty-two endured during this phase of her life, and for years afterward.

Again Mrs. Addams came through with a plan: Why not go to Europe for a complete change? Jane was enthusiastic. In 1883, Jane, her stepmother, and a party of six others went aboard the Cunard liner *Servia* headed for the Old World from which the Addams had migrated two centuries earlier. For an educated American in the 1880's, a journey to Europe was a kind of pilgrimage. Ancestral shrines, memories, and roots were here; so were the world's leading universities, academies, and cities. Europe's wealth, power, and prestige were unmatched. Politically independent for a century, Americans still suffered from a strong sense of cultural inferiority. "In truth," Matthew Arnold proclaimed in his haughty report of a visit made to America the same year Jane Addams was first visiting Europe, "everything is against distinction in America, and against the sense of elevation to be gained through admiring and respecting it." The United States had no castles, no sages, no medieval knights. If American writers like Emerson, Thoreau, and Whitman considered this an advantage, visitors like Harriet Martineau, Charles Dickens, and Mrs. Trollope often sneered at American newness and crudity. "Their cities are all provincial towns," Miss Martineau wrote. "It would be well if they loved the real less and the ideal more," Dickens complained. "I was quite oppressed by the serious and melancholy air of business." To escape this "provincialism" and taint of business, thousands of Americans flocked annually to Europe, tracking down "culture" in packs. They still do.

Fiction close to fact

Of all European nations, Americans then seemed to feel most in awe of Great Britain, at her imperial peak in the late nineteenth century. When Queen Victoria's government got effective control of the Suez Canal (1875) and

No skyscrapers loom on the New York skyline in this photograph of 1883, the year Jane sailed for Europe on the *Servia*.

Queen Victoria takes the air at Balmoral Castle. Her Scottish steward, John Brown, is at left, and a Sikh attendant is at right.

she became Empress of India (1876), one could truly say that Britannia ruled the waves. Almost a quarter of the globe's land surface was colored red on maps, to designate British control or allegiance; the sun never set on British soil. Her economic, political, and cultural influence permeated the world— a fact that the British had no notion of keeping secret.

No one was more fascinated by the Anglo-American connections than the novelist Henry James, born in America in 1843 but through choice a resident of England after 1876. He eventually became a British subject. By coincidence, James was also on the *Servia* when it sailed for Europe on August 22, 1883, and he sat at the same table with Jane Addams in the dining room. "He is very English in appearance," she wrote, "but not especially keen or intellectual." This remains perhaps the most astonishing judgment ever passed on Henry James, who was actually among the most "intellectual" men of his generation. But, apart from his Anglified reserve, which made it difficult for him to converse easily with strangers, the truth is that he and Jane could hardly have understood one another. James agreed with those Europeans who considered Americans crude, commercial-minded, and brash. Unsympathetic to the booming democracy that inspired Walt Whitman and Mark Twain, he found his ideal in the British aristocratic tradition that nurtured ladies and gentlemen of refined manners and established social position. While Jane Addams wanted to work out her destiny in her homeland, Henry James simply turned his back on it. She was an activist bent on changing society; he was a detached observer of the passing scene. Both became cosmopolitans interested in the people of foreign lands, but Jane would mingle with the poverty-stricken and downtrodden, while James preferred to circulate through the salons and country houses of the upper classes.

Still, Jane might have had a better opinion of her dining room acquaintance if she had read his latest novel, *The Portrait of a Lady*, a beautifully written study of a young American girl visiting Europe for the first time. James described, with a wealth of subtle nuances, the experiences of Isabel Archer entering an old, sophisticated society quite willing to take advantage of her wide-eyed American innocence—something that Jane might have appreciated during her own European experience.

Like Isabel, she saw fine country houses similar to the Gardencourt of James's novel, and she brushed against women who resembled his insidious Madame Merle. Unlike Isabel, however, Jane noticed how the other half lived—the masses, the larger segment of what Benjamin Disraeli called "the two nations" of the rich and the poor.

Jane Addams and Henry James went their separate ways after this one brief encounter on the high seas. It is a beguiling thought that two such different human beings ever got within speaking distance of one another.

Literary and social historians are also tempted to compare and contrast Jane Addams' life with that of her brilliant contemporary, Emily Dickinson, who was residing quietly in New England while Jane was seeking new experiences in Europe. Both were surcharged with nervous energy, baffled by the problems of finding a role for themselves in nineteenth-century America, given to introspection and self-analysis. The two did have somewhat different attitudes toward their fathers, for while Jane cherished a deep devotion to her father, Emily was sometimes quite skeptical about hers—as well as about the busy male world where her father played an active part. Emily heartily disliked people who "care about careers" to the exclusion of all other possible interests, and her attacks on a stuffy deity are accompanied by attacks on stuffy men. However, like the New England poetess, Jane Addams saw her life close twice—once when her father died, and again as she herself approached death. Both had a terror they "could tell to none," and came to know that "the soul selects its own society." Their solutions were quite different. Emily's surcease was poetry written in relative solitude; Jane had to get out into the world of action to find satisfaction. But are there any women of the present generation who tell us so much about our era as these two dedicated spinsters tell us about theirs?

Isabel Archer lived only in Henry James's novel; Emily Dickinson in distant Amherst, Massachusetts. The woman who had a direct effect on Jane's life, day after day, was Anna Haldeman Addams—but the effect was too often negative to please either. While they agreed on the importance of refinement, grace, and style in personal deportment, Jane refused to regard these passports to high society as the be-all and end-all that Mrs. Addams made of them. Jane's unwillingness to marry George Haldeman, or anyone else, remained as a barrier between stepdaughter and stepmother, for the latter could not sympathize with the determination of a girl in her early twenties to have a career rather than a husband. The quiet, intense conflict between the two was yet another burden for the frail, still-convalescent Jane.

Social vs. aesthetic reactions

During these months of mental struggle, physical pain was Jane's constant companion. But she would have nothing to do with self-pity or pampering. "Failure through ill health is just as culpable and miserable as failure through any other cause," she observed. In Europe, she would go to all the places she was supposed to go, see all the things she was supposed to see, learn whatever she was supposed to learn.

No one was more excited than twenty-three-year-old Jane Addams when she got her first

A YOUNG LADY WITH A TEMPER

The mature Jane Addams was famous for a tranquil disposition that she had not always possessed. The notebook she kept during her first European tour reveals her pronounced determination not to be imposed on and indicates that she had no aversion to starting a "fuss" whenever she and her traveling companions were vexed by anyone (see pages 132–134). Later, realizing that this was a character defect, she set out to eradicate it—and succeeded. Nicholas Kelley, son of Florence Kelley of Hull-House, has written: "My acquaintance with Hull-House began in 1891, in its second year, when as a small boy of six, I came here with my mother. . . . I never saw Miss Addams angry and never heard of her being angry. My mother once asked her how she could be so calm. Miss Addams replied that she had had a great struggle to master her temper when she was young."

Blarney Castle (above) holds the stone reputed to give eloquence to those who kiss it. Gustave Doré's engraving below shows a police patrol on duty in the London slums, keeping the wretched inhabitants under close surveillance.

glimpse of Europe—off Queenstown (now Cobh), Ireland, on August 29, 1883. Yet as early as the following day she began to find out what European "aristocracy" meant. The owner of nearby Blarney Castle, she learned, had an income of £13,000 (then over $60,000) a year. Men who worked for him got six shillings (then about $1.50) a week. Jane remembered this gross inequality as well as the striking beauty of the castle. She had hardly set foot in the Old World before the gulf between her *social* and *aesthetic* reactions began to emerge.

The next two months were devoted to "doing" the British Isles. In Dublin the Addams group bought art books. They went on to Edinburgh, "an enchanted city, filled with heroic associations." Stratford-on-Avon conjured up all the Shakespearean memories. But the traumatic experience that was to shape her whole thinking occurred farther south, in London. One Saturday evening, soon after their arrival in the capital, the American visitors went into the slums at Mile End Road. Jane "saw for the first time the overcrowded quarters of a great city at midnight." It was a sight that left her stunned and in disbelief. She had never imagined that such wretched, haggard people existed as the men, women, and children who pressed forward in a turbulent mob at the Saturday-night food auction, bidding frantically for vegetables that no member of the upper classes would have considered fit to eat. She noticed, too, that, as the auctioneer hawked his unsavory wares, skullduggery mingled with sorrow among the buyers. Since many an individual had to trade his last poor coin for a mildewed cabbage or wilted bunch of carrots, or else go without his Sunday meal, each tried to jostle his way to the front, and to outmaneuver the others before the last remnant of food was gone.

So this was glorious London, admired capital of a cultured nation and worldwide empire! The stinking vegetables, pinched faces, and raucous shouts were bad enough, but the myriad of clutching hands would haunt Jane more than anything else. From that day forward, she could never see a number of outstretched hands without being carried back to the horror of Mile End Road.

Not the fact that she had been unable to do anything, but that no one *expected* her to do anything, was the shock from which Jane Addams never fully recovered. As in London, so in every other city she visited, she found that an endless panorama of hideous human need and suffering lurked just behind the shining aristocratic exterior. On one occasion, in Saxe-Coburg, Germany, Jane tried to do something about conditions in a brewery. From her hotel she saw a line of working women carrying wooden tanks full of hot brew. Leaning forward under their back-breaking loads, they sometimes spilled scalding hot liquid on their bodies; large scars showed how many times such accidents had happened before. Stung into action, Jane found the brewery owner and complained. He received her with "exasperating indifference," evidently puzzled as to why anyone should object to the sight. The incident was a lesson in the indifference of employers to the suffering of their employees.

Little to dance about

On and on the Grand Tour went, lasting twenty-one months, and carrying Jane from northern Europe to Austria, Italy, Greece, back to Italy again, Switzerland, Britain, Berlin, and finally Paris. Jane looked at dozens of cathedrals, hundreds of pictures, and innumerable lovely views; studied German, Italian, and French; filled notebooks with her impressions. Her stepmother wanted her to take dancing lessons in Paris, but Jane's back hurt too much for that. Her diaries show conclusively that Jane Addams found a great deal to think about —but little to dance about—in nineteenth-century Europe.

One central lesson dominated all others: Artistic and intellectual effort was futile when disconnected from the ultimate test of the

German artist Kaethe Kollwitz caught the age-old anguish—and rising resentment—of Europe's ill-treated workers in her 1897 etching, "Marching Weavers." Such pictures encouraged the social-justice movements during this period.

A FASHIONABLE YOUNG LADY

When Jane toured Europe, she dressed well, befitting a young lady of her class, family, and upbringing. Her friends testified that this taste for fine clothing continued into her later life, when she preferred to appear in public garbed in the quiet elegance that became her. She liked smartly tailored dresses, and had a special fondness for elbow-length white kid gloves, which added to her appearance and made shaking hands easier at lectures and meetings. But, putting first things first, she never allowed fashion to get in the way of her work. Once when a secretary noted that her slip was showing, and began to adjust her dress, Jane paused for a minute, and then pulled away with the words: "Oh, never mind, I'm only going to speak."

Her generosity hampered her efforts to look as she wished, for she was constantly giving away the finery in her wardrobe. Thus, Louise de Koven Bowen presented her with a dozen pairs of gloves and sets of underwear, only to find Jane distributing them among her visitors who were too poor to buy such things. At Christmas, she rose to the spirit of the season so completely that Mrs. Bowen remarks ruefully: "It was difficult to get her to keep anything." She even gave away a beautiful coat tailor-made to fit her. The ladies of Hull-House understood this generosity for the virtue it was, while wishing she would show a little more of her famous practicality where her own clothes were concerned.

She wore dainty slippers to the opera, but did not scruple to kick them off if they felt uncomfortable, a surprising sight for any staid lady occupying the same box. In one way, Jane was decidedly unfashionable: She always wore rubbers on the streets, whether it was raining or not. At swank Bar Harbor, Maine, where she mingled with socialites like her Chicago acquaintance, Mrs. Potter Palmer, she emerged in her rubbers on the sunniest days. Her explanation was that the sidewalks made her feet cold, and she passed off the amusement of the others with a smile of her own that showed she too was amused.

As a young lady, she sported small modish hats appropriate to her age. In maturity, she switched to the large wide-brimmed variety popular with the women of the period. One of these received much notice in the press because she lost it while speaking at a public meeting, and had to ride bareheaded in a carriage with Theodore Roosevelt. On a visit to the White House to see T.R., Jane informed the butler: "I think I will take my hat off." He replied: "Madam, you can't take off your hat here, you must keep it on." She removed it in spite of him, and at table said to the President: "I had quite a scuffle with your butler. He didn't want me to take off my hat." T.R. answered: "Oh, dear, that was too bad. I often have scuffles with him."

Mary McDowell of the University Settlement once admired Jane's hat while the two were discussing a labor dispute in which Mary was involved. Despite their best endeavors, they could not decide what to do. As Jane was leaving she declared: "I can't do much to help you out of your troubles, but here is my hat. . . . I hope wearing it will make you feel better."

On her many travels, Jane carried sufficient luggage to provide for any predictable occasion, and invariably looked trim and neat, even in the hectic days when she took her pacifist message to the harassed statesmen of Europe during World War I. Her generosity extended to little things that mean so much. Receiving a box of roses to speed her recovery from an illness, she insisted on sending them to the sister of a Hull-House employee who was in the hospital. The employee was reluctant to take them, but Jane declared forthrightly: "They have served their purpose. They have got me out of bed, and I hope they will be successful in doing the same for her."

Mrs. Bowen adds an anecdote: "In later years Miss Addams came to live with me, and I had an elevator put in for her use. The other day a friend . . . remarked, 'I am glad you have the elevator you built for Miss Addams, which she was unable to give away'."

conduct it inspired. Until the *word* was made *flesh,* what did it mean to the millions who never attended operas or visited museums? What had she learned about real life in the cloister called Rockford Female Seminary? The young woman who returned first to New York and then to Cedarville could not ignore these questions, and could not begin to find answers. She wished that life might be molded closer to the heart's desire, but she had no idea of how to do it, or even where she should begin.

A bad period of her life followed. Jane called it "the nadir of nervous depression and sense of maladjustment." The family moved to Baltimore, where George was studying at Johns Hopkins. Mrs. Addams spent much time trying to climb the social ladder, a game in which her stepdaughter had no interest whatever. Jane felt as if she were being stifled by the politeness and pretension all around her. Courses in archaeology and Italian history provided the only real stimulation she had.

Anxious for the corporate religion that had eluded her at Rockford, she was baptized a Presbyterian in the summer of 1885. But, because the dedication of this church's members, rather than its specific theological tenets, motivated her, she remained nonsectarian, and some years later transferred, with no feeling of discomfort, to the Congregational church near Hull-House. She joined these religious bodies, her nephew James Weber Linn claims, as she might have joined a labor union, "because she thought her membership would help out." She was always glad to cooperate with any religious group engaged in humanitarian social work.

"I wish I had had a call to foreign missions as some of the girls at Rockford had," Jane wrote to Ellen Starr, who was now a schoolteacher. "They were fortunate; they knew what they wanted to do." Out of college several years, well-read and traveled, what had she *done*? That question became more acute during a visit to Girard, Kansas, where part of the funds from her father's estate had been used to buy mortgages. This type of investment had never bothered her before. Now, touring one of the farms that contributed to her personal income, she suffered a rude awakening. The farmhouse was badly rundown. The farmer's wife, "a picture of despair" after years of work and sorrow, stood in the doorway. Dirty, ragged children, too young to comprehend their own misery, shrank shyly behind her. The yard was filthy, the pigs in the pen half starved. The whole place had "poverty" written over it as surely as the slums of London. Jane's conscience revolted. She withdrew her investment in order to register a practical protest against the system that so demoralized human beings.

Personal doubts and spiritual unrest accompanied her home from Kansas. She still had no fixed resolution about what to do with her life when, in December 1887, she again went on shipboard, headed for Europe to join Ellen Starr. Perhaps this time she would find the purpose and the meaning she craved. At twenty-seven, six years out of college, she had accomplished nothing of consequence and had lost any sense of continuity or pattern in life that she had begun to develop in her teens. On her second European journey she wryly noted "the difference in my age and dignity between this trip and the one before. Then I was Mademoiselle and Fräulein; now everywhere it is 'Madame' with the utmost respect."

Revelation at the bullring

From Southampton and Paris she traveled to Germany. At Ulm, the glorious cathedral rose before her eyes. What impressed her most, however, was not the aesthetic beauty that has enchanted visitors to the town since the Middle Ages, but the mingling of people represented in the statues, paintings, and stained-glass windows. Here in this medieval building were portrayals of Hebrew prophets and Greek philosophers; Martin Luther, father of the Reformation, took his place amid Catholic

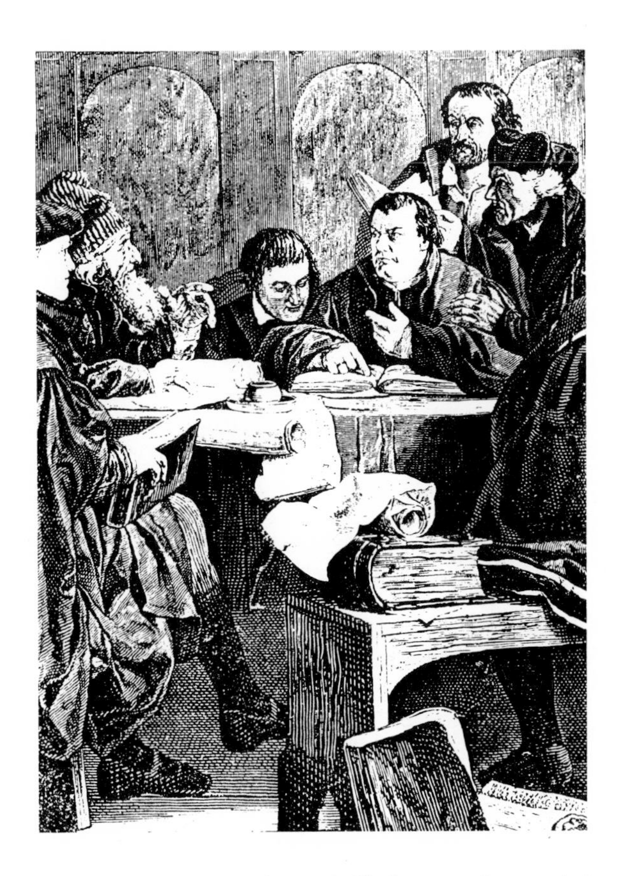

Jane admired the reforming zeal of Luther, seen here seated at right as he discusses translating the Bible into German.

In an 1891 issue, *Harper's Weekly* vividly revealed to its readers the violence involved in a Spanish bullfight.

saints. All mankind seemed welcome and at home in Ulm Cathedral. It was something new in the experience of Jane Addams—a "cathedral of humanity" dedicated to brotherhood, understanding, unity, and spiritual aspiration. A thought began to tease her mind: Why not build a modern "cathedral of humanity"? Surely so magnificent an ideal could not be dead, only waiting to be realized in a form that would meet contemporary needs? That thought became the cornerstone on which the edifice of her later life would be built (see pages 96–97).

Jane and Ellen Starr met in Munich, then went on to Rome. There Jane was ill for several weeks, and spent some time on the Riviera recuperating, after which she traveled to Madrid for Easter of 1888. Here the goal she had been seeking, and the idea she had been trying to formulate, would finally begin to clarify itself. Jane, like most tourists, was drawn to the spectacle of the bullfight. The others in her party, unable to stand it, left early; but Jane stayed, entranced by the "glories of the amphitheater." The bravery of the matadors reminded her of the trials of courageous men in past ages. This reverie, not the stark reality of the five dead bulls, held her. Finally leaving, and finding her friends waiting for her, she began, under their criticism, to mull over the incident. Suddenly she felt "tried and condemned"—for enjoying the violence, and for wasting her precious time on it.

Like a bolt, the realization of her inaction struck her speechless. She had been lulling her conscience with dreams, defending her continued idleness with self-righteous charges against others, and making some indefinite future reform a reason for going on with study and travel. "I had fallen into the meanest type of self-deception in making myself believe that all this was in preparation for great things to come," she confessed. In the stern terms of Christ's parable, she had been so busy pointing to the relatively small motes in others' eyes that she had not seen the relatively huge beam in her own eye. Such was her self-criticism outside the Madrid bullring.

From then on, she would act. The next morning she revealed to Ellen Starr a plan that had lingered in her mind for years, but had not begun to take any definite shape until her stay at Ulm. Why not rent a house in a city where many daily needs were urgent—where the battle for life was actually being fought—where one could try out the grand ideas learned in books and lectures by putting them to the ultimate test of the conduct they dictated or inspired? Why not *do* the truth? To Jane's astonishment and delight, Ellen Starr, the artist, understood precisely what she meant, and promised to join her in putting the new scheme into practice. The central principle on which the remainder of Jane Addams' long life would rest had been stated. Now she knew what she was seeking: ways and means of turning mere words into an inspiring, practical reality.

Chapter 4
FROM DREAMS TO INHABITING REALITY

THE FIRST THING the two excited reformers needed was a kind of model. Jane Addams and Ellen Gates Starr knew from their reading and their travel that the most suitable prototypes were to be found in Great Britain. As the leader of the Industrial Revolution, Britain was the first nation to confront some of its most bitter, agonizing consequences and pioneered in projects of social concern and urban relief. A long series of parliamentary reports had revealed the shocking misery of Britain's industrial cities, and had provoked remedial government legislation during the great ministries of Benjamin Disraeli and William Ewart Gladstone. Individual reformers attempted to restore order and dignity to labor. William Morris dreamed of a return to something like the medieval tradition of personal craftsmanship as an antidote to soulless mass production. John Ruskin, so admired by Jane Addams for his writings, also actually led an experiment in communal living, his short-lived Guild of St. George. Thomas Davidson founded the Fellowship of the New Life in 1883,.which became the Fabian Society, notable both for having Bernard Shaw among its members and for deeply influencing Britain's twentieth-century socialist governments of Ramsay MacDonald, Clement Attlee, and Harold Wilson.

Jane and Ellen knew of the London Charity Organization Society, established in 1869 and imitated in such American cities as Buffalo and Boston. But the chief model for these two aspiring American ladies was the social-settlement movement, culminating in London's Toynbee Hall. Arnold Toynbee (uncle of the later historian of the same name) had moved from Oxford University to London in 1875—while still a student—seeking a socially useful role among the poor. He joined Samuel Augustus Barnett, the Anglican vicar of St. Jude's Parish, an exponent of the "social gospel" who believed that the time had long since come to put Christian precepts into action in the lives of the people, both practically and effectively.

For Canon Barnett—as afterward for Jane Addams—a settlement was a group of individuals living in a poverty-stricken area, not only in order to understand the lives of those around them, but also to improve conditions in every possible way. The plan was to bring human beings together from all walks of life so they could learn from one another's example. The poor would thus not be merely ministered to by officials or philanthropists from the outside. Barnett believed that shared experience and personal concern could create a richer life for all in the chaotic new cities. As more young Oxford men rallied behind him, the University Settlement Association was born. Toynbee Hall (the first social settlement in the world) was erected in 1884 with the Reverend Mr. Barnett its first warden. It soon became a beachhead of social action in the London slums.

Canon and Mrs. Barnett repaid Jane's visit to Toynbee Hall by coming to Hull-House to open its first art show in 1891.

Chicago's challenge

Americans were quick to sense Toynbee Hall's importance. Stanton Coit visited and worked there; returning to New York, he set up his Neighborhood Guild—the first American settlement—in 1886. Even as he did this, Jane Addams was carefully examining Toynbee Hall for herself, formulating all the plans that she took back to Chicago. She could scarcely have found a more challenging place than the Windy City at that period of its history.

Chicago had grown by leaps and bounds since the day, back in 1844, when her parents had decided it was not the place for them. The focal point of Midwestern expansion, it was now a sprawling metropolis that had risen, phoenix-like, from the ashes left by the disastrous fire of 1871. The harbor handled scores of the biggest freighters plying the Great Lakes. Railroads converged on Chicago from the east, and fanned out into the west. An intricate banking system dealt with the high finances of manufacturing, wheat, lumber, and meatpacking. Chicago was already Carl Sandburg's "Stormy, husky, brawling,/City of the Big Shoulders."

Here, indeed, Darwinian "survival of the fittest" was law. Opportunities abounded for those astute and ruthless enough to rise above the herd into the wealthy class. Self-made men controlled industries, bought politicians and policemen, and lived in plush mansions on the shores of Lake Michigan. These tycoons had their labor pool in the city, especially in the squalid ghetto where lived vast numbers of easily exploited people who suffered from the misfortune of having been born abroad. From 1885 onward, Europeans fleeing their native lands came to America in the waves of the "new immigration." Hundreds of thousands poured in through New York every year and many of them went on to Chicago hoping to find work in the brawling hub of the Midwest. Chicago was prepared to accept their labor, but not to offer them anything approaching decent living conditions. They swarmed into a maze of slum areas, took menial jobs at low wages and long hours, and existed as best they could amid social evils and personal degradation.

Jane Addams, of course, was not the first humanitarian to notice the terrible condition of Chicago's poor. Various charitable organizations like the Y.M.C.A., the Ethical Culture Society, and the Relief and Aid Society assisted the dispossessed with everything from free meals to free libraries. But these groups could not eliminate the basic evils because they attacked, for the most part, the consequences rather than the causes of ghetto life. Besides, their activities were hampered by corrupt ward bosses who exchanged handouts for votes, and cared less about eradicating the slums than about making sure (in return for substantial bribes) that the magnates of manufacturing, transport, utilities, and real estate received the permits, charters, and franchises they wanted.

Violence was endemic to Chicago, much of it generated by strife between robber barons and their wage slaves. One terrible example came when a strike at the McCormick harvester plant led to the bloody Haymarket riot on May 4, 1886. A bomb was thrown as a group of police advanced, and they promptly opened fire on the crowd. Between the bomb and the shooting, seven people were killed and more than sixty injured. The authorities never discovered who really threw the bomb, but four of the accused were executed, and three more received long prison sentences. As these men were known to be radicals associated with anarchists, a wave of hysteria swept through Chicago enveloping legitimate social protests in dark suspicion.

This was the American city that journalist Lincoln Steffens described as "first in violence, deepest in dirt; loud, lawless, unlovely, ill-smelling . . . the 'tough' among cities, a spectacle for the nation. Criminally it was wide open, commercially it was brazen, and socially it was thoughtless and raw . . . . Everybody was for himself and none was for Chicago." If Christ came to Chicago, declared British observer William T. Stead in 1894, he would find "vice, criminality, corruption, and above all neglect such as no other late-nineteenth-century city would tolerate." Choosing to spend the rest of her life there was a bold decision on the part of the lady from Cedarville, Jane Addams. It was also realistic in terms of her own thinking—namely, that she should put her ideals to action and would personally benefit from such action. Additionally, it was realistic because the course she had adopted was one of the best possible ways to cope with the numerous problems raised by the growing urban slums.

American attitudes had changed since the Civil War. The sentimentality of the romantic era no longer found a congenial home in the new moral, economic, and artistic climate of the United States. Philosophers, writers, reformers, were turning more and more to hard-

This *Harper's Weekly* engraving of 1884 presents a panorama of bustling activity along the Chicago River, looking upstream.

In 1881, while manufacturers were demanding high protective tariffs, a *Puck* cartoon saw American industry as a clanking colossus "quite big enough to take care of myself!"

headed realism, looking facts in the face, and refusing to be fobbed off with pious and tarnished platitudes. Hence the rise of social realism in literature. "They will have the new truth in larger and larger degree," predicted William Dean Howells, a writer whom Jane Addams had long admired.

Once, after a lecture during which she had focused on one member of her audience (as was her custom), the man she had singled out approached her. Their conversation went as follows. "That was a wonderful speech, and do you know, I had the curious and delightful feeling all through that you were talking to me personally."

"In a way I was, and you helped me out so splendidly that I shall be very much obliged to you if you will tell me who you are."

"My name is William Dean Howells."

The literary and intellectual movement Howells led, and to which Jane Addams was emotionally committed, was a direct product of the American experience. At an earlier date, Howells himself had thought that "the more smiling aspects of life" were those most characteristically American. But after he took a more searching look at society, Howells came to the conclusion that idealism was often just a cloak for hypocrisy and selfishness. In his book *A Traveler from Altruria,* he developed this theme around the story of a visitor from an imaginary land who had admired American ideals from afar, and then had come to the United States to see those ideals in practice. The man from Altruria was astounded to find the leaders of American life busily cheating and exploiting their fellow citizens. The countermovement of which Howells was so articulate a spokesman, while drawing from European thought and experience, had few exact models to copy. Decidedly pragmatic and experimental, this American literary and social realism had to make its own way according to its own experience; it campaigned against actual grievances, fighting when and where the need arose, and was distinguished by its poignant simplicity and unquenchable zeal.

Three books by famous Americans were being utilized for reformist ideas at the time Jane Addams founded Hull-House. The first was by Henry "Single Tax" George who, in *Progress and Poverty,* raised the question of why masses of people were poverty-stricken at a time when the nation was progressing in such a spectacular way—or why "The House of Want" stood beside "The House of Have." George's diagnosis placed the blame on greedy land monopolists, who profited by selling or renting as values rose. He proposed to cure the economic ills of America by imposing a single, comprehensive tax on the land, and doing away with all other taxes. The second book was Edward Bellamy's *Looking Backward,* in which the author, outraged by the consequences of unbridled capitalism, imagined a purely collectivist society as it would exist in the year 2000.

Jane Addams knew the works of George and Bellamy. She later invited George to lecture at Hull-House, and recorded the warm welcome "this great leader" received from his audience "during his stirring address, filled, as all his speeches were, with high moral enthusiasm and humanitarian fervor."

She was never that close to the third author, Lester Ward, but he was perhaps the most important of all for her kind of thinking, since he showed in *Dynamic Sociology* that it was scientifically sound to accept Darwinism in the biological sense, while rejecting Social Darwinism. Explicitly contradicting the laissez-faire theories of William Graham Sumner, Ward argued that the evolutionary process becomes transformed in man, who has the intelligence to set aside "the survival of the fittest" in favor of evolution through mutual help. Legislation to sustain the weaker members of society is no violation of the natural law, but rather its highest manifestation. Jane Addams said amen to that.

The desire for reform was making itself felt when Jane came to Chicago, through the January snows of 1889, seeking a house that she could turn into a headquarters for the type of reform she had in mind. There was no hurry. Just any house wouldn't do, so she and Ellen Starr spent several months looking for precisely the right place. Journalists, architects, and city officials—even the former mayor—made suggestions. Jane finally discovered the ideal house. After "losing" it, and being vexed with herself for her forgetfulness of its location, she stumbled upon it again during a routine search with architect Allen Pond.

Occupying one corner of Halsted and Polk streets, the two-storied, high-windowed, red-brick mansion had been erected in 1856 by a real-estate speculator named Charles J. Hull, who wanted something in the "Italian villa style." A wide veranda, spaced off by clusters of Greek columns, gave the building a classical air. The rooms were large enough to allow for social gatherings of the local people, who would be the prime interest of the settlement. But the home of Charles J. Hull had come down in the world from its initial elegance. Miraculously, it had not been damaged during the Chicago fire of 1871, although the holocaust had started nearby (when, according to legend, Mrs. O'Leary's cow kicked over a lantern). A group of Catholic nuns occupied the premises four years

"STRANGE, WASN'T IT?"

The young Miss Addams was quite capable of getting angry. Later she not only kept her temper under the most trying circumstances but also became famous for her tolerance of both ingratitude and vituperation. Her personal physician, Dr. Alice Hamilton, who was also one of her oldest and closest colleagues at Hull-House, remembered:

"She never shrank from painful facts. She never refused to listen to damaging evidence. I well remember how indignant I was when she told me that she had invited a grief-stricken young couple to come for a visit, and I knew that those very people had treated her with a contemptible injustice born of panic and fear. When I reminded her of it she said vaguely, 'Why yes, that is true, they did. Strange, wasn't it?' And then she dropped the subject. She did not excuse them, for there was no excuse, but her pity was just as tender as if she had shut her eyes to the fact."

Graham Taylor remarked: "She tried to understand those who ignorantly or maliciously misinterpreted her; but rarely did she offer any self-defense. She was almost superhumanly without resentment—even extenuating their abuse as attributable more to prejudice than to evil intent. For years the publisher of the Chicago *Chronicle*, then the outstanding financial daily paper, persistently and with malice aforethought maligned both of us by name and urged the suppression of both settlements not only as seditious, but as encouraging delinquency and crime. Later he was himself convicted and sentenced to the federal penitentiary for violating the banking law. When I reported this to Miss Addams her only reply was, 'Poor old man!' "

A third friend, Mrs. Elia W. Peattie, wrote: "She has a patience which includes all men, all sins, all conditions, all prejudices, all superstitions. Whatever else may be said of her, she is largely tolerant. Possibly she is the most largely tolerant soul in this great community of souls who do not commune; this commonwealth which is not common; this industrial corporation called Chicago in which industry crushes and makes men."

later, and subsequently various rooms were rented to lodgers and businessmen. In 1889 a saloonkeeper and a furniture factory held leases on the first floor, while private families lived in the rooms above.

Only the unoccupied rooms were available to Jane Addams and Ellen Starr. They were lucky that the owner, Helen Culver, Hull's cousin and secretary, sympathized with their plans and allowed them to have the entire building rent free in 1890. Miss Culver eventually gave Jane the house itself and several nearby plots of land for expansion (see pages 150–151).

An urban ghetto

Hull-House opened on September 18, 1889, when three "new settlers"—twenty-nine-year-old Jane Addams, thirty-year-old Ellen Starr, and a matronly housekeeper named Mary Keyser—moved into the sooty, sagging mansion on Halsted Street. If they had been afraid of work, they would have been appalled by the amount of repairs that had to be done. If they had been bothered by incongruous neighbors, they would have winced when they looked out the windows and saw a saloon on one side and an undertaker's parlor on the other. For years the punsters of the area would refer to the settlement house, the undertaker's parlor, and the saloon as "Knight, Death, and the Devil," after Albrecht Dürer's engraving of that name.

Durer placed his Knight beside Death bearing an hourglass, with a bestial, misshapen Devil following close behind.

Jane Addams may have chuckled at the pun. She never chuckled at the reality that lay all around Hull-House. Too many drunken men reeled past from the multitude of gin mills that offered the bottle as a substitute for decency. Too many slatternly women, prematurely old through toil, poverty, and sorrow, peered from the dingy windows of rat-infested tenements. Too many ragged urchins ran in gangs through filthy streets littered with garbage, rags, and old newspapers. These people lived in a noxious atmosphere compounded of decaying food, stagnant water, primitive sewage, and coal soot. In summer, the heat seared their bodies; in winter, the cold chilled their bones; and their weakened physical condition left them vulnerable to tuberculosis and pneumonia. Usually too poor to afford a doctor, often too ignorant to know how to find one, the ill lay on wretched pallets in dismal rooms, surrounded by dejected families, until death came as a release.

Vice and crime germinated spontaneously in the drab, demoralizing life of the slums. It was enough to make the angels weep. City ghettos like this were the new frontier—harder, in many ways, than the frontier that John Addams had faced when he drove west from Chicago in 1844. The immigrants Jane Addams saw from her window were caught between two worlds, just as she had been when she wandered in the cities of Europe. But she had had money, comfort, education, while they had almost nothing but a handful of memories. Their Old World customs left them totally unfitted to understand, let alone to deal with, the New World to which they had come. Uprooted, their lives wrenched out of familiar patterns, they felt lost in the flux of America's urban change.

Chicago, on the other hand, did not know what to do about *them.* The city, a million strong now, was in the grip of a population explosion. About 400,000 Germans had come, 215,000 Irish, 54,000 Bohemians, thousands upon thousands of Poles, Italians, Greeks, Russians, Scandinavians, Jews. Chicago had more Germans than any place but Berlin and Hamburg, more Swedes than any cities but Stockholm and Göteborg. True, immigration was not the sole reason for Chicago's population problem. It had its enclaves of oppressed Negroes, and its share of other native-born Americans who had been submerged by the rising tide of poverty, many of them ex-farmers who had deserted the land for the city during the hard times that followed the depression of 1873. Nevertheless, the hordes of immigrants crowding in created dilemmas of a size and complexity never before known.

Americans did not take kindly to this invasion of foreigners. A residue still existed of the old nativism that had been so prevalent when the United States received an earlier influx of Europeans, especially Catholics, into what was basically an Anglo-Saxon, Protestant culture. Yet, the pre-Civil War immigration had not swamped the cities, and the immigrants, however different in their beliefs, had been able to find a place in American society. The post-Civil War newcomers met a much colder reception. Looked upon as another breed, they were subjected to a harsher mythology than mere nativism. They were said to be "un-American" —low in mentality, crude in manners, shifty in morals. Politically, the southern and eastern Europeans were held to be radical; socially, to be inferior. The melting pot, declared some of those who had only recently been melted in it themselves, could not be expected to assimilate the thousands of peasants who "threatened to break down American civilization."

Moreover, these new immigrants had reached America at a period when the nation's economic

Recently arrived immigrants, clad in their Old World costumes, head west by a railroad "Zulu car" in search of the American dream. Groups such as this, coming in a steady stream, helped to populate America's big cities.

situation was changing rapidly and drastically. New modes of production were destroying the old notion that one worked for wages primarily to save some money to be used as a stepping-stone toward starting a small business of one's own. Jane Addams' idol, Abraham Lincoln, had endorsed this, pointing out that the "prudent penniless beginner in the world labors for wages awhile, saves a surplus with which to buy tools or land for himself, then labors on his own account." The widespread dislocation, and even collapse, of this process was an important factor in social unrest. Business and farming enterprises alike were growing bigger and more complex, thus requiring a larger initial outlay than one man could now provide for himself.

The immigrants themselves also managed to exacerbate the social ills from which they suffered. Disliked by the Americans beyond the ghetto, they often disliked one another because of age-old animosities originating in Europe. Italians and Greeks, Poles and Germans, preferred not to mingle. Even the same religion frequently failed to bridge the culture gap. Bohemian Catholics resented Irish priests in their churches; Orthodox Jews from Russia avoided Reform Jews from Germany. Thus, instead of one big ghetto, there were a series of small ones, and the residents of each clung together tenaciously, cherishing their memories and language, and resisting Americanization.

Clearly, something had to be done about this welter of prejudices, misconceptions, and irrational hostilities if the slums of Chicago were ever to be cleaned up. Jane Addams had specific ideas on the subject when she selected Hull-House in the noisome Nineteenth Ward as her headquarters for a sustained endeavor. She resolved from the day she crossed its threshold that her house would be open to all creeds, races, and nationalities. The seething world outside her front door might be a jungle (a succession of gang murders took place not far away), but her door was, nonetheless, open to anyone at any time.

Hull-House was an integrated institution, although Negroes did not immediately take advantage of the settlement. At that time they formed only a small percentage of Chicago's population, numbering less than fifteen thousand in 1890, and were congregated in the South Division of the city—yet in time they came to know that they were as welcome as

"THE DOOR WAS OPEN"

One immigrant from Russia, Philip Davis, could barely speak English when he arrived in America as a young man. Yet he went to Harvard, became a social worker in Boston, and wrote an eloquent autobiography in which he cites Hull-House as an important milestone in his life: "In my neighborhood it was frequently mentioned as a kind of school which extended a helping hand to the immigrant. Upon making inquiries about it among the neighbors I found that everyone assessed it favorably, according to his needs and lights: The newsboy on the corner—'Oh yeah. Nice place. We play ball there.' . . . The old woman selling oranges on the sidewalk: 'It's kind of a "suspensary" ' [dispensary]. . . . A working girl passing by: 'Oh sure. I belong to the Choral Society. We sing there every Sunday.' . . . An Italian vegetable peddler: ' "Whole" House? Sure—she is open to everyone!' . . . The policeman on the beat: 'It's O.K. Takes the kids off the street!' . . .

"The first time I approached Hull-House the door was open and I walked in. No one was in the reception hall so I sat down near a table, eyeing the books and magazines. Presently Jane Addams appeared. . . . She greeted me cordially, then said: 'Don't you want to read the *Atlantic Monthly* just out?' . . . Miss Addams passed through several times. Realizing I was lingering rather than reading, she tried conversation: 'Living around here?' she ventured. 'On DeKoven Street,' I answered. 'Oh, then we are neighbors. You must come often,' she said warmly. That was what I had hoped for.

"Such was my introduction to Hull-House, the university of good will, good English, good citizenship—in brief, everything good that America stands for."

Davis greatly admired Jane Addams and fondly recalled how she had bolstered his confidence during his visits to the settlement: "Although very busy with the duties of the House, she always managed to talk with me and others like me. I have to smile now at the nature of those conversations, for she knew so much more about the subjects we discussed than I did. Gracious person that she was, she acted as if I were the authority on the subject and she an . . . amateur."

This open-air market near Hull-House was characteristically deep in mud and refuse when it was photographed in 1906.

anyone. Jane Addams, in turn, learned that *de facto* segregation in northern cities could be as deadly a social blight as legalized segregation in the South. She attacked it vigorously in her speeches and writings.

The essential point is that she was never a "do-gooder" in the pejorative sense of the term, never a dispenser of charity to the underdog in a purely personal way. She was that remarkable type of human being, the idealist who knows how to embody high principles in realistic, viable, enduring institutions. She has often been compared to St. Francis of Assisi, whose compassion bettered his society, and continued to do so after his death through the religious order he founded. Jane's "Franciscan Order" was Hull-House. She began, and the settlement continued, the process of bringing Christian morality to bear on social problems. Quite understandably, she has sometimes been called "Saint Jane."

William James, profound philosopher and brilliant phrasemaker, described Jane Addams accurately when he wrote to her: "The fact is, Madam, that you are not like the rest of us, who *seek* the truth and try to express it. You *inhabit* reality." Jane appreciated this accolade if only because of her high regard for the writer. She consistently followed the philosophy that James helped to formulate, and that John Dewey brought to a culmination—the typically American philosophy of pragmatism, which taught her to test her ideas by seeing how they worked when put into practice. She constantly adjusted her theories pragmatically to make them conform to experience. Thus, as experience proved that individual social workers could not cope by themselves with the immensely complicated problems of urban life, she laid increasing stress on the need of the state to shoulder more and more of the burden, and campaigned strenuously for social legislation and welfare boards to eradicate many of the evils that had brought Hull-House into existence. At the same time, she could see—pragmatically—that individual effort had a

Hull-House democracy is exemplified by this glimpse of Ellen Starr, second in command, pouring tea for the help.

unique effectiveness in some areas, and she never ceased to labor in those areas.

It took her friends—and even her close relatives—a long time to comprehend her principles, motives, and objectives. Why, they asked, would a refined girl of good family background want to live in the horrid slums of a rather terrifying city? Jane received little understanding at home; Mrs. Addams, a true believer in polite society and ladylike behavior, was dreadfully embarrassed by what her stepdaughter was doing, and flatly refused to provide financial assistance.

Jane and Ellen, however, remained undaunted. Their aim was to attract to Hull-House all whom they could assist in any way. A few of the neighbors came to tea, and then a few of the girls from the furniture factory to supper. The first program the two young women undertook was a reading class in George Eliot, the English novelist. Gradually the people along Halsted Street, conquering their shyness and their suspicion of these two "swells," began to frequent the old mansion where they could always find a welcome. Jane and Ellen treated everyone kindly. With their good education and European experience, they were able to speak Italian, German, and French as needed—a strong bond of sympathy and trust when so many immigrants possessed only the rudiments of English.

A changing dream

One besetting problem was to fill empty stomachs. Children, especially, found that milk and spaghetti were available at the "big house." There the fires burned throughout the bitter winter evenings; men and women knew that they could warm their hands and get hot coffee and sandwiches. But the wider economic dilemma remained. These immigrants had come to share in the American dream without realizing how sharply that dream was fading, even for native-born Americans, in an era of monopolies, trusts, strikes, and riots. How few of the foreign-born could hope to rise through competition into financial security!

Unable to move to a more respectable section of the city, they had to make the best of their situation. Hull-House did what it could for them. As its reputation grew, virtually every type of human problem arrived on its doorstep. "The demands which are brought to it," wrote the sociologist Dorothea Moore, "are varied enough. One man wants to be 'shown the sense of poetry,' another wants his wife 'converted to the evangelical religion' for the sake of a peaceful fireside, and a third wants—just the patrol wagon. One mother leaves her baby 'while she goes to the matinee,' and another hopes to find her boy, arrested she knows not where, for what, or by whom."

The demands on time and labor increased with success. Fortunately, volunteers also heard about Hull-House, and they came flocking in to help. Eventually more than one hundred full-time, part-time, or temporary workers were connected with the settlement, while more than twenty resided on the premises. Jane Addams and her closest collaborators—Ellen Starr,

Julia Lathrop, Alice Hamilton, Alzina Stevens, Florence Kelley, Louise de Koven Bowen, Mary Rozet Smith—constituted what is probably the most remarkable group of women, devoted to a single purpose, that the United States has ever known. Zona Gale termed the women of Hull-House "the great ladies of Chicago" because they "awakened the social conscience" [of the city] and "created a center of social energy for the nation."

Most of them left well-to-do families and pleasant homes to work in the urban ghetto. Why? Jane Addams had already answered that question with her phrase "the subjective necessity for social settlements," by which she meant that those who came to work had as much to gain as those who came for aid. She herself had suffered from the idleness that the possession of wealth encourages, from the feeling of uselessness engendered by an overprotected existence in an ivory tower. Her prescription for anyone so afflicted was meaningful, personal activity down among the masses of humanity. The rest of "the great ladies of Chicago" responded to that kind of thinking. Hull-House gave them an outlet into the real world (see pages 145–152).

Since several of the ladies had money, they contributed generously to its upkeep. Jane Addams and Ellen Starr had put their own funds into the project, and they managed to obtain aid from prosperous Chicagoans who admired their work. Thus Edward Butler, a successful businessman, contributed five thousand dollars for an art gallery. Yet, the financial burden became heavier as Hull-House activities expanded. So it was a real help when, for instance, Louise de Koven Bowen built Bowen Hall for the Woman's Club, and when Mary Rozet Smith opened her comfortable house for use by her colleagues at the settlement.

The success of Hull-House led to its incorporation in 1895. John Dewey, now a professor at the University of Chicago, was one of the trustees who supported the purposes summarized in the charter: "To provide a center for a higher civic and social life, to institute and maintain educational and philanthropic enterprises, and to investigate and improve the conditions [existing throughout] the industrial districts of Chicago."

JANE AS GARBAGE COLLECTOR

In her *Who's Who* listing, Jane included only a very few of her many and varied achievements—but one she always proudly listed in that sketch was her period as a garbage inspector! In 1898 one of her most indomitable colleagues, Florence Kelley, wrote the following account of the episode for *The New England Magazine:*

"In 1892 the condition of the alleys was such that epidemic cholera seemed inevitable. During that summer residents at Hull-House forwarded to the Board of Health more than one thousand complaints of violations of the sanitary laws. . . . The ward contractor made no attempt to live up to his contract; and he was stronger than the Board of Health. In 1895, Miss Addams filed a bid for the contract, which was not awarded to her; instead she was appointed ward [garbage] inspector. In the following year, when Miss Addams was about to be absent in Europe for several months, Miss Johnson, a resident who had been acting as her deputy, took the first civil service examination offered under the new law, passed at the head of the list, and . . . Miss Addams resigned. The struggle to enforce the contract is a daily recurring one, carried on with unwearied patience and ceaseless attention to detail. In consequence, the alleys are cleaner than they have ever been; and the interest of the neighbors in this aspect of the civil life is now so keen that, when Miss Johnson was temporarily removed to another ward during the last summer, daily complaints poured into the office of the Board of Health and more than one delegation called at the City Hall to ask for her return, which was ultimately granted. This wholly spontaneous action on the part of the neighbors who had never before taken any initiative may serve as an indication of the social effect of five years of patient effort on the spot for sanitary improvement. In 1892, when the alleys were in an intolerable condition, it was not possible to arouse any effective interest in them. In 1897, after two years of Miss Johnson's work as an official, the mere dread of a relapse into the old state of things called forth spontaneous protests."

A "cathedral of humanity"

By then, Jane Addams had made her point about "the objective value of a social settlement"—its value, that is, to the people of the neighborhood. She interpreted these words to mean much more than care and compassion for the suffering. Recalling how Ulm Cathedral seemed dedicated to the principle of reconciling all men and uplifting their souls, she built her own version of a "cathedral of humanity" on Halsted Street. Hull-House, ministering to spiritual no less than to bodily deprivations, dispensing beauty and culture along with food and clothing, showed its guests what to do with their leisure time. A program of adult education provided classes in painting, handicrafts, and music, and lectures in the sciences and humanities. William James and John Dewey were among the notable professors who lectured in Bowen Hall to huge crowds. The theater deserves special mention. The Hull-House Players achieved such renown for their repertoire—from the Elizabethans to Ibsen and Shaw—that they became pioneers of the little-theater movement in the United States. They gave the first American performance of John Galsworthy's *Justice* in 1911. The celebrated English man of letters visited Hull-House the next year, was impressed by the production, and granted the players permission to stage *The Pigeon*, his latest drama.

Amateur actor William Granata strikes a pose for a fine Hull-House production of Molière's *The Would-Be Gentleman.*

Hull-House "leavened the lump," to use the biblical figure of speech, in a multitude of ways. The Jane Club (a cooperative boarding-club for working women begun in 1891) and the public playground for children were imitated first in Chicago and then in other American cities. Under the prodding of Jane Addams, Chicago also undertook joint fund-raising for several worthy causes at once, a scheme that had been first fully endorsed at the Congress of Charities, Corrections and Philanthropy in 1893. Ideas propounded at Hull-House were practical enough to be implemented far beyond the boundaries of the Nineteenth Ward, among citizens who were not slum dwellers but solidly middle class.

It would be wrong, however, to give the impression that all Chicagoans revised their early unfavorable opinions of Hull-House. Respectable people continued to cast aspersions on the ladies who lived in the slums. Diehard defenders of laissez-faire suspected that radicalism was rampant at the settlement because it entertained men like Henry Demarest Lloyd, the author of *Wealth Against Commonwealth,* an excoriation of the brutal business practices of John D. Rockefeller and Standard Oil. Local politicians worried about the effect of social betterment on their constituents: Alderman John Powers made himself such a barrier to progress that Jane Addams threw her influence against him in elections—unsuccessfully, as she noted, since "one out of every five voters in the Nineteenth Ward held a job dependent on the good will of the alderman." Newspapers favorable to these interests fumed at Hull-House in news reports and editorials.

Still, Jane Addams had powerful advocates. Most influential of all, she had on her side John Peter Altgeld, who was elected governor of Illinois in 1892. Altgeld remains one of the great liberals of American history. Unafraid to adopt unpopular measures, he pardoned the Haymarket rioters who were still in jail. When workers at the Pullman Company walked off their jobs, Altgeld protested President Grover Cleveland's using federal troops against them, and he urged George Pullman to be more just to his employees, an appeal the sleeping-car magnate coldly rejected. "There is," Altgeld insisted, "at present neither Magna Charta nor Bill of Rights for the poor of our great cities." Clarence Darrow, who represented union leader Eugene V. Debs in court, was one of the Chicagoans who rallied to the side of the governor during the Pullman strike. Jane Addams was another. Although an old acquaintance of Pullman, she criticized his paternalistic attitude to labor in a searching analysis she titled *A Modern Lear* (see pages 157–161).

Of Altgeld's relation to the ladies of Hull-House, Charles Beard has written the following passage: "Nearly everything in his program was in their program: the demand for 'essential statistical information on industrial conditions in Chicago,' extension of child-labor legislation from mines to factories, extermination of sweatshops in cities, introduction of factory inspection, arbitration in labor disputes, regulation of public utilities, abolition of the exploitation of convict labor by private contractors, enlargement and improvement of state welfare institutions, lifting the state university to a high position as a center of learning and public service, and advancement of popular education in every department." Hull-House lost a good friend when Governor Altgeld was defeated in his bid for reelection in 1896.

A rebuke from Tolstoy

That same year Jane Addams took her first extended vacation in seven years. Since her arrival in Chicago in 1889, her duties as organizer, director, social worker, propagandist, fund-raiser, and gadfly of Chicago officialdom—she was by now the ward garbage inspector—had made it impossible for her to think about herself. In 1895, after a bad case of typhoid fever had left her weak and hollow-eyed, her doctor advised a complete rest and she decided to go abroad the next year. Her motives included more than physical recuperation. She wanted to meet Count Leo Tolstoy (see pages 164–169).

This 1909 *Collier's* print depicts vicious and corrupt people reveling at a ball in Chicago's First Ward, run by bosses "Bathhouse John" Coughlin and "Hinky-Dink" Kenna. John Powers (opposite page) was a similar boss in his ward.

"ONE LONG BAD DREAM"

Sidney and Beatrice Webb, an English couple who were almost exactly Jane's age and were both distinguished for their work on behalf of social democracy, stayed at Hull-House several times from 1893 onward. Mrs. Webb smoked cigarettes at a time when it was very daring indeed for a lady to do so, and in her effort to make the Englishwoman feel thoroughly at home, Jane smoked her first and last cigarette. "I was glad I didn't like them," she said later, "for if I had liked them I'd have had to smoke them!" Beatrice Webb, in turn, did not entirely like Hull-House, and wrote the following candid comments about it during a visit in 1898:

"Hull-House itself is a spacious mansion, with all its rooms opening, American fashion, into each other. There are no doors, or, more exactly, no *shut* doors; the residents wander from room to room, visitors wander here, there and everywhere; the whole ground floor is, in fact, one continuous passage leading nowhere in particular. The courtyard, in front of the house, is always filled with slum children. At the back, opening out of the kitchen, is a rough and ready restaurant. There is the usual scanty service; the front door being answered by the resident who happens, at that time, to be nearest to it. . . . Miss Jane Addams . . . is without doubt a remarkable woman, an interesting combination of the organizer, the enthusiast and the subtle observer of human characteristics. . . . She has a charming personality, gentle and dignified, shrewdly observant; above all she excels in persistency of purpose and unflinching courage. She has made Hull-House; and it is she who has created whatever spirit of reform exists in Chicago.

"In the evening of our arrival we underwent a terrific ordeal. First an uncomfortable dinner, a large party served, higgledy-piggledy. Then a stream of persons, labor, municipal, philanthropic, university, all those queer, well-intentioned or cranky individuals, who habitually center round all settlements! Every individual among them must needs be introduced to us (a diabolical custom from which we have suffered greatly in America). Gradually the crowd pressed us into a large hall, with chairs for some hundreds and a small platform. From this place [we] were expected to orate . . . on any topic we chose. . . . For a right down exhausting business, commend me to a dinner and a reception, preceding a lecture and a severe heckling! However, we seemed to give satisfaction. The other days . . . at Hull-House . . . seem like one long bad dream lightened now and again by Miss Addams' charming grey eyes and gentle voice and graphic power of expression."

The author of *War and Peace* was internationally famous not only as a novelist but as a humanitarian. Tormented by remorse over the way his class had ridden for centuries on the backs of the Russian serfs, Tolstoy made his personal atonement by renouncing his position, privileges, and wealth, by dressing and eating as the peasants did, and by joining them in the labor of the fields. "Christian socialism" and "the sermon of the deed" were his watchwords. Jane hoped to find out if they could be hers.

Mary Rozet Smith accompanied her on this tour. After a brief stay in London, they crossed over to the Continent, and went on to Moscow, where they arranged to see Tolstoy at his home in Yasnaya Polyana. The visit Jane had anticipated for so long did not go as she expected. In his outspoken fashion, Tolstoy remarked that her garment contained more than enough excess material to make one for a little girl. Learning that part of her income derived from an Illinois farm, he called her "an absentee landlord," and hinted that she should work on the land herself—a manifest absurdity for one whose explicit vocation was to effect reforms in the city. He did persuade her to consider the idea of practicing Tolstoyism by doing the chores at Hull-House, but she soon realized that this could only be self-defeating because it would cut into the vital demands on her time.

Chicago and Yasnaya Polyana were worlds apart; principles that worked with Russian peasants would not necessarily work with America's urban poor. Yet, as Jane left for home, she knew that Tolstoy was raising basic human questions applicable to any individual in any society—applicable, therefore, to her and her country. She let many of his ideas filter into her own thinking, and they influenced the writing she did at Hull-House in the years ahead. Accept the moral imperative, make a personal commitment to social righteousness, act now to break down the artificial barriers that sunder mankind, preach the dignity and worth of every human being—that was the philosophy of Leo Tolstoy. It was also the philosophy of Jane Addams.

Chapter 5
OLD BATTLES IN A NEW CENTURY

THE SEASONS and years went swiftly by for the ladies of Hull-House. One day Jane Addams glanced at the calendar and realized that, as the first decade of her social work drew to a close, so did the century. She was approaching forty. Born in the Midwest while the Civil War was erupting, she had lived to see the causes of that conflict largely disappear. She knew that in 1900 it was no longer a case of Yank versus Rebel, but of capitalist versus laborer, of native-born versus foreign-born, of Negro versus white society. The battlefields had shifted from Bull Run and Gettysburg to wherever men struggled for the life, liberty, and pursuit of happiness that had been promised to Americans long ago in the Declaration of Independence.

Progress had been made—Hull-House by itself testified to that—but much remained to be done. If hope was abroad in the land, so was despair. William Jennings Bryan—Jane's old intercollegiate debate rival—reflecting the hopeful attitude of America on the threshold of world power, optimistically proclaimed: "There is not a land upon God's footstool in which the power of the people is not growing, nor a country on earth where the forces of privilege are not retreating." Jane Addams felt that the world's evils were not retreating fast enough. Rhetoric such as Bryan's was not wholly right, nor was progress so smoothly automatic.

The reform movement, to which Hull-House was contributing so notably, had not conquered man's inhumanity to man. In 1900 the average workweek for laborers was fifty-nine hours; the average rate of pay was less than ten dollars a week. Marie and Bessie Van Vorst reported in *The Woman Who Toils* that multitudes of women and children earned barely a dollar for a twelve-hour day. Robert Hunter, who did part of his economic research at Hull-House, calculated in his 1904 book *Poverty* that at least ten million of America's seventy-six million inhabitants were so poor that they could not "obtain those necessaries which will permit them to maintain a state of physical efficiency." Humans, Hunter found, were denied "the standard that a man would demand for his horses."

Meanwhile, a professor at the University of Chicago was etching in acid words a picture of those who sat on top of this massive pyramid of human misery. Thorstein Veblen, in *The Theory of the Leisure Class,* took a long, hard look at America's men of wealth, and judged them to be relics of a "barbarian phase of life" —motivated by materialism and cupidity, proud of the fact that they were the "fittest" who "survived" in the economic struggle, and ostentatiously determined to flaunt their wealth in the "conspicuous consumption" of goods.

Socialism and capitalism

Under these circumstances, the American Socialist movement picked up momentum. Eugene V. Debs, who had become a Socialist while in prison for his role in the Pullman strike, ran as the party's candidate for President in 1900. In Chicago, the Socialists won appreciable support, were influential on the Chicago Trades Council, and elected several aldermen to the City Council. Some of the leading Socialists were friends and admirers of Jane Addams. She supported their program where its aims were in line with her own—better living conditions, integrity in government, more social action by the state, less power for the trusts. That is, she agreed with Socialist measures in the national tradition, which had previously been defended at one time or another by other American groups—such as the Greenbackers, the Populists, and the silverites. The ideology of the extreme Socialists, on the contrary, left her cold. Those who came to Hull-House were often Russian Marxists, "among whom," she noted, "a crude interpretation of the class conflict was the test of the faith." She never shared their faith—or their firm insistence (in her phrase) "that fellowship depends upon identity of creed."

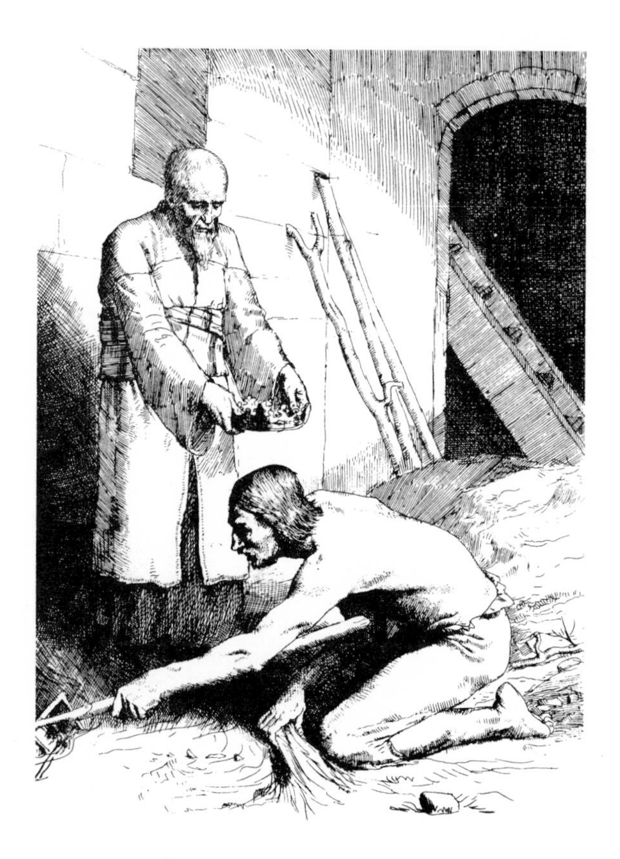

William Strang etched the "Man With the Muckrake" to illustrate the Bunyan episode mentioned on this page.

She was also well aware of the phenomenal gains of capitalism extolled by multimillionaire Andrew Carnegie, whose *Triumphant Democracy* revealed what a Scottish immigrant lad had been able to achieve in the United States. "The old nations of the earth creep on at a snail's pace," Carnegie wrote. "The Republic thunders past with the rush of the express." Statistics lent weight to his boast of rapid development. America was now the world's richest nation, possessor of the most powerful industrial system.

Jane Addams had no desire to break up that system, but rather to extend its benefits to more people. She therefore approved of the muckrakers, a brilliant group of crusading journalists who specialized during the early 1900's in socio-economic exposés of those in high places. They were named by Theodore Roosevelt from the Man with the Muckrake in John Bunyan's *Pilgrim's Progress*, who ignored a heavenly crown as he raked "the filth of the floor." There was "filth" enough on the "floor" of American life, and the muckrakers went at it with a right good will. They threw beams of light into the darkest corners of society, from shocking conditions in the slums and among immigrants, to child labor, the exploitation of Negroes, and the shady tactics of industrial corporations.

The horrified reaction of ordinary Americans, and the loud outcries of the guilty, proved that the muckrakers had hit a nerve center. As Jane Addams had long wished, many of the problems that Hull-House was attempting to deal with on a personal basis were now also being widely debated as public issues. The verdict of Edward A. Ross in *Sin and Society* became sounder every day: "The conclusion of the whole matter is this—our social organization has developed to a stage where the old righteousness is not enough." The new conditions cried aloud for new standards of political and social morality.

Despite the obstacles to so profound a change—the irresponsibility of individuals, the inertia of elected officials—Jane refused to mitigate her optimism. She still could do her bit, and she knew that it counted with the people of Halsted Street. Surrounded by greed, garbage, and gangsters, her mind, her heart, and her hands found the work for which she was best suited. Even if only a little good could be done, she would do it, joyfully, regardless of the evils that might remain untouched. Ellen Starr remarked to her on one occasion: "Jane, if the devil himself came riding down Halsted Street with his tail waving behind him, you'd say, 'What a beautiful curve he has in his tail!' " Jane is said to have answered: "Well, if he had a beautiful curve in his tail, I hope I should be able to appreciate it."

The struggle for justice

Her optimism sprang in part from the visible success of Hull-House, which flourished as the years went by, expanding its facilities and activities, becoming ever more significant as a center of the struggle for justice. Staff members went out daily on errands of mercy—washing newborn babies, counseling the young, ministering to the ill, consoling the aged, burying the dead. They badgered mayors and aldermen—and sometimes the governor down in Springfield—about rickety tenements, water pollution, poorly lit streets, and vermin.

Practicing Tolstoy's "sermon of the deed" left Jane Addams neither scarred nor hardened. When she lectured on gang warfare in the streets, or on the hideous sweatshops where little girls were callously exploited, she would clasp her hands demurely and lift her sweet aristocratic face toward her audiences, and they could only marvel that she had seen such terrible things. In speaking as in writing, she used a low-keyed rhetoric that was unemotional, logical, and persuasive. This quality was what made her so appealing on the platform.

Most of her thinking, writing, conferring, and planning was done in the Octagon Room of Hull-House—a comfortable room that functioned as the brain center of her operations. Looking out of the tall windows she could see the man-made courtyard garden and, beyond that, the man-made jungle of the Nineteenth Ward. The heavy Victorian furniture of the eight-sided room accommodated the visitors

A NEGRO COOK

The Abbott sisters, Grace and Edith, were both active workers at Hull-House. Grace later became the notable head of the Children's Bureau of the United States Department of Labor. Along with Jane, the Abbotts were directly involved in an episode of racial bigotry. Edith recalled:

"The unions were very difficult at times. Miss Addams tried hard to keep everything at the House pro-union in the letter as well as the spirit of union rules, but it wasn't always easy. Once when she had a difficult time about finding a new cook for the residents' dining-room and the coffee shop, she got a Negro—a tall fine-looking man—who was a very competent manager as well as a good cook. The young Greek man and the Bohemian girl who worked in the coffee shop and also in the dining-room liked the new cook at once, and everything was promising until Miss Addams wanted to have him join the cooks' union so that we would continue to have a union restaurant. He said that they wouldn't let him join the union because he was a Negro. Miss Addams was sure that he was mistaken; she couldn't believe that the unions were so narrow. . . . I was asked to 'try to do something.' I went downtown on a bitter cold, snowy day to see a woman whom I had known in the Women's Trade Union League, who was president of one of the women's unions, to see if she wouldn't help us. But she was uncompromising. 'Why does Miss Addams have a Negro cook?' she asked very sternly. 'Are none of the white cooks good enough for Hull-House?' I tried to explain the difficulties of the Hull-House situation. We needed a very special kind of cook—we were not a commercial profit-making restaurant—and this man was just what we needed. 'No.' She was firm. 'When every white cook, man or woman, in Chicago has a job, then you can begin to worry about how to get a Negro cook in the union.' I went home completely discouraged to report my failure to Miss Addams. When Grace finally got back and after she had had a conference with the union, she came home with a new and, as usual, very practical solution. The Negro cook was to join a Negro local in St. Louis, and Hull-House would still have its union restaurant."

The eight-year-old girls working in a cannery in 1911 were victims of the child labor that Jane Addams condemned. The same year, an Infant Welfare Society nurse on a house call (right) was helping cut the infant death rate sharply.

who came to her for advice. In that chamber she was psychiatrist, confessor, guide, disciplinarian, inspirer, or listening post, as the occasion demanded. On one wall hung a map of the ward neatly marked off into colored oblongs, block-by-block and street-by-street. This was the ghetto put into the terms of cartography: The colors represented nineteen nationalities that had come there to live. The two extremes were "native Americans"—black for Negroes and white for Caucasians—and in between came the multitude of immigrants in their densely packed sub-ghettos. Green indicated the Irish, blue the Italians, olive the Greeks, mauve the Germans, yellow the Bohemians, red the Russians (for the most part Russian Jews). Some of the smaller ethnic groups were the Chinese (orange), the Syrians (olive stripes), the Swiss (blue stripes), and the French Canadians (brown stripes). The overall pattern symbolized a living tapestry of personal hopes and fears felt by countless individuals. When she stared at her wall map (as she often did), the founder of Hull-House was inspecting, not merely a piece of multicolored paper, but an image of humanity under stress.

Here in the Octagon Room, Jane finished her first full-length book, *Democracy and Social Ethics* (1902). A compilation of twelve lectures delivered earlier, it dealt with matters like the Pullman strike, the campaign for child-labor legislation, and the workings of power politics in Chicago (see pages 173–175). The book was important less for what it exposed than for what it proposed: a shift from personal ethic to public ethic. She formulated this basic tenet of her philosophy in exact terms—as an evolutionist for whom society is a continuous, ever-changing process, and as a pragmatist for whom reforms must be pressed so long as they work, and no longer. Pointing out that the day had passed when the Good Samaritan could carry the whole load, she urged the whole of society to respond to human needs. Of course individual kindness remains important: The turkey left on the doorstep makes someone's Thanksgiving. But what happens when the Good Samaritan is too occupied elsewhere to leave a turkey on a particular doorstep? Should comfort be a mere matter of luck? Obviously not—and the only way to prevent this is to humanize democracy itself, so that the good of each becomes the concern of all.

Never striking sail

The best thing about Jane Addams was that she practiced what she preached. She never ceased to be a Good Samaritan who would leave the Octagon Room and hasten out into the streets to help those in distress; she never ceased to harass public officials about problems that were too big for Hull-House to handle all by itself. The typhoid epidemic in Chicago is a good example of her methods. She and her colleagues, while tending to the sick, dispensing advice about hygiene, and persuading individuals to join a program of fly control, were at the same time conducting a bacteriological survey to spur city officials into action. Dr. Alice Hamilton, who did most of the scientific research and wrote the report, described their success: "In Chicago the effect was most gratifying; a public inquiry resulted in a complete reorganization of the Health Department under a chief loaned by the [United States] Public Health Service, and an expert was put in charge of tenement-house inspection." Dr. Hamilton was then chosen to set up the Illinois Commission on Occupational Diseases, a bureau copied by states throughout the Union. The often cynical thinker Henry Adams was not in the least cynical when he took the influence of Hull-House into account in stating: "Chicago was the first expression of American thought as a unity; one must start there."

In 1902, John Peter Altgeld died. The former governor of Illinois had long been under attack by conservatives, but Jane Addams spoke at his funeral, ignoring warnings that her appearance would only harm herself and her settlement. Following Emerson's advice, she never struck sail to fear. Unafraid of the word "anarchist," she worked for the release of the anarchist editor Abraham Isaak. Isaak had been

DEFENDING THE ANARCHISTS

Jane Addams had a worthy ally in the ghetto: Graham Taylor, head of Chicago's second most prominent settlement. Taylor left a Congregational pastorate in Connecticut to become Professor of Christian Sociology at the Chicago Theological Seminary. He lectured to social workers at the University of Chicago; wrote articles for the Chicago *Daily News;* joined the Civic Federation and the Municipal Voters' League; and in 1894, inspired by Hull-House, founded the Chicago Commons Social Settlement in the Seventeenth Ward. Here, not far from Jane's Nineteenth Ward, and taking her work for his model, he ministered to the poor, acted as neighborhood adviser, and badgered corrupt officialdom.

He and Jane were constantly bracketed together by those who liked or disliked what they were doing. Thus, publisher John J. Walsh of the *Chronicle* deluged both with his editorial vituperation because they defended the constitutional rights of the city's extreme radicals during the anarchist "scare" that followed McKinley's assassination. Walsh wrote:

"The social settlements in this city have been made identical with opposition to the Constitution of the United States and hostile to the laws of Illinois. . . . To attempt to teach [anarchists] by ordinary means is as useless as to read the Riot Act to a pack of wolves. There is no middle way of dealing successfully with the anarchist. He must be wiped out or allowed to wrap the world in flame. He himself has decreed it, and Professor Taylor and Miss Addams are in poor business when they try to conceal this fact, and thus become the apologists of such a hideous creature. . . . The immigrants and the children they bring or bear after arrival are trained by the 'social settlements' in hostility to the lawful institutions of the country in which they seek liberty and the pursuit of happiness. . . . It is a cruel fate which guides the ignorant immigrant into the socialist precincts of Hull-House or Chicago Commons. It is a sad misuse of Chicago money which maintains these alluring pitfalls for the trustful and helpless."

However, another newspaper editorialized: "Because the settlements deal with conditions as they find them, and therefore are often associated necessarily with extremists, it is assumed that they encourage extreme views and support extreme acts. But the conditions are not created by the settlements. They are being studied and bettered by them. It is preposterous that any apology or any explanation should be called for in a community like Chicago on behalf of an institution like the social settlement."

Some journalists remained hostile, but the work of both settlements continued.

unjustifiably imprisoned after President McKinley's assassination by Leon Czolgosz, another anarchist with whom Isaak had no connection. Unafraid of the word "radical," she paid a public tribute to Altgeld. She could not abide blanket labels. Judgment should be administered by due process of law, not by slander. Guilt was a matter of evidence, not of association or hearsay. Those willing to dismiss a man with an epithet received a curt reply from Jane. When the English labor leader John Burns visited her at Hull-House, he announced: "I think your mayor is an ass." "But," Jane Addams replied, "he is so sincere!" Burns retorted: "All asses are sincere." "Perhaps. But sincerity is never asinine."

This remarkable capacity to judge people on their merits, and to look for the good in them, was one secret of her moral strength. It kept her from expecting too much of human nature. Unlike the would-be reformer who so often is disillusioned by disappointments, Jane Addams entertained no grandiose schemes and accepted realistic, attainable successes, even if limited, for their own sake. Nor did she ever permit her colleagues to forget that social work was its own reward. Louise de Koven Bowen recalled: "Miss Addams always had a very clear vision and a great sense of justice, and I can remember my mortification one day when I said, 'I have done everything in the world for that woman and she is not even grateful.' She looked at me quizzically and said, 'Is that the reason you helped her, because you wanted gratitude?' "

An understanding mayor

In 1905 Jane Addams received her most important municipal appointment, as a member of the school board, following a reformist triumph in the city elections. The new mayor was Edward F. Dunne, an opponent of the machine politics that had bedeviled Chicago for so long, and one of the powerful Chicagoans who understood and admired Hull-House. Dunne, whose principle it was to bring as many high-minded citizens as possible into his administration, quite naturally decided to give Chicago's most celebrated woman a voice in the running of the schools. She became chairman of the School Management Committee, a testimony to the respect she enjoyed among the members of the board. She hoped the city's schools might become what Hull-House aspired to be—a center for a higher civic and social life. "Our schools must give the children better and truer standards for judging life," she said. "Life does not ask whether a man can read and write, so much as it asks whether he can use whatever faculties have been given him." However, for the most part, it was a frustrating experience. Her plans to improve education in the city became bogged down in a long-drawn-out dispute between the Teachers' Federation and the school board, a paralyzing delay that she deplored, especially when there was so much constructive work to be done. Attempting to mediate on a basis of fact and reason, she irritated the extremists of both sides. Certain newspapers denounced her criticism of salaries, qualification tests, and promotions; many teachers did the same when she declared that all of their demands could not be satisfied. Her belief that "half a loaf is better than none" lacked persuasiveness in a quarrel of this nature: "I . . . became convinced that partisans would never tolerate the use of stepping-stones. They are much too impatient to look on while a beloved scheme is unstably balanced, and would rather see it tumble into the stream at once than have it brought to land in a halfhearted fashion." As a result, she became known derisively as "the Great Compromiser" and "the Henry Clay of Chicago." No doubt she wished that her attempted compromise had succeeded as well as some of those sponsored by Clay!

Apart from official wrangling, her school board position left her more exposed than ever to newspaper attacks. For instance, the news that Russian writer Maxim Gorki had brought his common-law wife to America shocked much of the reading public, but Jane asked that judgment be withheld until Gorki's side of the case could be heard. When the Chicago *Tribune* assailed her violently in print, Mayor Dunne

Jane encouraged the lighter things as grace notes in the symphony of life at Hull-House, praising "the desire of the young people to appear finer and better and altogether more lovely than they really are. . . . What might they not do to make our sordid cities more beautiful, more companionable?" Examples from the 1920's are: a youthful sculptor carving a bust of Washington after a heavy snowfall; the sixty-five-member band about to begin a rousing march; girls of the Dolls Club proudly showing off their dolls.

rushed to her defense, as on other occasions. But Dunne met political defeat in 1907, and his successor dropped Jane Addams from the school board within two years. She left the post feeling that Chicago was not ready for her type of educational philosophy. Hull-House might be a center for teaching a higher civic and social life; it might follow John Dewey's *The School and Society* in stressing stimulation and originality rather than dogma and discipline; but there was little hope of effecting this type of pedagogical reform in a big-city school-system racked by financial crises and political pay-offs.

Jane had used some of her spare time to work on a book that appeared in 1909, *The Spirit of Youth and the City Streets*. It dealt with the child's right to a happy childhood in a decent home, and with the unspeakable tragedy of allowing his environment to betray him. She argued that the police and the juvenile court would have less to do with youthful offenders if children were not subjected to unbearable physical and psychological burdens: unfeeling parents, slum conditions, long hours in sweatshops. She drew the moral that the tender years should be years of beauty—of art in the broadest sense. In turn, that was how Hull-House understood each of the arts it made available to children and adults alike. The classes in painting, crafts, drama, music, and dance were not merely paths to middle-class "cultivation." They served as occupational therapy, affording emotional release while developing skills and techniques, and embraced moral beauty no less than aesthetic beauty. "It is good," said Jane Addams, "for a social worker to be an artist too."

The myth of equality

In 1909, twenty years after the founding of Hull-House, two large gaps remained in the texture of American democracy, giving the lie to the myth of equality: Negroes and all women were still denied the full rights of citizenship. Jane Addams told an anecdote that makes this as plain as anything could. As the first woman president of the National Conference of Social Work, she labored, with two other dedicated women, Florence Kelley and Lillian Wald, to persuade President Theodore Roosevelt to call the first White House conference on children. As the speakers were gathering to take their places on the platform, the official in charge checked his list of names. "Are we all here?" he asked. "Yes, here is my Catholic speaker, my Jewish speaker, the Protestant, the colored man, and the woman. Let's all go on."

"You see, I am last," remarked "the woman" (Jane Addams) to "the colored man" (Booker T. Washington). "That is because I have no vote." "I'm glad to know the reason," Mr. Washington replied. "I have always before been the end of such a procession myself."

Jane's belief in women's rights was of long standing, dating back to the days when she heard her father speak on the subject. John Addams, committed to the Quaker concept of justice for all, agreed with the two outstanding leaders of the early feminist movement—Lucretia Mott and Elizabeth Cady Stanton, who organized the first women's rights convention in the United States at Seneca Falls, New York, in 1848. He had also sided with Susan B. Anthony, who strove after the Civil War to have the vote extended to women as well as Negroes by the

ON THE SUFFRAGE SOAPBOX

When Jane spoke for equal rights at home or abroad, she wielded a unique influence among the suffragettes because her renown extended far beyond the movement. Britain's Maude Royden noted of the women's international conference in Budapest in 1913: "She had no official position in the movement. She was not our President, or even on the . . . Board. She was an ordinary delegate, and although people tried very hard to get her away from her humble position on the floor of the hall and put on the platform, and although just to avoid any kind of a fuss she once or twice allowed herself to be put there, the next morning found her sitting among the other American delegates on the floor. And yet everyone realized that among the whole of the conference of women from all over the world, she was the one that was known to the whole world. Others were known in their own nation . . . but Jane Addams was a world figure. . . . When my mind goes back to that conference, I always have a feeling that Jane Addams wherever she sat was always the heart and soul of it."

Jane knew many leaders of the suffragettes, notably the redoubtable Carrie Chapman Catt. The New York *Times* reported in 1915: "Miss Jane Addams called yesterday on Mrs. Carrie Chapman Catt at the Empire State Campaign Headquarters, 303 Fifth Avenue, and promised the women her help in the campaign in October. The last month of the campaign will be the most important and Miss Addams will give probably a week of her time to New York in making speeches. She is also to visit . . . New Jersey, Massachusetts and Pennsylvania, and will speak for votes-for-women and urge the men to give the women their support." Miss Addams kept her word to Mrs. Catt, even though her thoughts were increasingly occupied with the ordeal of World War I.

Jane gained a reputation for repartee when opponents of suffrage heckled her—and could also show annoyance when she thought a meeting was mishandled by her fellow suffragettes. At New York's Carnegie Hall, finding herself last on the list of speakers, and not called on till 11:30 to give her address, she said, pointedly: "It is so late that I will just say that my address is 800 South Halsted Street." She felt irritated enough to let it go at that, but the loud applause of her audience finally drew from her the suffrage speech they had waited to hear.

She was willing to speak anywhere for the suffrage cause; if the crowd that came was too big for the hall, she stood on a soapbox outside to address the overflow audience there. At every opportunity, she also appeared before congressional committees and at major party conventions to advocate equal rights for women. Jane wryly recalled one such hearing when a committee member clearly showed "his drunken estate"—and she added: "On that occasion at least the time-honored argument, that women were not capable of using the franchise, was not advanced."

Fourteenth and Fifteenth Amendments to the Constitution. The youngest daughter of John Addams inherited his attitude. Then, at Rockford, she mingled with college girls much concerned about the influence of feminism on their future lives; one of these Rockford girls, Catherine Waugh, later became (under her married name of Catherine Waugh McCulloch) a prominent suffragette, and a colleague of Jane Addams in the movement. Jane herself took for the theme of "Bread Givers," her college address of 1880, the fact that "woman has gained a new confidence in her possibilities, and a fresher hope in her steady progress."

That theme grew more significant as the nineteenth century moved onward. The suffragettes continued to agitate, and Jane Addams remained one of their staunchest allies. She returned repeatedly to the fundamental point that men as well as women would benefit from an equalitarian franchise, first because the denial of dignity to some demeaned everybody, and second because inestimable feminine abilities were being lost to society under male supremacy. Women had not waited for equality to take an active role in combating child labor, sweatshops, and other evils. How much more might they not achieve if invited to participate in electing officials assigned to such matters?

Despite pressing duties at Hull-House, Jane attended the Congress of Representative Women at the Chicago World's Fair of 1893. When the Committee for Municipal Suffrage for Women was established in 1907, she accepted its chairmanship, in which capacity she shepherded trainloads of delegates to the Illinois state capital, Springfield, to talk to the governor. Six years later this group gained its objective in Chicago—the city extended the franchise to all qualified voters regardless of sex. By then, local battles had been won in various cities and states, but not until 1920, under the Nineteenth Amendment, did the United States declare the vote to be the right of every American.

Whatever the law might say, however, the reality did not automatically conform to it. American Negroes, legally citizens throughout

Mrs. Carrie Chapman Catt (opposite page) leads 20,000 eager suffragettes up New York's Fifth Avenue in 1918.

the country since Reconstruction, in fact ran into barriers nearly everywhere. Southern states used the "separate but equal" doctrine to systematize segregation, and prevented Negroes from voting by setting conditions that few could meet—poll taxes, literacy tests, and laws that ruled out the descendants of slaves. Northern states allowed Negroes to vote but practiced *de facto* segregation, which pushed them onto the fringes of civic life, leaving them impotent in the face of the white-power structure as well as the prey of demagogues.

Here again, Jane Addams felt the influence of her father, who had been an abolitionist in the days of slavery. Her interest in the problems of nonwhite Americans was deep, sincere, and continuous. Not only did she open Hull-House to Negroes on a basis of equality, but in 1910 she helped to found the National Association for the Advancement of Colored People. Two years later, at the first nominating convention of the Progressive party, she urged the seating of delegations, including those from below the Mason-Dixon line, without regard to race. In a subsequent article about that convention, she confessed that "I was assailed by the old familiar discomfort concerning the status of the colored man." Well might she feel so! There was little indication at the time, or for long afterward, that discrimination would ever be effectively challenged. She did not live to see the Supreme Court strike down the "separate but equal" doctrine in 1954, or the Negro revolt that began in 1956 with a bus boycott in Montgomery, Alabama. But she worked hard for the cause in the days when she served as a member of the NAACP, and advocated nonviolence in the drive for civil rights.

Campaigning for T.R.

Jane's decision to support the newly organized Progressive party was not made lightly. She disliked political labels because she knew from experience that reformers and reactionaries alike could be found in each major party on its national, state, and local levels. She backed certain candidates in elections strictly according to what they promised with regard to needed reforms, so that party lines meant nothing to her. She would not let herself be sidetracked by politics as such. Her most memorable book, *Twenty Years at Hull-House* (1910), left her readers convinced that she was not a party woman. In this autobiography, she appears as a sensitive, practical, energetic human being who would accept social justice from anyone. The fine prose style, never sentimental, never condescending to rhetorical embellishments, gave the book a permanent place on the shelf of American classics.

Jane Addams (at Yale, above) received fourteen honorary degrees as well as a number of other noteworthy awards.

Almost as it appeared, its author was achieving one of her most satisfying triumphs. Ninety thousand garment workers of Chicago struck for better wages. Jane Addams, serving on the arbitration panel, saw that an agreement about to be accepted by labor leaders would outlaw collective bargaining by employees. She therefore refused to sign, stood her ground, stated her intention to hold out indefinitely—and was vindicated when a new agreement made provision for collective bargaining in the future. Characteristically, her rectitude impressed both sides. When the tensions of the strike subsided, management agreed with labor that she had been the heroine of the occasion.

At fifty, Jane was much wiser in the ways of the world than when she rented Hull-House in 1889. And the world was wiser about her. Yale University acknowledged her universal reputation in 1910 by choosing her to be the first woman to receive its honorary degree. That spring Smith College awarded her an LL.D. at ceremonies attended by Julia Ward Howe, the ninety-year-old author of "The Battle Hymn of the Republic." After the famous Civil War anthem was sung, Mrs. Howe stated what Miss Addams, bedecked in her bright new hood, already knew full well: "We women have not won the battle yet, for the Lord or for ourselves."

Her desire to keep on fighting the battle for women, children, workers—indeed, for all Americans—was what actually moved Jane Addams to join the Progressive party in 1912.

Theodore Roosevelt ("fit as a bull moose") was running for another term in the White House. He had a good record on domestic affairs, by Hull-House standards, since during his Presidency (1901–1909) following the assassination of McKinley, he had introduced the Square Deal to the country, and had shown that he meant it by taking his "big stick" to the "malefactors of great wealth" (as well as to political and foreign opponents). Four years after stepping aside in favor of William Howard Taft in the 1908 election, T.R. was challenging Taft's conservatism. As Taft retained the allegiance of the Republican party regulars, Roosevelt bolted from the ranks, and split the party by accepting the Progressive nomination for President.

The Progressive platform covered a wide range of improvements—from woman suffrage and child-labor legislation to antitrust measures and greater federal control of the railroads. The platform embodied some of the basic social principles of Jane Addams, who, at Roosevelt's request, was a member of the platform committee. Inevitably there were planks she did not like, especially the one calling for two new battleships a year unless an international agreement on arms limitation could be reached. "I confess," she wrote, "that I found it very difficult to swallow those two battleships." But, being a realist, she understood that a compromise had to be made—and she made it.

Loyally doing her best for the cause, she campaigned vigorously for T.R., taking his message (and hers) from North Dakota to Colorado and Oklahoma. Expounding the Progressive platform, she entreated her audiences to send to Washington an Administration committed, as none ever had been before, to equality and justice. Politically, she failed. T.R. went down to defeat and dragged Taft with him. Democrat Woodrow Wilson, the beneficiary of the split in the Republican party, won the election of 1912. Still, Jane took consolation from the broader social dialogue that the campaign had started. She inferred, correctly, that much of the Progressive platform would filter into the policies of future Administrations.

POLITICKING FOR THE PROGRESSIVES

Historian Allen F. Davis has assessed the active role Jane played during Theodore Roosevelt's final candidacy for President:

"Jane Addams was the most famous and in many ways the most effective social worker in the 1912 Progressive campaign. She did much more than second Roosevelt's nomination at the convention. She was a member of the National Progressive Committee, the Illinois State Progressive Committee, and the Cook County Progressive Committee. She also wrote a series of six articles, syndicated in newspapers across the country, to attract attention to the Progressive party platform. During the last month of the campaign, she covered thousands of miles in a speaking tour that sometimes called for as many as three speeches a day. . . . One of the other Progressive campaigners remarked: 'Wherever I went I heard nothing but talk of Jane Addams. I suppose other political speakers had been out there, but you never would have guessed it from what people had to say.' . . . Her support of the Progressives attracted so much attention that the Democratic National Committee tried to persuade Lillian Wald to come out publicly in support of Wilson 'to counteract Jane Addams' support of the Progressive Party.' "

Many people disapproved of Jane's activity with the Progressive party. Mabel Boardman, the head of the American Red Cross, was a severe critic: "The great moral questions for whose furtherance the country owes a debt of gratitude to Miss Addams should not be handicapped by the limitations of party affiliation nor trammelled by becoming involved in the bitterness of controversies over candidates and utterly irrelevant policies." Jane's fellow social worker in Chicago, Graham Taylor, thought that she had "lost the heeding if not the hearing of the whole city which she had before."

But Jane's enthusiasm never flagged during the campaign. One of the residents of Hull-House remembered that "on one occasion after six consecutive nights on the train she returned . . . weary and uncomfortable, but she stayed up half the night regaling [us with her] experiences."

Could Jane Addams have carved out a political career for herself? Some people thought so. The Illinois Equal Suffrage Association wanted her to run for the Senate, and a group of Boston suffragettes actually endorsed her for President. Jane appreciated these compliments without ever taking them seriously.

Chapter 6
GREAT STRESSES OF WAR AND PEACE

WHILE AMERICA ENTERED its Progressive Era, Europe was moving ever closer to the nightmare of the Great War of 1914–1918. No one really wanted it. "It was something into which we glided, or rather staggered or stumbled," British Prime Minister Lloyd George said. "The lamps are going out all over Europe," his countryman, Sir Edward Grey, warned. "We shall not see them lit again in our lifetime." For years the European nations had played the old game of power politics and checkmate by alliance. Gradually the Continent divided into two armed camps with no real bridge between, each regarding the other with fear, suspicion, and hostility. In 1914, Europe was like the proud tower described by Barbara Tuchman. Suddenly, tragically, came the collapse. "To probe for underlying causes," this historian observes, "one must operate within the framework of a whole society and try to discover what moved the people in it." The causes and consequences of World War I will be debated as long as historians concern themselves with the subject.

This horror was the negation of everything Jane Addams represented—reason, compassion, compromise, peace. Reacting to it, she departed from her father's example. John Addams—a nonpacifist Quaker—had backed the Civil War, raised his Addams Guard to march off to battle, and voted for every military measure introduced into the Illinois legislature from 1861 to 1865. Jane Addams refused to back the war against Germany in any way. The two cases could certainly not be considered identical: Slavery posed a more clear-cut moral issue than the Kaiser did. Nevertheless, Jane took her stand on the pacifist principle that war is always wrong.

She intended to be realistic about pacifism. Her reading of Charles Darwin and Herbert Spencer had convinced her that man is by nature aggressive, so that only a misguided idealist could cherish the illusion of a society inhabited solely by altruists uninterested in personal triumphs. Moreover, the warlike impulses were not simply contemptible, for they implied undoubted virtues—such as comradeship, loyalty, courage, and steadfastness. William James had pointed the way out of this impasse when he published *The Moral Equivalent of War*. Taking the realities of human nature into account, the Harvard philosopher proposed that the passions and the ideals that produce armed conflict be channeled into peaceful pursuits, where they might find release without harming anyone. His principal proposal was to use conscription for training disciplined men to attack, not other men, but nature: by building bridges, planting forests, and, in general, doing anything emotionally satisfying and for the good of humanity.

Jane Addams was a Jamesian pacifist. She knew that mere nonviolence would not appeal to such a dynamic culture as America's, and she understood the magic spell of patriotism, having been raised in its golden glow. At the same time, she could not, would not, believe that her compatriots were beyond the reach of realistic pacifism. There *must* be a moral equivalent of war, and it *must* be brought to their attention. Disseminating this thought became one of the main tasks of her life. James gave her a rationale for the feelings that had been with her from her youth. Her opposition to violence had been an integral part of her thinking when she founded Hull-House, and war was violence of the most terrible kind. She was no late convert to pacifism, although she devoted more time to it during her later years because of her mature comprehension of the meaning of war, and because this was a period of United States engagement in wars.

From 1892 (when her first article on nonviolence appeared) until her death in 1935, she championed peace, a cause in some ways more difficult to explain than her activities at Hull-House. Her fight for social justice seemed to most people a positive effort to create what America lacked. But many of the same people saw in her peace crusade something negative. When she denounced nationalism, militarism, and the cost of armaments, when she openly opposed the emotional steamroller of public opinion during the war years, she got sneers instead of applause. Instead of being high on every list, she was blacklisted. World War I proved to be the most difficult and challenging period of Miss Addams' whole life.

On her trips to Europe in the 1880's, Jane had visited the Roman catacombs, studying early Christianity in an effort to find workable solutions for contemporary problems. "The early Christians were preeminently nonresistant," she wrote in 1892. "They believed in love as a cosmic force . . . . The spectacle of the Christians loving all men was the most

These richly bedecked monarchs gathered in London in 1910 for Edward VII's funeral. Left to right, seated are Alfonso XIII of Spain, George V of England, Frederick VIII of Denmark; standing are Haakon VII of Norway, Ferdinand I of Bulgaria, Manoel of Portugal, Wilhelm II of Germany, George I of Greece, Albert I of Belgium. The thrones of Bulgaria, Germany, Portugal, and Spain have vanished in the turbulence of war and rebellion during the twentieth century.

astounding Rome had ever seen." In 1896, noticing young men near Hull-House drilling with wooden guns, she urged them to drill with shovels and to apply them occasionally to the refuse cluttering the Chicago streets. As for internationalism—was not that the only principle by which the nationalities in the Nineteenth Ward could hope to live amicably together? Did not the principle also apply to the nations themselves, as well as to their emigrants settled in South Chicago?

Jane Addams took a strong stand against "imperialism" in reference to the annexation of the Philippines by the United States in 1898. And in 1904 she agreed to talk on pacifism at a Boston convention of national peace societies. "It is easy to kill a man," she declared. "It is not easy to bring him forward in the paths of civilization." Using her experiences within an interracial community, she developed this theme at length, and won such high praise that she was asked to lecture on the same subject at the University of Wisconsin summer school in 1906.

Revised and published under the title *Newer Ideals of Peace*, these Wisconsin lectures explored the concept of supplanting force with law. Jane traced the "European anarchy" to the nonexistence of a legal code crossing frontiers, to the fact that every nation made laws for itself alone, and was the sole determinant of the extent to which it would be bound by international mediation. The only sane, humane thing was to replace so unstable and dangerous a system with justice, the will to peace, and the setting aside of nationalist ambitions.

These ideas were widely discussed by those who agreed and those who disagreed. When one of Jane's Chicago friends, Mrs. Tiffany Blake, talked to President Theodore Roosevelt in 1907, mentioning that Miss Addams had sent her, she provoked an ambiguous response.

"WITHOUT HER, IT'S—NOTHING"

Francis Hackett, later a noted biographer and historian, was a journalist who claimed to be "totally ignorant of settlement work and devoid of missionary spirit" when he became a Hull-House resident in 1906. He lived there several years. His vivid account of what it was like to be there shows that Jane was the institution's central power and personality, even though the fact was not always outwardly apparent or desired by her:

"We who came there on probation before we were accepted as residents could hardly help feeling it was a sort of withdrawn community. But in its being withdrawn it was anything but mystical or dogmatic. Its faith was humanism. It 'warmed both hands before the fire of life.' No newcomer could resist its ease, its tolerance, or its cordiality. . . . Our probation, I suppose, did result in a real selection. Certain thorny people were not admitted. We who were there were in harmony. . . . The essential fact of Hull-House, the dominant fact, was the presence of Miss Addams. This is strange because while one was living there Miss Addams was away a good deal of the time, and when she was there one did not have a great deal to do with her; yet Hull-House, as one clearly felt at the time, was not an institution over which Miss Addams presided, it was Miss Addams, around whom an institution insisted on clustering. However she might deprecate it, and no one was more skillful than Miss Addams in deprecation, we often said, 'without her, it's—nothing.'

"A fine building, of course, and a fine group of people. A neighborhood that seethed with things to consider and do. But we returned to her personality for the overwhelming reason that our own personalities gained in value through contact with hers. She had the power to value human beings, to appreciate them, and to feel in terms of them. I do not mean to manipulate them. . . . Let me illustrate it. After the *Titanic* went down, someone spoke to her of the loss of the 'important' people on board. She shook her head. She felt sorry for W. T. Stead, for J. J. Astor, and the other headliners, but in that distinction of important and unimportant there was nothing final for Miss Addams. Each of the fourteen hundred had lost his own life, and her heart was moved alike for each of them, man, woman, and child."

Another observer, Helen Bennett, noted the same force of Miss Addams' personality: "At Hull-House Miss Addams was the dynamic force. So intense was this personal feeling that the spirits of the residents of the Settlement rose and fell with Miss Addams. 'When Miss Addams had a toothache,' said one visitor to Hull-House, 'the residents went about with hushed voices and soft tread, not that Miss Addams required it, but that they just naturally felt that way. When she recovered, everybody was gay.' "

T.R. was the most famous American to have fought in the Spanish-American War, and he had thoroughly approved of America's acquisition of the former Spanish colonies. He had no patience at all with the anti-imperialism of Jane Addams, or with her philosophy of pacifism. Mrs. Blake's allusion to Jane sent T.R. into one of his famous explosions: "Jane Addams—don't talk to me about Jane Addams! I have always thought a lot of her, but she has just written a bad book, a very bad book! She is all wrong about peace." Having disburdened himself of his unfavorable opinion of Jane, the President immediately added that this was not his entire opinion: "But she is a fine woman in every other way. Now that I've got that out of my system, she sent you here, did she? What can I do for you?"

T.R. meant that he greatly admired Jane's social work. Since she, on her part, admired his domestic policies, it is not difficult to understand why he wanted her on the platform committee of the Progressive party in 1912, or why she was so willing to campaign for him that year. World War I, and especially America's involvement in 1917, found these two great Americans again on opposite sides of a momentous public issue.

Harper's Weekly saw Theodore Roosevelt as a clown and side-show pitchman during the Progressive campaign of 1912.

Pacifism in wartime

When America's first national peace congress met in 1907, Jane Addams was on hand, helping to pass unequivocal resolutions against militarism. Other conferences followed, both national and international. In 1913, thanks to these global endeavors on the subject, an impressive Peace Palace—a gift of Andrew Carnegie—was opened at The Hague as a "tangible pledge" that nations would seek arbitration in disputes among themselves. Yet during this period the diplomatic situation worsened. One crisis after another plagued humanity—in Morocco, the Balkans, eastern Europe, and elsewhere. Jane Addams continued to preach pacifism in the sinister shadow of darkening war clouds. Her 1913 talk in New York's Carnegie Hall stressed her conviction that there was "rising in the cosmopolitan centers of America a sturdy and unprecedented international understanding which in time would be too profound to lend itself to war." Jane's use of the phrase "cosmopolitan centers" was significant, for it was her own urban living that led her to this insight—she had learned at first hand that great, polyglot cities provide their inhabitants with an experience qualitatively different from smaller towns or the countryside, where the crowding together of immigrant groups does not exist. That summer Jane traveled to Hungary with the American delegation to the International Suffrage Alliance, returning to New York to champion the Union Against Militarism. In January 1915 she joined three thousand women to organize the Women's Peace Party, and was elected chairman.

By then the European conflict was raging in all its fury. The German offensive having been halted on the Western Front, both sides dug in for a protracted, murderous struggle, their trenches running all the way from the English

Channel to the Swiss border. Millions of men either squatted in dismal squalor or rushed "over the top" into the desolation of no-man's-land to fight battles both horribly bloody and entirely inconclusive. Neither side would contemplate any cessation of hostilities short of victory. The United States was not yet involved. President Woodrow Wilson maintained an attitude of cautious neutrality during 1914 and 1915, a policy that Jane Addams supported as the right one for her country. (She would vote for Wilson in 1916 because, as his campaign posters said, "He kept us out of war.") But, being a private citizen, she had a wider freedom of personal action than the President, and she threw herself into an international effort to restore peace to Europe.

In April 1915 Jane Addams and some forty other Americans boarded the *Noordam* at New York, bound for a peace congress in The Hague. To make the trip was a major decision. Jane realized full well that it represented a radical break with public opinion at home, for most Americans were anxious to see the Allies triumph over the Central Powers, led by the Kaiser's Germany. Her old friend and critic, Theodore Roosevelt, reacted angrily to the women's peace movement, telling one of its representatives: "Pacifists are cowards, and your scheme is both silly and base." Jane Addams considered it neither silly nor base, although she regretted the unfavorable opinion that many of her countrymen were beginning to hold of her: "There were moments when one longed desperately for reconciliation with one's friends and fellow citizens. Solitude has always had its demons."

Hers was no sentimental pacifism, nor did she base her argument on religious grounds. She had invariably criticized war for solid

The Women's Peace Party organized this 1916 demonstration against compulsory military training in New York high schools.

social, political, and economic reasons. She opposed World War I on the same pragmatic grounds—it was destructive, wasteful, and ineffective, creating more problems than it solved, offering the final proof that physical force had ceased to be functional in international relations.

The Americans on the *Noordam* were allowed to proceed to Holland after an official delay for inspection in the English port of Dover. However, the English representatives were kept at home, and no women came from France, Russia, or Serbia. Nonetheless, delegations from the twelve nations got to work, under the chairmanship of Jane Addams. They adopted twenty resolutions, of which this was the most crucial: *"Continuous Mediation:* This International Congress of Women resolves to ask the neutral countries to take immediate steps to create a conference of neutral nations which shall without delay offer continuous mediation." Neutrals would serve as go-betweens.

This effort to "keep the doors open," and struggle *continuously* for new solutions, received wide acceptance. Mass meetings to initiate mediation were held in Switzerland, Holland, and Denmark. Brilliant speeches by Jane Addams, her friend Madame Rosika Schwimmer of Hungary, and others won the support of prominent American citizens. After hearing Madame Schwimmer in Detroit, Henry Ford agreed to back the plan. "We are going to get behind the work done by the Hague Peace Conference and carry that work forward," he told newspapermen.

The peace ship

In order to "get the boys out of the trenches by Christmas," Ford chartered a ship, the *Oscar II*, to sail over and speed negotiations.

Covered with flags and slogans, a vintage truck brings Wilson's 1916 campaign for reelection to the streets of New York.

Jane Addams was one of the eminent persons he consulted about his enterprise. She not only gave it her sanction but agreed to sail with the Ford group. Yet she had qualms. The project looked too much like a sideshow to suit her taste. The whole thing had been thrown together hurriedly, following Ford's snap decision to put his name and his money behind the peace ship; and the lack of methodical consultation as to aims and procedures meant that, once in Europe, improvisation would have to take the place of planning. Unable to give reporters a clear idea of his intentions, Ford left himself vulnerable to the cartoons that blossomed in the newspapers, which treated his "crusade" as a farce. They had a field day with such bizarre items as Ford's cable to Pope Benedict VII (who had died in A.D. 983—Benedict XV was now on the papal throne).

Fearful that Ford's venture would harm the peace movement by making it look ridiculous, Jane cabled staff officials at The Hague: "Keep the International Committee distinct from the Ford enterprise." Still, only a sudden illness prevented her from sailing on the *Oscar II*. Her absence proved a real loss to the party, for she would certainly have been a stabilizing influence.

Some notable Americans whom Ford wanted begged off for one reason or another. William Jennings Bryan came to say bon voyage. A clever photographer arranged a picture that prompted peals of laughter when it appeared in his paper—Bryan on deck holding a squirrel cage. Thomas A. Edison, who also showed up for the send-off, refused to go along even though Ford offered him, apparently in all seriousness, a million dollars to add his prestige to the project. The absurd climax came when, as the peace ship was pulling out, an exhibitionist who called himself "Mr. Zero" dived into the water and swam after it.

The carnival atmosphere accompanied the *Oscar II* to Europe. Henry Ford himself, pleading illness and stoutly denying disillusionment, left the expedition at Oslo. His followers, depressed by the defection of their leader, re-

THE BAYONET CONTROVERSY

Of all Jane's wartime pacifist speeches, one haunted her more than any other – the Carnegie Hall address of 1915 (following her return from Europe) in which she said: "We were told by young men everywhere who had been at the front, that men had literally to be stimulated to a willingness to perform the bloody work of bayonet charges. The English are in such cases given rum, the French, it is said, absinthe; the Germans, more scientifically, perhaps, inhalations of ether."

Criticism inundated her immediately. The most vehement rebuttal came from Richard Harding Davis, a popular novelist, an admirer of the martial, masculine virtues, and a much-traveled correspondent who considered himself an authority on the subject of war. Davis read with massive indignation what Jane Addams said about bayonet charges. It was, in his opinion, an atrocious slander, and he did not try to restrain his feelings as he picked up his pen to answer a woman he found tiresome and uncomprehending. "Since the war began," he wrote, "no statement has been so unworthy, or so untrue and ridiculous. The contempt it shows for the memory of the dead is appalling; the credulity and ignorance it displays are inconceivable. . . . Miss Addams desires peace. So does everyone else. But she will not attain peace by misrepresentation. I have seen more of this war and other wars than Miss Addams, and I know all war to be wicked, wasteful, and unintelligent, and where Miss Addams can furnish one argument in favor of peace I will furnish a hundred. But against this insult, flung by a complacent and self-satisfied woman at men who gave their lives for men, I protest. And I believe that with me are all those women and men who respect courage and honor." Davis considered his case unanswerable.

Alice Hamilton, who had been with Jane in Europe and understood her thinking, offered a different interpretation of the offending remark: "In the course of her speech she told of what we had heard repeatedly in England and on the Continent. . . . For some reason that simple statement of fact was taken as an insult to the brave Allies and, under the leadership of Richard Harding Davis, a newspaper campaign was launched against her which for bitterness cannot often have been exceeded. She was accused of insulting the heroic young men who were dying for their country, but nobody stopped to think that war does not mean only dying, it means killing; indeed no country wants its young men to die for it . . . but to kill for it. And surely it was no insult to say that decent young men, brought up in a Christian civilization, would not find it natural and easy to disembowel men like themselves whom they had never seen before. The English took it for granted that a stiff dose of rum was essential, but in 1915–and for some years after–many Americans romanticized the war and resented fiercely anything that disturbed the picture they had created. She returned therefore to a very painful time of misunderstanding and growing bitterness and the disappointment of all her hopes."

Richard Harding Davis

Jane herself wrote in 1922: "Only once did I try a public explanation. . . . I tried to remake my original statement to a young man of the Associated Press only to find it once more so garbled that I gave up in despair."

After America became a belligerent in 1917, Jane was increasingly subjected to public embarrassment. When she spoke in Chicago on one occasion, her audience listened in dead silence. Orrin N. Carter, Chief Justice of the Illinois Supreme Court, spoke up: "I have been a lifelong friend of Miss Addams. I have agreed with her on most questions in the past–." Jane interrupted with the observation: "That sounds as if you were going to break with me." Carter replied: "I *am* going to break. I think anything that may tend to cast doubt on the justice of our cause in the present war is very unfortunate. No pacifist measures, in my opinion, should be taken until the war is over."

The basic argument against pacifism throughout the war was that it both encouraged German aggression against peaceful nations, and discouraged the latter from resorting to the sword in self-defense. The New York *Times* said editorially that Jane Addams "has, in fact, been doing what she could for war, and . . . for the ultimate downfall of democratic institutions in Europe and for the extinction of the 'little peoples'; for more bloodshed, for more militarism, for the policy of conquest; for new Belgiums, more Serbias, for *Lusitanias* without end. It is well that the demonstration of the sad folly of peace-at-any-price should be given, but it is much to be regretted that it was Jane Addams who gave it."

The philosopher John Dewey disagreed: "The best statement which I have seen made of the pacifist position since we entered the war is that of Miss Addams. She earnestly protests against the idea that the pacifist position was negative. . . . She holds that the popular impression that pacifism meant abstinence and just keeping out of trouble is wrong; that it stood for a positive international policy in which this country should be the leader of the nations of the world 'into a wider life of coordinated activity'; she insists that the growth of nations under modern conditions involves of necessity international complications which admit 'of adequate treatment only through an international agency not yet created.' In short, pacifists 'urge upon the United States not indifference to moral issues and to the fate of liberty and democracy, but a strenuous endeavor to lead all nations of the earth into an organized international life.' That intelligent pacifism stands for this end, and that the more intelligent among the pacifists, like Miss Addams, saw the situation in this fashion, need not be doubted. But as Miss Addams [recognizes], there are many types of pacifists. I question whether any one who followed the pacifist literature which appeared in the year or two before we got into the war derived from it the conception that the dominant ideal was that ascribed to pacifism by Miss Addams, namely, that the United States should play a 'vitally energetic role' in a political reorganization of the world." Dewey lived to see this very development–although Jane did not.

Tugboats roil the water of New York harbor as they maneuver the "peace ship," a Scandinavian-American liner, into position.

mained in Europe long enough to arrange for American representation at the Neutral Conference for Continuous Mediation in Stockholm, after which they returned home. "The comedy of errors is over," proclaimed one newsman. Jane Addams objected to this contemptuous dismissal of the enterprise, and quoted with approval the following verdict: "The Ford Peace Ship may have been a gesture so futile as to be ridiculous—still it was a movement of generous faith at a time when more responsible politicians were afraid to act."

Events took the initiative away from the mediators. The war continued, mounting in fury, until America's entry in 1917—after Germany resumed unrestricted submarine warfare—put an end to the hopes for a compromise peace. The effect of famine, disease, and carnage became ever more bitter. Jane Addams and other pacifists saw in this a chance to take positive, helpful action. If they could not stop the fighting, they could at least come to the aid of millions of people victimized by war. Obviously the humanitarians faced a problem far beyond their personal resources. Here, if ever, Jane's principle held good that government assistance was mandatory—and the American government responded nobly. Herbert Hoover had been dispensing American relief in Europe since 1914. During 1915-1916 he concentrated on Belgium, then under the German heel, and saw to it that the Belgians received five million dollars' worth of food every month. The American ambassador to London, Walter Hines Page, declared: "But for Hoover, Belgium would have starved." In 1917, Hoover became United States Food Administrator. Jane Addams "experienced a great sense of relief" at this appointment, which Hoover accepted with the blunt warning that "the situation is more than war, it is a problem of humanity." He made the dedicated promise that "we will export every grain that the American people save from their normal consumption."

Joining the Food Administration when Hoover called for volunteers, Jane worked for it during and after the war, traveling widely through the country, asking Americans to grow more food on unused acres, to consume less in their own households, and to save as much as they could for shipment to the stricken people abroad. The resolute effort to rescue whole nations from mass starvation represented humane action on a scale unheard of before in human history. Jane Addams' book called *Peace and Bread in Time of War* sketches the epic tale of American relief activities.

The book also shows that the misconstruction, repudiation, and suppression of pacifism throughout the war had made Jane Addams a little bitter about the native land she had served so faithfully and in so many ways. "By the end of the war," she admitted, "we were able to understand, although our group certainly did not endorse the statement of Cobden, one of the most convinced of all internationalists: 'I made up my mind during the Crimean War that if ever I lived in the time of another great war . . . I would not as a public man open my mouth on the subject, so convinced am I that appeals to reason, conscience or interest have no force whatever on parties engaged in war, and that exhaustion . . . can alone bring a contest of physical force to an end.' "

Finally it did end; a shattered world prepared to draw up a shaky Versailles Treaty. Peace was a soiled dove. In 1919, Jane Addams went to Europe for the second conference of the Women's International League for Peace and Freedom. Some of her colleagues, having absorbed the slogan about the "war to end war" and having seen Wilson cast in the role of a new messiah, envisioned a brave new world emerging from the havoc of World War I. Never afraid of calling a spade a spade, Jane Addams reached no such conclusions from her own 1919 travels and talks. The same deadly nationalism that had brought on the war was still very much alive, not as a liberal influence (as some social reformers insisted) but as a destructive force. Millions of men had been killed, but the frenzied patriotism that sent

"A MAIDEN OUTLOOK UPON LIFE"

Some critics thought that Jane Addams was too sentimental. In her book *Counter-Currents*, published in 1916, the well-known American essayist Agnes Repplier wrote of Jane: "A lady lecturer, very prominent in social work, has made the gratifying announcement that 'the greatest discovery of the nineteenth century is woman's discovery of herself. It is only within the last fifty years that it has come to be realized that woman is human, and has a right to think and act for herself.'

"Now, after all, the past cannot be a closed page, even to one so exclusively concerned with the present. . . . If women failed to discover themselves a hundred or five hundred years ago, it was because they had never been lost; it was because their important activities left them no leisure for self-contemplation. Yet Miss Jane Addams, who has toiled so long and so nobly for the bettering of social conditions, and whose work lends weight to her words, displays in *A New Conscience and an Ancient Evil* the same placid indifference to all that history has to tell. What can we say or think when confronted by such an astounding passage as this:

" 'Formerly all that the best woman possessed was a negative chastity, which had been carefully guarded by her parents and duennas. The chastity of the modern woman of self-directed activity and of a varied circle of interests, which give her an acquaintance with many men as well as women, has therefore a new value and importance in the establishment of social standards.'

" 'Negative chastity'! 'Parents and duennas'! Was there ever such a maiden outlook upon life! It was the chastity of the married woman upon which rested the security of the civilized world—that chastity which all men prized, and most men assailed, which was preserved in the midst of temptations unknown in our decorous age, and held inviolate by women whose 'acquaintance with many men' was at least as intimate and potent as anything experienced today. Committees and congresses are not the only meeting-grounds of the sexes."

Armenian children, cold and hungry because of the Allied blockade, wait in line for food provided through American relief.

them off to die with slogans and songs on their lips was still viable. This new nationalism, she knew, was still in its early history. However, she thought it might be possible for the nations' representatives to meet in frank and fearless discussion of their national creeds—as the early church in its first centuries had called its ecumenical councils for creedal discussions. That, and not pious daydreaming, was Europe's best hope.

Old men's old game

There were few "frank and fearless" discussions at the Versailles peace table. Instead old men played the old game of power politics. Striving desperately to preserve his idealism through a newly established, powerful League of Nations, President Wilson gave in on some of his other Fourteen Points to preserve the one on the League. Then, ironically, he returned to an America which rejected his League, refused to join the World Court, and left him a broken, frustrated invalid. Embittered and half paralyzed, Woodrow Wilson left the White House on March 4, 1921, for retirement.

Into the Executive Mansion strode Warren G. Harding. What he intended to give the country that had elected him was "not nostrums but normalcy; not revolution but restoration; not surgery but serenity." Despite all her own psychic and physical pains, Jane Addams gathered her strength and prepared to confront the "normalcy" of a postwar generation. Her own vote for President in 1920 had gone not to Harding but to Socialist Eugene V. Debs. She was not so naïve as to suppose the traumatic effects of a world holocaust could be thrust aside with a few of Harding's phrases. A jittery America, watching the brutalities of the Russian despotism, suddenly became terrified of "Bolsheviks" at home. Throughout the 1920's social progress was hampered by the fear that any kind of state service was moving the United States closer to socialism. America had *not* returned to normal life, Jane noted, and she had no enthusiastic optimism about the future for those who consulted her.

Meanwhile, she did all she could to help her country and the world. In 1919 she concerned herself with the feeding of German and Austrian

These Chicago slum children were lucky enough to enjoy an outing at the Bowen Country Club, a facility of Hull-House in the area.

children, knowing what hunger can do to foes as well as friends. In the winter of 1922 she presided at a Conference for a New Peace called by the Women's International League for Peace and Freedom at The Hague. She accepted a commission from the delegates to visit various European states to urge support for a world economic conference, an international court for reparations, and the withdrawal of occupation armies. Accompanied by the indispensable Mary Rozet Smith, Jane Addams then took a nine-month trip around the world, visiting India, Japan, China, and the Philippines. A kidney operation temporarily confined her to a Tokyo hospital, where she was treated with great veneration. Remembering the coolness that had greeted pacifists in the United States, she commented that "an internationally minded person should be defined as a friend of every country except his own." And she deeply deprecated the actions of an America that "abandons the solemn covenants made in her name, restricts her immigration, increases her tariffs, and refuses to consider her war loans as part of the international responsibility she assumed."

India fascinated her with its ancient, intricate culture, and depressed her with its unspeakable poverty and pain. Always tolerant of other religions and government systems, Jane was impressed with Mahatma Gandhi and his program of nonviolence, derived (in part) from the writings of the American transcendentalist, Henry David Thoreau. Having visited Gandhi's *ashram* (or religious retreat) in India, she called him "the great teacher who more than any other living man is steadfastly committed to the typical Christian adventure, as yet untried, of nonresistance." This admiration for Gandhi continued throughout her life. She anticipated the success of his campaign.

Loving her enemies

As always, she was delighted to be back at Hull-House with her old friends and new demands. Despite her unpopular stand on pacifism, the settlement's income rose from $60,000 in 1917 to $70,000 in 1922 and $95,000 in 1929. Still, there was no denying that Jane Addams' courageous wartime views resulted in inevitable penalties in these years. "How well I remember,

"TIRELESS, GRACIOUS, EXEMPLARY"

Victor Weybright, later a well-known editor and author, met Jane Addams in the early 1920's: "I was a rapid typist in those days and, as her secretary, often could record Miss Addams' thought or handwriting almost as fast as she could speak or dash off rough drafts of speeches, letters, and memoranda. So I had a splendid opportunity to observe the greatest woman America had yet produced when dealing with the simplest and most abstract problems of the day. . . . Hull-House teemed with ideas. . . . Its dozen buildings were full of people, too. . . . The adult English classes for foreigners were based upon leftover Sears Roebuck catalogues donated by Julius Rosenwald. The little theatre was rampant with talent. The music school was an eyrie of singing birds. . . . Amid this never-ending round of education, research, social-service training, and good fellowship, Miss Addams was tireless, gracious, exemplary as a hostess, and warm-hearted as counsel and friend. She was the finest impromptu speaker I have ever heard. Though tolerant of human frailty, she was not a person to be bullied by the use of boring excuses or by overfamiliar appeals to her interests. Her dignity, her poise, and her beautiful voice commanded every situation. . . . She wrote well and with a sure touch, revising little. . . . But it is as a life force, a great person, that those who knew Jane Addams think of her. All who were touched by her idealism and character were transformed forever after by a sense of dedication that is impossible to define. One simply became more human and gently courageous, unafraid of criticism and impervious to flattery. One had partaken vicariously of greatness, through association with a natural teacher of the good life for one and all."

when I spoke in America in 1922 and 1923, the silence that greeted the name of Jane Addams," said Maude Royden, the British suffragette and pacifist. "The few faithful who tried to applaud her only made the silence more depressing." When the Daughters of the American Revolution circulated a "Spiderweb Chart" of fifty-one blacklisted individuals they considered subversives, Jane Addams' name was on it. She was also the target of a vicious attack by the American Legion in 1926, which accused her of being pro-German. "You know," Jane Addams said when she heard of this, "I am really getting old. I find it is not as easy to love my enemies as it used to be." Such flaggings of the spirit were rare. Let no one think that the haughty lists of the DAR or the threatening gestures of the American Legion intimidated tiny Jane Addams. In 1927, when her reputation was at a low ebb, she could still high-spiritedly remind a meeting of prominent lawyers and judges: "In every popular revolution the people begin their housecleaning by abolishing the courts."

That the quest for peace, in spirit as well as in word, continued long after the Armistice is demonstrated by books she read and preserved in her personal library: Ellen Key's *War, Peace and the Future*, Jessie W. Gibb's *Peace Sonnets*, Norman Thomas' *The Conscientious Objector in America*, Salvador de Madariaga's *Disarmament*, and Kathleen Norris' *What Price Peace*? But Miss Addams did not confine her campaign to the library. When the 1924 congress of the Women's International League for Peace and Freedom met in Washington, she was in the president's chair, apologizing for the cool reception given the overseas delegates by the American press. When some delegates chose to go from Washington to Chicago for a summer-school course, their train had to be diverted to another station in Cincinnati, since Ku Klux Klan members armed with sticks were waiting on the arrival platform. The bigotry and violence of the civil rights movement in the 1960's is no new thing to American life. Jane Addams saw more than her share of it in the 1920's.

In the summer of 1926 she traveled to Dublin for the Women's International League congress. Her opening address reflected the same faith that had motivated her for years: "We believe that new methods, free from physical violence, must be worked out for ending struggle." Now, as always, she refused to use unrealistic and high-sounding phrases. The only hope for a genuine adjustment, she knew, lay not in hiding from the truth, or gilding the lily, but in a patient effort to work problems out by daily experience. By practicing what she preached, day by day, she won her own immortality.

Chapter 7
PERSEVERANCE AND FINAL VICTORY

SUDDENLY everything nailed down seemed to be coming loose. In the fall of 1929 the New York stock market collapsed, signaling the beginning of the worst depression in American history. Within a month the loss in stock prices had totaled more than fifty billion dollars. Mass unemployment, bank failures, mob violence, and suicides followed; gaunt faces, hobo jungles, and relief projects were soon widespread. A long-proud nation came to have, in an incredibly short time, a new set of symbols reflecting hopeless despair: the slammed door; the endless walk; the shoes lined with newspapers; the straggling, sullen breadline; the dirt-caked hands warmed before gloomy fires; the hate-filled apathy of Hoovervilles. New popular songs had titles like "Can I Sleep in Your Barn Tonight, Mister?" and "Brother, Can You Spare a Dime?" Never had the American ship of state seemed closer to sinking.

Seventy years old in 1930, Jane Addams watched her country slide into the Great Depression during the closing years of her life. Though she had suffered much pain and undergone major surgery and long periods of confinement in hospitals, she fought the battles of the the 1930's as vigorously as she had those of the 1880's.

The book she published in 1930, her first in eight years, was called *The Second Twenty Years at Hull-House,* and continued her autobiography after 1910. Again it reflected her sense of mission, gift for organization, literary talent, and reflective insight. Belonging to the first generation of American women to be at all extensively college-trained, she had fought for half a century to escape Victorian standards, which said women's only proper work, when they had the temerity to leave the fireside, lay in the genteel areas of experience such as teaching well-brought-up children in pleasant classrooms. The first volume of Jane's autobiography had proved this attitude to be outdated by revealing what one woman had been able to achieve in the dismal slum of a rowdy city. The second volume dotted the *i*'s and crossed the *t*'s by following her activities into the broader fields of national politics and international pacifism. It was well received, attracting fewer snide masculine comments about feminine activism than had been the case earlier in her career.

The Nobel Peace Prize

Jane's reputation, nonetheless, continued to suffer—as she surmised it would—from her criticism of America's part in the war. She lived through a trying phase of partial eclipse, never recanting her pacifist principles, but never permitted to forget the aversion with which superpatriots regarded them. However, life often provides compensations. At this dark period Jane Addams had one of her brightest moments and highest honors. In November of 1931, she

Jane Addams, shown here convalescing, underwent an operation the day after receiving word of her Nobel Prize.

and Nicholas Murray Butler, the famed president of Columbia University, were jointly awarded the Nobel Peace Prize. The Nobel Committee chose Butler for his work with the Carnegie Endowment for International Peace, and Jane for her energetic career in the pacifist movement. Some of her friends resented the dual award on the ground that Butler, a supporter of the war against Germany, had forfeited his right to stand beside her in the eyes of the world; but Jane herself, whatever her private feelings, made no public comment on the subject.

Confined to a Baltimore hospital, and therefore unable to make the trip to Norway to receive her award in person, she joined the rest of the nation in reading what the Nobel citation said of her: "She clung to her idealism in the difficult period when other demands and interests overshadowed peace . . . . She was the right spokesman for all the peaceloving women of the world." That accolade would have been enough to immortalize the memory of Jane Addams, but she possessed too much vitality to be circumscribed by the neat formula devised in Oslo. She had shaped her time in so many ways!

Almost a half century before Jane began her social work, Henry Thoreau had gone to live in a cabin on the shores of Walden Pond. Jane Addams, just as committed as Thoreau to nonviolence, went to Hull-House. Both wanted to lead "authentic" lives (to use the term of twentieth-century existentialism). Only, where Thoreau "signed off" from society in protest against slavery, Jane found her life to be most authentic when she was actively engaged in transforming society. She labored in the ghetto so that she could live meaningfully. She left the woods and fields of Cedarville for the crowded streets of Chicago, because she knew the American experiment would succeed or fail there. In cities, man could, for the first time, control and direct his whole environment. No longer did he need to overcome slowly a great variety of natural forces; his intellect and skills could be put to work more directly and immediately. In the twentieth century the city would be home for most human beings. Once order and justice were established, a new freedom for humanity would flourish in a society transformed by technology. Here at last was the possibility of a fulfillment for individuals that the Founding Fathers had dreamed about when their nation was more than 95 percent rural.

But what would happen when technology bogged down—when the very heartbeat of the cities almost stopped? That was the terrifying question raised by the Great Depression, which began in 1929. All America's new urban problems could be solved, Jane Addams believed, by a pooling of individual minds, muscles, and wills. She refused to doubt that the American people could, if they would, successfully meet the challenge of the depression. The "moral equivalent of war" remained very much to the point in this crisis. The energy that had gone into World War I was precisely what was needed, except that now it should be channeled toward socially useful objectives. If each individual would pitch in and do his bit for the good of all, if private groups would undertake their own programs, if the government would vastly expand its assistance—then the nation might rise from the morass in which it was floundering.

Along with this credo, Jane offered her own stirring career as proof of its validity. She fervently maintained that a life of service to society would go a long way toward making society work. In her mind, it was as simple as that. But the depression worsened too rapidly for reasoned arguments. Political cliches and wild promises took turns dominating public opinion. Neurotics and fanatics pushed forward, with whole sections of the population following them. Schemes were advanced to share the wealth, soak the rich, collect foreign debts, and tap the pot of gold at the end of the rainbow.

The sad state of the nation made the election of 1932 a crucial one in American history. Republicans and Democrats alike invited Jane Addams to present her views to their platform committees in Chicago, and she urged a number of commitments such as lower tariffs and membership in the World Court. "Unless normal times return soon," she predicted, "the United States will be faced with the strange problem of taking care of a demoralized generation." No one denied that she spoke the truth.

Jane voted for Herbert Hoover in 1932. He was her old friend of wartime relief. He had, during his Presidency, received pacifist delegations cordially, attempted to get a program of disarmament accepted, declared a moratorium on war debts, and enunciated a good-neighbor policy toward the nations of Latin America. His domestic efforts had resulted in the establishment of the Federal Farm Board to expedite the marketing of agricultural commodities, the Reconstruction Finance Corporation to provide capital for financial institutions, and the Federal Home Loan Act. Jane, approving of all this, thought that Hoover deserved a second term in the White House. The American people did not. Demanding more drastic measures, they swept Franklin Delano Roosevelt into office on a tidal wave of votes.

"AMERICA'S UNCROWNED QUEEN"

Professor Frederick Stang, chairman of the Nobel Committee, used the phrase "America's uncrowned queen" in his brief address during the 1931 ceremonies in Oslo, and it quickly became a familiar term with reference to Jane Addams. On the same occasion, Professor Halvan Koht read the citation that accompanied the Nobel Peace Prize: "In honoring Miss Addams, we also pay homage to the work which women can do for the cause of peace and fraternity among nations. . . . Miss Addams . . . does not speak much, but her quiet, kind-hearted personality creates an atmosphere of good-will, which instinctively calls forth the best in all. For twenty-five years she has been the faithful spokesman of the idea of peace and little by little, without any effort to cause sensations, she has gained a prominent place in the love and esteem of her people.

"She became the first woman of the land, nearly its first citizen. She did not always have public opinion with her at home or abroad, but she never surrendered her faithfulness, and in her faithfulness she is genuinely American. . . . When the need was greatest she made the American woman's desire for peace an international interest. . . . In Jane Addams there are assembled all the best womanly attributes which shall help us to establish peace in the world. . . . She clung to her idealism in the difficult period when other demands and interests overshadowed peace. . . . She was the right spokesman for all the peaceloving women of the world."

Jane gave her Nobel Prize money to the International WILPF to carry on its work toward peace in the world. Not one cent of the $26,000 that she had been awarded from various sources during the year 1931 was kept for her personal use.

The New Deal

Jane Addams was too ill to go to Washington for the inaugural in 1933. It was a gray bleak day. Winter clouds hung over the scene, as if reflecting the despair in many hearts. The vast throng gathered at the Capitol seemed drawn by curiosity as much as hope. Down Pennsylvania Avenue drove Herbert Hoover, the humanitarian who had been baffled by the depression, who had failed in putting "a car in every garage and a chicken in every pot." Bugles blew at noon. Leaning on the arm of his son James, Franklin D. Roosevelt walked onto the platform. Chief Justice Charles Evans Hughes, a ramrod of a man, administered the oath on the Dutch Bible that had been in the Roosevelt family for three hundred years. Then came the voice of the new President, destined to symbolize democracy at bay: "In every dark hour of our national life a leadership of frankness and vigor has met with that understanding and support of the people themselves which is essential to victory . . . . Let me assert my firm belief that the only thing we have to fear is fear itself."

Jane Addams liked his voice and his analysis. The problem was to expand the areas of national concern for the people; to promote the general welfare—measured primarily in terms of human values rather than vested property rights. The government had to establish new rules of the game, so that everyone could play. The New Deal would write these new rules.

Roosevelt's strategy was direct: Meet the emergency with emergency action. Attack the cause of the crisis. "We are against revolution," Roosevelt insisted. "Therefore we wage war against those conditions which make revolutions—against the inequalities and resentments which breed them." Jane Addams knew what he meant. She had been using such tactics for forty years—"the more things change, the more they remain the same."

The nation "rediscovered" Jane Addams' program and vitality in the early Roosevelt years. The rise of the New Deal reinstated her as a national heroine. During the final years of her life she was officially feted as no other woman had been in this country ever before. Miss Frances Perkins, Roosevelt's Secretary of Labor and the first woman Cabinet officer in our history, was on record as saying: "Jane Addams really invented social work and social welfare as a department of life in the United States." Even more significant was the admiration the President's wife showed for her. It

EARTHQUAKE IN THE GHETTO

The Great Depression was "the American earthquake" to writer-critic Edmund Wilson, who devoted his essay "Hull-House in 1932" to the conditions he found on a tour of the area:

"Hull-House had always stood for tolerance; all the parties and all the faiths had found asylum there. . . . With its strong walls, its enclosed staircased courts, and a power plant of its own, it stands like a medieval chateau protected by a moat and portcullis. Inside it there is peace and a sort of sanctity. Jane Addams at seventy-two still dominates [it] with her singular combination of the authority of a great lady and the humility of a saint. In the large refectory-like dining room with its copper and brass and bare brick, the quick glances of the 'seeing eye' which fascinated young women in the nineties and excited them to go in for settlement work—that glance at once penetrating and shy—still lights its responses around her table."

Wilson found "a sea of misery" extending from Hull-House on every side. The sorrows of the depression seemed magnified in the ghetto, where unemployment and want—terrifying specters at the best of times—were now more demoralizing than ever. The slum dwellers huddled in unheated rooms, depending on relief for their scanty meals. Some had too much pride to ask for aid until they became desperate; they were "pale and thin with undernourishment." Many immigrants, confused about how to obtain government charity, never had it until relief workers knocked on their doors. They sat in stolid suffering amid their "Slavic saints and Madonnas, bristling with spiky gold crowns, Byzantine embroidery and Polish inscriptions." Ironically, here and there a room looked neater than before because the husband, chronically out of work, had finally had the time to paint the walls or nail down the floorboards.

Jane Addams shared their sorrows, as she had ever since her arrival at Hull-House. Her old friend, Elia W. Peattie, for whom Jane was a "woman of the hour," gives this perspicacious assessment:

"They say that Jane Addams always had a sad face, even before she became a professional neighbor and a conscious patriot. Certainly her face is sad now, though the eyes are luminous and the lips adapt themselves readily to smiles. She has the look of one who has seen a vast deal and learned . . . lessons of patience and courage. I am quick to add the 'courage' to the 'patience,' for the sort of patience that Jane Addams has is not at all of that sodden, dejected variety which is to be classed with indigestion. . . . Her patience is of the heavenly kind . . . and . . . enables her to keep from getting discouraged while she is busied doing the best she can to remedy the wrong which has awakened the patience. . . . It is her habit to be rather silent, and yet . . . she has brought about her at one time or another, the most brilliant thinkers and talkers in the country. At the long table with its simple fare, where the residents of Hull-House break bread after their day of diverse duties, have gathered . . .

Depression street scene.

most persons of original, peculiar or dominating thought of the present time. Some have been refugees, some revolutionists; some have represented the conventions and have been distinguished as achievers of modern forms of prosperity; some have been passionate theorists, others heroic demonstrators of this or that system. But one and all, speaking in this tongue or that, have done their best to explain and justify themselves to Jane Addams. I don't know why. No one quite knows why. Perhaps no one ever understood why people and pope deferred to [Saint] Catherine of Siena. . . .

"Miss Addams is not the woman to see visions, to indulge in mysticism, or to think of herself as a martyr or a spiritual leader. These things are not according to her temperament. Her compassion for the world takes a curiously practical and immediate form. She has, perhaps, not absolute confidence in the hereafter. . . . She does not intrude her ideas on that subject upon others. What she does do is to try to mitigate the difficulties of the present life, and to study the sources of the discontent, the inequality, the submergence of unfortunate men. . . . She listens to whoever comes to her by day or night. . . .

"Miss Addams has walked a long road, and she has come at last to a beautiful and windless place, a plateau of high altitude, where a wonderful peace lies brooding. . . . She has . . . attained to a true and unaffected understanding of brotherhood. . . . She accepts humanity. She is the never-wearied investigator of it. . . .

"She is wanted where her opinion can be freely heard. At the biennial meeting of women's clubs of Los Angeles, where the consideration of the admission of clubs of colored women came up . . . Miss Addams was conspicuous. Her opinions were opposed to those of an overwhelming majority. . . . But that fact did not deter the vast gathering of women from giving her the closest, most respectful . . . affectionate attention. When her clear contralto voice made its way from the left of the gallery where she sat, complete silence fell. . . . She was talking against compromise, speaking for a broad, general principle of humanity and sublime democracy. . . . And we voted for compromise. Miss Addams, patient and calm and sad, knew her ideas would have to wait a few generations more—perhaps a few centuries more. . . .

"She is always trying to be inconspicuous. She likes some of the elegancies, for she was born to them. . . . I remember one pleasing evening gown of [blue] trimmed with rich Japanese embroidery of deep contrasting tints of blue chrysanthemums piled one upon the other. . . . She takes very great pride in her nephew, Mr. James Weber Linn, to whom she has been almost a mother. Mr. Linn is making a happy reputation for himself as a young novelist, and he is one of the corps of English instructors at the University of Chicago. He gives what time he can to Hull-House, and he made haste to dedicate his first book to Miss Addams."

Edmund Wilson and Elia W. Peattie alike show that Jane Addams always felt the compassion for the downtrodden that brought her to the ghetto in the first place. She remained a "good neighbor."

A confident Franklin Roosevelt faces the crowd, the microphones, and the nation during his campaign for President in 1932. He was the first nominee to exploit the radio fully.

was Eleanor Roosevelt who would eventually take Jane Addams' place as the outstanding American woman on the world scene. Their convictions ran along parallel lines.

Both believers in internationalism, they became ever more disturbed as dictators stalked the earth. The same year Mrs. Roosevelt's husband took office in America, Adolf Hitler got the top post in Germany. Mussolini continued to strut about the stage, bullying his opponents and imagining he could establish a new Roman Empire along the Mediterranean. Japan moved against Manchuria, and cast hungry glances at Southeast Asia. Stalin was consolidating his power in the Soviet Union and extending his influence everywhere else, through local Communist parties and admirers. History was traveling along a darkened river, and all too few people were asking where it might lead or what rocks and whirlpools lay ahead.

A hatred of hypocrisy

In America itself, people were much more apt to ask when the depression, or the lawlessness brought on by Prohibition, might end. Jane Addams lived in the city of lawlessness personified. Chicago had its gangsters and bootleggers, and its corrupt politicians who worked hand-in-glove with them. The Roaring Twenties saw the rise of Al Capone, an unsavory underworld czar who dominated the illegal vice and liquor trade in the Chicago area, killed off his rivals in gang wars, and terrorized decent citizens.

The residents of Hull-House noticed telltale signs of the worst effects of Prohibition—the abandoned car used to transport liquor, the drunk staggering out of an apparently respectable club that was actually a speakeasy, the morbidly curious crowds flocking to the scene of a gangland slaying.

If it seemed incredible that Chicago, and other American cities to a lesser degree, should permit such enormities to continue, the reason became increasingly plain. Millions of otherwise law-abiding Americans denied that the government had any right to prevent them from taking a drink. Treating the Eighteenth Amendment as a bad law, they flouted it, and went to bootleggers for the whiskey and gin they could not obtain legally. Jane Addams realized what was happening. She felt that Prohibition had its good points and did not advocate its repeal, but she criticized it for violating her principle of not attempting to force rectitude on others. She told a graduating class at her alma mater (now known as Rockford College): "One does good, if at all, *with* people, not *to* people. It is easy, for instance, for us to take liquor away from the Negro in the South for his good, and from the immigrant laborer in the North for his good, but the curious result is this—a law passed by people who are quite sure that they themselves do not need the law at all . . . . Democracy is perhaps not an attainment, but a process—the process according to which we do not force law upon others, but make it for ourselves, and morally binding on ourselves therefore as its makers."

This thinking paralleled that of F.D.R., who, looking at Prohibition from the broad national perspective of the White House, pressed for the repeal of the Eighteenth Amendment; this end came about with ratification of the Twenty-first Amendment in 1933. Repeal prompted no protest from Jane Addams, although she voted against it. A teetotaler and nonsmoker herself, she never begrudged others their liquor and tobacco, nor could she be classified as a "wet" or a "dry" in any absolute sense. The consequences remained her criterion. She lived through the Gilded Age and the Jazz Age without being besmirched by the excesses of either one.

Hers, after all, *was* a great success story, a tale of high achievement in troubled times. She moved onward, upward, outward—from the countryside to the big city, to the nation, to the wide world. Her healing words, spoken first in the Chicago ghetto, were later heard at the ends of the earth.

Some critics hold that Jane Addams was entirely too serious, that her solemn commitment to human betterment drained her of all wit and humor. Jill Conway, a twentieth century scholar and admirer of "the great ladies of Chicago," puts it this way: "They were high-spirited but not witty, happy but never gay, and curiously one-dimensional. Like characters in a Dickens novel, one always knows what they are going to say." The judgment is too harsh. Jane may not have had spontaneous humor, but she certainly did have a touch of wit and irony. Thus, when the DAR, exasperated with her pacifism, expelled her from its ranks, she commented dryly: "I supposed at the time that [membership] had been for life, but it was apparently only for good behavior."

We should also note, in a rounded appraisal, that her life was one of intense loneliness. Emotionally frozen since her father's death, she never knew the pleasures of a husband and children of her own. She was happy in her close

In this painting by Ben Shahn, a government agent supervises the destruction of illegal wine. Prohibition outlawed all liquors with more than one-half of one percent alcohol.

association with women friends such as Mary Rozet Smith and Louise de Koven Bowen, but most of her tremendous energy went into her public role. When great decisions had to be made at critical moments in her life, she alone made them.

She had to accept the fact that some of her reforms involved the loss of old virtues. The attack on entrenched wealth meant that there would be fewer Carnegies to endow public libraries. The appearance of young women in social work meant the erosion of delicate feminine values. If the gain far outweighed the loss, the loss was still regrettable. Jane, therefore, could not examine the consequences without second thoughts. Preaching acceptance of the world around her, she never fully accepted it herself. And yet, as Walter Lippmann pointed

"I AM VERY MUCH ALIVE"

Hull-House was a very popular spot among visitors to Chicago, and its residents were well accustomed to showing strangers around the premises. Bus companies, conducting sight-seeing tours, often stopped at the settlement and guided people through it. One summer it was estimated that one thousand people a day visited on these trips. Of course, Jane herself was subjected to the scrutiny of total strangers craning their necks to get a look at America's most famous woman. She heard the guides describe her many a time, and rarely protested against anything they said. The most noteworthy exception was the time she happened to be sitting in a corner of the main room while a guide described her memorable career, from start to finish, to the tourists grouped around him. "How long has Miss Addams been dead?" inquired one of them. Jane was astounded by his answer: "Oh, about three or four years." Her patience snapped. Approaching the group, she stated emphatically: "I am sorry to disappoint you, but I assure you I am very much alive." This particular guide did not linger on the premises that day. Jane had undermined his credibility with this group, so he hurried back to the bus.

out, she had compassion without condescension, pity without retreat into vulgarity, and sympathy for common things without forgetting the uncommon. Lippmann concluded: "That, I think, is why those who have known her say that she was not only good but great."

Excellence and permanence

Jane Addams' health continued to deteriorate after her seventieth birthday, and her heart weakened. In the winter of 1931 she went to Florida to gain strength, and did not return to Hull-House until the following April. Thoughts of immortality assumed a larger role in her thinking, as the last book published in her lifetime, *The Excellent Becomes the Permanent*, demonstrates. The title, taken from Plato, expresses her belief that a life's excellence assures it of immortality. Eternity is not a duration of time but a certain quality of the soul that, once attained, can never cease to exist.

Such thoughts comforted her as one after another of her lifelong associates passed away—Julia Lathrop, Florence Kelley, Mary Smith. Word of Miss Smith's death, in the Smith house where Jane herself was confined to a sickbed, brought Miss Addams as close as she ever came to the death-urge. "I thought over everything," she declared later. "I suppose I could have willed my heart to stop beating, and I longed to relax into doing that, but the thought of what she had been to me for so long kept me from being cowardly."

Instead, Jane willed that renewed activity would follow her long convalescence. She lived with enough vigor to help Hull-House and Chicago during the 1933 "Century of Progress" celebration marking her adopted city's centennial. She also continued to assist her country, still caught in the grip of the depression; she conferred with scores of people, advised officials, spoke whenever she was strong enough to travel outside the city. Her "funny old heart," she told friends, was "behaving splendidly." A physician commented: "She will have to wear herself out. She can't rust out; it isn't her way."

Awards and honorary degrees continued to come. Gone was the coldness and animosity of the war and postwar eras; she was not just accepted, but venerated, by her fellow Americans. Through all the acclaim she kept her faithfulness to the daily particulars of American life, her almost obsessive concern for the good of individual human beings here and now. But she insisted that these individuals be fitted into patterns of behavior. "Wisdom to deal with a man's difficulties comes only through some knowledge of his life and habits as a whole," she observed. As with a man, so with a nation. Her critique of the United States is still very much to the point. Here, in her customary manner, she had an air of storming heaven's gates fully armed with the pertinent facts.

Frail though she was, Jane Addams could be neither bent nor broken by opposition. To grow and improve was the fulfillment of her life and America's destiny. Like President Franklin Roosevelt, whom she came more and more to admire in her last years, she was pragmatic, optimistic, and flexible. In discussing his political outlook, Roosevelt liked to say he stood "a little to the left of center." Jane Addams described herself as "always in the middle of the road; in politics as well as social reform I have been for 'the best possible.' " By no means everyone would place her in "the middle of the road," but a revealing episode in 1934 provides a telling justification for this appraisal. The University of California simultaneously gave honorary degrees to Jane Addams, Herbert Hoover, and Secretary of Labor Frances Perkins. While Hoover and Miss Perkins both refused to be photographed together, each was quite willing to be photographed separately with Jane. The former Republican President and the Democratic Cabinet member classified each other as extremists, but thought Jane was safely in between!

That "best possible" for which she aimed was good enough to win for her the 1935 American Education Award, which cited her "willingness to learn from life" and her teaching of "tolerance and peaceful community living, first at home and then in the world at large." The ceremony was broadcast internationally. Back in Chicago, Miss Addams spent her mornings working on a biography, never completed, of Julia Lathrop. Her afternoons were for visitors and programs at ever-active Hull-House.

Thanks for "being yourself"

Nobody can choose the one supreme moment of triumph in so full and rich a life as Jane Addams', yet anyone who writes about her is tempted to try. For this biographer that moment occurred on May 2, 1935, when she was in Washington for the twentieth anniversary dinner of the Women's International League for Peace and Freedom. In her seventy-fifth year, obviously near the close of her life, Jane Addams received tumultuous acclaim, both privately and publicly. "It is for being yourself that I thank you tonight," said her symbolic heir-apparent, Eleanor Roosevelt. "When the day comes when difficulties are faced and settled without resorting to the type of waste which war has always meant, we shall look back in this country upon the leadership you have given us, Miss Addams."

The celebrations culminated the next day in a radio linkup with London, Paris, Moscow, and Tokyo—an international symposium.

At the dinner described on this page, Jane Addams (right) chats with Mrs. Roosevelt (left) and Mrs. Cordell Hull, wife of the Secretary of State. Despite the heavy toll of age and illness, Jane had full command of herself when she spoke.

"SHE GOES IN PEACE"

Poignant stories were told of the funeral at Hull-House, and Linn recorded a number of them: "Workmen, coming in at six in the morning with their lunchboxes, placed them on a bench at the side of the room, then knelt as at a *prie-dieu*, and prayed in low voices. Once, a Greek, when he discovered that she was not to be buried 'by state,' as he had supposed, not after services in a church, nodded in approval. 'Her no just one people, her no just one religion,' he said, 'Her all peoples, all religions.' Children, in their best clothes, came and passed silently by hundreds, her own six-year-old great-grandniece among them. She looked about curiously; she had never been at Hull-House. 'Are we all Aunt Jane's children?' she whispered. . . . At Halsted and Twelfth . . . an officer was directing a tangle of traffic. When he saw the hearse coming down from the direction of Hull-House, he stopped everything in both directions and came over to the hearse. 'Is it her?' he asked respectfully. 'Yes,' said the driver. 'She goes in peace,' said the policeman, and when the car had turned left across the traffic, he was still standing, holding up his hand for quiet."

The tombstone set up over her grave in the Cedarville cemetery records in its simple legend the two achievements of her life of which she was most proud: JANE ADDAMS OF HULL-HOUSE AND THE WOMEN'S INTERNATIONAL LEAGUE FOR PEACE AND FREEDOM.

When her turn came to speak, Jane Addams put down her script and spoke impromptu to the listening world, giving her final message, her final advice: "Nothing could be worse than the fear that one had given up too soon and had left one effort unexpended which might have saved the world."

On May 10, she attended her last public meeting—of the Cook County Commissioners. Five days later she suffered a severe pain in her left side, and a surgeon who examined her advised an operation. When Louise de Koven Bowen entered her room with word that the ambulance would arrive in fifteen minutes, Jane replied calmly: "Then I can finish this novel. There are only a few pages left, and I'd like to get through them." The discipline and perseverance that had marked her life remained firm to the very end. The operation revealed a cancer so advanced that her doctors feared she would never regain consciousness. But she did; and for three days she struggled valiantly with her fatal illness. Her mind was clear enough for a mild jest: "When I was a child, I had an old doctor friend who told me that the hardest thing in the world to kill was an old woman. He seems to have been right." Sinking rapidly, she died on May 21, 1935. Her last words, when asked if she would like a sip of water, were: "Always, always, water for me."

The mortal remains of Jane Addams lay in state at Hull-House, where thousands of mourners, many in tears, passed through to pay their last respects. Then she was taken back to Cedarville to be buried near the mother she had scarcely known, the father who had been lost to her more than half a century before. The announcement of her death had brought a flood of tributes—from the White House, from the ghetto, from around the world. It is difficult to single out one of them for special mention, but the chief executive of her native state came as close as anyone to writing a fitting epitaph for her. Said Governor Henry Horner of Illinois: "I think of her as of the evening star, drawing the imagination of man through the clouds to the knowledge of a light that cannot fail."

PICTURE PORTFOLIO

Hull-House, restored to look much as it did when Jane Addams leased it in 1889, is now on the Chicago campus of the University of Illinois.

CHILD OF A VICTORIAN MIDWEST

JANE ADDAMS represented a triumph of heredity over environment. The rural town of Cedarville, Illinois, where she was born on September 6, 1860, was typically Midwestern and Victorian. Her childhood was darkened by her mother's death when Jane was less than three, and was hardly enhanced by her looks—she "was small, frail, and pigeon-toed, and carried her head to one side, as a result of a slight spinal curvature." Even so, her early years were idyllic. She loved to play in the gristmill (below) her father built among

trees he had planted; she engaged in endless games with a stepbrother in nearby caves, bluffs, and hills. She began her higher education at seventeen at Rockford Female Seminary—an ivy-clad school emphasizing Greek, Latin, and the preparation of young ladies for missionary work among far-off heathen. Birthplace, childhood, and schooling all seemed unlikely to produce an intellectually vital woman who would dedicate her life to Chicago's slum dwellers. But Jane Addams was the daughter of a bookish doer who was as kind as he was incorruptible. When Jane was a mere seven she foretold her future to her adored father. Shocked by the dingy homes of the poor in Cedarville, she announced that some day she would live in a "big house" amid "horrid little ones."

Jane was eleven when the picture (left) of her father's mill was drawn in 1871, and sixteen when she was photographed (above) with her stepmother, Anna, and one of her two stepbrothers, George. A year later she entered Rockford where Sill Hall below, named for the school's first principal (a woman with whom Jane differed), had already been built.

WOMAN ADRIFT IN EUROPE

IF THE CHILD sensed her destiny, the young woman at first forgot. Jane was graduated from Rockford in 1881—the year her father died—and matriculated in a medical school. But physical collapse, an operation on her crooked spine, and six months abed cut short her studies. Exhausted emotionally and bodily, she welcomed the prescription of her surgeon and stepbrother, Harry Haldeman, that she pass two years in Europe. With her stepmother and six friends, she sailed in August 1883. For twenty-one months Jane drifted spiritually, vaguely seeking "culture." Her first impressions were a jumble of pleasure and distress. In Ireland's County Kerry (right) she noted that the poor lived in mean huts and often had to sit in the dark. In London (far right) she complained that she "could scarcely breathe" for "the dreadful yellow fog." In Scotland's Ayrshire, where the River Afton (below) had inspired Robert Burns, she read him on the way to the cottage of his birth and "liked Tam O'Shanter as I never did before." In Italy (bottom right) she found "wonder and beauty." One brief excursion, however, proved formative if not decisive. Two

months after her arrival in Europe, she visited London's East End; there shrivelled women begged in doorways (left), children had only the streets for playgrounds (right), and the hungry bargained (above) for food that the rest of the city spurned. "It was enough to make one thoroughly sad & perplexed," she wrote to her brother. The East End's horror haunted her wherever she traveled afterward. She concluded that the pursuit of culture was not enough, and recalled the aphorism that "conduct, and not culture is three fourths of human life."

From Italy, she described "the paralyzing sense of the futility of all artistic and intellectual effort when disconnected from the ultimate test of the conduct it inspired," and her sense of futility gradually gave way to "the desire to live in a really living world . . . refusing to be content with a shadowy intellectual or esthetic reflection of it." She concluded also that the first generation of American college women, to which she belonged, had been educated too quickly, with too much emphasis on the mere acquisition of learning;

GINGER
AND ICE

Figure of Seneca (left), the Roman philosopher whose Stoic egalitarianism contributed to the French Revolution, adorns a choir stall in Ulm Cathedral. London's Toynbee Hall (below) was named for Arnold Toynbee, who died in 1883, aged thirty-one, exhausted by work for social reform.

in the process, she feared, they had lost the simple humanity and healthy emotions of their mothers and grandmothers. Pampered and sheltered, they were cut off from the "really living world" and felt helpless to do anything about its evils.

Jane herself still felt helpless, unable to harness her vague idealism to practicality. When, after several years at home, she sailed again for Europe in December 1887, she was twenty-seven and as bewildered and planless as she had been on her sickbed. Germany, out of its past and present, provided a sense of direction. In Ulm's soaring cathedral (above left) she found carvings of Greek and Roman philosophers, Hebrew prophets, and pagan temple builders among Christian saints. But in the streets outside such noble structures, the poor—personified in *The Weavers* of Gerhart Hauptmann's drama and illustrated in Kaethe Kollwitz's etching (above)—seethed with outrage at their plight. Inspired and moved, Jane dreamed of a "cathedral of humanity" big enough to shelter "a fellowship of common purpose." After twenty years, she had returned to her childhood vision of a "big house" amid "horrid little ones." Back in London, she visited such a place—the East End's Toynbee Hall, first of the settlement houses. "I found myself at Toynbee Hall," she wrote, "with high expectations and a certain belief that whatever perplexities and discouragement concerning the life of the poor were in store for me, I should at least know something at firsthand. . . . I had at last finished with 'preparation for life,' however ill-prepared I might be." Toynbee Hall showed her that organized social workers could raise a drab community to a higher level through shared experience—and the example inspired her.

FROM RICHES TO THE RAGGED

JANE was better prepared than she knew for the challenge she had set herself. Blessed with a substantial income, she chose for home and headquarters an aging, battered mansion surrounded by the misery of a slum in the nation's most raucous city. She called it Hull-House. In the 1890's—Hull-House's first decade—Chicago sprawled and brawled, drank and stank. It spewed its sewage into Lake Michigan (foreground, right), giving its million people, in 1891, the highest typhoid death rate in America. More than two fifths of the million were clannish, suspicious, unlettered immigrants from Europe, peppered with Negro refugees from the South. When the festivities of the great 1893 Columbian Exposition (left) gave way to economic depression and strikes, Chicago flamed with

Hull-House (below), rural when built in 1856 by Charles Hull, had been engulfed by the city when Jane Addams took it over. It stood in the center of the lithograph (top), above the Chicago River. Jane had worked there three years when the gleeful Democrat with the whip (center, in picture at left) collected his 1892 election bet on Grover Cleveland by having his Republican friend haul him in a carriage through the city's teeming streets.

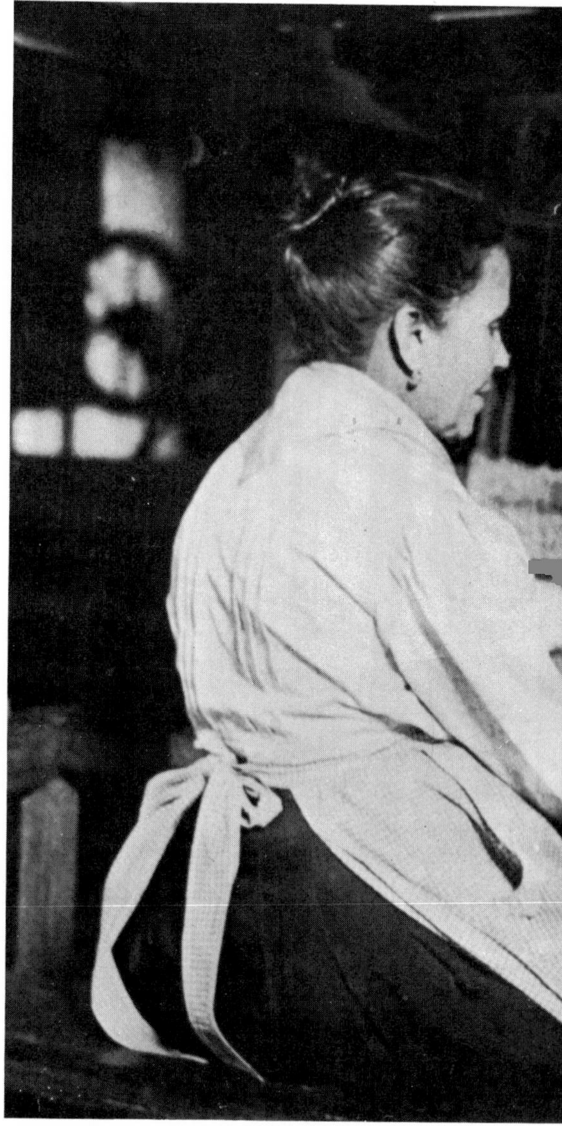

gunfire and bloodshed. But nothing fazed Jane; she did whatever needed doing. She and her friends and co-workers, of whom Mary Rozet Smith (right, painted by Alice Kellogg Tyler) was closest to her, had no preconceived ideas for Hull-House beyond refurbishing it (above left) and making it a center for the neighbors, rich or poor, young or old. It grew astonishingly. To imbue children with respect for their parents' Old World skills, Jane established a Labor Museum (above center) where older women delighted in weaving as they had in their homelands.

Hull-House quickly acquired an art school for children (above right), an art gallery, a coffee house, a gymnasium, a boys' club, a girls' boarding club, a men's club, a women's club, a nursery, a theater, a children's building, an apartment house. Each developed as Jane saw the need for it.

"Jane Addams had many talents," the historian Henry Steele Commager has noted, "but none more remarkable than her ability to work from the immediate to the general, from practical problems to philosophy, and even from the local to the national and the international. She always began with the job at hand, no matter how elementary or undignified; she took on the job of inspector of garbage removal for her ward to show how it

should be done—and did it so well that the [political] boss had to abolish the job itself in order to protect those collectors who held their jobs as sinecures; she went to the Illinois legislature with case histories of working women to push through labor legislation. ...What she saw of youth on the city streets ended up as a program of school playgrounds; what she learned of children in trouble with the law ended as the first juvenile courts in the nation."

Hull-House did serious chores: Jane Addams classified its activities as social, educational, humanitarian, and civic. As early as 1895 she and her colleagues published *Hull-*

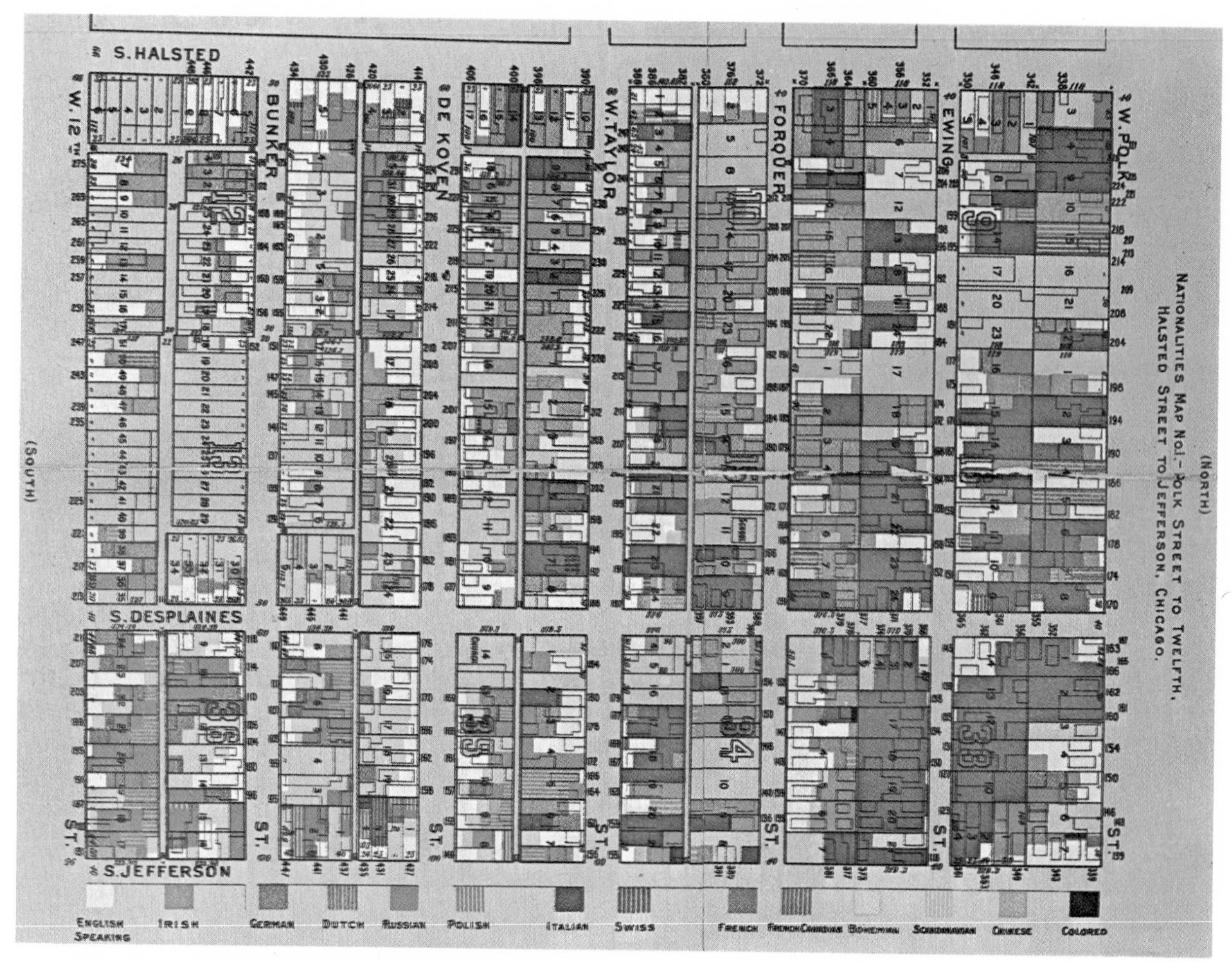

Map of a Nineteenth Ward area, keyed by color to its residents' national origin, was prepared for *Hull-House Maps and Papers* on the basis of information collected by a Hull-House worker for the U.S. Bureau of Labor. "This ward has a population of about 50,000," said an accompanying study. "It has had no unusual political scandal connected with it, but its aldermen are generally saloon-keepers and its political manipulations are those to be found in the crowded wards where the activities of the petty politicians are unchecked."

House Maps and Papers, a sociological study of the Nineteenth Ward, in which Hull-House was located. Her settlement attracted as volunteers William Lyon Mackenzie King, later Prime Minister of Canada; Julia Lathrop, the first chief of the United States Children's Bureau; Gerard Swope, who became president of General Electric Company; Judge Ben Lindsey, who founded Denver's juvenile court; and many other future notables. But Jane Addams exercised such tactful skill that Hull-House beneficiaries never considered themselves the objects of "social work," or Hull-House a great pioneering institution. They knew it as a place of fun and friendship, where, miraculously, they developed talents they were unaware they possessed. Band leader and clarinetist Benny Goodman got his first musical training at Hull-House; Norah Hamilton, head of its art school, said of her pupils: "The children seem to find in their inner lives a world of color and beauty in which they are perfectly at home." Generation after generation trekked to Hull-House. The grandmother of Eleanore Pasquale (right, with Miss Addams in 1934) learned to rejuvenate clothes there; and her daughter, and then Eleanore, followed. Even instructors learned. Wallace Kirkland, who made the picture opposite and many others in this book, acquired his expertise during fifteen years of residence at Hull-House, where he taught

boys to use cameras. More than twenty years after he first photographed Eleanore, he visited her as a LIFE photographer. Eleanore, whose own children by then had attended Hull-House, recalled: "That Miss Addams, she was a doll." "We always thought of Jane Addams," says Kirkland himself, "as a lovable grandmother, never as an old maid, or a social worker. One of her great assets was a complete absence of jealousy—she didn't care who got the credit, just so the thing was done." She got many things done, in many fields, but her delight never waned in "the spontaneous joy . . . the unworldly ambitions, the romantic hopes" of the young, and her delight inspired others. Louise de Koven Bowen (left), a benevolent Chicagoan, gave Hull-House an estate overlooking Lake Michigan where city-bred children could romp in field and wood (right), and sketch or paint flowers they had never seen before (below). Every Hull-House art student visited it for at least a weekend yearly; most got two-week vacations there. A dedicated Hull-House trustee, Mrs. Bowen herself was often on hand, living in the house (background, left) she had built on a knoll and entertaining her guests there.

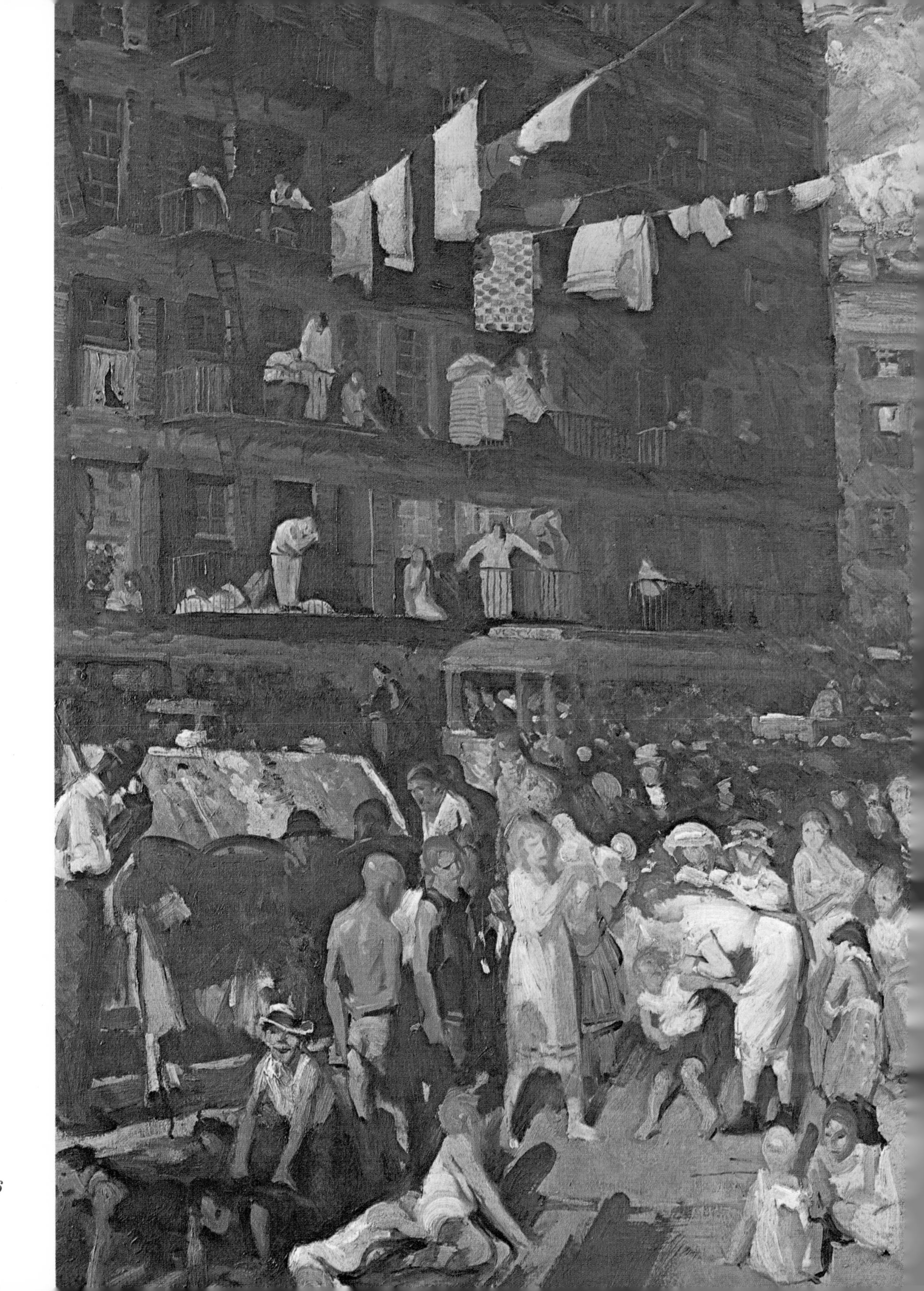

THE URBAN POOR

MOST OF THE CHILDREN who studied at Hull-House and frolicked on Mrs. Bowen's estate dwelt in the fetid poverty common to America's great cities. The environs (below) of Hull-House were even worse than the towering slum (left) painted by George Bellows, for in the Nineteenth Ward most of the houses were small, wooden, and ramshackle; many had been moved on rollers to the sites where they stood. Built for single families, they now sheltered—after a fashion—as many as could crowd in. Hundreds had no sewer connections and got their water from lone taps in the back yards. Streets, lined with overflowing garbage boxes, were foul and dimly lit; where it existed, paving was broken, and the wooden sidewalks were decaying. Huge flies swarmed in the filthy stables, and huge rats in the houses. Schools were drab, poorly equipped, and too few in number. Factories, which employed "pitifully sweated garment workers" (in the words of Jane Addams' friend Emily Balch), were almost as bad as the houses, but nobody enforced the factory laws. Such conditions impelled Jane Addams and her associates to sponsor a wide variety of reform movements.

SOCIAL AND POLITICAL REFORMS

JANE ADDAMS' BATTLES for social reforms began with the birth of Hull-House. Ignorant of the conditions of child labor, she was startled to discover, at the settlement's first Christmas party, some little girls refusing candy because they toiled in a candy factory from 7 A.M. to 9 P.M. and could not "bear the sight of it." A wearying campaign in which she mobilized trade unions, churches, and clubs won passage of a state law restricting employment to persons over fourteen, and cleaning up sweatshops. Other Addams-powered drives involved garbage, milk, playgrounds, and women's work hours. At the same time Jane helped unionize women garment workers, arbitrated labor disputes, and led trainloads of delegates to the state capital to demand woman suffrage. Women in Illinois won the vote in 1913, seven years before women won it as a basic national right.

Competition for jobs made immigrants unpopular with many Americans. The February 11, 1888 cover (right) of the magazine *Judge* quotes the portly employer thus: "As long as I am plentifully supplied with Immigrant Labor, I shall be deaf to the demands of the native workingman." When immigration was later restricted, Jane Addams vigorously fought inequities in the laws. During the 1894 Pullman strike, in which President Cleveland sent gun-carrying federal troops to Chicago (below), Jane participated in a futile attempt at arbitration. Her long, untiring campaign for woman suffrage often demanded her public appearance. The 1912 parade pictured below (she is at far right) preceded by a year the triumph of woman suffrage in Illinois.

A PRAGMATIC PACIFIST

TWO DECADES of everbroadening activity took Jane from brief obscurity in the Nineteenth Ward to municipal, statewide, and national celebrity. With the outbreak of World War I, her endeavors to restore peace —and later to alleviate war-created misery— made her internationally famous and perhaps the best-known woman of her era. She had always opposed war and force as a means of settling disputes, but she was a rare sort of pacifist. She did not decry patriotism; she considered it "one of the finest instincts of the human spirit." She did not merely condemn violence; she considered aggression too deep-seated in man to be uprooted, but believed, with William James, it could be guided to better uses than bayonet charges and gas warfare. At Hull-House she had seen initially antagonistic folk of diverse origins learn to work together. She thought nations could do so, too. To keep America out of the war, she organized the Women's Peace Party and became its chairman; she led a 1915 meeting in Europe of women from twelve countries who sought to prevent the war's spread; she

When the Women's Peace Party gathered in New York's Washington Square in 1915 (left), war was becoming grotesque as well as horrible: the ghouls at bottom left are ordinary French soldiers transformed by gas masks. Wilfred Owen, the English poet who died in the war, described a gas attack thus: "Gas! Gas! Quick, boys!—An ecstasy of fumbling/ Fitting the clumsy helmets just in time/ But someone still was yelling out and stumbling/ And floundering like a man in fire or lime—/ Dim through the misty panes and thick green light,/ As under a green sea, I saw him drowning." But old-fashioned bayonet fighting—being used below by American troops to overrun a German trench at Verdun—was even worse. Jane Addams heard from hospital nurses that "delirious soldiers are again and again possessed by the same hallucination—that they are in the act of pulling their bayonets out of the bodies of the men they have killed."

founded and became president of the Women's International League for Peace and Freedom (often called WILPF or WIL), which advocated a conference of neutrals to mediate between nations. Jane and her friend Mary McDowell (far left) led peace demonstrations. But once the U.S. entered the war, WILPF refrained from word or action that might impede victory. After the war, Jane led the organization in striving to remove the causes of war, and in demanding both disarmament and a revision of the Versailles Treaty. The Daughters of the American Revolution, satirized above by Grant Wood, believed she was unpatriotic, denounced her—with unconscious irony—as "revolutionary," and revoked the honorary DAR membership it had bestowed on her in 1900. Unperturbed, Jane went on to help feed starving Russians (right) and Germans (top right). Never abandoning Hull-House, she made international peace a major concern all through her later years.

A PRAGMATIC PACIFIST

After the war, Jane Addams surveyed German needs, and found ten million desperately hungry children, personified above in Kaethe Kollwitz's sketch for a poster. Jane also helped to obtain funds for succoring famished Russians like those below, who haul a sledge laden with American Relief Association food. She did much work for Herbert Hoover's U.S. Food Administration and the American Friends Service Committee.

CONCERNS FOR ALL HUMANITY

FOR JANE ADDAMS, the words "peace" and "freedom" applied not just to nations, but to every individual in the world, of which she saw a great deal in her last fifteen years. Of her many trips abroad, the longest, in 1923, took her, via Paris, to India, the Philippines, Manchuria, Korea, China, and Japan, where schoolgirls (left) and officials deferentially greeted her. Overseas again in 1926, she found Europeans vastly more concerned and better informed about the Sacco-Vanzetti case (subject of Ben Shahn's montage below) than were most Americans. She herself fought for clemency for the two men, as much because she detested capital punishment as because she believed they had been convicted by political intolerance rather than evidence. When Sacco and Vanzetti were executed, she said the U.S. had wasted a unique opportunity to show that "we are here attaining a conception of justice broad and fundamental enough to span the reach of our population and their kinfolk throughout the world."

One journey abroad Miss Addams could not make. She was in a hospital when her Nobel Peace Prize medal (below) was presented. She gave most of her prize money to the Women's International League for Peace and Freedom.

For six years two Italian anarchists, Nicola Sacco and mustachioed Bartolomeo Vanzetti, dominated international attention as they dominate Ben Shahn's montage (left). Between July 14, 1921, when they were convicted of the murder of a South Braintree, Mass., paymaster and his guard, and August 23, 1927, when they were executed, demonstrators around the world (far left) appealed, marched, and destroyed American property to protest "political martyrdom" of the two men. Governor A. T. Fuller of Massachusetts, the small figure with upraised hand in the painting, denied clemency after a personal investigation and after a three-man committee headed by Harvard's President A. Lawrence Lowell (in middle of group beside coffins) decided the facts did not warrant a retrial. Alfred Nobel, who founded the Nobel Peace Prize represented by the medal above, bore a different kind of burden from Fuller's and Lowell's. A Swedish chemist, he invented dynamite and other explosives to enhance safety in blasting, only to see them used to kill.

HER LEGACY TO THE WORLD

TWENTY-ONE YEARS after Jane Addams' death, the 1956 International Congress of the Women's International League for Peace and Freedom, in a resolution on "The Sacredness of Human Life," urged that the killing of a human being be declared a crime against humanity. It equated with individual murder the practice of capital punishment, the waging of civil or international war, and atomic or hydrogen tests that emit deadly radiation.

The resolution might have been written by Jane Addams herself, for she had spoken out against wars and capital punishment and would have opposed "The Bomb," all three of which are symbolized in these photographs. Her voice is silenced, but her work continues. Today the WILPF favors disarmament under United Nations control, an end to all wars and all nuclear testing, a strengthened United Nations including mainland China in its membership, broadened economic assistance to underdeveloped countries, and full racial equality. A long-time WILPF sponsor, Marian Anderson, has often represented the United States on the U.N. Trusteeship Committee, urging Jane's humanitarianism.

The first H-bomb test (above) in 1952 destroyed a Pacific islet, and later hydrogen bombs have been many times more powerful. Radiation from such bombs affects all living things, so Jane Addams' WILPF ranks bomb-testing with capital punishment and war among crimes against humanity. America no longer tests bombs above ground. Capital punishment in the United States has perceptibly waned since the execution in 1960 of Caryl Chessman, whose sentence by a California court stirred worldwide protest (above right). Jane Addams opposed capital punishment with the pragmatism that marked her pacifism. Doubting it served any purpose, she said: "Perhaps the historians could tell us whether in those places wherein witches were executed others were deterred from becoming witches." At right, the agony of a wounded American soldier being given first aid in Vietnam epitomizes Jane Addams' reasons for hating all war.

HER LEGACY TO HULL-HOUSE

WHILE JANE ADDAMS' work for humanity has reached out to all the world, it also continues where it began, in Chicago, with ever-increasing vigor. Ten Hull-House buildings in the old Nineteenth Ward succumbed to wreckers in the early 1960's to accommodate the University of Illinois campus, and only Hull-House mansion and the dining hall survive there, as memorials to Miss Addams. But the Hull-House Association has spread far afield, embracing six bustling, widely separated neighborhood centers—one of which boasts seven subcenters—and serving areas that were still prairie in Miss Addams' lifetime. In the Addams tradition, they not only feed, clothe, shelter, and counsel the needy, but make the lives they save worth living. Hull-House centers teach everything from baby care and cooking to ballet and sculpture. They provide gymnasiums and athletic fields, conduct medical and dental examinations, organize museum and camping trips, produce plays, and even operate a theater that tours the Midwest. The clients are no longer mostly immigrants. Well ahead of the rest of the country, Hull-House never practiced any kind

The Negro children gazing wistfully into a playground they may not enter (above) represent a social condition that Jane Addams denounced. Today segregation of this kind is disappearing—partly due to the NAACP, of which she was a founding member. But integration is an old story at Hull-House; in these recent pictures, the amateur actors at far left are rehearsing *The Threepenny Opera* and the boys at immediate left are happily playing on the gymnasium floor. "The goals of our gym program," Hull-House explains, "include giving children in a crowded community the opportunity to have fun, to learn to play, to learn to get along with the other children, to have experience in making group decisions, to learn special physical skills and to learn to control their own behavior." The melting pot, Jane Addams style, works so well that one cooking class, made up almost entirely of Spanish-speaking young girls, delightedly concentrates on preparing such non-Spanish delicacies as brownies and pizza; a cooperating Jewish group tutors Spanish-speaking adults in English. Thus, shared experience continues.

HER LEGACY TO HULL-HOUSE

of discrimination, but one center, because of its location, serves chiefly Southern whites and American Indians, another an area 99 percent Negro. Jane Addams came by her anti-segregationist sentiments early. Her father hated slavery, and Jane recalled: "I must have been less than four years old when I saw a slave, but I have never forgotten the black man sitting in quiet conversation with my father as I entered a room one sunny morning. He was being helped to Canada, where he would become free, and how valiantly I prayed that he would have a safe journey." She warned that segregation put the Negro "outside the immediate action of that imperceptible but powerful social control which influences the rest of the population" and produced a "readiness to irritation" inevitable "when one race is forced to demand as a right from the other those things which should be accorded as a courtesy." The group below, enjoying a Hull-House Association benefit ball game, epitomizes the ideals she so deeply cherished.

HER OWN WORDS

A MODEL FATHER

Jane Addams was a prolific writer who turned out a long list of books and articles, most of them tracts for the times, dealing with subjects bearing on her philosophy, social work, and pacifism. Somehow, amid her arduous labors in the Chicago ghetto, she also found time to publish two volumes of autobiography. The first volume, Twenty Years at Hull-House, *which appeared in 1910, is by all odds the best thing she ever wrote. Moved by introspective meditation on her early years, she tells her story with feeling and sensitivity, in personalized, concrete terms. The fine prose runs smoothly in balanced sentences. The author's characteristic moral energy infuses every page.*

If Jane Addams is the heroine of Twenty Years at Hull-House, *its hero is assuredly John Addams, her father. He was her idol and her guide; his influence pervaded her life; and he is the subject of the most moving reminiscences she ever wrote, excerpted here:*

Elias Hicks, whose concepts so deeply influenced John Addams, lived to repent of a youth spent in "learning to sing vain songs, and to take delight in running horses." A Long Island farmer, he became a "concerned Friend" during the Revolution and began to meditate on the Quaker writings of George Fox and others. Gradually he came to doubt the literal truth of certain biblical passages, especially those in which the Deity seems to favor war. The "inner light" presented no such problem to him, so he placed full reliance on it in his moral life. Many Quakers held that the Bible and the "inner light" taught the same message, so they considered Hicks a heretic. The dispute was too fundamental to be settled and Hicks chose to lead his adherents into the Hicksite "separation."

■ On the theory that our genuine impulses may be connected with our childish experiences, that one's bent may be tracked back to that no-man's-land where character is formless but nevertheless settling into definite lines of future development, I begin this record with some impressions of my childhood.

All of these are directly connected with my father, although of course I recall many experiences apart from him. I was one of the younger members of a large family and an eager participant in the village life, but because my father was so distinctly the dominant influence and because it is quite impossible to set forth all of one's early impressions, it has seemed simpler to string these first memories on that single cord. Moreover, it was this cord which not only held fast my supreme affection, but also first drew me into the moral concerns of life, and later afforded a clue there to which I somewhat wistfully clung in the intricacy of its mazes.

It must have been from a very early period that I recall "horrid nights" when I tossed about in my bed because I had told a lie. I was held in the grip of a miserable dread of death, a double fear, first, that I myself should die in my sins and go straight to that fiery Hell which was never mentioned at home, but which I had heard all about from other children, and, second, that my father—representing the entire adult world which I had basely deceived—should himself die before I had time to tell him. My only method of obtaining relief was to go downstairs to my father's room and make full confession. The high resolve to do this would push me out of bed and carry me down the stairs without a touch of fear. But at the foot of the stairs I would be faced by the awful necessity of passing the front door—which my father, because of his Quaker tendencies, did not lock—and of crossing the wide and black expanse of the living room in order to reach his door. I would invariably cling to the newel post while I contemplated the perils of the situation, complicated by the fact that the literal first step meant putting my bare foot upon a piece of oilcloth in front of the door, only a few inches wide, but lying straight in my path.

I would finally reach my father's bedside perfectly breathless and, having panted out the history of my sin, invariably received the same assurance that if he "had a little girl who told lies," he was very glad that she "felt too bad to go to sleep afterward." No absolution was asked for or received, but apparently the sense that the knowledge of my wickedness was shared, or an obscure understanding of the affection which underlay the grave statement, was sufficient, for I always went back to bed as bold as a lion, and slept, if not the sleep of the just, at least that of the comforted.

John Addams rarely displeased Jane, but she recalled one time when he did so:

■ Although I constantly confided my sins and perplexities to my father, there are only a few occasions on which I remember having received direct advice or admonition; it may easily be true, however, that I have forgotten the latter, in the manner of many seekers after advice who enjoyably set forth their situation but do not really listen to the advice itself. I can remember an admonition on one occasion, however, when, as a little girl of eight years, arrayed in a new cloak, gorgeous beyond anything I had ever worn before, I stood before my father for his approval. I was much chagrined by his remark that it was a very pretty cloak—in fact so much prettier than any cloak the other little girls in the Sunday School had that he would advise me to wear my old cloak, which would keep me quite as warm, with the added advantage of not making the other little girls feel bad. I complied with the request but I fear without inner consent, and I certainly was quite without the joy of self-sacrifice as I walked soberly

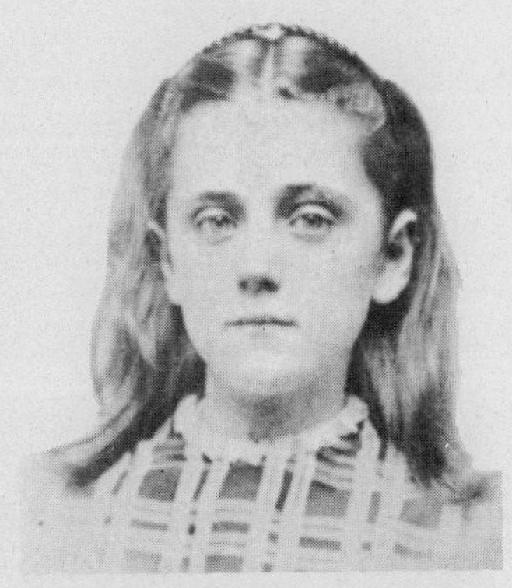

Jane Addams was a thoughtful eight-year-old when this photograph was taken. Her father had recently married the widowed Anna Haldeman, who brought her children with her to the house (left) that John Addams had built for his first wife in 1854. Its quiet elegance suited a Quaker patriarch who shunned the shoddy and gaudy aspects of his era. He resided there except when serving in the state legislature. His house was so durably constructed that it still serves as a private residence, one of the most notable in its section of Illinois. Despite extensive remodeling, the elegance is still there—and the house is plainly recognizable as the one where Jane Addams was born back in 1860, and in which her father presided over the most impressionable years of her life.

through the village street by the side of my counselor. My mind was busy, however, with the old question eternally suggested by the inequalities of the human lot.

The storm and stress of the Civil War convulsed America during Jane's early childhood. In placid Cedarville, young men joined up as banners waved, bands played, and local leaders including John Addams delivered patriotic speeches. Far away, Yanks and Rebels clashed at Bull Run, Chancellorsville, Gettysburg, Cold Harbor, and many other bloody battlefields. Finally peace came, but the national rejoicing quickly turned to profound grief at the sudden, violent, tragic death of the President. One of Jane's touching vignettes in Twenty Years at Hull-House *presents her father in desolation after learning of Lincoln's assassination.*

■ I suppose all the children who were born about the time of the Civil War have recollections quite unlike those of the children who are living now. Although I was but four and a half years old when Lincoln died, I distinctly remember the day when I found on our two white gateposts American flags companioned with black. I tumbled down on the harsh gravel walk in my eager rush into the house to inquire what they were "there for." To my amazement I found my father in tears, something that I had never seen before, having assumed, as all children do, that grown-up people never cried. The two flags, my father's tears, and his impressive statement that the greatest man in the world had died, constituted my initiation, my baptism, as it were, into the thrilling and solemn interests of a world lying quite outside the two white gateposts. . . .

Is it not Abraham Lincoln who has cleared the title to our democracy? He made plain, once for all, that democratic government, associated as it

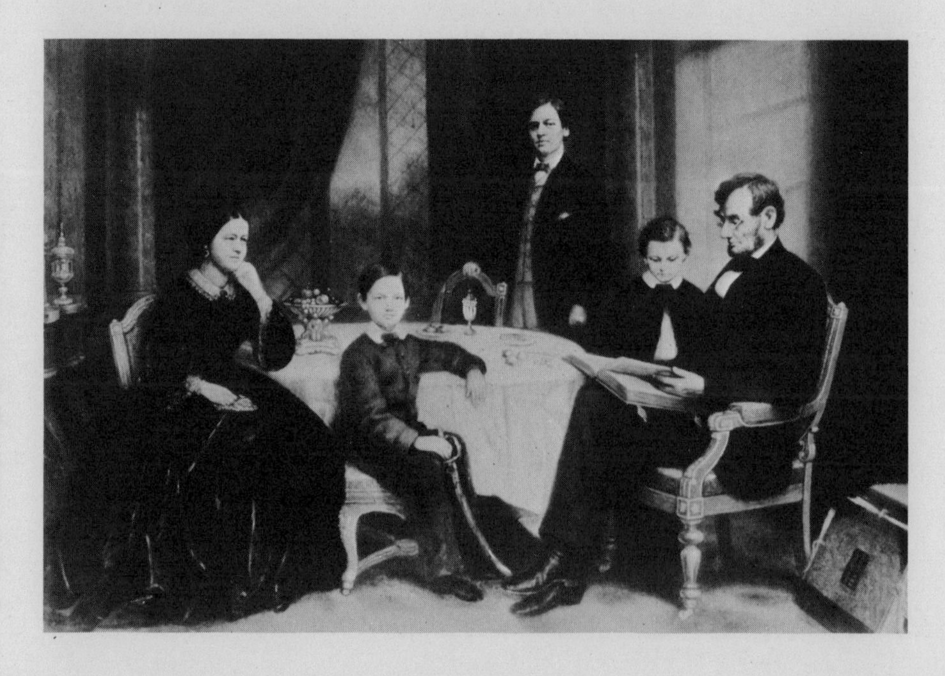

Francis B. Carpenter painted this group portrait of the Lincolns and their sons in the White House in 1861. Mary Todd Lincoln sits near William Wallace ("Willie"), Robert Todd stands behind the table, and the President shows Thomas ("Tad") the pages of a book. By now it is difficult to visualize the Lincoln family in the White House without recalling Carpenter's portrayal of the five of them together. Carpenter also did portraits of Presidents Tyler, Fillmore, and Pierce, and painted "The Emancipation Proclamation," which hangs in the Capitol in Washington. Later the artist wrote *Six Months in the White House with Abraham Lincoln*.

is with all the mistakes and shortcomings of the common people, still remains the most valuable contribution America has made to the moral life of the world.

Another notable man deeply admired by Jane was George Washington, who, as she notes below, wished his slaves to be free. Washington was "principled against selling Negroes, as you would cattle in the market," and had vowed "never again to become the master of another slave by purchase," if it could be avoided. His will, accordingly, provided that his slaves were to be freed at the death of his wife, Martha, and he also specified that his body servant, William, be given his freedom immediately upon Washington's death if William so desired, "as a testimony of my sense of his attachment to me and for his faithful services during the Revolution." Jane gave the following speech in 1903:

Richard J. Oglesby, here depicted in his uniform as a major general in the Union army during the Civil War, turned abolitionist when the family slaves were sold after his parents' death. He later bought back and liberated "Uncle Tim," an old servant. After fighting in the Mexican War, he panned for gold as a forty-niner, helped found the Republican party in the 1850's, and became governor of Illinois three times. Like his good friend John Addams, he strongly supported Lincoln. John's daughter Jane always remembered a red-letter day of her childhood "when Governor Oglesby, whom all Illinois children called 'Uncle Dick,' spent a Sunday under the pine trees in our front yard."

■ We meet together upon these birthdays of our great men, not only to review their lives, but to revive and cherish our own patriotism. This matter is a difficult task. In the first place, we are prone to think that by merely reciting these great deeds we get a reflected glory, and that the future is secure to us because the past has been so fine. In the second place, we are apt to think that we inherit the fine qualities of these great men, simply because we have had a common descent and are living in the same territory. As for the latter, we know full well that the patriotism of common descent is the mere patriotism of the clan—the early patriotism of the tribe. We know that the possession of a like territory is merely an advance upon that, and that both of them are unworthy to be the patriotism of a great cosmopolitan nation whose patriotism must be large enough to obliterate racial distinction and to forget that there are such things as surveyor's lines. Then when we come to the study of great men it is easy to think only of their great deeds, and not to think enough of their spirit. What is a great man who has made his mark upon history? Every time, if we think far enough, he is a man who has looked through the confusion of the moment and has seen the moral issue involved; he is a man who has refused to have his sense of justice distorted; he has listened to his conscience until conscience becomes a trumpet call to like-minded men, so that they gather about him and together, with mutual purpose and mutual aid, they make a new period in history.

Let us assume for a moment that if we are going to make this day of advantage to us, we will have to take this definition of a great man. We will have to appeal to the present as well as to the past. We will have to rouse our national conscience as well as our national pride, and we will all have to remember that it lies with the young people of this nation whether or not it is going to go on to a finish in any wise worthy of its beginning. If we go back to George Washington, and ask what he would be doing were he bearing our burdens now, and facing our problems at this moment, we would, of course, have to study his life bit by bit; his life as a soldier, as a statesman, and as a simple Virginia planter.

First, as a soldier. What is it that we admire about the soldier? It certainly is not that he goes into battle; what we admire about the soldier is that he has the power of losing his own life for the life of a larger cause; that he holds his personal suffering of no account; that he flings down in the gage of battle his all, and says, "I will stand or fall with this cause." That, it seems to me, is the glorious thing we most admire, and if we are going to preserve that same spirit of the soldier, we will have to found a similar spirit in the civil life of the people, the same pride in civil warfare, the spirit of courage, and the spirit of self-surrender which lies back of this. If we look out upon our national perspective, do we not see certainly one great menace which calls for patriotism? We see all around us a spirit of materialism—an undue emphasis put upon material possessions; an inordinate desire to win wealth; an inordinate fear of losing wealth; an inordinate desire to please those who are the possessors of wealth. Now, let us say, if we feel that this is a menace, that with all our power, with all the spirit of a soldier, we will arouse high-minded youth of this country against this spirit of materialism. We will say today that we will not count the opening of markets the one great field which our nation is concerned in, but that when our flag flies anywhere it shall fly for righteousness as well as for increased commercial prosperity; that we will see to it that no sin of commercial robbery shall be committed where it floats; that we shall see to it that nothing in our commercial history will not bear the most careful scrutiny and investigation; that we will restore commercial life, however complicated, to such honor and simple honesty as George Washington expressed in his business dealings.

Let us take, for a moment, George Washington as a statesman. What was it he did, during those days when they were framing a constitution, when they were meeting together night after night, and trying to adjust the rights and privileges of every class in the community? What was it that sustained him during all those days, all those weeks, during all those months and years? It was the belief that they were founding a nation on the axiom that all men are created free and equal. What would George Washington say if he found that among us there were causes constantly operating against that equality? If he knew that any child who is thrust prematurely into industry has no chance in life with children who are preserved from that pain and sorrow; if he knew that every insanitary street, and every insanitary house, cripples a man so that he has no health and no vigor with which to carry on his life labor; if he knew that all about us are forces making against skill, making against the best manhood and womanhood, what would he say? He would say that if the spirit of equality means anything, it means like opportunity, and if we once lose like opportunity we lose the only chance we have toward equality throughout the nation.

Let us take George Washington as a citizen. What did he do when he retired from office, because he was afraid holding office any longer might bring a wrong to himself and harm to his beloved nation? We say that he went back to his plantation on the Potomac. What were his thoughts

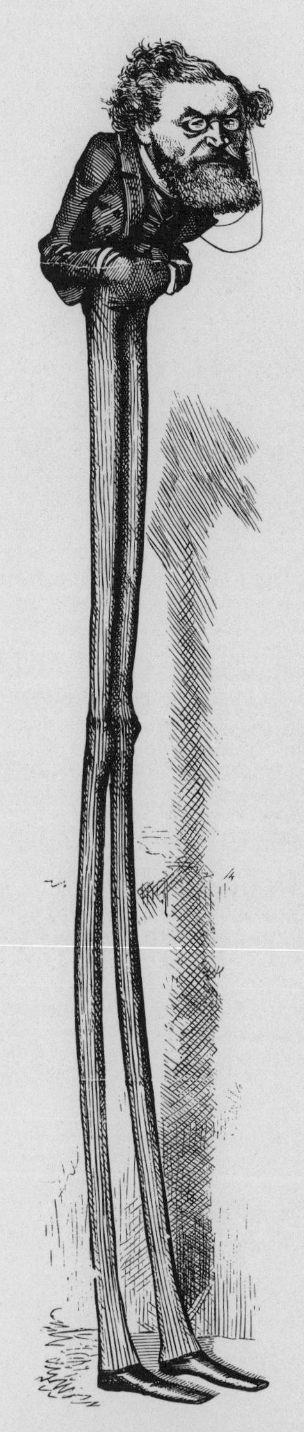

Thomas Nast drew Carl Schurz as "The Tower of Strength." A German immigrant who became an American statesman and man of letters, Schurz firmly backed Lincoln; Jane gave twenty-five copies of his book on Lincoln "to a club of boys . . . the very first Christmas we spent at Hull-House."

during the all too short days that he lived there? He thought of many possibilities, but, looking out over his country, did he fear that there should rise up a crowd of men who held office, not for their country's good, but for their own good? Would he not have foreboded evil if he had known that among us were groups and hordes of professional politicians who, without any blinking or without any pretense that they did otherwise, apportioned the spoils of office, and considered an independent man as a mere intruder, as a mere outsider; if he had seen that the original meaning of officeholding and the function of government had become indifferent to us, that we were not using our foresight and our conscience in order to find out this great wrong which was sapping the foundations of self-government? He would tell us that anything which makes for better civic service, which makes for a merit system, which makes for fitness for office, is the only thing which will tell against this wrong, and that this course is the wisest patriotism. What did he write in his last correspondence? He wrote that he felt very unhappy on the subject of slavery, that there was, to his mind, a great menace in the holding of slaves. We know that he neither bought nor sold slaves himself, and that he freed his own slaves in his will. That was a century ago. A man who a century ago could do that, would he, do you think, be indifferent now to the great questions of social maladjustment which we feel all around us? His letters breathe a yearning for a better condition for the slaves as the letters of all great men among us breathe a yearning for the better condition of the unskilled and underpaid. A wise patriotism, which will take hold of these questions by careful legal enactment, by constant and vigorous enforcement, because of the belief that if the meanest man in the republic is deprived of his rights, then every man in the republic is deprived of his rights, is the only patriotism by which public-spirited men and women, with a thoroughly aroused conscience, can worthily serve this republic. Let us say again that the lessons of great men are lost unless they reenforce upon our minds the highest demands which we make upon ourselves; that they are lost unless they drive our sluggish wills forward in the direction of their highest ideals.

Jane's most fantastic tale of her Rockford days concerns Thomas De Quincey, who made a hit with his *Confessions of an English Opium Eater,* not because he admitted taking drugs (which were easy to buy in his time), but because he described in fine prose his vivid experiences with them. Jane and her classmates were not fearful of imitating De Quincey because he denied feeling any ill effect after swallowing opium. His reaction took the form of sharpened sense perceptions, and a marked mental clarity. But he ended up wandering from lodging to lodging, unable to remain anywhere peacefully. Jane's shorter bout with opium (see page 30) produced no such loss of self-discipline or control.

COLLEGE DAYS AND AFTER

When John Addams insisted that his youngest daughter attend Rockford Female Seminary, Jane was far from enthusiastic. Yet she came to love it. The literary curriculum at Rockford naturally included several of Shakespeare's plays. Jane read them so often and with such concentration that they saturated her mind, giving a permanent bent to her outlook on life. As a mature woman, confronted with the Pullman strike, she went to King Lear *for an appropriate text* *(see pages 157–161)**. As an undergraduate, she had written a striking analysis of* Macbeth:

■ In the eleventh century Duncan and Macbeth were two grandsons of the reigning king of Scotland. In course of time the old king peacefully

Washington Irving, who died the year before Jane's birth, was established as a classic writer when she read him as a child (see page 15). Edgar Allan Poe had hailed him as "the most deservedly eminent among all the pioneers of American literature." Gifted with a leisurely and charming style, beguiled by strange legends and romantic history, Irving wrote both comic tales based on fiction *(Rip Van Winkle, The Legend of Sleepy Hollow)* and true tales based on fact. His long biography of Washington helped to mold Jane's high opinion of the first President.

died, and Duncan ascended the throne. He had but the shadow of a claim over his cousin, he was not as gifted a man, he probably made no greater effort toward the crown, and yet he gained it. The divine right of kings was bestowed upon him while Macbeth was merely one of his subjects. We should take Duncan to be one of those men who in some way have the material universe on their side, a "great vague backing" in all they do or undertake, the word "luck" somewhat expresses their success. . . . Macbeth is not envious, but he continually thinks of these things; he is a nervous man and cannot think calmly.

Shakespeare leaves us to imagine all this. He does not present Macbeth until these thoughts have begun to pursue and control him. . . .

All the scenes of the play are laid at night, and we are hurried on with feverish rapidity—we do not know the Macbeth of the daytime, how he appears in council or battle—we meet only the nervous, high-strung man at night, pursued by phantoms and ghosts, and ever poetically designing a murder.

Shakespeare presents the man's thoughts ere he presents the man himself, and in the very first scene the three witches frighten us before we know what they are to represent. As Macbeth enters they hail him with the three titles his heart most desires; he starts, who wouldn't? The thoughts he has been thinking and thinking have suddenly embodied themselves, and stand before him on the . . . bare heath. They have all at once grown into definite purposes, have spoken out before a third person, Banquo, and he knows that ever afterwards he must acknowledge them, that they will pursue and harass him. We have all had the experience—how we prepare ourselves for sudden deeds by the intuitive choice of good and evil, or, as our thoughts go forth never to be recalled, how they increase and gain enormous proportions until we lose all control of them.

The lines at the right, from a notebook Jane kept at college in 1878, show her efforts to systematize evolution and ethics. Her references to "the struggle for existence" and "the survival of the fittest" echo Darwin and Spencer. She is obviously quoting from the books she read, rather than setting down her personally developed ideas on "conscience," "utility," and "sense of duty." The last quotation of this excerpt is a tag from Roman law: *Fiat justitia, ruat coelum* ("Let justice be done, though the sky fall"). Jane had not fully formulated her moral concepts at this time, but she already understood many of the problems posed by evolution.

"Conscience is the struggle for existence become aware of itself in the mind of a thinking person."
"Utility is scientifically the result of the conflict of individual rights, with survival of the fittest.
Sense of duty" "The pleasure resulting from intelligent acquiescence in self-sacrifice that makes self sacrifice possible."
"From the primitive thought "self-preservation is the first law of nature" up to the highest abstract expression of moral duty "Fiat justitia, ruat coelum"

But Macbeth had this experience in a way that was simply frightful. His thought grew so powerful as to assume form and shape, as to be endowed with life and a distinct physical existence. . . . His first impulse is one of fear and terror at the metaphysical confusion in which he is entangled. He is lost in a maze of his own thoughts, he knows not what is real and what is fantastical, he is filled with horrible imaginings and doubts; but slowly from all this confusion there arises a phantom distinctly before him. It seems afar off, he detaches it from himself, and yet he knows it is his own creation. He says: "Why do I yield to that suggestion/ Whose horrid image doth unfix my hair?"—That image is murder. . . . Here he yields to that impulse of a sort of self-preservation, that shielding of his inner character; he wishes not to harm or shock himself, he would gain a deadly end, but without the illness that should attend it. With this purpose he reorganizes the witches and phantoms, and shifts upon them the entire moral responsibility of his future actions. He follows them mechanically and saves himself—it is a phantom that murders Duncan.

He discloses his purpose to Lady Macbeth, and thus gives to her the physical or material responsibility. She plans and contrives, does all coolly and calmly, for she is but murdering a man. . . . Macbeth meanwhile is struggling throughout with murder itself, invisible yet clinging and horrible, the phantom that pursues him until the last moment. Just before the final deed he soliloquizes: "Now o'er the one half world/ Nature seems dead, and withered murder/ Alarmed by his sentinel wolf/ Moves like a ghost"—'Tis "withered murder" that leads him on to his destruction, and he follows it as something inevitable. . . . He kills Duncan and comes back to his wife horror-struck and frightened, not because of the bloody deed, but because he has murdered sleep, because he has heard a voice cry "Sleep no more! Macbeth does murder sleep!" No matter how often we read it, it always produces the same thrilling effect; the idea of a man murdering sleep; think of being pursued by withered murder and a sleepless sleep.

This then is the result, by getting rid of his will and following merely the poetical idea, he kills not a man, but an imaginary, an invisible horrible being. It is frightful. . . .

Macbeth is driven from murder to murder, ghosts and phantoms pursue him, he consults again the weird sisters, gains courage and is lost through his own daring—a poetical man doing the worst deeds in a poetical sense—the philosophy of murder.

Historian John Lothrop Motley (1814-1877) aspired to be America's Thomas Carlyle, and he came close to this aspiration in his books on the Dutch republic. He was a committed democrat who, serving in embassies abroad, saw European freedom movements at first hand. Since the spirit of liberty seemed in peril, he defended it in fiery, eloquent prose, picturing Holland as a David withstanding a Goliath (Spain), and as a model for other oppressed nations to imitate. His books sold well, bringing his libertarian message to a wide public—including Jane Addams and the other students who studied him at Rockford.

After leaving Rockford, Jane suffered two severe shocks—the death of her father (1881) and her spinal operation (1882). Then came her first tour of Europe (1883–1885). The notebook she kept during the tour reveals an eye for scenery and social conditions, an ear attuned to the cadences of local dialects, and a mind no less curious about legends than about historical antiquities and cultural monuments. The abbreviated entries have an immediacy unique in her writings, and are therefore worth reading in order to recapture the excitement of the moment. Jane "could not kiss the Blarney Stone" because her

During the tour described on these pages, Jane encountered many echoes of Thomas Moore (above, in an 1833 engraving), Ireland's gift to the Romantic movement. Possessing a genuine lyric talent and a passion for the exotic, Tom Moore published poems on Oriental themes in the manner of Byron (whose biography he wrote, but whose memoirs he destroyed as being too scandalous). But he was above all an Irish patriot who expressed most of his authentic feeling through treatment of Irish causes. He defended the men who struggled to free his beloved country, denounced the harshness of British rule, and turned out scores of verses whose meters perfectly fitted various tunes in *Irish Melodies,* a collection of traditional folk airs. Since so much of his poetry was set to eminently singable music, it reached a wide transatlantic audience, including Jane's stepmother—an adept at strumming the guitar and warbling Moore's stanzas.

physical condition prevented her from leaning out the small aperture and stretching to the point on the wall where the stone is embedded. But otherwise, she was game for all the adventures that came her way after arriving at the Irish port of Queenstown (now Cobh) in 1883.

■ August 29. Made the passage [across the Atlantic] in seven days. Three hours beautiful drive up Queenstown Harbor just at sunset. . . . Rode from Queenstown to Cork . . . the same evening. Slept six in a room. Spent the morning hunting up tickets to send our trunks in to Glasgow . . . to be held until called for.

In the afternoon went to Blarney Castle, eight in an open omnibus. The beautiful drive . . . along the River Lee [past] the Queen's College, the insane asylum with elegant grounds [and] two beautiful country places with holly and laurel overhanging the walls. One stone wall after another all the way through two little villages consisting of rows of cottages most of them with flowers in the window and lots of children—a squad of them following the bus on and on until we threw them pennies. . . . Blarney Castle . . . perfectly beautiful, a tower 120 feet high. Could not kiss the Blarney Stone. Young Englishman kissed it and offered to kiss my hand. . . .

August 31. Left Cork on Thursday morning at eight o'clock. After three hours arrived at Killarney Railway Hotel. At once made arrangements to [do] the round of the lakes and were off by twelve. Took lunch in the boat about two—wine offered to the boatmen. . . . In the morning, first a ride of nine miles through a beautiful country with stone walls and smooth roads to the opening of Dunloe Pass. Beggars, thirteen children at once and an old man. . . . The long winding path up to the very opening of the gap. . . . Then the donkey ride of four miles through Dunloe Pass—the purple and . . . the eagle perched way up. The balanced rock that Tom Moore compared to the poet's heart: the lightest touch sets moving but all earth can't shake from its base. Down through the black valley where the sun [doesn't] shine for three months of the year. Poor people with only goats and cows and land enough to raise hay and potatoes. No windows in some of the houses: "Don't need to see in the winters, ma'am, they sit in the dark."

Met the boat at the foot of the upper lake, four oarsmen with lunch. A beautiful ride through the lake . . . saw the place where the chief and his lady . . . ferried across and left footprints in the rock. Went past eagle nest rock . . . and the meeting of the waters to the third lake. The legend of O'Donahue who comes back every May to read in his library (books piled up along the shore in the rocks). Puts on his eyeglasses (another rock). Whoever sees him will have a rich and handsome husband before the end of the year. Mouse Island, seven white mice to be seen on it, only come out Sunday after services. Landed at Ross Castle, a beautiful old ruin covered with ivy. Went back to the hotel by dinner time. Anecdotes told by the old driver. Devil's punch bowl on top of the mountain. A man once dropped through to Australia where a woman was weeding her garden. . . . The Dunloe gap so healthy people in it live to be 115. "English can take everything away from us but our blarney." Innisfallen is such rich land, put a sheep in it at night, it comes out fat in the morning ("I won't say what morning").

Saw lovely floating clouds in the mountains like volcanoes. The highest in Ireland, 3414 feet. Saw quite a large good-looking stone house entirely deserted because haunted by fairies. Serpent's lake where St. Patrick banished the serpents, they try to get out every Monday morning. One inlet of water into the lake but no outlet because the serpents drink up all the water. Father Mathew story: A girl one evening after service shut up in the church. At midnight a ghostly priest came out and offered to hear Mass. She told Father Mathew . . . who went in the next night. He found the ghostly priest was uneasy because he had been paid for a Mass that he had never said. Father Mathew offered to say it and asked for his reward that he have power over intemperance. And, sir, if he raised his hand over a man in blessing, that man would sooner cut his throat than have a smell of whiskey—"I've seen them." . . .

Saw the mountain the Devil had taken a bite out of but afterward dropped it into the Lake as a little island. "And where is the Devil now?" "Gone over to London, ma'am."

From Cork, Jane and her party moved up to Dublin. These entries in her notebook cover a gamut of subjects from her solicitude about her stepmother's illness to the intriguing fact that Susan B. Anthony, with whom Jane would later cooperate in the suffrage movement, had been at Trinity College just before her. Some notes encapsulate whole segments of Irish history. The "murder" she mentions had occurred only a year earlier (1882), when a band of Irish rebels stabbed to death two officials of the British administration as they walked through Phoenix Park. The "battlefield of Boyne" refers to the successful defense of Belfast (1690) against the troops of James II, who hoped to use Ireland as a springboard from which to regain the English throne occupied by William of Orange.

■ Sunday morning . . . went to English service at Christ's Cathedral—beautiful music from a full choir. We then walked in the rain through the Castle courtyards to St. Patrick's Cathedral. . . . After leaving the Castle, took two hacks in the pouring rain, and drove to the birthplace of Thomas Moore, in a house . . . back of St. Patrick's. Three-story red brick house with a liquor shop below. Then to Phoenix Park. . . . The big monument of the Duke of Wellington. Saw the spot of the murder. Guide very much impressed by it and inclined to go into details. Came back to the hotel for . . . dinner. Ma had a chill in the evening, and was quite sick. . . . Impressed by the quantity of British soldiers we saw everywhere.

September 4. Ma felt the effect of her last night's chill, and was feverish all day. . . .

September 5. Ma was no better. . . . I bought a scrap album and pasted in a few pictures. . . .

Edward Gibbon was an eighteenth-century rationalist who described "the triumph of barbarism and religion" in his *Decline and Fall of the Roman Empire.* Later scholars differ with his phrase without compromising his basic work, which remains the greatest history in the English language. It is also one of the longest, so if, as Jane Addams reports, she and two other Rockford girls read him in one summer vacation, they must have been rapid readers indeed. Jane notes: "Each became skeptical of the other two. We fell upon each other with a sort of rough-and-tumble examination, in which no quarter was given or received; but the suspicion was finally removed that anyone had skipped." The girls might have been more at ease with Gibbon's autobiography, with its sentence (humorous to later generations) about his one romance, his father's opposition, and his own decision on the proper course to follow: "I sighed as a lover, I obeyed as a son."

September 6. Ma gave me a handsome Brussels lace tie for my birthday. . . .

September 7. Ma some better today but still has the weak times early in the morning, and about three in the afternoon. Bought some books. . . .

September 9. Ma sat up today and is better. This afternoon I rode in the streetcar to the Botanic Gardens. . . . Riding back in the streetcar on top, an old gentleman talked with me. Has an appointment from the Queen as Irish poplin manufacturer; was a conservative, but said that "England had gone too far, too far. We have given her all her famous men, and what has she done for us?" . . .

[September 17]. Spent about ten minutes in the old Trinity College Library. . . . The name above ours in the register as follows: "Equal rights for women, political and social, advocated by Susan B. Anthony, Rochester, N.Y., U.S.A." At two o'clock we took the train to Belfast. Our fears and fidgets lest some one else would come into our carriage. One woman who tried it and then got out. . . . Saw the battlefield of Boyne. . . . Reached Belfast by seven in the evening.

September 18. Rode around the city . . . and out to [the] linen manufactury where it is all made by hand. The rows of cosy-looking cottages and the big low building where they weave. . . . Everyone was very kind in showing us the mill.

Ellen Terry joined Sir Henry Irving to play Ophelia to his Hamlet, and remained with his company for twenty-four years, performing feminine leads so well that she set standards against which other actresses were measured. Toward the end of her career she suffered from a failing memory. John Gielgud, her nephew, recalled a time when she was cast in the role Jane mentions on this page—Portia in *The Merchant of Venice*, for which she is costumed here—with her daughter, Edith Craig, as prompter: "When she came to the line, 'This bond doth give thee here no jot of ____' She stopped dead. The actor standing nearest to her on the stage . . . was preparing to whisper the missing word into her ear, when the voice . . . from the prompt corner shattered the silence with the words, 'Blood, mother, blood!' "

Scotland was full of historical and literary associations for the recent graduate of Rockford, who encountered the familiar names of Mary Queen of Scots, John Knox, Robert Burns, and Sir Walter Scott. On at least two occasions, the Scottish scenery reminded Jane of her native land. Then came England. The memory of Wordsworth attracted Jane to the Lake District; from there the route lay through historic English cities down to London. Here she made all of the usual tourist rounds of the British metropolis, not forgetting the fashionable London shops that catered to fashionable women with money to spend. An interesting sidelight provided by these entries in her notebook is the frequency with which these peripatetic American ladies got into a "fuss" with one individual or another. The hapless male was often a cabdriver.

■ September 19. Found ourselves in Glasgow in a pouring rain. . . . Took the night train to Edinburgh. Our first view of the city was perfectly wonderful and amazing—the old Castle, the deep ravine, and the buildings. . . . For the next three days, sick in bed. . . . Friday we drove about the city and went through Queen Mary and Darnley's room at the old Abbey. Old Giles Church on Sunday where John Knox preached. . . . Heard Henry Irving . . . in *The Merchant of Venice.* Saw Ellen Terry as Portia.

September 24. Left Edinburgh . . . caught a view of Linlithgow Castle. . . . The wild mountainous scenery, cascades, etc. like the Pennsylvania mountains. . . .

September 25. This morning found us in . . . Inverness. Took a ride after breakfast, six in a carriage, all over the little town. . . . Took the boat . . .

on the Caledonian Canal. Rode through the Ness River and Loch Ness, the high hills with rugged rocks about like the Hudson. . . .

September 28. Left Glasgow . . . for Ayr. Read Burns on the way and liked *Tam O'Shanter* as I never did before. Got carriage and proceeded at once to the cottage where he was born. The room still with the very bed in it, the stone floor, Highland Mary's spinning wheel. Saw the fields that he plowed, the well where "Mary's mither hanged herself," and the Road of Tam O'Shanter. Alloway Kirk without any roof, the old walls standing, and old men pointing into it and repeating in broad Scots the dreadful scene from *Tam O'Shanter*. . . .

October 2. Started from the Windsor Hotel. . . . Reached Melrose. . . . Took a carriage three miles to Abbotsford [Sir Walter Scott's baronial mansion]. A guide took us through Scott's little study . . . his library and drawing room. . . . Drove to the beautiful remains of Melrose Abbey. . . . Took dinner . . . and the drive to Dryburgh Abbey. . . . Walked over the suspension bridge on the Tweed, three quarters of a mile to the Abbey. . . . The Abbey the most beautiful ruin we have seen. . . .

Arrived at Grasmere. . . . Walked to Wordsworth House, where he had lived for nine years and brought his wife in 1802. Plain little whitewashed house towards the road, but back in the garden the cottage is beautiful. Little vine-covered porch. . . . Saw Wordsworth's grave. . . .

October 6. Elegant station hotel at York. . . . The old walls of white stone forming a promenade built by Edward I in 1239. . . . From York went to Leeds. Fuss about the second- or third-class tickets. From Leeds drove to Nottingham. . . . From Nottingham went to London. . . .

October 8. This morning spent at the bankers etc. Called at the American Exchange. . . . In the afternoon went to the Tower. . . . Hard time to make the cabman stop at a drugstore. . . .

October 10. Shopped at Jay's on Regent Street. . . . Bought a cloak, black silk dress, gloves, etc. Was measured . . . tried on dress . . . and [it] is to be sent home finished on Monday. Skirts all ready-made to select from.

October 11–12. Rode to Windsor. Fuss about the guides, "official" and non-official. . . . Ride to Stratford-on-Avon. . . . Streets full of people. . . . Walked to Shakespeare's birthplace. Little room where he was born. Drunken man at the gate reciting "All the world's a stage, etc." Hotel Red Horse. Three very pleasant ladies from Pittsburgh.

October 13. This morning went to the church where Shakespeare is buried. . . . Hard to think of Shakespeare alone. . . .

October 14. Sunday morning went to St. Margaret's Chapel. . . . Canon Farrar, very finished and elegant but hard to follow. Subject—The Judgment Day.

October 15. Spent the morning shopping. . . .

October 16. Saw about our dresses at Jay's and reached Westminster Abbey. . . . Wonderful first impression of the gray air and magnificent arches—as if it had never been built, but [was] a pure creation of mind. Straight to the Poets' Corner. . . .

When John Henry Brodribb went on the stage, he felt disinclined to see his real name on theater marquees. So he chose the more euphonious "Henry Irving" for the benefit of the public, adding the "Sir" after Queen Victoria knighted him—the first actor to be so honored. He played dozens of roles, including Shylock (above), before electrifying London in 1874 with his Hamlet, which Tennyson considered the finest performance he had ever seen. Success led Irving to become an actor-manager with his own company and theater. One member was an American, Edwin Booth, with whom he alternated the roles of Othello and Iago. Another member, Ellen Terry, called Irving "an egoist of the great type." Drama critics in Britain and the United States (he toured America eight times) called him the king of actors.

Sir Walter Scott built Abbotsford with the royalties from his brilliant series of historical novels, which were international best sellers in the early nineteenth century. He had been dead for decades when Jane visited his home, but it still held memories of the days when he played the host there on a grand scale to a steady stream of admirers from Britain, the Continent, and America. He lived like one of his own characters, except that they lacked his literary genius.

Robert Burns wrote *Tam O'Shanter* in one day, and it has charmed readers such as Jane ever since. It tells how Tam, riding homeward through the night after a long stay at the tavern, interrupts a witches' orgy at Alloway Kirk, is pursued in a headlong chase toward running water, and dashes across the bridge in the nick of time, leaving the tail of his mare in the grasp of the leading witch. The poem is a masterpiece of the supernatural, tellingly treated in a rowdy comic vein.

October 17. Left the Waterloo Station . . . to Richmond . . . drove through Richmond Park. . . . Out through Kingston to Hampden Court. . . . Into the Kew Gardens. Fuss with fat, toothless driver. . . .

October 18. Pictures taken. . . . To Hyde Park and Rotten Row. . . .

October 20. Parliament Houses . . . St. Paul's. . . . Came home past Covent Garden Markets. . . .

October 26. Party of nine to the East End. . . . Took a streetcar . . . down to Bethnal Green. Came back the Mile End Road. . . . The thousands of poor people who were marketing at the booths and market stalls along the streets.

Jane's notebook reference to Mile End Road is a mere thumbnail statement. She later expanded it into an arresting passage of Twenty Years at Hull-House, *wherein recording her discovery of the harrowing condition of the poor in the sordid slums of London.*

■ One of the most poignant of these experiences, which occurred during the first few months after our landing upon the other side of the Atlantic, was on a Saturday night, when I received an ineradicable impression of the wretchedness of East London, and also saw for the first time the overcrowded quarters of a great city at midnight. A small party of tourists were taken to the East End by a city missionary to witness the Saturday-night sale of decaying vegetables and fruit, which, owing to the Sunday laws in London, could not be sold until Monday, and, as they were beyond safekeeping, were disposed of at auction as late as possible on Saturday night. On Mile End Road, from the top of an omnibus which paused at the end of a dingy street lighted by only occasional flares of gas, we saw two huge masses of ill-clad people clamoring around two hucksters' carts. They were bidding their farthings and ha'pennies for a vegetable held up by the auctioneer, which he at last scornfully flung, with a gibe for its cheapness, to the successful bidder. In the momentary pause only one man detached himself from the groups. He had bidden in a cabbage, and when it struck his hand, he instantly sat down on the curb, tore it with his teeth, and hastily devoured it, unwashed and uncooked as it was. He and his fellows were types of the "submerged tenth," as our missionary guide told us, with some little satisfaction in the then new phrase, and he further added that so many of them could scarcely be seen in one spot save at this Saturday night auction, the desire for cheap food being apparently the one thing which could move them simultaneously. They were huddled into ill-fitting, cast-off clothing, the ragged finery which one sees only in East London. Their pale faces were dominated by that most unlovely of human expressions, the cunning and shrewdness of the bargain hunter who starves if he cannot make a successful trade, and yet the final impression was not of ragged, tawdry clothing nor of pinched and sallow faces, but of myriads of hands, empty, pathetic, nerveless and workworn, showing white in the uncertain light of the street, and clutching forward for food which was already unfit to eat.

Perhaps nothing is so fraught with significance as the human hand, this oldest tool with which man has dug his way from savagery, and with which he is constantly groping forward. I have never since been able to see a number of hands held upward, even when they are moving rhythmically in a calisthenic exercise, or when they belong to a class of chubby children who wave them in eager response to a teacher's query, without a certain revival of this memory, a clutching at the heart reminiscent of the despair and resentment which seized me then.

For the following weeks I went about London almost furtively, afraid to look down narrow streets and alleys lest they disclose again this hideous human need and suffering. I carried with me for days at a time that curious surprise we experience when we first come back into the streets after days given over to sorrow and death; we are bewildered that the world should be going on as usual and unable to determine which is real, the inner pang or the outward seeming. In time all huge London came to seem unreal save the poverty in its East End. During the following two years on the Continent, while I was irresistibly drawn to the poorer quarters of each city, nothing among the beggars of South Italy nor among the salt miners of Austria carried with it the same conviction of human wretchedness which was conveyed by this momentary glimpse of an East London street. It was, of course, a most fragmentary and lurid view of the poverty of East London, and quite unfair. I should have been shown either less or more, for I went away with no notion of the hundreds of men and women who

These flower girls selling bouquets at London's Covent Garden market were photographed in 1877, and may have been still there in 1883 when Jane saw the slums she describes here so movingly. The lives of such women were not as romantic as that of Eliza Doolittle, the flower girl in George Bernard Shaw's *Pygmalion*, with her amusing new acquaintances and triumphant success. The reality was made up of dingy rooms, skimpy meals, long hours on the streets in rain or shine, repeated appeals to unfeeling passersby to "buy a bunch of vi'lets," and—at best—a few coins at the end of the day. British reformers, unlike Shaw's Professor Higgins, took a humanitarian interest in the flower girls, and used them as prime examples of the crying need for a new kind of decency to improve the intolerable conditions in cities corroded by the excesses that followed the Industrial Revolution.

When Jane wrote this letter to Ellen Gates Starr on February 7, 1886, she was in Baltimore with her stepmother and her stepbrother George, who was working for his doctorate at Johns Hopkins University. Her leisure allowed her to attend lectures, practice her French, and read a list of great books, including the one mentioned here. Ellen had fervent artistic interests and, understandably, she had encouraged Jane to read Ruskin's *Modern Painters*, with its high appreciation of the blazing canvases of William Turner. Jane, in turn, called Ellen's attention to Voltaire. Later on in this same letter, Jane makes the suggestion: "If we are to meet next summer, we might try reading something before then and have opinions . . . ready to 'exchange.' "

My dear Ellen
I have been
reading "Modern Painters"
most of the afternoon, I
have remembered your
injunction given "Read it,
and don't let the grass grow
under your feet." One is
always impressed by
Ruskin, in addition to the

had gallantly identified their fortunes with these empty-handed people, and who, in church and chapel, "relief works," and charities, were at least making an effort toward its mitigation.

FROM THE IDEA TO THE DEED

The poverty of the laboring classes haunted Jane until the end of her second European tour in 1888, when she decided irrevocably to dedicate herself to social work. From then on, she never looked back. All of her agonizing soul-searching came to an abrupt end, for now she knew exactly what to do—establish a settlement in the Chicago slums, where life was real, earnest, and grim. Her thoughts on the subject were remarkably precise from the very beginning, and she was able to go into details about the theory and practice of social work when she twice addressed a summer school at Plymouth, Massachusetts, in 1892, less than three years after the opening of Hull-House.

In My Friend, Julia Lathrop, *Jane explains how these two addresses got into print. Julia was a Rockford contemporary who specialized in child welfare, and served as an active member of the Illinois Board of Charities before going on to Washington to become the energetic head of the federal Children's Bureau. She urged Jane to publish the addresses, so the two ladies from Hull-House took them to Walter Hines Page, editor of* The Forum *(and later, during World War I, American ambassador to London, where Jane met him again). Jane, the author, felt diffident, but Julia (known for her sense of humor) counseled firmly: "Don't cave in, J.A., this is our chance to give the public the pure milk of the word!" Jane adds that "much to our astonish-*

ment Mr. Page took both articles and afterward sent a generous check in payment, which astonished us even more."

It was her habit to rework these and other articles for use in her books. Since Twenty Years at Hull-House *is readily available, and the original articles reveal her ideas and attitudes at important stages of her life, the articles have been drawn on extensively for these excerpts. The first Plymouth address concerns the objective reason for social work—the fact that those in distress need help:*

Walter Hines Page (1855–1918) had two notable careers—in publishing and in diplomacy—during both of which he met Jane Addams. A native of North Carolina, Page grew up in the post-Civil War period, advocated reconciliation after Reconstruction, and urged the South to modernize itself. In 1885 he went to New York, where he soon joined *The Forum* and was thus in a position to buy the two articles Jane brought to him. Later he edited the *Atlantic Monthly*, founded *The World's Work*, and helped to form the publishing firm of Doubleday, Page. In 1913, President Wilson appointed him ambassador to Great Britain. His post in London did not at once enchant him; he complained: "The English have only two vegetables—and both of them are cabbage." (The second was Brussels sprouts.) But World War I made an ardent Anglophile of Page, and when Jane arrived in 1915 with her plea for a negotiated peace, he received her courteously at the embassy, but refused to back a scheme he thought would help the Central Powers and hurt the Allies. In 1917 an English friend met Page the day after America declared war. "Thank God," said the friend, "that there is one less hypocrite in London today." Page asked what he meant. "I mean you. Pretending all this time that you were neutral; that isn't necessary any longer." Page laughed and replied: "You are right!"

■ Hull-House, Chicago's first social settlement, was established in September 1889. It represented no association, but was opened by two women, supported by many friends, in the belief that the mere foothold of a house, easily accessible, ample in space, hospitable and tolerant in spirit, situated in the midst of the large foreign colonies which so easily isolate themselves in American cities, would be in itself a serviceable thing for Chicago. It represents an attempt to make social intercourse express the growing sense of the economic unity of society, to add the social function to democracy. It was opened in the theory that the dependence of classes on each other is reciprocal, and that "as the social relation is essentially a reciprocal relation, it gives a form of expression that has peculiar value."

Hull-House stands on South Halsted Street, next door to the corner of Polk. South Halsted Street is thirty-two miles long and one of the great thoroughfares of Chicago. Polk Street crosses Halsted midway between the stockyards to the south and the shipbuilding yards on the north branch of the Chicago River. For the six miles between these two dignified industries the street is lined with shops of butchers and grocers, with dingy and gorgeous saloons, and pretentious establishments for the sale of ready-made clothing. Polk Street, running west from Halsted Street, grows rapidly more respectable; running a mile east to State Street, it grows steadily worse and crosses a network of gilded vice on the corners of Clark Street and Fourth Avenue. Hull-House is an ample old residence, well built and somewhat ornately decorated after the manner of its time, 1856. It has been used for many purposes, and although battered by its vicissitudes, it is essentially sound and has responded kindly to repairs and careful furnishing. Its wide hall and open fires always insure it a gracious aspect. It once stood in the suburbs, but the city has steadily grown up around it and its site now has corners on three or four distinct foreign colonies. Between Halsted Street and the river live about ten thousand Italians: Neapolitans, Sicilians, and Calabrians, with an occasional Lombard or Venetian. To the south on Twelfth Street are many Germans, and side streets are given over almost entirely to Polish and Russian Jews. Further south, these Jewish colonies merge into a huge Bohemian colony, so vast that Chicago ranks as the third Bohemian city in the world. To the northwest are many Canadian-French, clannish in spite of their long residence in America, and to the north are many Irish and first-generation Americans. On the streets directly west and farther north are well-to-do English-speaking families, many of whom own their

Julia Lathrop (pronounced *Laythrop*) was born and raised in Rockford, and attended the seminary there for a year before transferring to Vassar. Jane Addams met her at a performance of the Rockford drama group, but their paths diverged until Jane founded Hull-House, to which Julia came as a resident during its first year. Trained as a lawyer, Julia proved to be an important recruit, able to cope with fine legal points when the settlement was embattled in court cases. Her keen professional mind made her the guiding spirit behind *Hull-House Maps and Papers.* She held many important posts in America and abroad, heading the United States Children's Bureau from 1912 to 1921 and later serving as adviser on child welfare to the League of Nations. The other Hull-House residents respected her as a sharp-witted conversationalist who was also a peacemaker no matter how heated the debate. Her mere presence made them feel better. Whenever she returned to the settlement after an absence, she was usually greeted by the first to see her with the joyful shout: "J. Lathrop's here!"

houses and have lived in the neighborhood for years. I know one man who is still living in his old farmhouse. . . .

The streets are inexpressibly dirty, the number of schools inadequate, factory legislation unenforced, the street-lighting bad, the paving miserable and altogether lacking in the alleys and smaller streets, and the stables defy all laws of sanitation. Hundreds of houses are unconnected with the street sewer. The older and richer inhabitants seem anxious to move away as rapidly as they can afford it. They make room for newly arrived emigrants who are densely ignorant of civic duties. This substitution of the older inhabitants is accomplished also industrially in the south and east quarters of the ward. The Hebrews and Italians do the finishing for the great clothing manufacturers formerly done by Americans, Irish, and Germans, who refused to submit to the extremely low prices to which the sweating system has reduced their successors. As the design of the sweating system is the elimination of rent from the manufacture of clothing, the "outside work" is begun after the clothing leaves the cutter. For this work no basement is too dark, no stable loft too foul, no rear shanty too provisional, no tenement room too small, as these conditions imply low rental. Hence these shops abound in the worst of the foreign districts, where the sweater easily finds his cheap basement and his home finishers. There is a constant tendency to employ school children, as much of the home and shop work can easily be done by children. The houses of the ward, for the most part wooden, were originally built for one family and are now occupied by several. They are after the type of the inconvenient frame cottages found in the poorer suburbs twenty years ago. Many of them were built where they now stand; others were brought thither on rollers, because their previous site had been taken for a factory. The fewer brick tenement buildings which are three or four stories high are comparatively new. There are few huge and foul tenements. The little wooden houses have a temporary aspect, and for this reason, perhaps, the tenement-house legislation in Chicago is totally inadequate. Back tenements flourish; many houses have no water supply save the faucet in the back yard; there are no fire escapes; the garbage and ashes are placed in wooden boxes which are fastened to the street pavements.

Jane's basic principle was to treat the area as a unit, inviting to Hull-House all of the social elements that made up the complex welter of the Nineteenth Ward. She wanted to lift the whole community to a higher level, as is shown here:

■ This site for a settlement was selected in the first instance because of its diversity and the variety of activity for which it presented an opportunity. It has been the aim of the residents to respond to all sides of the neighborhood life: not to the poor people alone, nor to the well-to-do, nor to the young in contradistinction to the old, but to the neighborhood as a whole, "men, women, and children taken in families as the Lord mixes them." The activities of Hull-House divide themselves into . . . the social, educational, and humanitarian. I have added civic—if indeed a settlement of women can be said to perform civic duties. These activities spring from no preconceived notion of what a social settlement should be, but have increased gradually on demand. . . .

A settlement which regards social intercourse as the terms of its expression logically brings to its aid all those adjuncts which have been found by experience to free social life. It casts aside nothing which the cultivated man regards as good and suggestive of participation in the best life of the past. It ignores none of the surroundings which one associates with a life of simple refinement. The amount of luxury which an individual indulges in is a thing which has to be determined by each for himself. It must always be a relative thing. The one test which the settlement is bound to respect is that its particular amount of luxury shall tend to "free" the social expression of its neighbors, and not cumber that expression. The residents at Hull-House find that the better in quality and taste their surroundings are, the more they contribute to the general enjoyment.

Immigrants, however maltreated in their unfamiliar environment, at least had warm memories of the Old Country to fall back on. Their children, born in Chicago, wishing to be considered Americans, neither possessed nor desired this consolation, which, indeed, they frequently despised in their parents. Hull-House was one of the first institutions to bring the generations together:

■ It is much easier to deal with the first generation of crowded city life than with the second or third, because it is more natural and cast in a simpler mould. The Italian and Bohemian peasants who live in Chicago still put on their bright holiday clothes on Sunday and go to visit their cousins. They tramp along with at least a suggestion of having once

Maxwell Street, typical of the Chicago slums around Hull-House, was a thoroughfare that Jane Addams knew well. This photograph of 1906 shows the kinds of people and shops that characterized it and the rest of the area. Rag collectors unload their wagon at the edge of this unpaved street in the middle of a huge city. In the background, from right to left, are a Jewish meat market with barrels of refuse outside, a rag dealer's store, a leather repair shop, a house for sale, and the scanty furniture of a family about to move elsewhere. The camera has caught a split second of ghetto life as it was early in the twentieth century.

walked over ploughed fields and breathed country air. The second generation of city poor have no holiday clothes and consider their cousins "a bad lot." I have heard a drunken man in a maudlin stage babble of his good country mother and imagine he was driving the cows home, and I knew that his little son, who laughed loud at him, would be drunk earlier in life, and would have no such pastoral interlude to his ravings. Hospitality still survives among foreigners, although it is buried under false pride among the poorest Americans. One thing seemed clear in regard to entertaining these foreigners: to preserve and keep for them whatever of value their past life contained and to bring them in contact with a better type of American. For two years, every Saturday evening, our Italian neighbors were our guests; entire families came. These evenings were very popular during our first winter at Hull-House. Many educated Italians helped us, and the house became known as a place where Italians were welcome and where national holidays were observed. They come to us with their petty lawsuits, sad relics of the *vendetta*, with their incorrigible boys, with their hospital cases . . . and with their needs for an interpreter.

Friday evening is devoted to Germans and is similar in purpose; but owing to the superior education of our Teutonic guests and the clever leading of a cultivated German woman, we can bring out the best of that cozy social intercourse which is found in its perfection in the "Fatherland." They sing a great deal in the tender minor of the German folksong or in the rousing spirit of the Rhine. They are slowly but persistently pursuing a course in German history and literature. The relationship by no means ends with social civilities, and the acquaintance made there has brought about radical changes in the lives of many friendless families. I recall one peasant woman, straight from the fields of Germany. Her two years in America had been spent in patiently carrying water up and down two flights of stairs and in washing the heavy flannel suits of iron-foundry workers. For this her pay had averaged thirty-five cents a day. Three of her daughters had fallen victims to the vice of the city. The mother was bewildered and distressed, but understood nothing. We were able to induce the betrayer of one daughter to marry her; the second, after a tedious lawsuit, supported his child; with the third we were able to do nothing. This woman is now living with her family in a little house seventeen miles from the city. She has made two payments on her land and is a lesson to all beholders as she pastures her cow up and down the railroad tracks and makes money from her ten acres. She did not need charity. She had an immense capacity for hard work, but she sadly needed "heading." She is our most shining example, but I think of many forlorn cases of German and Bohemian peasants in need of neighborly help.

Because of its community approach to urban problems, Hull-House played host to young and old, educated and uneducated, immigrants and native Americans. In this same speech of 1892, explaining the multifarious programs undertaken by the settlement, Jane expresses her appreciation for the vital assistance provided by her alma mater, Rockford College.

Jane Addams was connected with William Rainey Harper (above) by way of the University of Chicago, with which Hull-House had an unofficial but quite vital relationship. Known as "the steam engine in pants," Harper was the first president (1891–1906) of the new university and rapidly made it one of the nation's great centers of learning. His educational commission laid down the rules for Chicago's teachers that led to the strike in which Jane became caught as a member of the school board (see pages 60–61). Harper liked the connection between his institution and Jane's, but it proved something of an embarrassment to her. The university had been founded with money donated by leading "robber barons," much of it from John D. Rockefeller—and this was "tainted money" in the view of many reformers. Challenged to explain her position, Jane confessed to feeling disquietude about the source, but she could not see any clear moral imperative to sever her relations with a university that was certainly helping to improve Chicago. Harper himself felt justified in accepting "tainted money," because he maintained his intellectual and administrative freedom, even in dealing with Rockefeller.

■ But our social evenings are by no means confined to foreigners. Our most successful clubs are entirely composed of English-speaking and American-born young people. Those over sixteen meet in two clubs, one for young men and one for girls, every Monday evening. Each club dispatches various literary programmes before nine o'clock, when they meet together for an hour of social amusement before going home at ten. Dancing they always prefer, although they will devise other amusements. The members of the Tuesday evening clubs are from fourteen to sixteen years old; a few of them are still in school, but most of them are working. The boys who are known as the Young Citizen's Club are supposed to inform themselves on municipal affairs, as are the Hull-House Columbian Guards who report alleys and streets for the Municipal Order League. We have various other clubs of young people that meet weekly; their numbers are limited only by the amount of room. We hold the dining room, the reception room, and the octagon each evening for the College Extension classes, and can reserve only the large drawing room and gymnasium for the clubs and receptions. The gymnasium is a somewhat pretentious name for a building next door which was formerly a saloon, but which we rented last fall, repaired, and fitted up with simple apparatus. A "real gymnasium" is at present being built for Hull-House. During the winter the old one sheltered some enthusiastic athletic classes. The evenings were equally divided between men and women. The children came in the afternoon. This may answer for a description of the formal social evenings, although there is much social life going on constantly which cannot be tabulated....

Every Thursday evening for three years, save during the three summer months, we have had a lecture of some sort at Hull-House. This has come to be an expected event in the neighborhood. These lectures are largely attended by the College Extension students, and the topics are supposed to connect with their studies, but many other people come to them and often join a class because of the interest a lecturer has awakened. This attraction is constantly in mind when these lectures are planned. For two years a summer school has been held at Rockford, Ill., in connection with the College Extension classes. From one-third to one-half the students have been able to attend it, paying their board for a month and enjoying outdoor study quite as much as the classes. I would recommend for imitation the very generous action on the part of the Rockford College trustees in placing at our disposal their entire educational apparatus, from the dining room to the laboratories. On the borderland between social and educational activity are our Sunday afternoon concerts, and the Plato Club which follows them.

The industrial education of Hull-House has always been somewhat limited. From the beginning we have had large and enthusiastic cooking classes, first in the Hull-House kitchen and later in a tiny cottage across the alley which has been fitted up for the purpose. We have also always had sewing, mending, and embroidery classes. This leads me to speak of the children who meet weekly at Hull-House, whose organization is between classes and clubs. There are three hundred of them who come on

William Rainey Harper (opposite) termed Thorstein Veblen (above) "not an asset" to the University of Chicago, but he allowed Veblen to teach there from 1893 to 1906. Veblen, the son of Norwegian immigrants, grew up as a farm boy who knew the rigors of life on the Middle Border. Too aloof to suit the gregarious Harper, Veblen rejected activism of any kind, preferring to indulge an "idle curiosity" about the evolution of institutions, and remaining an unsocial sociologist. Jane Addams had little to do with him, but they shared a common desire for a new kind of democracy. According to Veblen, society develops through instincts (constant) and habits (malleable). Habits, therefore, are vulnerable to change, and the problem for America is to change the habits of the robber barons, replacing their "conspicuous waste" with enlightened behavior. He thought this could be achieved through technocracy—engineers (rather than businessmen) would run the system, and stress production rather than profits. Otherwise, Veblen predicted, the instability of the price structure would cause recurrent crises. His warning was recalled in 1929, when the Great Depression struck two months after his death.

Sidney Webb (1859–1947), who visited Hull-House with his wife Beatrice (1858–1943) and got an interesting reception (see page 54), was a prime figure in the trend toward public responsibility described by Jane Addams on this page. The Webbs studied economics and joined the Fabian Society and the Labor party. Sidney served in both of Britain's socialist governments during the 1920's and became Lord Passfield. Beatrice, a more intransigent egalitarian, firmly refused to be called Lady Passfield. The Webbs strongly believed that Soviet Communism represented "a new civilization," and the sardonic British social commentator Malcolm Muggeridge says of their writings on it:

"They sorted out and tabulated the spurious information made available to them about the U.S.S.R.; analyzed a constitution that had never existed except on paper, and explained the inalienable right of Soviet citizens to subject themselves wholly to an all-powerful and tyrannous state. The last time I saw Mrs. Webb, she asked me if I would like to see a portrait presented to her by Stalin. . . . The portrait hung in a room upstairs, lighted from below. It was of Lenin. . . . Mrs. Webb, I could see, was in a state of exaltation, and I reflected then, in one of those moments of almost agonizing illumination that come so very rarely, that I was witnessing the final prostration of Victorian high-mindedness before the naked brutality of our time."

three days, not counting, of course, the children who come to the house merely as depositors in the Penny Provident Fund Savings Bank. A hundred Italian girls come on Monday. They sew and carry home a new garment, which becomes a pattern for the entire family. Tuesday afternoon has always been devoted to schoolboys' clubs: they are practically story-telling clubs. The most popular stories are legends and tales of chivalry. The one hundred and fifty little girls on Friday afternoon are not very unlike the boys, although they want to sew while they are hearing their stories. The value of these clubs, I believe, lies almost entirely in their success in arousing the higher imagination. We have had a kindergarten at Hull-House ever since we have lived there. Every morning miniature Italians, Hebrews, French, Irish, and Germans assemble in our drawing room, and nothing seems to excite admiration in the neighborhood so much as the fact that we "put up with them."

Although Hull-House was not a charity organization as such, its residents performed countless charitable works when these were the most effective way of bringing immediate relief to the downtrodden. Jane Addams gladly co-operated with public agencies, and felt very relieved as they took upon themselves more of the common burden.

■ In addition to the neighbors who respond to the receptions and classes are found those who are too battered and oppressed to care for them. To these, however, is left that susceptibility to the bare offices of humanity which raises such offices into a bond of fellowship. These claim humanitarian efforts. Perhaps the chief value of a settlement to its neighborhood, certainly to the newly arrived foreigner, is its office as an information and interpretation bureau. . . .

From the very nature of our existence and purpose we are bound to keep on good terms with every beneficent institution in the city. Passing by our telephone last Sunday morning, I was struck with the list of numbers hung on the wall for easy reference. They were those of the Visiting Nurses' Association; Cook County Hospital; Women's and Children's Hospital; Maxwell Street Police Station for city ambulance; Health Department; City Hall; Cook County Agent, etc. We have been on very good terms with the Hebrew Relief and Aid Society, the Children's Aid, the Humane Society, the Municipal Order League, and with the various church and national relief associations. Every summer we send out dozens of children to the country on the *Daily News* Fresh Air Fund and to the Holiday Home at Lake Geneva. Our most complete cooperation has been with the Visiting Nurses' Association. One of the nurses lives at Hull-House, pays her board as a resident, and does her work from there. Friends of the house are constantly in need of her ministrations, and her cases become friends of the house. Owing to the lack of a charity organization society in Chicago we have been obliged to keep a sum of money as a relief fund. Five bathrooms in the rear of Hull-House are open to the neighborhood and are constantly in use. . . .

The more definite humanitarian effect of Hull-House has taken shape in a day nursery, which was started during the second year of our residence on Halsted Street. A frame cottage of six rooms across our yard has been fitted up as a *crèche*. At present we receive from thirty to forty children daily. A young lady who has had kindergarten training is in charge; she has the assistance of an older woman, and a kindergarten by a professional teacher is held each morning in the playroom. This nursery is not merely a convenience in the neighborhood; it is, to a certain extent, a neighborhood affair. Similar in spirit is the Hull-House Diet Kitchen, in a little cottage directly back of the nursery. Food is prepared for invalids and orders are taken from physicians and visiting nurses of the district. . . . We sometimes have visions of a kitchen similar in purpose to the New England Kitchen of Boston, but on a more cooperative plan, managed by the Hull-House Woman's Club. This club meets one afternoon a week. It is composed of the most able women of the neighborhood, who enjoy the formal addresses and many informal discussions. The economics of food and fuel are often discussed. The Hull-House household expenses are frankly compared with those of other households. I have always felt that "friendly visiting," while of great value, was one-sided. To be complete the "friendly visitor" should also be the "friendly visited." It is quite possible that looking over her expense book with that of her "case" would be beneficial to her. The residents at Hull-House find in themselves a constantly increasing tendency to consult their neighbors on the advisability of each new undertaking. We have lately opened a boarding club for working girls near Hull-House on the cooperative plan. I say advisedly that we have "opened" it; the running of it is quite in the hands of the girls themselves. The furniture, pictures, etc., belong to Hull-House, and

The members of this Hull-House cooking class—one of the home-economics ventures mentioned here by Jane—appear to have been enjoying themselves when the camera caught them. Some are in animated discussion; others are obviously aware that they are about to be photographed. The stoves and utensils of the settlement kitchen were primitive by present-day standards, but the meals always attracted a good turnout of Hull-House residents and guests. At dinner, Jane Addams herself customarily presided with her special blend of relaxed warmth and genuine interest in all the concerns of everyone around her.

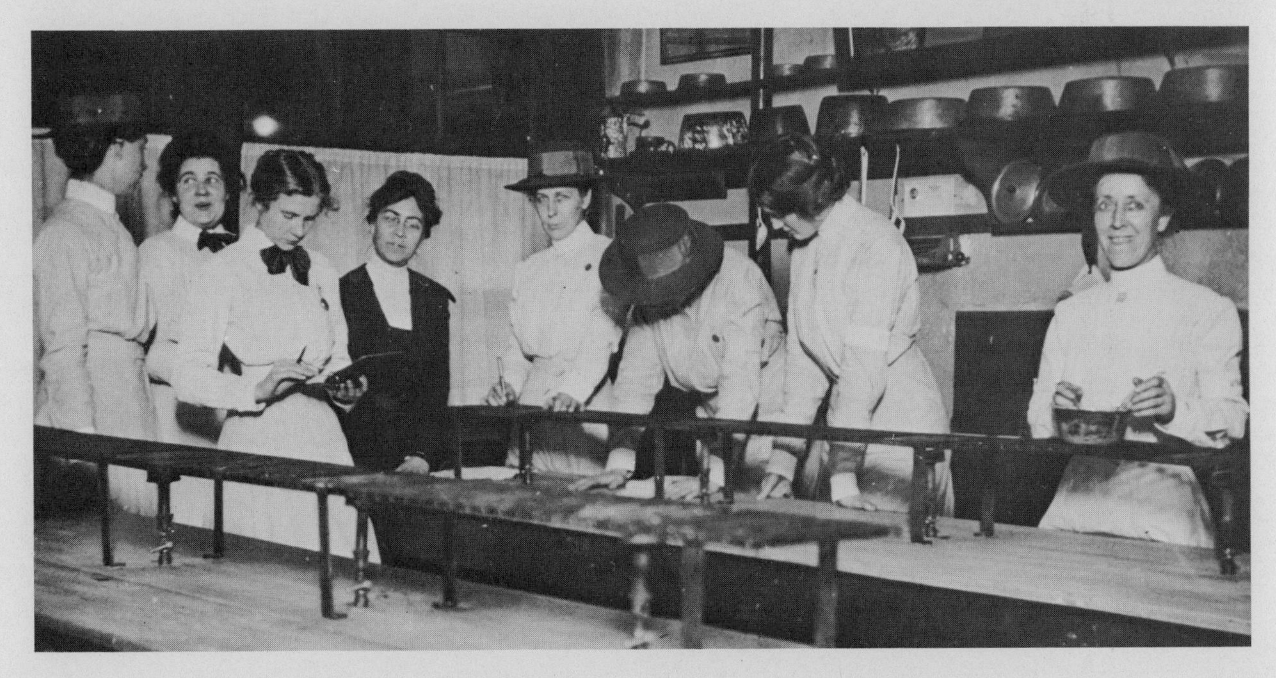

whatever experience we have is at their disposal; but it is in no sense a working-girls' "home," nor is it to be run from the outside. We hope a great deal from this little attempt at cooperative housekeeping. The club has been running three months and has twenty-five members.

Educational activities at Hull-House went much further than the mere imparting of information. There was a constant give-and-take between teachers and pupils, lecturers and listeners, advocates of diverse viewpoints. Thus, capitalists and socialists mingled at debates, and the cross-fertilization of ideas produced understanding where it had never existed before.

■ It is difficult to classify the Working People's Social Science Club, which meets weekly at Hull-House. It is social, educational, and civic in character, the latter chiefly because it strongly connects the house with the labor problems in their political and social aspects. This club was organized at Hull-House in the spring of 1890 by an English workingman. It has met weekly since, save during the months of summer. At eight o'clock every Wednesday evening the secretary calls to order from forty to one hundred people. A chairman for the evening is elected and a speaker is introduced who is allowed to talk until nine o'clock; his subject is then thrown open to discussion and a lively debate ensues until ten o'clock, at which hour the meeting is declared adjourned. The enthusiasm of this club seldom lags. Its zest for discussion is unceasing, and any attempt to turn it into a study or reading club always meets with the strong disapprobation of the members. Chicago is full of social theorists. It offers a cosmopolitan opportunity for discussion. The only possible danger from this commingling of many theories is incurred when there is an attempt at suppression; bottled up, there is danger of explosion; constantly uncorked, open to the deodorizing and freeing process of the air, all danger is averted. Nothing so disconcerts a social agitator as to find among his auditors men who have been through all that and who are quite as radical as he in another direction.

The economic conferences which were held between businessmen and workingmen during the winter of 1888–89 and the two succeeding winters doubtless did much toward relieving this state of effervescence. Many thoughtful men in Chicago are convinced that if these conferences had been established earlier the Haymarket riot and all its sensational results might have been avoided. The Sunset Club is at present performing much the same function. There is still need, however, for many of these clubs where men who differ widely in their social theories can meet for discussion, where representatives of the various economic schools can modify each other, and at least learn tolerance and the futility of endeavoring to convince all the world of the truth of one position. To meet in a social-science club is more educational than to meet in a single-tax club, or a socialistic chapter, or a personal-rights league, although the millennium may seem further off after such a meeting. In addition to this modification of view there is doubtless a distinct modification of attitude. This spring the Hull-House Social Science Club heard a series of talks on municipal and county affairs by the heads of the various departments. During the discussion following the address on "The Chicago Police," a workingman had the pleasure of telling the chief of police that he had been arrested, obliged to pay two dollars and a half, and had lost three days' work, because he had come out of the wrong gate when he was working on the World's Fair grounds. The Chief sighed, expressed his regret, and made no defense. The speaker sat down bewildered; evidently for the first time in his life he realized that blunders cut the heart of more than the victim.

Is it possible for men, however far apart in outward circumstances, for the capitalist and the workingman, to use the common phrase, to meet as individuals beneath a friendly roof, open their minds each to each, and not have their "class theories" insensibly modified by the kindly attrition of a personal acquaintance? In the light of our experience, I should say not.

Jane's second 1892 Plymouth address presents the obverse of the coin. Having treated the objective reason for social work, she now treats the three subjective reasons: many well-to-do people need this outlet; there is an innate desire "to share the race life"; and there is a growing urge to put Christianity into actual practice. Here she views the wealthy as essentially sound human beings who deserve to be rescued from a life of indolence, pride, and frustration, who have much to gain from accepting a useful function among their fellow citizens.

In this news drawing of 1886 from *Harper's Weekly*, a bomb explodes among the policemen in Chicago's Haymarket Square as a labor spokesman furiously harangues the crowd. This Haymarket riot, which cast somber reflections over social movements for more than a decade afterward—and which, as Jane Addams notes on the opposite page, might never have occurred had Hull-House and other organizations come into existence a little sooner—long remained a symbol of the struggle of the working class. The great issue at that time was the eight-hour day at the McCormick reaper plant, and, as Jane suggests, the issue might have been settled peacefully except for a grievous lack of communication between labor and management. Partly due to Hull-House, such communication later evolved; in the twentieth century, it finally led to collective bargaining as one of the keys to effective coexistence.

The British reform movement developed largely from the labors of the seventh Earl of Shaftesbury, an aristocrat who devoted most of his long life (1801–1885) to protecting the working class through parliamentary acts. Avoiding party discipline in order to gain wide support for his humanitarian efforts, he introduced bills that reformed the lunacy laws, cut the working day, and took women and children out of the coal mines. The Climbing Boys Act of 1840 protected chimney sweeps; the crusading novelist Charles Dickens considered the Lodginghouse Act of 1851 the best legislation ever passed by Parliament. Lord Shaftesbury stressed education, housing, and public health. He built a model village on his own estate, where each family had a cottage, an acre of land, and rent of only one shilling a week. To bring spiritual consolation to the poor, he sponsored religious services in theaters and music halls, thereby drawing sharp criticism from his staid colleagues in the House of Lords, who accused him of turning religion into a spectacle.

■ The social organism has broken down through large districts of our great cities. Many of the people living there are very poor, the majority of them without leisure or energy for anything but the gain of subsistence. They move often from one wretched lodging to another. They live for the moment side by side, many of them without knowledge of each other, without fellowship, without local tradition or public spirit, without social organization of any kind. Practically nothing is done to remedy this. The people who might do it, who have the social tact and training, the large houses, and the traditions and customs of hospitality, live in other parts of the city. The clubhouses, libraries, galleries, and semipublic conveniences for social life are also blocks away. We find workingmen organized into armies of producers because men of executive ability and business sagacity have found it to their interests thus to organize them. But these workingmen are not organized socially; although living in crowded tenement houses, they are living without a corresponding social contact. The chaos is as great as it would be were they working in huge factories without foreman or superintendent. Their ideas and resources are cramped. The desire for higher social pleasure is extinct. They have no share in the traditions and social energy which make for progress. Too often their only place of meeting is a saloon, their only host a bartender; a local demagogue forms their public opinion. Men of ability and refinement, of social power and university cultivation, stay away from them. Personally, I believe the men who lose most are those who thus stay away. But the paradox is here: When cultivated people do stay away from a certain portion of the population, when all social advantages are persistently withheld, it may be for years, the result itself is pointed at as a reason, is used as an argument, for the continued withholding.

It is constantly said that because the masses have never had social advantages they do not want them, that they are heavy and dull, and that it will take political or philanthropic machinery to change them. This divides a city into rich and poor; into the favored, who express their sense of the social obligation by gifts of money, and into the unfavored, who express it by clamoring for a "share"—both of them actuated by a vague sense of justice. This division of the city would be the more justifiable, however, if the people who thus isolated themselves on certain streets and used their social ability for each other gained enough thereby and added sufficient to the sum total of social progress to justify the withholding of the pleasures and results of that progress from so many people who ought to have them. But they cannot accomplish this. The social spirit discharges itself in many forms, and no one form is adequate to its total expression. We are all uncomfortable in regard to the insincerity of our best phrases, because we hesitate to translate our philosophy into the deed.

It is inevitable that those who feel most keenly this insincerity and partial living should be our young people, our so-called educated young people who accomplish little toward the solution of this social problem, and who bear the brunt of being cultivated into unnourished, oversensitive lives. They have been shut off from the common labor by which they live and which is a great source of moral and physical health. They feel a fatal want of harmony between their theory and their lives, a lack of coordination between thought and action. I think it is hard for us to realize how seriously many of them are taking to the notion of human brotherhood, how eagerly they long to give tangible expression to the democratic ideal. These young men and women, longing to socialize their democracy, are animated by certain hopes. These hopes may be loosely formulated thus: that if in a democratic country nothing can be permanently achieved save through the masses of the people, it will be impossible to establish a higher political life than the people themselves crave; that it is difficult to see how the notion of a higher civic life can be fostered save through common intercourse.

The blessings which we associate with a life of refinement and cultivation can be made universal and must be made universal if they are to be permanent. The good we secure for ourselves is precarious and uncertain, is floating in mid-air, until it is secured for all of us and incorporated into our common life.

As usual, Jane links her detailed facts to a philosophical interpretation of the reality to which they belong. She places residents of the social settlements against the shifting background of man's evolution and progress down the centuries, and appropriately quotes Thomas Henry Huxley, next to Darwin himself the foremost proponent of the Darwinian theory.

■ I find it somewhat difficult to formulate the second line of motives which I believe to constitute the trend of the subjective pressure toward the settlement. There is something primordial about these motives, but I am perhaps overbold in designating them as a great desire to share the race life. We all bear traces of the starvation struggle which for so long made up the life of the race. Our very organism holds memories and glimpses of that long life of our ancestors which still goes on among so many of our contemporaries. Nothing so deadens the sympathies and shrivels the power of enjoyment as the persistent keeping away from the great opportunities for helpfulness and a continual ignoring of the starvation struggle which makes up the life of at least half the race. To shut one's self away from that half of the race life is to shut one's self away from the most vital part of it; it is to live out but half the humanity which we have been born heir to and to use but half our faculties. We have all had longings for a fuller life which should include the use of these faculties. These longings are the physical complement of the "Intimations of Immortality" on which no ode has yet been written. To portray these would be the work of a poet, and it is hazardous for any but a poet to attempt it. . . .

There is nothing after disease, indigence, and a sense of guilt so fatal to health and to life itself as the want of a proper outlet for active faculties. I have seen young girls suffer and grow sensibly lowered in vitality in the first years after they leave school. In our attempt then to give a girl pleasure and freedom from care we succeed, for the most part, in making her pitifully miserable. She finds "life" so different from what she expected

Charles Darwin resembles a sage in this portrait made toward the end of his life—a resemblance appropriate for the man who transformed major areas of human thought. Before he was born in 1809, the idea of evolution had already been suggested, but most scientists, and nearly all laymen, remained unconvinced. Darwin was persuaded during the 1830's when he visited the Galapagos Islands in the Pacific on a scientific expedition. Finding different species of plants and animals on different islands, he theorized that those adapted to local conditions survived and bred, while natural selection killed off the unfit. This was the basis of his *Origin of Species* (1859), which set forth a theory of evolutionary development. His *Descent of Man* (1871) traced humanity's heritage back to the anthropoids. By the time he died in 1882, evolution was well on its way to becoming the fundamental biological theory. After more than a century of criticism, discussion, and research, there is no absolute unanimity about its processes, but the fact of evolution is undoubted.

it to be. She is besotted with innocent little ambitions and does not understand this apparent waste of herself, this elaborate preparation, if no work is provided for her. There is a heritage of noble obligation which young people accept and long to perpetuate. The desire for action, the wish to right wrong and alleviate suffering, haunts them daily. Society smiles at it indulgently instead of making it of value to itself. . . . There are a few girls who, by the time they are "educated," forget their old childish desires to help the world and to play with poor little girls "who haven't playthings." Parents are often curious about this. They deliberately expose their daughters to the knowledge of the distress in the world. They send them to hear missionary addresses on famines in India and China; they accompany them to lectures on the suffering in Siberia; they agitate together over the forgotten region of East London. In addition to this, from babyhood the altruistic tendencies of these daughters are persistently cultivated. They are taught to be self-forgetting and self-sacrificing, to consider the good of the Whole before the good of the Ego. But when all this information and culture begins to show results, when the daughter comes back from college and begins to recognize her social claim to the "submerged tenth" and to evince a disposition to fulfil it, the family claim is strenuously asserted; she is told that she is unjustified, ill-advised in her efforts. If she persists the family too often are injured and unhappy, unless the efforts are called missionary, and the religious zeal of the family carry them over their sense of abuse.

We have in America a fast-growing number of cultivated young people who have no recognized outlet for their active faculties. They hear constantly of the great social maladjustment, but no way is provided for them to change it and their uselessness hangs about them heavily. Huxley declares that the sense of uselessness is the severest shock which the human system can sustain, and, if persistently sustained, it results in atrophy of function. These young people have had advantages of college, of European travel and economic study, but they are sustaining this shock of inaction.

After philosophy, religion. Jane finds the Christian conscience becoming an ever stronger force for social change, with religious people increasingly unwilling to sit idle before the suffering of the masses:

■ The third division of motives which I believe make toward the settlement is the result of a certain *renaissance* going forward in Christianity. The impulse to share the lives of the poor, the desire to make social service, irrespective of propaganda, express the spirit of Christ, is as old as Christianity itself. . . .

That Christianity would have to be revealed and embodied in the line of social progress is a corollary to the simple proposition that man's action is found in his social relationships in the way in which he connects with his fellows, that his motives for action are the zeal and affection with which he regards his fellows. By this simple process was created a deep enthusiasm for humanity, which regarded man as at once the organ and object of revelation; and by this process came about that wonderful fellowship, that true democracy of the early Church, that so captivates the imagination. . . .

I believe that there is a distinct turning among many young men and women toward this simple acceptance of Christ's message. They resent the assumption that Christianity is a set of ideas which belong to the religious consciousness, whatever that may be, that it is a thing to be proclaimed and instituted apart from the social life of the community. They insist that it shall seek a simple and natural expression in the social organism itself. The settlement movement is only one manifestation of that wider humanitarian movement which throughout Christendom, but preeminently in England, is endeavoring to embody itself, not in a sect, but in society itself. Tolstoy has reminded us all very forcibly of Christ's principle of nonresistance. His formulation has been startling and his expression has deviated from the general movement, but there is little doubt that he has many adherents, men and women who are philosophically convinced of the futility of opposition, who believe that evil can be overcome only with good and cannot be opposed by evil. . . .

I cannot of course speak for other settlements, but it would, I think, be unfair to Hull-House not to emphasize the conviction with which the first residents went there, that it would simply be a foolish and an unwarrantable expenditure of force to oppose and to antagonize any individual or set of people in the neighborhood; that whatever of good the House had to offer should be put into positive terms; that its residents should live with opposition to no man, with recognition of the good in every man, even the meanest. I believe that this turning, this *renaissance* of the early Christian humanitarianism, is going on in America, in Chicago, if you please, without leaders who write or philosophize, without much speaking, but with a bent to express in social service, in terms of action, the spirit of Christ. Certain it is that spiritual force is found in the settlement movement, and it is also true that this force must be evoked and must be called into play before the success of any settlement is assured. . . .

If you have heard a thousand voices singing in the "Hallelujah Chorus" in Handel's *Messiah*, you have found that the leading voices could still be distinguished, but that the differences of training and cultivation between them and the voices of the chorus were lost in the unity of purpose and the fact that they were all human voices lifted by a high motive. This is a weak illustration of what a settlement attempts to do. It aims, in a measure, to lead whatever of social life its neighborhood may afford, to focus and give form to that life, to bring to bear upon it the results of cultivation and training; but it receives in exchange for the music of isolated voices the volume and strength of the chorus. It is quite impossible for me to say in what proportion or degree the subjective necessity which led to the opening of Hull-House combined the three trends: first, the desire to interpret democracy in social terms; secondly, the impulse beating at the very source of our lives urging us to aid in the race progress;

This is how Thomas Henry Huxley appeared to *Vanity Fair* in 1871—a pugnacious Victorian ready to defend his creed against all comers. His creed was science; he coined the word "agnostic" to cover his religious doubts, and appointed himself "Darwin's bulldog" to defend evolution. His debate with Bishop Samuel Wilberforce at Oxford in 1860 became famous. Wilberforce asked whether Huxley was descended from the ape on his grandmother's or his grandfather's side of the family. Huxley is said to have murmured: "The Lord hath delivered him into mine hands." The debate was a solid victory for Huxley and created a wide feeling that religion was at a disadvantage when its advocates were unthinkingly opposed to science.

and, thirdly, the Christian movement toward Humanitarianism. It is difficult to analyze a living thing; the analysis is at best imperfect. Many more motives may blend with the three trends; possibly the desire for a new form of social success due to the nicety of imagination, which refuses worldly pleasures unmixed with the joys of self-sacrifice; possibly a love of approbation, so vast that it is not content with the treble clapping of delicate hands, but wishes also to hear the bass notes from toughened palms, may mingle with these.

Hull-House was formed into a corporation in 1895. This was something Jane Addams bowed to because of the legal argument that the settlement would be in a stronger position if treated as a unified institution, rather than merely as a group of individual residents using the same house as their headquarters. But she disliked the move for reasons set forth in her 1892 address, where she stresses adaptability rather than legality:

■ The one thing to be dreaded in the settlement is that it lose its flexibility, its power of quick adaptation, its readiness to change its methods as its environment may demand. It must be open to conviction and must have a deep and abiding sense of tolerance. It must be hospitable and ready for experiment. It should demand from its residents a scientific patience in the accumulation of facts and the steady holding of their sympathies as one of the best instruments for that accumulation. It must be grounded in a philosophy whose foundation is on the solidarity of the human race, a philosophy which will not waver when the race happens to be represented by a drunken woman or an idiot boy. Its residents must be emptied of all conceit of opinion and all self-assertion, and ready to arouse and interpret the public opinion of their neighborhood. They must be content to live quietly side by side with their neighbors until they grow into a sense of relationship and mutual interest. Their neighbors are held apart by differences of race and language which the residents can more easily overcome. They are bound to see the needs of their neighborhood as a whole, to furnish data for legislation, and use their influence to secure it. In short, residents are pledged to devote themselves to the duties of good citizenship and to the arousing of the social energies which too largely lie dormant in every neighborhood given over to industrialism. They are bound to regard the entire life of their city as organic, to make an effort to unify it and to protest against its over-differentiation.

Our philanthropies of all sorts are growing so expensive and institutional that it is to be hoped the settlement movement will keep itself facile and unincumbered. From its very nature it needs no endowment, no roll of salaried officials. Many residents must always come in the attitude of students, assuming that the best teacher of life is life itself and regarding the settlement as a classroom. Hull-House from the outside may appear to be a cumbrous plant of manifold industries, with its round of clubs and classes, its day nursery, diet kitchen, library, art exhibits, lectures, statistical work and polyglot demands for information, a thousand people coming

Mackenzie King (1874–1950) met Jane Addams in 1895, when she spoke in Toronto on Arnold Toynbee and social settlements. Stirred by the speech, he noted in his diary: "I love Toynbee and I love Jane Addams." He was inspired to become a resident of Hull-House while doing graduate work at Chicago University, and his biographer says: "Miss Addams was reluctant to lose him and offered him . . . a small salary which would have enabled him to stay at Hull-House." His college duties later forced him to leave, but the experience taught him the value of social work. Returning to Canada, he entered politics, was elected to the federal parliament, took over leadership of the Liberal party, and became Prime Minister in 1921. He then welded together a powerful combination of political forces that dominated Canada's public life for more than twenty years. On April 20, 1948, he set a record for statesmen of the English-speaking world by surpassing the 7,620 days in office of Sir Robert Walpole, Britain's eighteenth-century Prime Minister. As King was receiving felicitations, a reporter hung this legend on a nearby portrait of Walpole: "SCRATCHED!"

and going in an average week. But viewed as a business enterprise it is not costly, for from this industry are eliminated two great items of expense—the cost of superintendence and the cost of distribution. All the management and teaching are voluntary and unpaid, and the consumers—to continue the commercial phraseology—are at the door and deliver the goods themselves. In the instance of Hull-House, rent is also largely eliminated through the courtesy of Miss Culver, the owner. Life is manifold and Hull-House attempts to respond to as many sides as possible. It does this fearlessly, feeling sure that among the able people of Chicago are those who will come to do the work when once the outline is indicated. It pursues much the same policy in regard to money. It seems to me an advantage—this obligation to appeal to businessmen for their judgment and their money, to the educated for their effort and enthusiasm, to the neighborhood for their response and cooperation. It tests the sanity of an idea, and we enter upon a new line of activity with a feeling of support and confidence.

In closing her Plymouth addresses of 1892, Jane looks forward to the day when the settlement will be pronounced obsolete. Having transformed society and convinced every man that he is his brother's keeper, it can disappear, leaving behind a job well done:

■ At first we were often asked why we came to live there when we could afford to live somewhere else. I remember one man who used to shake his head and say it was "the strangest thing he had met in his experience," but who was finally convinced that it was not strange but natural. There was another who was quite sure that the "prayer-meeting snap" would come in somewhere, that it was "only a question of time." I trust that now it seems natural to all of us that the settlement should be there. If it

Young Benny Goodman, son of a Jewish tailor in Chicago's slums, came to Hull-House in 1921 with a burning desire to learn the clarinet and play in the band, which had, in his words, "new instruments and swell uniforms." His ability soon earned him a place in the band, and he marched in many a parade through Chicago. The rowdiness of the city affected even its music; Benny recalls: "If we couldn't outplay them, we'd get into a scrap and bang up their instruments." He and his friends experimented with Dixieland rhythms during their spare time, and some were good enough to get professional bookings. Benny went on to greater success than any of them. The photograph below was taken in 1938, when the King of Swing returned to Hull-House to show its music students what an old grad had achieved. The beaming woman at left is Charlotte Carr, who became head of the settlement after Jane Addams died in 1935. Later in his career Benny married an aristocratic English lady. At least one London butler announced the couple's arrival at a party with the formula: "Her Ladyship and the King of Swing."

is natural to feed the hungry and care for the sick, it is certainly natural to give pleasure to the young and to minister to the deep-seated craving for social intercourse all men feel. Whoever does it is rewarded by something which, if not gratitude, is at least spontaneous and vital and lacks that irksome sense of obligation with which a substantial benefit is too often acknowledged. The man who looks back to the person who first put him in the way of good literature has no alloy in his gratitude.

I remember when the statement seemed to me very radical that the salvation of East London was the destruction of West London; but I believe now that there will be no wretched quarters in our cities at all when the conscience of each man is so touched that he prefers to live with the poorest of his brethren, and not with the richest of them that his income will allow. It is to be hoped that this moving and living will at length be universal and need no name. The settlement movement is from its nature a provisional one. It is easy in writing a paper to make all philosophy point one particular moral and all history adorn one particular tale; but I hope you forgive me for reminding you that the best speculative philosophy sets forth the solidarity of the human race, that the highest moralists have taught that without the advance and improvement of the whole no man can hope for any lasting improvement in his own moral or material individual condition. The subjective necessity for social settlements is identical with that necessity which urges us on toward social and individual salvation.

Over the years, Jane returned repeatedly to her vision of the ideal settlement. Perhaps her best brief statement of its essence is in her article "A Function of the Social Settlement," which she submitted to the American Academy of Political and Social Science in 1899:

■ This, then, will be my definition of the settlement: that it is an attempt to express the meaning of life in terms of life itself, in forms of activity. There is no doubt that the deed often reveals when the idea does not, just as art makes us understand and feel what might be incomprehensible and inexpressible in the form of an argument. And as the artist tests the success of his art when the recipient feels that he knew the thing before, but had not been able to express it, so the settlement, when it attempts to reveal and apply knowledge, deems its results practicable, when it has made knowledge available which before was abstract, when through use, it has made common that knowledge which was partial before, because it could only be apprehended by the intellect.

The chief characteristic of art lies in freeing the individual from a sense of separation and isolation in his emotional experience, and has usually been accomplished through painting, writing, and singing; but this does not make it in the least impossible that it is now being tried, self-consciously and most bunglingly we will all admit, in terms of life itself. A settlement brings to its aid all possible methods to reveal and make common its conception of life. All those arts and devices which express kindly relations from man to man, from charitable effort to the most specialized social intercourse, are constantly tried. There is the historic statement, the literary presentation, the fellowship which comes when great questions are studied with the hope of modifying actual conditions, the putting forward of the essential that the trivial may appear unimportant, as it is, the attempt to select the more typical and enduring forms of social life, and to eliminate, as far as possible, the irrelevant things which crowd into actual living. There are so-called art exhibits, concerts, dramatic representations, every possible device to make operative on the life around it, the conception of life which the settlement group holds. The demonstration is made not by reason, but by life itself. There must, of course, be a certain talent for conduct and unremitting care lest there grow to be a divergence between theory and living, for however embarrassing this divergence may prove in other situations, in a settlement the artist throws away his tools as soon as this thing happens. He is constantly transmitting by means of his human activity, his notion of life to others. He hopes to produce a sense of infection which may ultimately result in identity of interest.

A sixteen-year-old girl, refusing to take a wage cut at a Hart, Schaffner & Marx shop in Chicago's garment district, quit her job in 1910. This seemingly trivial incident triggered a massive walkout that closed down the industry. The strikers shown above are demanding not only better wages and working conditions, but also the right to picket—a significant step in labor's growing insistence on its rights. Jane Addams told the labor leaders involved, who were willing to set aside collective bargaining: "Your own people will never agree." Nor did they. Hart, Schaffner & Marx, accepting collective bargaining, became leaders in good labor relations. The company's president, Harry Hart, remained a friend of Jane Addams. So did Sidney Hillman, head of the garment workers, who later became a prominent political ally of Franklin D. Roosevelt.

HULL-HOUSE AND THE UNIONS

Six years after the establishment of Hull-House, its residents pooled their knowledge, insights, and talents, and published Hull-House Maps and Papers, *a penetrating sociological study of Chicago's Nineteenth Ward. Jane Addams took the labor movement for her subject, as she would again and again during her career. Having been involved with workingmen and workingwomen ever since her arrival on Halsted Street, she knew their problems in a personal way. She had seen the powerlessness of the individual confronting the industrial giants, and the evils that came of workers undercutting one another in the market. Hence, "organization" is a key word in her chapter, "The Settlement as a Factor in the Labor Movement," excerpted here:*

■ A settlement accepts the ethics of its contemporaries that the sharing of the life of the poor is essential to the understanding and bettering of that life; but by its very existence it adopts this modern code somewhat formally. The social injury of the meanest man not only becomes its concern, but by virtue of its very locality it has put itself into a position to see, as no one but a neighbor can see, the stress and need of those who bear the brunt of the social injury. A settlement has not only taken a pledge towards those thus injured, but it is placed where the motive-power for the fulfilment of such a pledge is constantly renewed. Propinquity is an unceasing factor in its existence.

A review of the sewing trades, as seen from a settlement, will be sufficient to illustrate this position. Hull-House is situated in the midst of the sweaters' district of Chicago. The residents came to the district with the general belief that organization for working people was a necessity. They

The exploitation of women and children in the garment industry is the subject of this *Harper's Weekly* drawing, which appeared in the issue dated April 26, 1890. It was titled: "Cheap Clothing—The Slaves of the 'Sweaters.'" The little girl and her mother carry to their employer the clothing they have stitched together from piecework provided by him. This was the common system during the period described by Jane Addams in these pages. It did not disappear until after the rise of the labor unions—a movement that Jane backed wholeheartedly—and the development of the new social conscience that she repeatedly called for after establishing Hull-House and realizing the tragic conditions that were commonplace in Chicago and other crowded urban areas.

would doubtless have said that the discovery of the power to combine was the distinguishing discovery of our time; that we are using this force somewhat awkwardly, as men use that which is newly discovered. In social and political affairs the power to combine often works harm; but it is already operating to such an extent in commercial affairs, that the manufacturer who does not combine with others of his branch is in constant danger of failure; that a railroad cannot be successfully projected unless the interests of parallel roads are consulted; and that working people likewise cannot be successful until they, too, learn skillfully to avail themselves of this power.

This was to the residents, as to many people, an accepted proposition, but not a working formula. It had not the driving force of a conviction. The residents have lived for five years in a neighborhood largely given over to the sewing trades, which is an industry totally disorganized. Having observed the workers in this trade as compared to those in organized trades, they have gradually discovered that lack of organization in a trade tends to the industrial helplessness of the workers in that trade. If in all departments of social, political, and commercial life, isolation is a blunder, and results in dreariness and apathy, then in industrial affairs isolation is a social crime; for it there tends to extermination. This process of extermination entails starvation and suffering, and the desperate moral disintegration which inevitably follows in their train, until the need of organization in industry gradually assumes a moral aspect. The conviction arrived at entails a social obligation.

No trades are so overcrowded as the sewing trades, for the needle has ever been the refuge of the unskilled woman. The wages paid throughout the manufacture of clothing are less than those in any other trade. In order to meet the requirements of the workers, lack of skill, and absence of orderly life, the work has been so subdivided that almost no skill is required after the garment leaves the cutter. It is given practically to the one who is at hand when it is ready, and who does it for the least money. This subdivision and low wage have gone so far that the woman who does home finishing alone cannot possibly gain by it a living wage. The residents of Hull-House have carefully investigated many cases, and are ready to assert that the Italian widow who finishes the cheapest goods, although she sews from six in the morning until eleven at night, can only get enough to keep her children clothed and fed, while for her rent and fuel she must always depend upon charity or the hospitality of her countrymen. If the American sewing-woman, supporting herself alone, lives on bread and butter and tea, she finds a Bohemian woman next door whose diet of black bread and coffee enables her to undercut. She competes with a wife who is eager to have home finishing that she may add something to the family comfort; or with a daughter who takes it that she may buy a wedding outfit.

The Hebrew tailor, the man with a family to support, who but for this competition of unskilled women and girls, might earn a wage upon which a family could subsist, is obliged, in order to support them at all, to put his little children at work as soon as they can sew on buttons. It does not help his industrial situation that the woman and girl who have brought it about have accepted the lower wages in order to buy comforts for an invalid child, or to add to the earnings of an aged father. The mother who sews on a gross of buttons for seven cents, in order to buy a blue ribbon with which to tie up her little daughter's hair, or the mother who finishes a dozen vests for five cents, with which to buy her children a loaf of bread, commits unwittingly a crime against her fellow workers, although our hearts may thrill with admiration for her heroism, and ache with pity over her misery. . . .

If the settlement, then, is convinced that in industrial affairs lack of organization tends to the helplessness of the isolated worker, and is a menace to the entire community, then it is bound to pledge itself to industrial organization, and to look about it for the lines upon which to work. And at this point the settlement enters into what is more technically known as the labor movement. . . .

It was perhaps natural, from the situation, that the unions organized at Hull-House should have been those in the sewing trades. The shirtmakers were organized in the spring of 1891. . . . The cloakmakers were organized at Hull-House in the spring of 1892. . . . The first meeting at Hull-House was composed of men and girls, and two or three of the residents. The meeting was a revelation to all present. The men, perhaps forty in number, were Russian-Jewish tailors, many of whom could command not even broken English. They were ill-dressed and grimy, suspicious that Hull-House was a spy in the service of the capitalists. They were skilled workers, easily superior to the girls when sewing on a cloak, but shamefaced and constrained in meeting with them. The American-Irish girls were well-dressed, and comparatively at ease. They felt

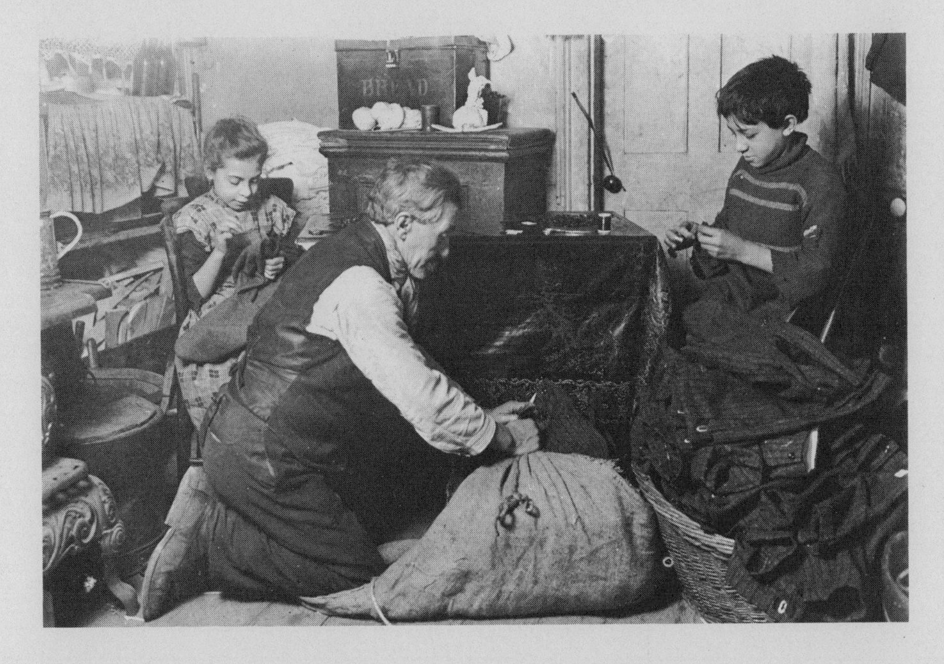

The tots on the left are working at home, pressed into service by their parents to add to the meager family income. Many parents wanted something better for their children than this sort of servitude. Jane Addams later recognized this hope when she spoke to women on the need for a child labor law: "I am happy to remember that I never met with lack of understanding among the hard-working widows. . . . There was always a willingness, even among the poorest women, to keep on with the hard night-scrubbing or the long days of washing, for the children's sake." Opponents of the law were mainly manufacturers—"self-made men," as Jane wryly classified them.

chaperoned by the presence of the residents, and talked volubly among themselves. These two sets of people were held together only by the pressure upon their trade. They were separated by strong racial differences, by language, by nationality, by religion, by mode of life, by every possible social distinction. The interpreter stood between the two sides of the room, somewhat helpless. He was clear upon the economic necessity for combination; he realized the mutual interdependence; but he was baffled by the social aspect of the situation. The residents felt that between these men and girls was a deeper gulf than the much-talked-of "chasm" between the favored and unfavored classes. The working girls before them, who were being forced to cross such a gulf, had a positive advantage over the cultivated girl who consciously, and sometimes heroically, crossed the "chasm" to join hands with her working sisters.

There was much less difference of any sort between the residents and working girls than between the men and girls of the same trade. It was a spectacle only to be found in an American city, under the latest conditions of trade life. Working people among themselves are being forced into a social democracy from the pressure of the economic situation. It presents an educating and broadening aspect of no small value. . . .

The crucial question of the time is, "In what attitude stand ye toward the present industrial system? Are you content that greed and the seizing upon disadvantage and the pushing of the weaker to the wall shall rule your business life, while in your family and social life you live so differently? Are you content that Christianity shall have no play in trade?" If these questions press upon all of us, then a Settlement must surely face the industrial problem as a test of its sincerity, as a test of the unification of its interests with the absorbing interests of its neighbors. Must it, then, accept the creeds of one or the other of these schools of social thought, and work for a party; or is there some underlying principle upon which the settlement can stand, as in its Christianity it endeavors to stand on something more primitive than either Catholicism or Protestantism? Can it find the moral question involved? Is there a line of ethics which its action ought to follow? Is it possible to make the slow appeal to the nobler fibre in men, and to connect it with that tradition of what is just and right?

A glance at the labor movement shows that the preponderating force has been given to what may be called negative action. Unions use their power to frustrate the designs of the capitalist, to make trouble for corporations and the public, such as is involved, for instance, in a railroad strike. It has often seemed to be the only method of arresting attention to their demands; but in America, at least, they have come to trust it too far. A movement cannot be carried on by negating other acts; it must have a positive force, a driving and self-sustaining motive power. A moral revolution cannot be accomplished by men who are held together merely because they are all smarting under a sense of injury and injustice, although it may be begun by them. . . .

Is it too much to hope that as the better organized and older trades unions are fast recognizing a solidarity of labor, and acting upon the literal notion of brotherhood, that they will later perceive the larger solidarity which includes labor and capital, and act upon the notion of brotherhood . . . and . . . universal kinship?

Before this larger vision of life there can be no perception of "sides" and no "battle array?" In the light of the developed social conscience the "sympathetic strike" may be criticised, not because it is too broad, but because it is too narrow, and because the strike is but a wasteful and negative demonstration of ethical fellowship. In the summer of 1894 the Chicago unions of Russian-Jewish cloakmakers, German compositors, and Bohemian and Polish butchers, struck in sympathy with the cause of the American Railway Union, whom they believed to be standing for a principle. Does an event such as this, clumsy and unsatisfactory as its results are, prefigure the time when no factory child in Chicago can be overworked and underpaid without a protest from all good citizens, capitalist and proletarian? Such a protest would be founded upon an ethical sense so strong that it would easily override business interests and class prejudices.

Manifestations of the labor movement are erratic and ill-timed because of the very strength of its motive power. A settlement is not affrighted nor dismayed when it sees in labor meetings, in caucuses, and turbulent gatherings, men who are—

"Groping for the right, with horny, calloused hands,
And staring round for God with bloodshot eyes,"

although the clumsy hands may upset some heavy pieces of convention, as a strong blindman overturns furniture, and the bloodshot eyes may be wild and fanatical. The settlement is unworthy of its calling if it is too timid or dull to interpret this groping and staring. But the settlement should be affrighted, and bestir itself to action, when the groping is not for the right, but for the mere purpose of overturning; when the staring is not for God, but for Mammon—and there is a natural temptation towards both. . . .

The despair of the labor movement is, as Mazzini said in another cause long ago, that we have torn the great and beautiful ensign of Democracy. Each party has snatched a rag of it, and parades it as proudly as if it were the whole flag, repudiating and not deigning to look at the others. It is this feeling of disdain to any class of men or kind of men in the community which is dangerous to the labor movement, which makes it a class measure. It attacks its democratic character, and substitutes party enthusiasm for the irresistible force of human progress. The labor movement must include all men in its hopes.

CHICAGO'S KING LEAR

The most unusual of Jane Addams' writings is "A Modern Lear," in which she uses a Shakespearean analogy to dissect the behavior of a Chicago tycoon. This was originally an address delivered before the Chicago Woman's

Club in 1894, at the time of the Pullman strike. Some of her friends advised against publication because they thought her handling of George Pullman too caustic, and she withheld the address until 1912, when it appeared in The Survey. *By then, Pullman was dead, and the strike was no longer a burning issue. But Jane still continued to believe that she was right in drawing a parallel between the sleeping-car magnate and Shakespeare's tragic monarch. The play begins with King Lear doting on his three daughters, but completely misunderstanding their characters. When he decides to parcel his kingdom among them, asking only that they express unbounded affection for him, Cordelia, the youngest, refuses the bargain that her unworthy sisters accept with glib words of praise for their father. Lear disinherits Cordelia, who loves him, is subsequently betrayed by his two oldest daughters, who loathe him—and crushing tragedy results from his incomprehension. In Jane's analysis, a similar fault could be charged to George Pullman, who built a model town for his employees without trying to understand them as human beings. Determined to do everything* for *them rather than* with *them, Pullman responded with outraged indignation when they went on strike against the conditions he imposed.*

■ Historically considered, the relation of Lear to his children was archaic and barbaric, holding in it merely the beginnings of a family life, since developed. We may in later years learn to look back upon the industrial

This old engraving depicts King Lear, in plumes and ermine, pointing toward Cordelia with a menacing gesture. His wicked daughters, Goneril and Regan, remain discreetly silent—happy to see Cordelia out of the way, and planning to turn upon their father as soon as they have the power. The courtiers are shocked by the violence with which Lear rejects his favorite child. Kent (left) is about to protest. The balanced man of the drama, Kent foresees that calamity must result from Lear's anger, and it does; by the time the curtain falls, all the principals are dead. Tolstoy thought that Lear's motive was implausible, but psychologists hold that masculine vanity sometimes craves an exaggerated expression of affection—Lear's underlying thought. Despite Tolstoy's opinion, this remains one of literature's great tragedies.

relationships in which we are now placed as quite as incomprehensible and selfish, quite as barbaric and undeveloped, as was the family relationship between Lear and his daughters. We may then take the relationship of this unusually generous employer at Pullman to his own townful of employees as at least a fair one, because so exceptionally liberal in many of its aspects. King Lear doubtless held the same notion of a father's duty that was held by the other fathers of his time; but he alone was a king and had kingdoms to bestow upon his children. He was unique, therefore, in the magnitude of his indulgence, and in the magnitude of the disaster which followed it. The sense of duty held by the president of the Pullman Company doubtless represents the ideal in the minds of the best of the present employers as to their obligations toward their employees, but he projected this ideal more magnificently than the others. He alone gave his men so model a town, such perfect surroundings. The magnitude of his indulgence and failure corresponded, and we are forced to challenge the ideal itself: the same ideal which, more or less clearly defined, is floating in the minds of all philanthropic employers.

Eugene V. Debs (1855–1926) headed the American Railway Union during its bitter struggle with the Pullman Company. He had come up the hard way, working as a railroad fireman in Indiana at the age of sixteen before joining the drive to organize a railroad union. As a result of the Pullman strike, he went to jail, on a charge of criminal conspiracy to defy the government. Debs studied socialism in his cell, and emerged to become the leader of American Socialists, and editor of their weekly, *Appeal to Reason.* He was his party's candidate for President with almost unfailing regularity from 1900 through 1920. Jane Addams voted for him the last time, though at that moment he was again in the penitentiary serving a ten-year sentence on charges of sedition during World War I. Far from considering Debs a criminal, Jane admired him as a stalwart champion of peace and human welfare —and thus added her ballot to some 920,000 that Debs polled in 1920. Released in 1921 by order of President Harding—who did not, however, restore his citizenship—Debs was widely venerated as a martyr to high principles.

The two cases, of course, were not identical. King Lear simply wanted to govern the lives of his daughters. George Pullman wanted more than that in the case of his employees—a corporate profit from their labor.

■ In shops such as those at Pullman—indeed, in all manufacturing affairs since the industrial revolution—industry is organized into a vast social operation. The shops are managed, however, not for the development of the workmen thus socialized, but for the interests of the company owning the capital. The divergence between the social form and the individual aim becomes greater as the employees are more highly socialized and dependent, just as the clash in a family is more vital in proportion to the development and closeness of the family tie. The president of the Pullman Company went further than the usual employer does. He socialized not only the factory but the form in which his workmen were living. He built and, in a great measure, regulated an entire town. This again might have worked out into a successful associated effort if he had had in view the sole good of the inhabitants thus socialized, if he had called upon them for self-expression and had made the town a growth and manifestation of their wants and needs. But, unfortunately, the end to be obtained became ultimately commercial and not social, having in view the payment to the company of at least 4 percent on the money invested, so that with this rigid requirement there could be no adaptation of rent to wages, much less to needs. The rents became static and the wages competitive, shifting inevitably with the demands of trade. The president assumed that he himself knew the needs of his men, and so far from wishing them to express their needs he denied to them the simple rights of trade organization, which would have been, of course, the merest preliminary to an attempt at associated expression. If we may take the dictatorial relation of Lear to Cordelia as a typical and most dramatic example of the distinctively family tragedy, one will asserting its authority through all the entanglement of wounded affection, and insisting upon its selfish ends at all costs, may we not consider the absolute authority of this employer over his town as a typical and dramatic example of the industrial tragedy? One will directing the energies of many others, without regard to their desires, and having in view in the last analysis only commercial results? . . .

The president of the Pullman Company doubtless began to build his town from an honest desire to give his employees the best surroundings. As it developed it became a source of pride and an exponent of power, that he cared most for when it gave him a glow of benevolence. Gradually, what the outside world thought of it became of importance to him and he ceased to measure its usefulness by the standard of the men's needs. The theater was complete in equipment and beautiful in design, but too costly for a troupe who depended upon the patronage of mechanics, as the church was too expensive to be rented continuously. We can imagine the founder of the town slowly darkening his glints of memory and forgetting the common stock of experience which he held with his men. He cultivated the great and noble impulses of the benefactor until the power of attaining a simple human relationship with his employees, that of frank equality with them, was gone from him. He, too, lost the faculty of affectionate interpretation, and demanded a sign. He and his employees had no mutual interest in a common cause.

George M. Pullman patented his Pullman sleeping car, organized the Pullman Palace Car Company, and in 1880 founded the town of Pullman just outside Chicago. His literature proclaimed it to be "a town from which all that is ugly, discordant, and demoralizing is eliminated" and "a solution of the industrial problem." But one of his employees living in the town explained graphically what was wrong with Pullman's thinking: "We are born in a Pullman house, fed from the Pullman shop, taught in the Pullman school, catechized in the Pullman church, and when we die we shall be buried in the Pullman cemetery and go to the Pullman hell." Pullman's refusal to deal with the strikers prompted a snort from Mark Hanna, McKinley's campaign manager in 1896: "A man who won't meet his men halfway is a goddamned fool!" Today, with the strike largely forgotten, the name Pullman stands for its originator's contribution to the amenities of life. It remains the word for the sleeping car, which, with slight variations around the world, is still based on the principles Pullman applied. The facing seats are formed into lower berths, with the uppers folding down from overhead; the beds are frequently screened off by heavy curtains placed on either side of the car's center aisle.

Sharing Lear's psychological defect—blindness to the realities of the case—Pullman was baffled by the dilemma that he had himself created.

■ Without pressing the analogy too hard, may we not compare the indulgent relation of this employer to his town to the relation which existed between Lear and Cordelia? He fostered his employees for many years, gave them sanitary houses and beautiful parks, but in their extreme need, when they were struggling with the most difficult question which the times could present to them, when, if ever, they required the assistance of a trained mind and a comprehensive outlook, he lost his touch and had nothing wherewith to help them. He did not see the situation. He had been ignorant of their gropings toward justice. His conception of goodness for them had been cleanliness, decency of living, and above all, thrift and temperance. He had provided them means for all this; had gone further, and given them opportunities for enjoyment and comradeship. But he suddenly found his town in the sweep of a worldwide moral impulse. A movement had been going on about him and through the souls of his workingmen of which he had been unconscious. He had only heard of this movement by rumor. The men who consorted with him at his club and in his business had spoken but little of it, and when they had discussed it had contemptuously called it the "Labor Movement," headed by deadbeats and agitators. Of the force and power of this movement, of all the vitality within it, of that conception of duty which induces men to go without food and to see their wives and children suffer for the sake of securing better wages for fellow workmen whom they have never seen, this president had dreamed absolutely nothing. But his town had at last become swept into this large movement, so that the giving up of comfortable homes, of beautiful surroundings, seemed as naught to the men within its grasp.

The domestic arrangements of King Lear ended in catastrophe. The Pullman strike ended in apparent victory for the tycoon after President Cleveland sent federal troops to break it. But Pullman's version of benevolent despotism would soon be as dead as Lear's.

■ Day after day during that horrible suspense, when the wires constantly reported the same message, "The president of the company holds that there is nothing to arbitrate," one longed to find out what was in the mind of this man, to unfold his ultimate motive. One concludes that he must have been sustained by the consciousness of being in the right. Only that could have held him against the great desire for fair play which swept over the country. Only the training which an arbitrary will receives by years of consulting first its own personal and commercial ends could have made it strong enough to withstand the demands for social adjustment. He felt himself right from the commercial standpoint, and could not see the situation from the social standpoint. For years he had gradually accustomed himself to the thought that his motive was beyond reproach, that his attitude to his town was always righteous and philanthropic. Habit held him persistent in this view of the case through all the changing conditions. . . .

The new claim on the part of the toiling multitude, the new sense of responsibility on the part of the well-to-do, arise in reality from the same source. They are in fact the same "social compunction," and, in spite of their widely varying manifestations, logically converge into the same movement. Mazzini once preached, "The consent of men and your own conscience are two wings given you whereby you may rise to God." It is so easy for the good and powerful to think that they can rise by following the dictates of conscience, by pursuing their own ideals, leaving those ideals unconnected with the consent of their fellowmen. The president of the Pullman Company thought out within his own mind a beautiful town. He had power with which to build this town, but he did not appeal to nor obtain the consent of the men who were living in it. The most unambitious reform, recognizing the necessity for this consent, makes for slow but sane and strenuous progress, while the most ambitious of social plans and experiments, ignoring this, is prone to the failure of the model town of Pullman.

That Jane Addams was a hardheaded social scientist, as well as a softhearted social worker, is clear from the articles she submitted to the technical journals. This is another one—"Trades Unions and Public Duty," which appeared in the 1899 volume of The American Journal of Sociology. *Here,*

Grover Cleveland ordered the soldiers to march against the Pullman strikers when told that Chicago was in the grip of anarchy, but the Illinois lawyer-poet Edgar Lee Masters judged that "there was no rioting or disturbance of moment . . . until after the federal troops arrived." This was a stormy event of Cleveland's second Administration. His first (1885–1889) had been relatively peaceful, highlighted by his marriage in the White House. He opposed pressure groups, vetoed pensions, curtailed land giveaways, and urged Congress to lower tariffs. Running for reelection in 1888, he polled more popular votes than Benjamin Harrison—but lost in the electoral vote. Four years later, Cleveland won again, and soon had to grapple with the panic of 1893. He got Congress to repeal the Silver Purchase Act, thus infuriating Western silverites. When the gold drain forced him to retain J. P. Morgan, critics charged that he had yielded to the exorbitant terms of the financial magnate. In 1895, again receiving bad advice, Cleveland threatened the British with war before an agreement was reached on the boundary between Venezuela and British Guiana. He left office with a record as one of our stronger Presidents, but perhaps too inclined to hasty action—as in the case of the Pullman strike.

she follows her argument about the labor movement to its logical conclusion, and insists that the unions are simply trying to do, haltingly and piecemeal, what society should do in the most comprehensive manner.

■ In this paper I have assumed that the general organization of trades unions and their ultimate purposes are understood, and also that we recognize that the public has a duty toward the weak and defenseless members of the community. With these assumptions granted, two propositions are really amazing: first, that we have turned over to those men who work with their hands the fulfillment of certain obligations which we must acknowledge belong to all of us, such as protecting little children from premature labor, and obtaining shorter hours for the overworked; and, second, that while the trades unions, more than any other body, have secured orderly legislation for the defense of the feeblest, they are persistently misunderstood and harshly criticized by many people who are themselves working for the same ends.

The first proposition may be illustrated by various instances in which measures introduced by trades unions have first been opposed by the public, and later have been considered praiseworthy and valuable, when the public as a whole has undertaken to establish and enforce them. For years trades unions have endeavored to secure laws regulating the occupations in which children may be allowed to work, the hours of labor permitted in those occupations, and the minimum age below which children may not be employed. Workingmen have accepted women into their trades unions, as an inevitable development of industrial conditions, but they resent the entrance of children into their trades, not only because children bring down wages, for women do that as well, but because children are injured by premature labor. The regulation of child labor is one of the few points in which society as a whole has made common cause with the voluntary efforts of trades unions, but the movement was initiated and is still largely carried forward by them. It is quite possible to understand the reasons for this.

We may imagine a row of people seated in a moving streetcar, into which darts a boy of eight, calling out the details of the last murder in the hope of selling an evening newspaper. A comfortable-looking man buys a paper from him, with no sense of moral shock; he may even be a trifle complacent that he has helped along the little fellow who is making his way in the world. The philanthropic lady sitting next to him may perhaps reflect that it is a pity that such a bright boy is not in school. She may make up her mind in a moment of compunction to redouble her efforts for various newsboys' missions and homes, that this poor child may have better teaching and perhaps a chance of manual training. She probably is convinced that he alone, by his unaided efforts, is supporting a widowed mother, and her heart is moved to do all she can for him. Let us imagine that next to her sits a workingman trained in trades-union methods. He will probably view with indignation the spectacle of a heedless child jumping on moving cars at the risk of his limbs, shouting out facts and reports that should be unknown to him for many years, and he may wonder for the hundredth time why it is that society allows this utter waste of its immature members. He knows that the boy's natural development is arrested, and that the abnormal activity of his body and mind uses up the force which should go into growth. He is forced to these conclusions because he has seen many a man enter the factory at eighteen and twenty so worn out by premature work that he is laid on the shelf within ten or fifteen years. He knows very well that he can do nothing in the way of ameliorating the lot of this particular boy; that his only possible chance is to agitate for proper child-labor laws in order to regulate, and, if possible, prohibit, street vending by children, so that the child of the poorest may have his school time secured to him, and may have at least his short chance for growth.

These three people sitting in the streetcar are all honest and upright, and recognize a certain duty toward the forlorn children of the community. The self-made man is encouraging one boy's own efforts. The philanthropic lady is helping on a few boys. The workingman alone is obliged to include all the boys of his class. Workingmen, in their feebleness in all but numbers, have been forced to the state to secure protection for themselves and for their children. They cannot all rise out of their class, as the occasionally successful man has done; some of them must be left to do the work in the factories and mines, and they have no money to spend in ameliorating philanthropy. In order to secure help from the state they have been obliged to agitate, and to make a moral appeal to the community as a whole—that most successful appeal which has ever distinguished great popular movements, but which we seem to distrust, and

Hull-House welcomed crowds of children such as these three who were there during the 1920's. The two boys above are mugging in front of the camera, showing aplomb, good humor, and complete confidence in their surroundings. For them and many other youngsters, such genial characteristics of life were largely confined to their hours at the settlement—and disappeared once they had returned to their dismal homes. Jane Addams often sorrowed over the street gangs running at random through the city. She wanted to give the members of these gangs pleasanter surroundings for their spare time, and these pictures show how well she succeeded. The little gamin at left posed in the Boys' Club for an engaging photograph.

do not ordinarily use so often as the appeals to self-interest, national tradition, or class prejudice. Almost all the labor legislation which has been secured in this country to protect the workman against the harshest conditions of industry has been secured through the efforts of trades unions, the training in which naturally leads men to appeal to the state, and to use those tools which democracy affords. . . .

To consider the second proposition: For many years I have been impressed with the noble purposes of trades unions, and the desirability of the ends which they seek; and at the same time I have been amazed at the harshness with which their failures are judged by the public, and the undue stress which is laid upon the violence and disorder which sometimes accompany their efforts. How far is this violence and the consequent condemnation of the public the result of ignoble purposes on the part of the trades unions, and how far is it the result of the partial effort and failure which we thrust upon them, when the trades unions alone are obliged to do what the community as a whole should undertake? Scenes of disorder and violence are enacted because trades unions are not equipped to accomplish what they are undertaking. The state alone could accomplish it without disorder. The public shirks its duty, and then holds a grievance toward the men who undertake the performance of that duty. It blames the union men for the disaster which arises from the fact that the movement is a partial one. The public is forced to one of two alternatives: that the state should not attempt to ameliorate the lot of workingmen . . . or that the trades unions, unassisted, are doing that for which we are all responsible, and which we all ought to undertake. . . .

Bernard Shaw had not yet dazzled the world when Jane Addams paused in London in 1896. He was a journalist specializing in drama and music criticism, and a prominent figure of the Fabian Society. Jane says that "a reception given by Karl Marx's daughter . . . to Liebknecht [a German Marxist] gave us a glimpse of the old-fashioned orthodox Socialist who had not yet begun to yield to the biting ridicule of Bernard Shaw, although he flamed in their midst that evening." For Jane, Shaw was primarily a left-wing theorist, although when his plays (with their social criticism and incisive wit) began to appear, some of them were performed at the Hull-House theater. Over the years, she found that she continued to disagree with many of Shaw's beliefs and theories.

Is it too much to hope that in time other citizens, as well as trade unionists, may be educated to ask themselves: "Does our industrial machinery, or does it not, make for the greatest amount and the highest quality of character?" And that when it is answered, as it must be at the present moment, that the state does not concern itself with the character of the producer, but only with the commercial aspects of the product, is it again too optimistic to predict that those other citizens will feel a certain sense of shame and recognize the fact that the trades unions have undertaken a duty which the public has ignored?

THE INFLUENCE OF TOLSTOY

Although Jane Addams looked to life itself as the chief source of human understanding, she never ceased to consult the great writers of the world who interpreted life. Leo Tolstoy remained her prime favorite, and she went to his books for apt quotations with which to grace the pages of her own, especially Twenty Years at Hull-House, *where she has much to say about him. Wanting to make her readers feel the stark reality of urban life at its worst, she introduces into her autobiography a passage from Tolstoy that perfectly expresses the thought in her mind—and that is still quite germane to the urban problems facing America in the last third of the twentieth century:*

■ As I review these very first impressions of the workers in unskilled industries, living in a depressed quarter of the city, I realize how easy it was for us to see exceptional cases of hardship as typical of the average lot, and yet, in spite of alleviating philanthropy and labor legislation, the indictment of Tolstoy applied to Moscow thirty years ago still fits every American city: "Wherever we may live, if we draw a circle around us of a hundred thousand, or a thousand, or even of ten miles circumference, and look at the lives of those men and women who are inside our circle, we shall find half-starved children, old people, pregnant women, sick and weak persons, working beyond their strength, who have neither food nor rest enough to support them, and who, for this reason, die before their time; we shall see others, full-grown, who are injured and needlessly killed by dangerous and hurtful tasks."

Like many admirers of Tolstoy, Jane Addams longed to have a personal conversation with him. Her chance came when illness interrupted her unremitting labor at Hull-House and forced her to take the rest she so badly needed, giving her a good reason for the European vacation that reached its high point at Tolstoy's Russian home.

Jane Addams and Mary Smith, traveling across Europe in the style to which they were accustomed, presented something of a contrast to most of the pilgrims who came to Yasnaya Polyana to sit at the feet of the Russian count whose social conscience would not permit him to live like the aristocrat he was. According to Aylmer Maude, "both ladies were very well dressed" when they met Tolstoy in his rude blouse and heavy boots. Maude felt that Tolstoy was benign rather than severe when he greeted his two American guests, but Jane, nervous in the presence of the great man, and unfamiliar with his mannerisms, received quite a different impression:

■ I had time to review carefully many things in my mind during the long days of convalescence following an illness of typhoid fever which I suffered in the autumn of 1895. The illness was so prolonged that my health was most unsatisfactory during the following winter, and the next May I went abroad with my friend Miss Smith, to effect if possible a more complete recovery.

The prospect of seeing Tolstoy filled me with the hope of finding a clue to the tangled affairs of city poverty. I was but one of thousands of our contemporaries who were turning toward this Russian, not as to a seer—his message is much too confused and contradictory for that—but as to a man who has had the ability to lift his life to the level of his conscience, to translate his theories into action. . . .

We had letters of introduction to Mr. and Mrs. Aylmer Maude of Moscow, since well known as the translators of *Resurrection* and other of Tolstoy's later works, who at that moment were on the eve of leaving Russia in order to form an agricultural colony in South England where they might support themselves by the labor of their hands. We gladly accepted Mr. Maude's offer to take us to Yasnaya Polyana. . . .

John Burns (above, haranguing London strikers), met Jane Addams and Mary Rozet Smith in London on their way to visit Tolstoy, and "showed us his wonderful civic accomplishments at Battersea, the plant turning street sweepings into cement pavements, the technical school teaching boys bricklaying and plumbing, and the public bath in which the children of the Board School were receiving swimming lessons —these measures anticipating our achievements in Chicago by at least a decade and a half." Burns did not underestimate his achievements in the British labor movement. Asked by Jane what Chicago needed most, he replied: "A hundred John Burnses!" His verdict on Jane herself was succinct: "The only saint that America has produced."

Jane stresses the humanitarianism of Leo Tolstoy (above), but she knew he represented far more than that. Starting life as a typical Russian aristocrat, Tolstoy (1828–1910) accepted a military commission as his due, and commanded a battery of guns in the Crimean War. Then he retired from the army to devote himself to writing. In 1861 he freed his serfs as ordered, thereby supporting the Czar, although he was opposed to czarism on principle as a despotic system from which Russia needed to be liberated. In 1866 he published *War and Peace*, generally considered the greatest novel ever written. In 1876 he experienced the religious conversion that transformed his life, impelling him both to practice and preach the ideal of nonresistance that turned idealists everywhere into Tolstoyans. Developing a moralistic cultural criticism, he disparaged masters like Shakespeare and Wagner, but he was just as severe with himself when he reread his earlier writings. By the time of his death, he was the best-known Russian opponent of the czarist system.

Tolstoy, standing by clad in his peasant garb, listened gravely but, glancing distrustfully at the sleeves of my traveling gown which unfortunately at that season were monstrous in size, he took hold of an edge and pulling out one sleeve to an interminable breadth, said quite simply that "there was enough stuff on one arm to make a frock for a little girl," and asked me directly if I did not find "such a dress" a "barrier to the people." I was too disconcerted to make a very clear explanation, although I tried to say that monstrous as my sleeves were they did not compare in size with those of the working girls in Chicago and that nothing would more effectively separate me from "the people" than a cotton blouse following the simple lines of the human form; even if I had wished to imitate him and "dress as a peasant," it would have been hard to choose which peasant among the thirty-six nationalities we had recently counted in our ward. Fortunately the countess came to my rescue with a recital of her former attempts to clothe hypothetical little girls in yards of material cut from a train and other superfluous parts of her best gown until she had been driven to a firm stand which she advised me to take at once. But neither Countess Tolstoy nor any other friend was on hand to help me out of my predicament later, when I was asked who "fed" me, and how did I obtain "shelter"? Upon my reply that a farm a hundred miles from Chicago supplied me with the necessities of life, I fairly anticipated the next scathing question: "So you are an absentee landlord? Do you think you will help the people more by adding yourself to the crowded city than you would by tilling your own soil?" This new sense of discomfort over a failure to till my own soil was increased when Tolstoy's second daughter appeared at the five o'clock tea table set under the trees, coming straight from the harvest field where she had been working with a group of peasants since five o'clock in the morning, not pretending to work but really taking the place of a peasant woman who had hurt her foot.

Tolstoy's wife, who did not object to living like a countess, and who could be disconcerting in her own genteel way, wanted to know why Mary, sitting next to her, had never married. Aylmer Maude summarizes their conversation: "The Countess did not approve of young women remaining so long unmarried. . . . Miss Smith pleaded as an excuse for herself that she had never been asked, but the Countess pooh-poohed the suggestion." Jane, meanwhile, was preoccupied with Tolstoy himself:

■ That summer evening as we sat in the garden with a group of visitors from Germany, from England and America, who had traveled to the remote Russian village that they might learn of this man, one could not forbear the constant inquiry to one's self as to why he was so regarded as sage and saint that this party of people should be repeated each day of the year. It seemed to me then that we were all attracted by this sermon of the deed, because Tolstoy had made the one supreme personal effort, one might almost say the one frantic personal effort, to put himself into right relations with the humblest people . . . who tilled his soil. . . .

Doubtless all of the visitors sitting in the Tolstoy garden that evening had excused themselves from laboring with their hands upon the theory that they were doing something more valuable for society in other ways. No one among our contemporaries has dissented from this point of view so violently as Tolstoy himself, and yet no man might so easily have excused himself from hard and rough work on the basis of his genius and of his intellectual contributions to the world. So far, however, from considering his time too valuable to be spent in labor in the field or in making shoes, our great host was too eager to know life to be willing to give up this companionship of mutual labor. . . .

At the long dinner table laid in the garden were the various traveling guests, the grown-up daughters, and the younger children with their governess. The countess presided over the usual European dinner served by men, but the count and the daughter, who had worked all day in the fields, ate only porridge and black bread and drank only *kvass*, the fare of the haymaking peasants. Of course we are all accustomed to the fact that those who perform the heaviest labor eat the coarsest and simplest fare at the end of the day, but it is not often that we sit at the same table with them while we ourselves eat the more elaborate food prepared by someone else's labor. Tolstoy ate his simple supper without remark or comment upon the food his family and guests preferred to eat, assuming that they, as well as he, had settled the matter with their own consciences. . . .

The conversation at dinner and afterward, although conducted with animation and sincerity, for the moment stirred vague misgivings within me. Was Tolstoy more logical than life warrants? Could the wrongs of life be reduced to the terms of unrequited labor and all be made right if each person performed the amount necessary to satisfy his own wants? Was it not always easy to put up a strong case if one took the naturalistic view of life? But what about the historic view, the inevitable shadings and modifications which life itself brings to its own interpretation? Miss Smith and I took a night train back to Moscow in that tumult of feeling which is always produced by contact with a conscience making one more of those determined efforts to probe to the very foundations of the mysterious world in which we find ourselves.

Keir Hardie was a Scot who did more than any other individual to found Britain's Labor Party. Jane Addams was greatly impressed by him in 1896: "We heard Keir Hardie before a large audience of workingmen standing in the open square of Canning Town . . . and we joined the vast body of men in the booming hymn—'When wilt Thou save the people/ O God of Mercy, when!'—finding it hard to realize that we were attending a political meeting. It seemed that moment as if the hopes of democracy were more likely to come to pass on English soil than upon our own." Hardie had recently returned from America, where he met Eugene Debs, still in jail for his part in the Pullman strike. Debs amused him by saying: "Walk right in and make [yourself] at home." On another visit to America in 1912, Hardie's feminine audiences gave him an ovation when he advocated woman suffrage in these terms: "It is only by recognizing the perfect right of every human being to equal treatment because they are human beings that we can hope for better days."

When Jane wrote her thank-you note to Aylmer Maude, she explained why, although moved by the humanitarian philosophy of Tolstoy, she could not accept the more radical tenets of Tolstoyism. Briefly, Tolstoy's unyielding adherence to a stern creed collided with her policy of accepting compromises for the sake of practical goals. Maude considered Jane's letter so significant that he had it published in The Humane Review *in 1902:*

■ "The glimpse of Tolstoy has made a profound impression upon me—not so much by what he said as the life, the gentleness, the Christianity in the soul of him. . . . A radical stand such as Tolstoy has been able to make throws all such effort as that of settlements into the ugly light of

This letter, written from Berlin, is dated July 31, 1896. Jane was still in a flush of exhilaration from her meeting with Tolstoy seven days before—and still agitated in mind about Tolstoyism—when she sat down in her hotel room to tell her good friend Henrietta Barnett, wife of the warden of Toynbee Hall, about the experiences she and Mary Rozet Smith had just had at Yasnaya Polyana. For this letter, as for her later writings concerning Tolstoy, she drew on the notebook she had kept in Russia. Under the July 24 heading, she set down succinct notes, such as the following: "Mr. Maude called for us. Went to little village beyond Tula. Drove to Tolstoy's estate. Countess' reception. Daughter trots us to the village. Supper. The Count drove to station at 11 P.M." As Jane notes in the opening sentence of this letter to Mrs. Barnett, she felt "quite illuminated" by her visit.

My dear Mrs Barnett
We have just come out of Russia quite illuminated from a visit to Tolstoy which we made in company with an ardent friend and disciple of his — Mr Maude. We enjoyed the time in Russia very much and

compromise and inefficiency—at least so it seemed to me—and perhaps accounts for a certain defensive attitude I found in myself.

"Our effort at Hull-House has always been to seize upon the highest moral efforts we could find in the labor movement or elsewhere, and help them forward—to conserve the best which the community has achieved and push it forward along its own line when possible. We have always held strongly to the doctrine of nonresistance, selecting the good in the neighborhood and refraining from railing at the bad. Gradually I have come to believe even further than that in nonresistance—that the expectation of opposition and martyrdom, the holding oneself in readiness for it, was in itself a sort of resistance and worked evil or at best was merely negative.

"No doubt a Christian who preached against the holding of private property would arouse much opposition on the part of the property holders; he might give up his own in a way which would work as a constant source of irritation to them. But I can imagine the thing being done in a way which would make it merely incidental to the great wave of fellowship and joy which would swallow it—the coming of the spirit was so great an event to the followers in Jerusalem that the division of goods received but little comment.

"So I would imagine the new Social Order (if it could come ideally) would gather to itself all that was best and noblest in the Old, all the human endeavor which has been put into it in the right direction, and which has become sacred because it is so human and pathetic; that its joy and righteousness would sweep men into it. The *ideal* is always admired; it is only when it begins to work itself out and to compromise with the world and circumstances that it becomes hated and misunderstood. This is doubtless inevitable, but it is a great pity to consider the hate essential, to confuse the result which the imperfect presentation of the ideal makes upon men, with the effect which the ideal might have. This belief has come to be part of my method of living, and I should have to start quite over again and admit the value of resistance if I gave it up. . . . I am sure you will understand my saying that I got more of Tolstoy's philosophy from our conversations than I had gotten from Tolstoy's books. I believe so much of it that I am sorry to seem to differ so much."

The "new Social Order" Jane Addams mentions near the end of the opposite page was also very much in the mind of Prince Peter Kropotkin (1842–1921) a Russian aristocrat who formulated an anarchist theory that local voluntary groups should replace the centralized state. Jane later wrote of Kropotkin's 1899 visit: "When he came to America to lecture, he was heard throughout the country with great interest and respect; that he was a guest of Hull-House during his stay in Chicago attracted little attention at the time, but two years later, when the assassination of President McKinley occurred, the visit of this kindly scholar . . . was made the basis of an attack upon Hull-House." Jane knew Kropotkin, often forced to live in exile, was not the "red revolutionary" of the anarchist scare that followed the assassination. Not surprisingly, Kropotkin subsequently condemned the Bolsheviks as "gangsters" when they seized power.

THE SOCIAL FUNCTION OF THE "BOSS"

Tolstoy had to deal with petty officials representing the Czar. Jane Addams had to deal with the "czar" of the Nineteenth Ward, alderman John Powers, who maintained his position through the skillful manipulation of the electorate. She did not mention Powers by name when she wrote "Ethical Survivals in Municipal Corruption," published in the International Journal of Ethics *in 1898, but all Chicago knew that "Johnny the Pow" was the subject of this pen portrait, and that its author was bent on his political defeat. Although Jane failed to unseat Powers, who remained an alderman until his death in 1913, she produced a realistic analysis of his perennial victories at the polls—an analysis that still stands up as one penetrating example of how to think about urban problems:*

■ Nothing is more certain than that the quality which a heterogeneous population, living in one of the less sophisticated wards, most admires is the quality of simple goodness; that the man who attracts them is the one whom they believe to be a good man. . . . Abstract virtues are too difficult for their untrained minds to apprehend, and many of them are still simple enough to believe that power and wealth come only to good people. The successful candidate, then, must be a good man according to the standards of his constituents. He must not attempt to hold up a morality beyond them, nor must he attempt to reform or change the standard. His safety lies in doing on a large scale the good deeds which his constituents are able to do only on a small scale. If he believes what they believe, and does what they are all cherishing a secret ambition to do, he will dazzle them by his success and win their confidence. . . .

The alderman, therefore, bails out his constituents when they are arrested, or says a good word to the police justice when they appear before him for trial; uses his "pull" with the magistrate when they are likely to be fined for a civil misdemeanor, or sees what he can do to "fix up matters" with the state's attorney, when the charge is really a serious one.

Lincoln Steffens discovered that many American cities suffered from the conditions Jane describes here. He was a "gentleman reporter" who possessed a strong claim to being called the first muckraker. He certainly caught public attention as no American journalist had before him when he published the articles that became his book *The Shame of the Cities* (1904). The novelty lay in the lengths to which he went to get the sordid facts, his fearlessness in naming names, and his stark conclusion (which had been anticipated by Jane Addams, but never previously published so widely or in such mordant detail) that America's municipal corruption mirrored the nation's social corruption. Steffens wrote biting sentences that were repeated by his readers. "Politics is business. That's what's wrong with it." "The spirit of lawlessness is the American spirit." "The 'foreign element' excuse is one of the hypocritical lies that save us from the clear sight of ourselves." That last sentence might easily have come from the pen of Jane Addams.

A gray-faced woman visited Hull-House one morning and asked that her son be helped out of the city prison, because he was her last support. The alderman had always done it for her, but the boy had been arrested so often that even his patience, the most colossal she had ever known, had given way. One of her boys was in the penitentiary, and one of them in the reform school for a term of years, and if this one, her Benjamin, were sent up she would have no wages forthcoming. The alderman had bailed them out and spoken to the judges many times since they were little fellows. He had begun when her husband was still living, but he had kept on long after she was a widow and when the boys were still too young to vote, which the neighbors all said was "mighty good of him." The mother had no notion of the indifference for law which this course had fostered in her sons; she was only in despair that her long-suffering and powerful friend had at last come to the position when he could no longer serve her and could only give his sympathy. It did not occur to any of those concerned that the sense of justice was thus slowly undermined and lawbreaking encouraged. . . .

Because of simple friendliness, the alderman is expected to pay rent for the hard-pressed tenant when no rent is forthcoming, to find jobs when work is hard to get, to procure and divide among his constituents all the places which he can seize from the city hall. The alderman of the Nineteenth Ward at one time made the proud boast that he had 2,600 people in his ward upon the public payroll. This, of course, included day laborers, but each one felt under distinct obligations to him for getting the job. When we reflect that this is one third of the entire vote of the ward, we realize that it is very important to vote for the right man, since there is, at the least, one chance out of three for a job. If we recollect, further, that the franchise-seeking companies pay respectful heed to the applicants backed by the alderman, the question of voting for the successful man becomes as much an industrial as a political one. An Italian laborer wants a job more than anything else, and quite simply votes for the man who promises him one.

But if the workers placated the alderman because he had so much control over employment, they also liked him for his munificence, and admired him for his style. "Johnny the Pow" knew where to find the money with which to finance handouts on a grand scale, especially at election time. Historian Anne Firor Scott has termed him "literally Johnny-on-the-spot" where his constituents were concerned. Jane Addams goes into some detail regarding this function of the ward boss as a political phenomenon, for she sees him answering a genuine social need, and therefore not to be dislodged except by an alternative performing the same function in a better way:

■ The alderman gives presents at weddings and christenings. He seizes these days of family festivities for making friends. It is easiest to reach people in the holiday mood of expansive goodwill, but on their side it seems natural and kindly that he should do it. The alderman procures passes from the railroads when his constituents wish to visit friends or to attend the funerals of distant relatives; he buys tickets galore for benefit entertainments given for a widow or a consumptive in peculiar distress; he contributes to prizes which are awarded to the handsomest lady or the most popular man. At a church bazaar, for instance, the alderman finds the stage all set for his dramatic performance. When others are spending pennies he is spending dollars. Where anxious relatives are canvassing to secure votes for the two most beautiful children who are being voted upon, he recklessly buys votes from both sides, and laughingly declines to say which one he likes the best, buying off the young lady who is persistently determined to find out, with five dollars for the flower bazaar, the posies, of course, to be sent to the sick of the parish. The moral atmosphere of a bazaar suits him exactly. He murmurs many times, "Never mind; the money all goes to the poor," or "It is all straight enough if the church gets it," or "The poor won't ask too many questions." The oftener he can put sentiments of that sort into the minds of his constituents, the better he is pleased. Nothing so rapidly prepares them to take his view of money-getting and money-spending. . . .

If the alderman seizes upon festivities for expressions of his goodwill, much more does he seize upon periods of sorrow. At a funeral he has the double advantage of ministering to a genuine craving for comfort and solace, and at the same time of assisting at an important social function. That curious feeling of remorse, which is an accompaniment of quick sorrow, that desire to "make up" for past delinquencies, to show the world how much, after all, we loved the person who has just died, is as natural as it is universal. In addition to this, there is among the poor, who have few social occasions, a great desire for a well-arranged funeral, the grade of which almost determines their social standing in the neighborhood. The alderman saves the very poorest of his constituents from that awful horror of burial by the county; he provides carriages for the poor, who otherwise could not have them; for the more prosperous he sends extra carriages, so that they may invite more friends and have a longer procession; for the most prosperous of all there will be probably only a large "flower piece." It may be too much to say that all the relatives and friends who ride in the carriages provided by the alderman's bounty vote for him, but they are certainly influenced by his kindness, and talk of his virtues during the long hours of the ride back and forth from the suburban cemetery. . . .

The alderman of the Nineteenth Ward owns several saloons, one downtown within easy access of the city hall, where he can catch the more important of his friends. Here again he has seized upon an old tradition and primitive custom—the good-fellowship which has long been best expressed when men drink together. The saloons offer a common meeting-ground, with stimulants enough to free the wits and tongues of the men who meet there. Last Christmas, our alderman distributed six tons of turkeys, and four or more tons of ducks and geese; but each luckless biped was handed out either by himself or one of his friends with a "Merry Christmas." Inevitably, some families got three or four apiece, but what

Andrew Carnegie was not a churchgoer—on Sundays he preferred to bob about in his swimming pool "while a Highlander . . . plays sacred music on his pipes." Arriving from Scotland in 1848, virtually penniless and aged twelve, he found a job in Pennsylvania at $1.20 a week, moved steadily on to better ones, and ended by selling his self-developed steel empire for almost half a billion dollars in 1901. He preached a "gospel of wealth," asserting that true charity meant giving "to help those who will help themselves." Unlike many tycoons, however, Carnegie had a social conscience. He sympathized with labor, deplored the accumulation of wealth for selfish reasons, and spent many of his millions on philanthropic enterprises. Sharing Jane Addams' concern about the war clouds gathering over Europe (but with the means to do more about it in a material way than she could), he financed the Peace Palace at The Hague and the Carnegie Endowment for International Peace —only to see with horror, as Jane did, the eruption of war in 1914.

of that? He had none of the nagging rules of the charitable societies, nor was he ready to declare that, because a man wanted two turkeys for Christmas, he was a scoundrel who should never be allowed to eat turkey again.

Of course, there are those who see through the schemes. Some constituents merely suspect, others connive, and still others glory in the fact that they can thus "soak the alderman." The young man who fills his pockets with handfuls of cigars, giving a sly wink at his companions, takes a step downward to the position where he is willing to sell his vote to both parties, and then scratch his ticket as he pleases. Less than a year ago a man in ordinary conversation with the writer complained quite openly, and with no sense of shame, that he had sold his vote for only two dollars this year, and that he was awfully disappointed. The writer happened to know that his income during the nine months previous had been but twenty-eight dollars; that he was in debt thirty-two dollars; and she could well imagine the eagerness with which he had counted upon this source of revenue. The situation revealed once more the difficulty of attaining virtue by those hardest pressed in the industrial struggle; and in the revelation the writer felt the familiar grip that silences us all in the presence of temptations which have never been ours. . . .

Dickensie scene full of
Christmas cheer – and every
thing is going on extra great-
great. One hundred & thirty
turkeys have been sent in.
A barrel of cranberries one
of apples and Mr Warner has
sent a large share of his
store full of groceries – so
that all is going merry
as merry as can be.

In this letter of December 23, 1894, Jane speaks of the "Christmas cheer" at Hull-House. Her handwriting is often hard to decipher, but she mentions that "one hundred and thirty turkeys" had been distributed, that "cranberries" were much in evidence, and that the atmosphere was "merry as merry can be." Christmas had an oldtime jollity when the ladies of the settlement presided over the festivities. The people of the ghetto were lifted out of their drab existences at the big house with its roaring fires, glasses of punch (non-alcoholic), and array of good things to eat. It was a Dickensian scene, often enhanced by passages read aloud from *A Christmas Carol* and *The Pickwick Papers.* But the ladies never forgot the neighbors who could not get to Hull-House because of illness or other circumstances. The residents went to them, bringing food, gifts, and the true spirit of Christmas to many of those who were unable to leave their rooms even at the height of the holiday season.

The question does, of course, occur to many minds, Where does the money come from with which to dramatize so successfully? The more primitive people accept the truthful statement of its sources without any shock to their moral sense. To their simple minds he gets it "from the rich," and so long as he again gives it out to the poor, as a true Robin Hood, with open hand, they have no objections to offer. Their ethics are quite honestly those of the merrymaking foresters. The next less primitive people of the vicinage are quite willing to admit that he leads "the gang" in the city council, and sells out the city franchises; that he makes deals with the franchise-seeking companies; that he guarantees to steer dubious measures through the council, for which he demands liberal pay; that he is, in short, a successful boodler. But when there is intellect enough to get this point of view, there is also enough to make the contention that this is universally done; that all the aldermen do it more or less successfully, but that the alderman of the Nineteenth Ward is unique in being so generous; that such a state of affairs is to be deplored, of course, but that that is the way business is run, and we are fortunate when a kindhearted man who is close to the people gets a large share of the boodle; that he serves these franchised companies who employ men in the building and construction of their enterprises, and that they are bound in return to give jobs to his constituency. It is again the justification of stealing from the rich to give to the poor. Even when they are intelligent enough to complete the circle, and to see that the money comes, not from the pockets of the companies' agents, but from the streetcar fares of people like themselves, it almost seems as if they would rather pay two cents more each time they ride than give up the consciousness that they have a big, warmhearted friend at court who will stand by them in an emergency. The sense of just dealing comes apparently much later than the desire for protection and kindness. On the whole, the gifts and favors are taken quite simply, as an evidence of good and loving kindness, or are accepted as inevitable political measures.

The ward boss reflects the society he rules. Such is the moral at which Jane Addams arrives after a close study of John Powers and his political bastion in the Hull-House area. Therefore, to get rid of him, the community must be raised to so high a level that it will no longer tolerate politicians of his stripe, but will turn his function over to honest men in an administration dedicated to the public welfare. In time, this truth enunciated in her 1898 article came to be a working principle of Chicagoans, and indeed of Americans in general, who curtailed the authority of the "boss" in the public life of the nation.

■ The alderman is really elected because he is a good friend and neighbor. He is corrupt, of course, but he is not elected because he is corrupt, but rather in spite of it. His standard suits his constituents. He exemplifies and exaggerates the popular type of a good man. He has attained what his constituents secretly long for. . . . We must also remember that the imitative impulse plays an important part in life, and that the loss of social estimation, keenly felt by all of us, is perhaps most dreaded by the hum-

John Powers professed that his feelings were hurt by Jane's opposition. "After all," he asked, "aren't we both working to help the immigrants? Shouldn't we be allies?" Jane pointed to a significant difference: He was making a fortune out of the slums, and she wasn't. He said to her: "Miss Addams, if you want any little favor from me, just tell me and I'll see to it." Jane responded politely: "Thank you, Mr. Powers." But she never accepted his offer, which prompted his lament: "I wish just once she'd ask me, and not fight me all the time." His demeanor changed when she challenged him in the 1898 local election. He told the press: "The trouble with Miss Addams is, she is just jealous of my charitable work in the ward." And he predicted: "Hull-House will be driven from the ward." He raised the cry of "petticoat government," and persuaded some respectable Chicagoans to censure Jane for her "unfeminine" activities. The result of this confrontation was a standoff: Powers won the election, but Hull-House remained active and influential. Historian Allen Davis comments: "The picture of Jane Addams as a kindly social worker and gentle pacifist should be altered to include Jane Addams the realistic reformer who battled Johnny Powers in the Nineteenth Ward."

Mrs. Potter Palmer was a socialite with a social conscience. The unquestioned queen of Chicago society, she supported liberal Governor Altgeld, served with the Civic Federation, and frequented Hull-House while community crusades were discussed. Prominent at the Chicago World's Fair of 1893, she kept her temper when a Spanish princess called her "an innkeeper's wife" (the "inn" was the sumptuous Palmer House, built by her husband). On the American committee at the Paris Exposition of 1900, she caused her friend Jane Addams to be appointed a juror. In the anarchist scare following McKinley's assassination, Mrs. Palmer became alienated from Hull-House. But Chicago's grande dame remained devoted to her city, so she and Jane still worked for the same causes. When Potter Palmer died, he left his multimillion-dollar estate to his widow; this provoked Marshall Field, another man of considerable means, to comment: "A million dollars is enough for any woman." However, she proved to be a shrewd manager of her millions, using them wisely for personal, family, and philanthropic enterprises. Chicago still bears the imprint of Mrs. Potter Palmer's generosity in many areas—from medical facilities to old-master paintings.

blest. It is doubtless true that freedom for individual conduct, the power to give only due weight to the opinions of one's neighbors, is one of the latest developments of civilization. A form of constraint, gentle but powerful, is afforded by the simple desire to do what others do, in order to share with them the approval of the community. Of course, the larger the number of people among whom an habitual mode of conduct obtains, the greater the constraint it puts upon the individual will. Thus it is that the great corruption of the city presses most heavily where it can least be resisted and is most likely to be imitated. . . .

This lowering of standards, this setting of an ideal, is perhaps the worst of the situation, for daily by our actions and decisions we not only determine ideals for ourselves, but largely for each other. We are all involved in this political corruption, and as members of the community stand indicted. This is the penalty of a democracy—that we are bound to move forward or retrograde together. None of us can stand aside, for our feet are mired in the same soil, and our lungs breathe the same air.

During a campaign a year and a half ago, when a reform league put up a candidate against our corrupt alderman, and when Hull-House worked hard to rally the moral sentiment of the ward in favor of the new man, we encountered another and unexpected difficulty. Finding that it was hard to secure enough local speakers of the moral tone which we desired, we imported orators from other parts of the town, from the "better element," so to speak. Suddenly we heard it rumored on all sides that, while the money and speakers for the reform candidate were coming from the swells, the money which was backing our corrupt alderman also came from a swell source; it was rumored that the president of a streetcar combination, for whom he performed constant offices in the city council, was ready to back him to the extent of fifty thousand dollars; that he, too, was a good man, and sat in high places; that he had recently given a large sum of money to an educational institution, and was therefore as philanthropic, not to say good and upright, as any man in town; that our alderman had the sanction of the highest authorities, and that the lecturers who were talking against corruption, and the selling and buying of franchises, were only the cranks, and not the solid businessmen who had developed and built up Chicago.

All parts of the community are bound together in ethical development. If the so-called more enlightened members of the community accept public gifts from the man who buys up the council, and the so-called less enlightened members accept individual gifts from the man who sells out the council, we surely must take our punishment together. There is the difference, of course, that in the first case we act collectively, and in the second case individually; but is the punishment of cynicism which follows the first any lighter or less far-reaching in its consequences than the arousing of this imitative impulse which follows the second? . . .

If we would hold to our political democracy, some pains must be taken to keep on common ground in our human experiences, and to some solidarity in our ethical conceptions. Just because, in America, we have a wide difference in our traditions, customs, religion, and language, must we cherish our moral awakenings, our mutual compunctions, and strivings for better things. A strenuous moral appeal meets with a much surer response than one based upon prejudice or patriotism. Kinship of a common moral nature is the last and most comprehensive of all bases of union. The meaning of life is, after all, to search out and then to conform our activities to our new knowledge. And if we discover that men of low ideals and corrupt practice are forming popular political standards simply because such men stand by and for and with the people, then nothing remains but to obtain a like sense of identification before we can hope to modify ethical standards.

Jane Addams was considered Chicago's leading citizen, while Julius Rosenwald (above) was ranked second by many observers. He made a fortune as head of Sears, Roebuck, and devoted most of it to philanthropies such as the Chicago Museum of Science and Industry and his Rosenwald Fund "for the well-being of mankind." His work for the betterment of the city brought him into close contact with Hull-House, and he served as a trustee for many years. His admiration for Jane Addams was so great that he told his wife: "One feels that it is a benediction to have her in one's home." He thought she was wrong to join the Progressive campaign in 1912, but later wrote her: "I have no hesitancy in admitting now that I believe that you acted wisely, and that I was mistaken." With this letter he enclosed a check for $50,000 for Hull-House—generosity characteristic of him, for he sent both a congratulatory note and a $10,000 check on her seventieth birthday. His biographer has written: "Rosenwald valued . . . the important efforts of Miss Addams and her associates. He was one of [the] business men to whom [she] referred in *Twenty Years at Hull-House* as those 'to whom the practical world of affairs seems so supremely rational.' "

AN ELEGY FOR A DEAD CHILD

Fortunately for Chicago, there were better people in the city than ward bosses like John Powers. None ranked higher in the estimation of Jane Addams than the Dewey family—philosopher John Dewey, his wife Alice, and their five children. Virtual neighbors since Dewey taught at the University of Chicago while Jane was directing Hull-House, they became such fast friends that he named a daughter after her. Dewey resigned from Chicago in 1904 to go to Columbia University. It was at this time that he lost his promising son Gordon; Hull-House held a memorial service for him, with Jane Addams delivering an elegy marked by philosophical musing on the meaning of death in so pathetic a case. This address, excerpted here, forms a moving chapter of her book The Excellent Becomes the Permanent:

■ When he who has gone from our familiar living is a little child, who has surrounded us with that affection which Mr. Dewey has himself described as "the most appealing and most rewarding of all affections," almost as hard to endure as the immediate loss itself is the realization that his future will exist without relation to ourselves, that his growth will go forward without our fostering and defense, without the fulfilling of all those hopes which fasten themselves so securely upon a child of unusual ability and suggestive charm.

And yet in a distinct and sturdy personality, such as Gordon Dewey possessed, which had already unfolded itself for eight years in the midst of exceptional surroundings for feeding its nascent powers and for supplying the equipment with which to reproduce that which the active, persistent mind most vividly apprehended, we have in our own hands a key, an artifice, as it were, by which we may read his future. We cannot read it absolutely as though it were written in a book—life as it is lived on the earth does not unfold itself in that way—but we may read it in a very remarkable degree by our perceptions, by our knowledge of what his personality implied and was destined to achieve. . . .

He possessed in a remarkable measure that trait which we are accustomed to associate only with the mature mind of wide and tolerant experi-

John Dewey (1859–1952) had the longest career of any American philosopher. A Vermont Yankee, he went from Johns Hopkins into university teaching, and ranked in fame and influence with Britain's Bertrand Russell. Dewey was called "the most American of philosophers" because of his commitment to pragmatism, experimentalism, and the democratic process. Like the early pioneers, he refused to be bound by traditional usages that hindered progress. During his years in Chicago, he ran the "Dewey School"—often accused of being too permissive with its pupils, but much admired by Jane Addams. Like her, Dewey supported Theodore Roosevelt in 1912 and La Follette in 1924, but despite his appreciation of her pacifist thought, he disagreed with her about America's entry into World War I. His opposition to Communism became even more stringent than hers when he investigated the Moscow purge trials and concluded that Stalin had framed Trotsky. One of his daughters wrote that Dewey's faith in his principles took on "a sharper and deeper meaning because of Hull-House and Jane Addams."

ence, a sense of the humor in life and the ability to meet a situation by a flank movement, as it were, by giving it the unexpected turn, pulling out the sting from any childish disappointment by a perception of the gentle incongruity and the ironic charm in the disappointment itself. This can only be illustrated; I remember my astonishment when I first encountered it in the little red-frocked baby of three. His mother had bidden him show me a Christmas book, and he had trotted down the hall in search of "Father Goose," only to come gleefully back again without the book, but holding a tiny white feather in his hand, as he chuckled: "I couldn't find Fazzer Goose, but I found a goose fezzer in the hall." The independence of mind with which he ventured the little joke, the complete sense of comradeship with which he took me into it and gave me at once to understand that although we might differ in our tastes for books there could be but one right way to turning an awkward situation into a pleasure, secured for me from that moment a new and intimate friend.

Our minds are all filled with reminiscences of him. One pictures the grave little figure as he shakes hands through the car window with Admiral Dewey, restraining his boundless enthusiasm with a quaint sense of the dignity which is befitting one who bears the same great name. When asked what he said to his hero, he replied: "I couldn't say much because I am a Dewey, too." [There was a distant relationship.]

When John Dewey reached his seventieth birthday on October 20, 1929, he was universally regarded as America's foremost living philosopher. Two thousand of his students and friends came to New York to pay their respects, Jane Addams among them, and she offered "A Toast to John Dewey," the eloquence of which has not been lost because The Survey *published her remarks that November.*

■ John Dewey was a member of the first board of Hull-House trustees. It consisted of two or three businessmen, two or three philanthropic women, and the philosopher, to keep us from becoming either hardboiled or sentimental in this new undertaking, which the English somewhat heavily called "residential study of the problems of poverty." Unlike many trustees, he actually worked on the job: he took Julia Lathrop's Plato Club for a series of Sunday afternoons one midwinter, some days so stormy that only the "cranks" came. The Plato Club was an epitome of all discussions held on social questions in the nineties. You propounded your theory and stuck to it through thick and thin, and no compromise was permitted! You either believed in heredity or you believed in environment, and the very high schools debated the question with the same fervor brought to bear upon the problem of the priority of the chick or the egg. It was therefore most significant when John Dewey, who came to the new University of Chicago in 1894, announced the theory, or rather when the theory slowly leaked out, of an ever changing society in constant need of exploration and rediscovery; but stranger still was his ultimate test of the utility of any social scheme. Even Mr. Dooley said to Mr. Hennessy in the

Chicago *Tribune* itself, "The question is, Hennessy, does it work? The jawing isn't worth a tinker's dam."

It was still more useful then, when John Dewey began a little practice school which he established near the University of Chicago, and demonstrated among other things the interaction between the individual and his environment. He studied the response of each child, not to a static environment but to various surroundings largely produced by the child himself. An historic period having made itself at home in the child's imagination, he energetically dug, built, wove, and cooked according to his needs, in a primitive hut or a moated castle. John Dewey's little yellow-covered book, *School and Society,* made so clear the necessity for individualizing each child that it is quite fair, I think, to say that his insistence upon an atmosphere of freedom and confidence between the teacher and pupil, of a common interest in the life they led together, profoundly affected all similar relationships, certainly those between the social worker and his client. We were used to saying that the welfare of the community is a mutual responsibility, but John Dewey told us that the general intelligence is dormant, with its communications broken and faint, until it possesses the public as its medium.

He, who had so highly individualized the children in his school as to drive their parents into alarmed protest, warned us not to make exceptions of ourselves in regard to the experiences of life. But as he had socialized the children by giving them an almost empirical consciousness of the race life, so he individualized us by the corollary that the dear public itself—for which we were so much concerned—comes into existence through the extension of the acts of individuals beyond those personally involved.

Perhaps the entire psychological approach to the problems of social welfare was implicit in the situation when that group of brilliant men formed the Department of Philosophy at the new University of Chicago. . . . Perhaps we may trace back to this group of men the movement now culminating in the brand new psychiatric social worker and in the institutes of juvenile research. It began, in Chicago at least, when a student of John Dewey's was put in charge of the Child Study Department in the public schools. It was largely the prestige of Dr. Dewey himself which enabled the department to come into existence, and perhaps it is not a mere coincidence that it was Chicago that founded the first psychopathic clinic attached to its Juvenile Court, which in its turn had been the pioneer ten years earlier, because children were entitled to a court adapted to their own needs. We are impatient for the time when such a treatment may be extended to the adult criminal. At the moment the data supplied by the psychologists is often left on the hands of the embarrassed judge as extralegal material; he cannot permit it to affect the judicial decision, although it may be convincing enough to weigh heavily upon his conscience.

Whatever may be the outcome of these newer experiments, many of John Dewey's contemporaries are certain of one thing: that the problems of social welfare in our own time have never been so squarely faced as by the philosopher who deliberately made the study of men and their intelli-

Edward F. Dunne rose in Chicago politics with backing from the reformers. Irish by descent, he had studied at Trinity College, Dublin, and served as a circuit judge of Cook County. He failed in his attempted reforms as mayor of Chicago (1905–1907) because he was, in the words of one historian, "a fine man . . . but he surrounded himself with starry-eyed idealists like himself." Jane Addams, his appointee to the school board, blamed the educational fiasco of this administration on the lack of a "concerted policy of any kind." Yet she and Dunne admired one another, and she viewed his defeat with regret. Dunne proved more successful as governor of Illinois (1913–1917); he was responsible for better roads, factory regulations, and food laws—and for partial woman suffrage in the state.

gences a foundation for the study of the problems with which men have to deal. In those years when we were told by the scientists, or at least by the so-called scientists, that the world was in the grasp of subhuman forces against which it was absurd to oppose the human will, John Dewey calmly stated that the proper home of intelligence was the world itself and that the true function of intelligence was to act as critic and regulator of the forces which move the world. . . .

Although Dr. Dewey is not easy to read nor, in the Chautauqua sense, a popular lecturer, through the conscious use of his luminous mind he has almost made over the connotations on the very word philosopher for thousands of people. This has been the result of his deliberate convictions. May we quote his own words which one of his students has placed on the title page of his last book: "Better it is for philosophy to err in active participation in the living struggles and issues of its own age and times, than to maintain an immune monastic impeccability. To try to escape from the snares and pitfalls of time by recourse to traditional problems and interests—rather than that, let the dead bury their own dead." It is such winged words as these which have endeared John Dewey to those who live in settlements or undertake other lines of social welfare.

I remember during certain strenuous days in Chicago when we were under cross fire in a bewildering situation of a strike turned into a lockout, that I thought with primitive green envy of university professors on the other side of town secure from the bludgeonings of both trade unionists and capitalists. But at least one of these professors promptly entered the industrial arena. It was part of his lifelong effort to embody truth in conduct. He has qualified for a preeminent position among all those committed to the long struggle for social betterment. It is a toast rather than a topic—John Dewey and Social Welfare!

GIVING AND RECEIVING

"Of the various struggles which a decade of residence in a settlement implies," Jane Addams wrote, "none have made a more definite impression on my mind than the incredibly painful difficulties which involve both giver and recipient when one person asks charitable aid of another." This theme is elaborated in her Atlantic Monthly *article of February 1899, "The Subtle Problems of Charity," which formed the basis for a central chapter of her first book,* Democracy and Social Ethics *(1902). Jane put the following passage into her article: "For most of the years during a decade of residence . . . my mind was sore and depressed over the difficulties of the charitable relationship. The incessant clashing of ethical standards, which had been honestly gained from widely varying industrial experience—the misunderstandings inevitable between people whose conventions and mode of life had been so totally unlike—made it seem reasonable to say that nothing could be done until industrial conditions were made absolutely democratic. . . . Recently, however, there has come to my mind the suggestion of a principle, that while the painful condition*

of administering charity is the inevitable discomfort of a transition into a more democratic relation, the perplexing experiences of the actual administration have a genuine value of their own. . . . The social reformers who avoid the charitable relationship with any of their fellowmen take a certain outside attitude toward this movement. . . . The doctrinaire . . . avoids the perplexity, and at the same time loses the vitality."

Jane frequently toned down her thought between her articles and her books, and the above passage does not appear in Democracy and Social Ethics*— another good reason for going back to the magazine piece excerpted below to see how strongly she felt when she first broached the subject:*

■ Let us take a neighborhood of poor people, and test their ethical standards by those of the charity visitor, who comes with the best desire in the world to help them out of their distresses. A most striking incongruity, at once apparent, is the difference between the emotional kindness with which relief is given by one poor neighbor to another poor neighbor, and the guarded care with which relief is given by a charity visitor to a charity recipient. The neighborhood mind is immediately confronted not only by the difference of method, but also by an absolute clashing of two ethical standards.

A very little familiarity with the poor districts of any city is sufficient to show how primitive and frontierlike are the neighborly relations. There is the greatest willingness to lend or borrow anything, and each resident of a

The woman solicitously applying a surgical dressing to an elderly Negro patient in the scene below was a member of Chicago's Visiting Nurse Association—an organization that existed, in the words of Jane Addams, "for the care of the sick poor in their own homes." This need was one of the first Jane noticed in making her rounds of the Nineteenth Ward. In New York, it led Lillian Wald to establish the Henry Street Settlement, devoted to public nursing (see page 200). The visiting nurse was, for many slum dwellers, their only contact with the medical profession. For some, her arrival meant, quite literally, the difference between life and death.

given tenement house knows the most intimate family affairs of all the others. The fact that the economic condition of all alike is on a most precarious level makes the ready outflow of sympathy and material assistance the most natural thing in the world. There are numberless instances of heroic self-sacrifice quite unknown in the circles where greater economic advantages make that kind of intimate knowledge of one's neighbors impossible. An Irish family, in which the man has lost his place, and the woman is struggling to eke out the scanty savings by daywork, will take in a widow and her five children who have been turned into the street, without a moment's reflection upon the physical discomforts involved. . . .

Another woman, whose husband was sent up to the city prison for the maximum term, just three months before the birth of her child, having gradually sold her supply of household furniture, found herself penniless. She sought refuge with a friend whom she supposed to be living in three rooms in another part of the town. When she arrived, however, she discovered that her friend's husband had been out of work so long that they had been reduced to living in one room. The friend at once took her in, and the friend's husband was obliged to sleep upon a bench in the park every night for a week, which he did uncomplainingly, if not cheerfully. Fortunately it was summer, "and it only rained one night." The writer could not discover from the young mother that she had any special claim upon the "friend" beyond the fact that they had formerly worked together in the same factory. The husband she had never seen until the night of her arrival, when he at once went forth in search of a midwife who would consent to come upon his promise of future payment.

The evolutionists tell us that the instinct to pity, the impulse to aid his fellows, served man at a very early period as a rude rule of right and wrong. There is no doubt that this rude rule still holds among many people with whom charitable agencies are brought into contact, and that their ideas of right and wrong are quite honestly outraged by the methods of these agencies. When they see the delay and caution with which relief is given, these do not appear to them conscientious scruples, but the cold and calculating action of the selfish man. This is not the aid that they are accustomed to receive from their neighbors, and they do not understand why the impulse which drives people to be good to the poor should be so severely supervised. . . . They cannot comprehend why a person whose intellectual perceptions are stronger than his natural impulses should go into charity work at all. The only man they are accustomed to see whose intellectual perceptions are stronger than his tenderness of heart is the selfish and avaricious man, who is frankly "on the make." If the charity visitor is such a person, why does she pretend to like the poor? . . . In moments of indignation they have been known to say, "What do you want, anyway? If you have nothing to give us, why not let us alone, and stop your questionings and investigations?"

Infant welfare quickly became a separate and vital branch of public health. Peasants from European farm areas, especially, were baffled by the complex, impersonal American urban environment, where milk for the baby was not merely a matter of rounding up the cow in the pasture. They required professional advice from the women of Infant Welfare, such as the young lady in the picture above. Hull-House worked closely with the Infant Welfare Society to raise health standards. In 1910 there were 122 deaths per 1,000 live births in Chicago. In 1911 the Infant Welfare Society was formed, and the death rate for babies under the care of the IWS promptly dropped to 42 per 1,000. (Five decades later, the death rate for babies served by Chicago's IWS had dropped down to only 2.3 per 1,000.)

The poor, understandably, do not simply accept humanitarian assistance as something to be thankful for. They tend to regard the welfare worker as personally an intruder, and also as the representative of an impersonal system devoid of human feelings.

■ Doubtless we all find something distasteful in the juxtaposition of the two words "organized" and "charity." The idea of organizing an emotion is in itself repelling, even to those of us who feel most sorely the need of more order in altruistic effort and see the end to be desired. We say in defense that we are striving to turn this emotion into a motive: that pity is capricious, and not to be depended on; that we mean to give it the dignity of conscious duty. But at bottom we distrust a little a scheme which substitutes a theory of social conduct for the natural promptings of the heart, and we ourselves feel the complexity of the situation. The poor man who has fallen into distress, when he first asks aid, instinctively expects tenderness, consideration, and forgiveness. If it is the first time, it has taken him long to make up his mind to the step. He comes somewhat bruised and battered, and instead of being met by warmth of heart and sympathy he is at once chilled by an investigation and an intimation that he ought to work. He does not see that he is being dealt with as a child of defective will is cared for by a stern parent. There have been no years of previous intercourse and established relation, as between parents and children. He feels only the postponement or refusal, which he considers harsh. He does not "live to thank his parents for it," as the disciplined child is reported to do, but cherishes a hardness of heart to his grave. The only really popular charity is that of visiting nurses, who carry about with them a professional training, which may easily be interpreted into sympathy and kindness, in their ministration to obvious needs without investigation. . . .

The most serious effect upon the individual comes when dependence upon the charitable society is substituted for the natural outgoing of human love and sympathy, which, happily, we all possess in some degree. . . . If a poor woman knows that her neighbor next door has no shoes, she is quite willing to lend her own, that her neighbor may go decently to mass or to work; for she knows the smallest item about the scanty wardrobe, and cheerfully helps out. When the charity visitor comes in, all the neighbors are baffled as to what her circumstances may be. They know she does not need a new pair of shoes, and rather suspect that she has a dozen pairs at home, which indeed she sometimes has. They imagine untold stores which they may call upon, and her most generous gift is considered niggardly, compared with what she might do. She ought to get new shoes for the family all round; "she sees well enough that they need them." It is no more than the neighbor herself would do. . . .

The subject of clothes, indeed, perplexes the visitor constantly, and the result of her reflections may be summed up something in this wise: The girl who has a definite social standing, who has been to a fashionable school or to a college, whose family live in a house seen and known by all her friends and associates, can afford to be very simple or even shabby as to her clothes, if she likes. But the working girl, whose family lives in a tenement or moves from one small apartment to another, who has little social standing, and has to make her own place, knows full well how much habit and style of dress have to do with her position. Her income goes into her clothing out of all proportion to that which she spends upon other things. But if social advancement is her aim, it is the most sensible thing which she can do. She is judged largely by her clothes. Her house furnishing with its pitiful little decorations, her scanty supply of books, are never seen by the people whose social opinions she most values. Her clothes are her background, and from them she is largely judged. It is due to this fact that girls' clubs succeed best in the business part of a town, where "working girls" and "young ladies" meet upon an equal footing, and where the clothes superficially look very much alike. Bright and ambitious girls will come to these downtown clubs to eat lunch and rest at noon, to study all sorts of subjects and listen to lectures, when they might hesitate a long time about joining a club identified with their own neighborhood, where they would be judged not solely on their personal merits and the unconscious social standing afforded to good clothes, but by other surroundings which are not nearly up to these. . . . Have we worked out our democracy in regard to clothes farther than in regard to anything else? . . .

The charity visitor is still more perplexed when she comes to consider such problems as those of early marriage and child labor; for she cannot deal with them according to economic theories, or according to the conventions which have regulated her own life. She finds both of these fairly upset by her intimate knowledge of the situation, and her sympathy for those into whose lives she has gained a curious insight. She discovers how incorrigibly bourgeois her standards have been, and it takes but a little time to reach the conclusion that she cannot insist so strenuously upon

I am sorry for I would have
grateful for the opportunity
to serve the Philippine
Independence Committee
and hope that you will give
me another chance.
Faithfully yours
Jane Addams

An anti-imperialist during the Spanish-American War, Jane Addams soon thereafter joined those who demanded freedom for the Philippine Islands. She wrote this letter on April 30, 1904, to Edward Ordway of the Philippine Independence Committee, explaining in the first part (not reproduced here) that his appeal for her services arrived while she was away from Chicago. She then goes into this passage, expressing her regret that they missed connections the first time, and declaring her "hope that you will give me another chance." Despite the efforts of Jane and the Committee, the Philippine Republic did not attain full independence until 1946, more than a decade after her death.

the conventions of her own class, which fail to fit the bigger, more emotional, and freer lives of working people. The charity visitor holds well-grounded views upon the imprudence of early marriages; quite naturally, because she comes from a family and circle of professional and business people. A professional man is scarcely equipped and started in his profession before he is thirty; a businessman, if he is on the road to success, is much nearer prosperity at thirty-five than at twenty-five. . . . But this does not apply to the workingman. In many trades he is laid upon the shelf at thirty-five, and in nearly all trades he receives the largest wages of his life between twenty and thirty. . . . He naturally regards his children as his savings bank; he expects them to care for him when he gets old, and in some trades old age comes very early. A Jewish tailor was quite lately sent to the Cook County poorhouse, paralyzed beyond recovery at the age of thirty-five. Had his little boy of nine been a few years older, the father might have been spared this sorrow of public charity. He was, in fact, better able to support a family when he was twenty than when he was thirty-five, for his wages had steadily become less as the years went on. Another tailor whom I know, a Socialist, always speaks of saving as a bourgeois virtue, one quite impossible to the genuine workingman. He supports a family, consisting of himself, a wife and three children, and his parents, on eight dollars a week. He insists that it would be criminal not to expend every penny of this amount upon food and shelter, and he expects his children later to take care of him.

In her 1899 article Jane found one of the more "subtle problems of charity" in the slum dwellers' habit of spending their welfare money on trivialities and luxuries. She realized, as many social workers did not, that such improvidence could be considered useful to the community, for example, when it kept youngsters out of mischief by providing them with legitimate pleasures. This was another case of her opposing condemnation of a social ill until a better means of doing the same thing could be introduced:

■ There are an impressive number of children who uncomplainingly hand over their weekly wages to their parents, sometimes receiving back ten cents or a quarter for spending money, but quite as often nothing at all; and the writer knows one daughter of twenty-five who for six years has received two cents a week from the . . . wages which she earns in a large factory. Is it habit or virtue which holds her steady in this course? If love and tenderness had been substituted for parental despotism, would the mother have had enough affection, enough power of expression, to hold her daughter's sense of money obligation through all these years? This young woman, who spends her paltry two cents on chewing gum, and goes plainly clad in clothes of her mother's choosing, while many of her friends spend their entire wages on clothes which factory girls love so well, must be held by some powerful force. . . .

The first impulse of our charity visitor is to be somewhat severe with her shiftless family for spending money on pleasures and indulging their

John Peter Altgeld was a liberal Democrat who denounced conservative Democrat Grover Cleveland's intervention in the Pullman strike: "As Governor of the State of Illinois, I protest . . . and ask the immediate withdrawal of the Federal troops from active duty in this State." The President refused, and Altgeld himself was attacked by businessmen who resented his unwillingness to support their interests. His enemies called him a "dastardly anarchist" for pardoning the men jailed after the Haymarket riot. One newspaper, referring to his German birth, termed him "a sausage-maker from Württemberg" and a "foreign adventurer." He was accused of encouraging immigrants, especially those with radical ideas, to the detriment of American institutions. Demands for his impeachment failed, but the controversy contributed to his defeat in 1896, when he supported Bryan and free silver. Altgeld's death in 1902 brought an outpouring of sentiment from a legion of admirers who agreed with Jane Addams that he belonged to the authentic American tradition. Vachel Lindsay put the sentiment into memorable verse: "Sleep softly, eagle forgotten, under the stone/ Time has its way with you there, and the clay has its own/ Sleep on, O brave-hearted, O wise man, that kindled the flame/ To live in mankind is far more than to live in a name."

children out of all proportion to their means. The poor family which receives beans and coal from the county, and pays for a bicycle on the installment plan, is not unknown to any of us. But as the growth of juvenile crime becomes gradually understood, and as the danger of giving no legitimate and organized pleasure to the child becomes clearer, we remember that primitive man had games long before he cared for a house or for regular meals. There are certain boys in many city neighborhoods who form themselves into little gangs with leaders somewhat more intrepid than the rest. . . . They have the excitement of knowing that they may be seen and caught by the "coppers," and at times they are quite breathless with suspense. In motive and execution it is not the least unlike the practice of country boys who go forth in squads to set traps for rabbits or to round up a coon. It is characterized by a pure spirit of adventure, and the vicious training really begins when they are arrested, or when an older boy undertakes to guide them into further excitements. From the very beginning the most enticing and exciting experiences which they have seen have been connected with crime. The policeman embodies all the majesty of successful law and established government in his brass buttons and dazzlingly equipped patrol wagon. The boy who has been arrested comes back more or less a hero, with a tale to tell of the interior recesses of the mysterious police station. The earliest public excitement the child remembers is divided between the rattling fire engines, "the time there was a fire in the next block," and the patrol wagon "the time the drunkest lady in our street was arrested." In the first year of their settlement the Hull-House residents took fifty kindergarten children to Lincoln Park, only to be grieved by their apathetic interest in trees and flowers. On the return an omnibusful of tired and sleepy children were galvanized into sudden life because a patrol wagon rattled by. Eager little heads popped out of the windows full of questioning. "Was it a man or a woman?" "How many policemen inside?" and eager little tongues began to tell experiences of arrests which baby eyes had witnessed.

The excitement of a chase, the chances of competition, and the love of a fight are all centered in the outward display of crime. The parent who receives charitable aid, and yet provides pleasures for his child and is willing to indulge him in his play, is blindly doing one of the wisest things possible; and no one is more eager for playgrounds and vacation schools than the charity visitor whose experience has brought her to this point of view.

Although Jane expressed herself best in prose, she occasionally resorted to verse as a means of conveying her sentiments on some subject close to her heart. In April 1905 she published the following stanzas on Hull-House:

A house stands on a busy street,
Its doors are opened wide,
To all who come it bids 'Good Cheer,'
To some it says: 'Abide.'

Gathered within its friendly walls
A club of women find
The joys of glad companionship,
Contentment for the mind.

For they have learned what all must learn,
That in life's hardest storm
The shelter we together build
Is all that keeps us warm;
That fellowship is heaven-sent,
That it alone can free
The human heart from bitterness,
And give it liberty.

Some hours they spend in quiet mood,
On poet's wings up-borne,
They lose themselves in other's joys
Or weep with those who mourn.
Some hours by traveled mem'ry led
To foreign lands they roam;
Some hours they bide beside the hearth
And talk of things of home.

Some hours they sit 'neath music's spell,
And when the air is rife
With all the magic of sweet sound,
It heals the pang of life.
Some hours they dream with civic pride
Of cities that shall be,
Within whose streets each citizen,
Shall live life worthily.

Some hours they sew with tender thought,
To keep one mem'ry green;
They talk of those whose lives are hard,
Who suffer wrongs unseen.
They ever open wide their hearts
To all who are oppressed,
And in life's strange perplexities
They strive for what is best.

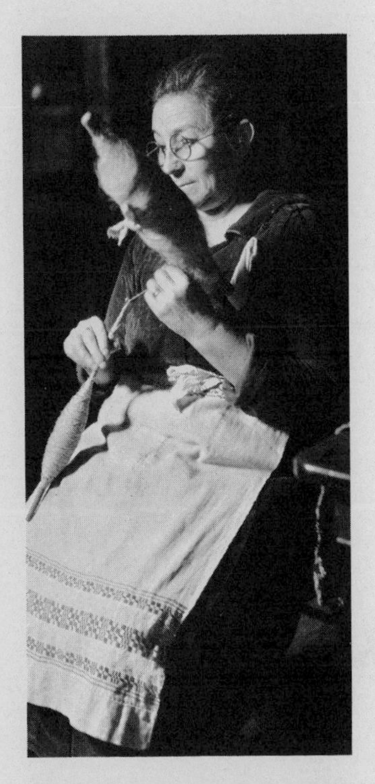

This woman spinning in the Hull-House Labor Museum recalls Jane's memoirs, where she says the museum "was first suggested to my mind when I saw an old Italian woman. . . . I was walking down Polk Street, perturbed in spirit, because it seemed so difficult to come into genuine relations with the Italian women and because they themselves so often lost their hold upon their Americanized children. . . . Suddenly I looked up and saw the old woman with her distaff. . . . She might have served as a model for one of Michelangelo's Fates, but her face brightened as I passed and . . . she called out that when she had spun a little more yarn, she would knit a pair of stockings for her goddaughter. The occupation of the old woman gave me the clue that was needed. Could we not interest the young people . . . in these older forms of industry, so that, through their own parents and grandparents, they would . . . lay a foundation for reverence of the past which Goethe declares to be the basis of all sound progress. . . . Within a month a room was fitted up to which we might invite those of our neighbors who were possessed of old crafts." By this and other means (see page 100), Hull-House vitally enhanced appreciation of the dignity of labor.

HER POLITICAL ROLE

By joining the Progressive party in 1912, Jane Addams played the most direct political role of her life. She would have been attracted by the party's social welfare principles in any case, but her allegiance was strengthened when she was requested, first to help write the platform, and then to deliver the seconding speech, at the Progressive nominating convention. Her heartfelt tribute to Theodore Roosevelt received a thundering ovation from the delegates, and was read into the Congressional Record:

■ I rise to second the nomination, stirred by the splendid platform adopted by this convention. Measures of industrial amelioration, demands for social justice, long discussed by small groups in charity conferences and economic associations, have here been considered in a great national convention and are at last thrust into the stern arena of political action. A great party has pledged itself to the protection of children, to the care of the aged, to the relief of overworked girls, to the safeguarding of burdened men. Committed to these humane undertakings, it is inevitable that such a party should appeal to women, should seek to draw upon the great reservoir of their moral energy so long undesired and unutilized in practical politics—one the corollary of the other; a program of human welfare, the necessity for women's participation.

We ratify this platform not only because it represents our earnest convictions and formulates our high hopes, but because it pulls upon our faculties and calls us to definite action. We find it a prophecy that democracy shall not be actually realized until no group of our people—certainly not ten million so sadly in need of reassurance—shall fail to bear the responsibilities of self-government and that no class of evils shall lie beyond redress. The new party has become the American exponent of a worldwide movement toward juster social conditions, a movement which the United States, lagging behind other great nations, has been unaccountably slow to embody in political action. I second the nomination of Theodore Roosevelt because he is one of the few men in our public life who has been re-

Jane Addams and Theodore Roosevelt, here speaking from the rear of a train in Tennessee, got along famously during the Progressive campaign of 1912. Even their differences were good-humored. "Peace," Jane wrote, "was forever a bone of contention between us, although the discussions were never acrimonious and sometimes hilarious, for he loved to remind me that it was he who had received the Nobel Peace Prize and that he had therefore been internationally recognized as the American authority on the subject." This anecdote refers to Roosevelt's success in mediating the Russo-Japanese War in 1905, while he was President. T.R. did not live to see Jane join him in the select list of Nobel laureates nineteen years after their badinage of 1912.

sponsive to the social appeal and who has caught the significance of the modern movement. Because of that, because the program will require a leader of invincible courage, of open mind, of democratic sympathies, one endowed with power to interpret the common man and to identify himself with the common lot, I heartily second the nomination.

While the Progressive party appeared committed to equality, some powerful members were making the customary exception of the period, and ruling out racial equality. As soon as she realized this, Jane Addams registered a strong protest, but she remained loyal to the party because it "had at least taken the color question away from sectionalism and put in a national setting which might clear the way for a larger perspective." She explained her position in "The Progressive Party and the Negro," which was published as a magazine article in The Crisis *in 1912:*

■ At the Progressive convention held in Chicago last August, disquieting rumors arose concerning the Negro delegates. It was stated that although two groups from Florida, one of colored men and one of white, had been excluded because of a doubt as to which had been authorized to elect delegates, the colored men only from Mississippi had been excluded; and that this was done in spite of the fact that the word "white" had been inserted in the call for the State convention which elected the accredited delegates. It did not seem sufficient to many of us that the credentials committee in seating the Mississippi delegation had merely protested against the use of the word "white," and some of us at once took alarm on behalf of the colored men.

With several others, who were also members of the National Association for the Advancement of Colored People, I appeared before the resolutions committee to point out the inconsistency of pledging relief to the overburdened workingman while leaving the colored man to struggle unaided with his difficult situation, if, indeed, the action of the credentials committee had not given him a setback. . . .

When I asked myself most searchingly whether my Abolitionist father would have remained in any political convention in which colored men had been treated slightingly, I recalled an incident of my girlhood which was illuminating and somewhat comforting. I had given my father an explanation of a stupid decision whereby I had succeeded in bungling the plans of a large family party, and I ended my apology with the honest statement that I had tried to act upon what I thought his judgment would have been. His expression of amused bewilderment changed to one of understanding as he replied: "That probably accounts for your confusion of mind. You fell into the easy mistake of substituting loyalty and dependence upon another's judgment for the very best use of your own faculties. I should be sorry to think that you were always going to complicate moral situations, already sufficiently difficult, by trying to work out another's point of view. You will do much better if you look the situation fairly in the face with the best light you have."

After seeing the play *Justice* at Hull-House, Theodore Roosevelt became a hearty admirer of playwright John Galsworthy (above), who, on his arrival in Chicago in 1912, seemed the quintessential Englishman: a graduate of Oxford who affected a monocle and was reserved in manner and speech. As one of Britain's foremost writers, he was lionized on his visit with an American exuberance he dreaded, and his wife, understanding his social limitations, hovered at his elbow so that she could intervene whenever the conversation began to drag. Jane Addams invited him to Hull-House, where he saw and applauded a performance of *Justice*. Jane's nephew and biographer, James Weber Linn, a professor of English literature at the University of Chicago, had been telling his students that Galsworthy was no pessimist, "and what the hell difference if he is?" Galsworthy himself answered in more genteel terms: "I am distressed to hear that any reader of my books thinks me a pessimist. Really, I'm not." He left that verdict with Chicagoans, returned to London, wrote many notable plays dealing with social problems, and finished his realistic masterpiece—a trilogy collectively titled *The Forsyte Saga*. He was awarded the Nobel Prize in Literature in 1932.

William James (1842–1910) belonged to one of America's most remarkable families. He was the son of Henry James, Sr., a metaphysician, mystic, writer, and friend of Carlyle; he was the brother of Henry James, one of the ranking masters in world literature; he was himself both the most influential and the most eminent American philosopher and psychologist of his era. He declared that he had learned more from relatives and from traveling than he ever had from teachers, who tended to treat their students "as so many small slices cut from the loaf of life" on which "to dab the butter of arithmetic and spelling." It has been said: "Henry James wrote fiction like psychology, and William James wrote psychology like fiction." But, unlike the Anglicized Henry, William remained unmistakably American—optimistic, progressive, experimental, pragmatic. In fact, William developed a philosophical system of pragmatism, and also insisted: "The community stagnates without the impulse of the individual. The impulse dies away without the sympathy of the community." His pragmatism emphasized the finding of usable truths and the avoidance of those abstract problems that could never be solved by anything that could be learned from actual human experience. He emphasized free will, personal responsibility, and the reality of religious experience. No wonder Jane Addams, also unmistakably American and pragmatic, found a close friend and kindred spirit in William James.

Certainly the Abolitionists followed the best light they had, although it differed from that possessed by the framers of the Constitution, whose light had also come from the eighteenth-century doctrines of natural rights and of abstract principles, when ideas were pressed up to their remotest logical issues, without much reference to the conditions to which they were applied. Shall we be less fearless than they to follow our own moral ideals formed under the influence of new knowledge, even although the notion of evolution has entered into social history and politics, and although "abstract" in the tongue of William James has come to imply the factitious, the academic, and even the futile?

When some newspapers declared that the support of Jane Addams was worth one million votes to Theodore Roosevelt in the election of 1912, Jane deprecated her role: "Like the report of Mark Twain's death, the report is greatly exaggerated." Another rumor held that, if elected, T.R. intended to offer Miss Addams a place in his Cabinet, but the candidate himself scotched the rumor by saying: "Indeed, there could be no better representative than she, but I would not have done so. I think she is so much more needed . . . at Hull-House." Talk like this became completely academic when Roosevelt lost to Woodrow Wilson. The issues of the campaign, however, remained alive, and only a few weeks after publicizing her qualms about the treatment of Negroes at the Progressive convention, Jane returned to the subject of prejudice. The fiftieth anniversary of the Emancipation Proclamation on January 1, 1913, gave her the opportunity to ask: "Has the Emancipation Proclamation Been Nullified by National Indifference?" The Survey *ran her answer under that title in February:*

■ Although our very prosperity and political tranquillity were achieved through the efforts of the previous generation of reformers, it is our mood to accept their work with a nod of recognition for its sacrifices but with no sense of obligation to carry on the strenuous task. Does our mood repeat that worldwide yielding to race antagonism, or does it partake of the growing self-assertion of the so-called "superior" races who exact labor and taxes from black and yellow men with the easy explanation of "manifest destiny"? Scrutiny of reactionary developments are, of course, valuable only as they indicate possible ways of escape, otherwise they were best left untouched. But is it not possible at this fiftieth anniversary of the issuance of the Emancipation Proclamation, that most compelling and far-reaching document of democracy, to seriously test our national trend, using as a touchstone our attitude towards those whose freedom was achieved with such an expenditure of moral energy and devotion?

What have we done to bring to the status of full citizenship the people Lincoln's proclamation raised from the conditions of slavery, who were thereby enabled at once to legitimatize family life and to make contracts, but who inevitably looked forward to the civil and political rights implied in the great document? How far are we responsible that their civil rights are often rendered futile, their political action curtailed, their equality before the law denied in fact, industrial opportunities withheld from them and, above all, that for twenty-five years they have been exposed to the black horrors of lynching? How far has the act of the Great Emancipator been nullified by our national indifference? It would be difficult to state just when the tide of indifference set in but certainly we would all admit that the attitude both in the North and South towards colored men has been responsible for strange inhibitions and limitations operating on the spirits of the entire white population. If we would carefully study the souls of white folks to discover the cause of this spiritual bondage, it would not be difficult to find in the South a loyalty to a lost cause. . . . Memories of a caste relationship, which permitted great intimacy but perpetuated differences in opportunity, blind whole communities to the inconsistencies practised in many parts of the South today. Whenever Southern men thoughtlessly brand every black man as a menace to the virtue of white women, they forget the loyal protection given by black men to white women and children during the continuance of Negro slavery. Conditions of the shameful carpetbagger and the corrupt political practices after the war are still used by the young South to justify a similar system of political corruption and oppression toward those whom the Northerner so unwisely befriended. These, among other things, account for the treatment of the blacks by the white South when education, economic opportunity, civil rights, personal justice, and political capacity are in practice often successfully, and apparently conscientiously, denied to the Negro.

But what of the white North which, ignoring the glory of its inheritance, careless of the principles for which the war was fought at such terrible cost, submits to the chains forged, not by the Southerner as is often asserted, but by its own indifference? The consequence of such bondage upon the life of the nation can be formulated only when we have a wider and more exact knowledge. What has been and is being lost by the denial of opportunity and of free expression on the part of the Negro, it is now very difficult to estimate; only faint suggestions of the waste can be perceived. There is, without doubt, the sense of humor, unique and spontaneous, so different from the wit of the Yankee, or the inimitable storytelling prized in the South; the Negro melodies which are the only American folksongs; the persistent love of color expressing itself in the bright curtains and window boxes in the dullest and grayest parts of our cities; the executive and organizing capacity so often exhibited by the headwaiter in a huge hotel or by the colored woman who administers a complicated household; the gift of eloquence, the mellowed voice, the use of rhythm and onomatopoeia which is now so often travestied in a grotesque use of long words.

Jane Addams did not end on a despairing note when she wrote of the racial problem. On the contrary, she was encouraged by the solid progress of American Negroes during her lifetime, and in 1933, when only two years were left to her, she told the readers of School Life *that educational statistics proved the ability and tenacity of these segregated citizens of the United States and that they deserved far better treatment from their native land:*

Booker T. Washington (1856–1915), who was a fellow speaker with Jane Addams at many major conferences (see pages 62 and 198 for examples), was the leading Negro spokesman of his time. Born a slave, he worked in the West Virginia coal mines after the Civil War, graduated from Hampton Institute, where he later taught, and from 1881 to his death headed Tuskegee Institute in Alabama. Henry Watterson, a Confederate veteran whose Louisville *Courier-Journal* was for decades recognized as the voice and conscience of Dixie, wrote of this ex-slave: "No man, since the war of sections, has exercised such beneficent influence and done such real good for the country—especially to the South." Washington won recognition as a great educator with a clear-cut philosophy for the advancement of his race; he believed in industrial training as the entering wedge that would allow Negroes to rise to the status of first-class citizens—and his students formed a large percentage of successful Negroes for more than a generation. That philosophy seems too narrow and too tepid for Negro militants now, but those who follow it are still succeeding. He vigorously shared the view Jane Addams expresses on this page—that all Americans are the losers when Negroes are denied their rightful opportunity. And, like Jane Addams, Booker Washington was never bitter. He said: "No man, black or white, from North or South, shall drag me down so low as to make me hate him."

■ Perhaps the most remarkable graphic chart of the thousands published annually by the various departments of the United States Government is one issued last year from the Office of Education, Department of the Interior, which shows the rise in literacy among Negroes. It records the percentage of increase in literacy among Negroes from 2 percent in 1850 to 84 percent in 1930. The graph is the cold report of a herculean effort, for it is almost impossible to overestimate the difficulties confronting the ambitious adult whose forebears have never had any advantages of education. No group of people in our country have been more successful in overcoming all these difficulties than have the Negroes through three generations.

The Negroes, perhaps above any group in our population, are persistent in sending their children to school in the midst of difficulties. Their school attendance is high in spite of the fact that in fourteen of the Southern states 93 percent of the schools for Negroes are rural schools, often difficult of access, with the one teacher sometimes poorly equipped, and with a shortened term. It is obvious that the development of the Negro race in the United States depends more directly upon the elementary-school teacher than on any other factor. The teachers themselves are conscious of this. Despite their meager pay, the Negro teachers are eager to improve their professional equipment. It has been estimated that more than 30,000 Negro teachers were enrolled last year in summer schools throughout the country. The high schools for Negro young people, although inadequate in number, are gradually adding vocational guidance, and the pupils are at least made aware of the variety of occupations and of the careful preparation demanded of those who enter them. I wish we could say that they always found positions in their chosen occupations.

The strongest challenge to Booker T. Washington's Negro leadership came from William Edward Burghardt Du Bois (above), who anticipated the militant mood of later generations. "The problem of the twentieth century," Du Bois wrote in 1900, "is the problem of the color line—the relation of the darker to the lighter races of man." Born in Massachusetts, Du Bois—who lived from 1869 to 1963—was of mixed ethnic origins he himself described as "a flood of Negro blood, a strain of French, a bit of Dutch, but, thank God, no Anglo-Saxon!" A skilled sociologist, Du Bois dropped Washington's concept of Negro progress through industrial training, and urged the "talented tenth" to take the lead. He and Jane Addams both helped found the National Association for the Advancement of Colored People (NAACP), but unlike Jane, he later became disillusioned with peaceful methods of securing civil rights, resigned from the organization, and ended up a Communist. In the latter part of his life, he was often consulted on African affairs by the United Nations and also worked on an encyclopedia of Africa.

THE DEVIL BABY

The immigrants in the Chicago ghetto were often superstitious. Jane Addams did not deny the fact, but rather probed for the social reality that nearly always underlay the superstition. The great test of her method was the incredible mass delusion concerning the "Devil Baby" of Hull-House, a case that fascinated her so much that she recounted the details in at least four different writings—one of them The Second Twenty Years at Hull-House, *from which this excerpt is taken:*

■ In the late winter and early spring following the Progressive campaign, my friend, Mary Rozet Smith, and myself spent three months in Egypt and Syria. The panoramic procession of Egyptian women filling their jars from the waters of the Nile and bearing them upon their heads to the parched fields which at best produced barely enough to keep their children alive, the glimpses into the smoking huts at the end of the day when each child received his meager portion from his anxious mother, induced a new sense of the unending effort of women throughout the earth that human life might be maintained upon its surface. These somber reflections may have prepared me for the visit of the Devil Baby at Hull-House which occurred soon after our return. . . .

The knowledge of his existence burst upon the residents of Hull-House one day when three Italian women, with an excited rush through the door, demanded that the Devil Baby be shown to them. No amount of denial convinced them that he was not there, for they knew exactly what he was like with his cloven hoofs, his pointed ears and diminutive tail; the Devil Baby had, moreover, been able to speak as soon as he was born and was most shockingly profane.

The three women were but the forerunners of a veritable multitude; for six weeks from every part of the city and suburbs the streams of visitors to this mythical baby poured in all day long and so far into the night that the regular activities of the settlement were almost swamped. The Italian version . . . dealt with a pious Italian girl married to an atheist. Her husband in a rage had torn a holy picture from the bedroom wall, saying that he would quite as soon have a devil in the house as such a thing, whereupon the devil incarnated himself in her coming child. As soon as the Devil Baby was born, he ran around the table shaking his finger at his father, who finally caught him and in fear and trembling brought him to Hull-House. . . .

THE WHITE HOUSE
WASHINGTON

SHADOW LAWN,
October 17, 1916

My dear Miss Addams:

I cannot deny myself the pleasure of telling you how proud I am and how much strengthened

May I not also say with what interest I read your article in the Atlantic Monthly on "The devil baby at Hull House?" The pathos and revelation of it all are indeed poignant and I carried away from reading the article what I am sure will be a very permanent impression.

Cordially and sincerely yours,

Woodrow Wilson

When Woodrow Wilson (above) wrote this letter (left), he and Jane were mutual admirers. She was backing him for reelection the next month, and the section omitted here continues "... I feel that I should have your approval and support. I know that you always act with such genuineness that no support could hearten me more than yours." The next year, the two were estranged by America's entry into World War I. Wilson denied any contradiction in his switch from neutrality to belligerence, which he blamed on the German ruthlessness that forced America to "make the world safe for democracy." But Jane criticized "this myth... that democracy is to be secured through war." Although backing his postwar campaign for the League of Nations, she thought he made a mistake in binding the League to the peace treaties instead of making it a separate issue. Wilson's second wife, Edith Bolling Galt, attracted caustic comment in Jane Addams' circle. Told that the President was "walking humbly with God," Florence Kelley snorted: "You mean walking humbly with Galt."

Although the visitors to the Devil Baby included persons of every degree of prosperity and education, the story constantly demonstrated the power of an old wives' tale among thousands of men and women in modern society who are living with their vision fixed and their intelligence held by some iron chain of silent habit. To such primitive people the metaphor apparently is still the very stuff of life, or rather, no other form of statement reaches them; the tremendous tonnage of current writing for them has no existence. It was in keeping with their simple habits that the reputed presence of the Devil Baby should not reach the newspapers until the fifth week of his sojourn at Hull-House—after thousands of people had already been informed of his whereabouts by the old method of passing news from mouth to mouth.

For six weeks as I went about the house I would hear a voice at the telephone repeating for the hundredth time that day, "No, there is no such baby"; "No, we never had it here"; "No, he couldn't have seen it for fifty cents"; "We didn't send it anywhere because we never had it"; "I don't mean to say that your sister-in-law lied, but there must be some mistake"; "There is no use getting up an excursion from Milwaukee, for there isn't any Devil Baby at Hull-House"; "We can't give reduced rates, because we are not exhibiting anything"; and so on and on. As I came near the front door I would catch snatches of arguments that were often acrimonious: "Why do you let so many people believe it, if it isn't here?" "We have taken three lines of cars to come and we have as much right to see it as anybody else"; "This is a pretty big place—of course you could hide it easy enough"; "What are you saying that for, are you going to raise the price of admission?"

Among the visitors to the Devil Baby were many foreign-born peasant women. . . . To them this simple tale with its direct connection between cause and effect, between wrongdoing and punishment, brought soothing and relief, and restored a shaken confidence as to the righteousness of the universe. Because the Devil Baby embodied an undeserved wrong to a poor mother whose tender child had been claimed by the forces of evil, his merely reputed presence had power to attract to Hull-House hundreds of women who had been humbled and disgraced by their children; mothers of the feebleminded, of the vicious, of the criminal, of the prostitute. In their talk it was as if their long role of maternal apology and protective reticence had at last broken down, as if they could speak out freely because for once a man responsible for an ill-begotten child had been "met up with" and had received his deserts.

This cartoon of 1914, "Equal Suffrage," suggested that the suffragettes coveted some of Uncle Sam's masculine characteristics along with the vote. Many men objected to the movement, but some ladies also urged legislatures to reject equal suffrage. Such members of the fair sex mortified the suffragettes, including Carrie Chapman Catt: "When an anti with an ingratiating smile said, 'Gentlemen, we trust you to take care of us and the government,' almost any legislative committee could be counted on to beam with self-satisfaction in response. Then it was that suffragists felt . . . the poignant difference between the appeal of a just claim and a clinging vine. However, even this experience stirred a new suffrage zeal, so was not without its uses." That "zeal" led to eventual victory.

DEFENDING WOMEN'S RIGHTS

Universal suffrage was one cause that frequently took Jane Addams away from her work in the ghetto. As the director of famous Hull-House, she was an authoritative speaker and a moral force adding prestige to the campaign; and she rarely said "No" to an appeal from her suffragette sisters when they con-

vened at home or abroad. In "Aspects of the Woman's Movement," an article in The Survey, *Jane recorded some high drama at a meeting in Central Europe the year before the outbreak of World War I, when feminine representatives from many lands came together to agitate for equality with men, and circumvented an old rule about women remaining silent in church.*

■ There are certain days which remain in our memories in the light of *species aeternitatis,* days which seem to break through into the reality which lies beneath the outward seeming. I spent such a day on the Danube in the summer of 1913, with delegates to the International Suffrage Alliance, meeting that year in Budapest. These women from many nations, sitting upon the deck of the river steamer, felt that curious stimulus which comes from the discovery of likemindedness between people of varied cultures, for there is something of the same interest in discovering the underlying likenesses as there is in the patriotic cherishing of distinctive national traits. Not a breath, not a tremor of the future, ruffled the polished surface of the Danube on that summer day. There was no haunting apprehension that these bordering states within a year's time would be firing the opening shots of the most terrible war recorded in history. . . .

That convention in the summer of 1913, in the old Hungarian capital, was the first I had attended of the International Suffrage Alliance, although for several years I had served as vice-president of the National American Women's Suffrage Association when Dr. Anna Shaw was its brilliant president. I recall her vivid personality in many striking situations, but one in Budapest remains most clearly in my mind. The old city on the Danube had long been a stronghold of Calvinism, with the result that one of the most beautiful churches belonged to the Presbyterians. It had been decided that Dr. Shaw was to give the "Congress sermon" there, but when the day arrived there was great difficulty as to a woman occupying the pulpit. The matter was finally arranged by placing a platform, with a reading desk upon it, in what had been at one time the junction of the transept and the nave of the stately old church, while the audience was seated around the platform in four different directions. In scholastic cap and gown, she stood on her raised dais and with the eloquence of which she had been past master since her early days as a pioneer Methodist preacher, she filled the vast arches with a valiant plea for the rights of women based on the old historic pleas for the rights of the individual, so dear to Calvin's heart.

But for Americans, the main suffrage battle had to be won at home in the United States. Across the country, crowds came out to hear Jane Addams when she appeared on the platform; the women were generally friendly, the men were often satirical—like the mere male who was squelched at a meeting in Kansas when he interrupted the ladies.

■ Through all my experiences in the woman's movement and in the stirring conventions held every year, there remained in my mind certain

Like Jane Addams, Susan B. Anthony (satirized above) had for a father a Hicksite Quaker who taught her self-reliance. In 1869 she helped found the National Woman Suffrage Association. Arrested for attempting to vote in 1872, she pressured masculine opponents so insistently that her co-worker, Elizabeth Cady Stanton, wrote: "Whenever I saw that stately Quaker girl . . . I knew that some happy convocation of the sons of Adam was to be set by the ears." It was said of these two suffragettes: "Mrs. Stanton forged the thunderbolts, and Miss Anthony fired them." In 1892, Miss Anthony replaced Mrs. Stanton as president of the association. She died in 1906, missing the triumph of the "Anthony Amendment" for which she had so valiantly fought—ratification of the Nineteenth Amendment in 1920.

stories of simple women who could not do otherwise than make an effort for the franchise because they needed it so bitterly. There was a sanction quite outside of the organized movement. In the suffrage campaign during which I had spoken in five of the Western states, I had come away with a tremendous admiration for Western women. I recall an outdoor meeting on the steps of a county building in a Kansas town. A man in the crowd ventured one of the cheap jibes to which woman suffragists had been so long subjected. An old lady who had come from Wisconsin to help in the campaign suddenly mounted the seat of the automobile in which she was sitting and begged leave to reply to him. To our surprise she evidently knew his name and the very county in Kansas from which he came. She told of her experiences in Kansas fifty years earlier when she had campaigned there to secure the school vote for women, and had then known the speaker's mother, who was living in a remote part of the new state. This pioneer mother had borne six children without medical attendance or the ministrations of any woman, and had buried two without the benefit of clergy. She had been eager for the school vote because she wanted a school for her growing family, and in the midst of her cares had worked hard in the campaign. The simple tale of courageous living and high thinking was unfolded before her son and ended with the question directed to him: "Who can better vote on the needs of this state of yours or on the needs of this great country of ours than a woman like that?" He had of course no reply, and sheepishly disappeared in the crowd.

The suffragettes believed that women had an indisputable claim to the vote if only because of their proven ability to deal with social and political problems,

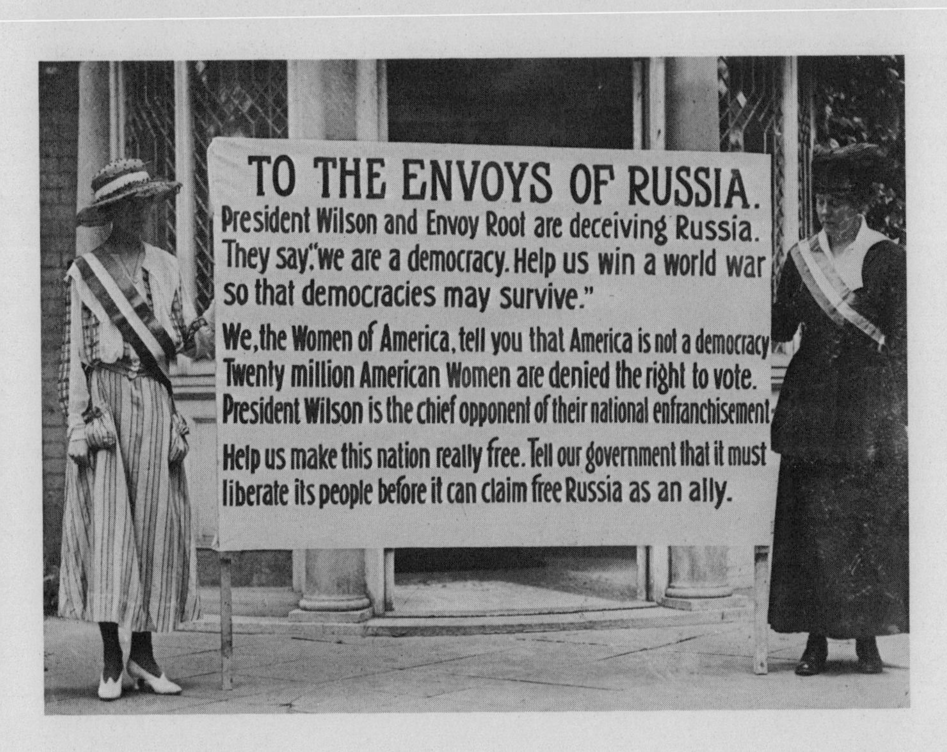

These two suffragettes carried their banner to a White House gate on June 22, 1917. The message indicts Woodrow Wilson, but he later came out in favor of the Nineteenth Amendment. The words "free Russia" refer to the women's voting rights introduced by the provisional regime that had overthrown the Czar in March. Wilson's concern was to keep the Russians in World War I in order to maintain pressure on Germany along the Eastern Front. The new Russian government tried to do so but was defeated and demoralized by the enemy. Seizing power late in 1917, the Bolsheviks forced Premier Alexander Kerensky into exile in the United States. Lenin came to terms with the Germans, thus allowing them to concentrate on the Western Front.

which by now crowded the agenda at sessions of the women's clubs. One passage in The Second Twenty Years at Hull-House *mentions some of the less genteel, but socially necessary, activities in which they engaged:*

■ During these prewar years the settlement groups met constantly for civic discussion. I recall an incident connected with the City Club which, when it was first built in Chicago, was used as a meeting place for all sorts of organizations. We talked over all our causes as we ate luncheon under its hospitable roof. One day as I entered the elevator, the boy who knew me well said casually: "What are you eating with today—with garbage or with the social evil?" I replied: "Garbage," with as much dignity as I could command under the circumstances and he deposited me on the fourth floor where I found Mary McDowell, head of the University of Chicago Settlement, pinning on the wall blueprints of a certain garbage reduction plant. I had been a little disturbed by my conversation in the elevator, and remarked: "Isn't it amazing the way we eat and at the same time talk about these disagreeable subjects?" She went on pinning up her blueprints as she replied: "If you lived near Bubbly Creek, into which the five largest slaughterhouses in the world discharge their refuse, you would be so interested in garbage that you would talk about it at luncheon or any other time." I assured her that I was interested in garbage, and instanced the fact that I had once been a garbage inspector myself. "Yes," she said, "you are interested, but if you lived back of the Yards you could not think that any mere talk about it was disagreeable."

And so the woman's clubs were ready at least to investigate any civic situation which seemed to call for vigorous action; and because cooperation among women was new and the companionship exhilarating they were continually "borne onward with that flood of freedom which to the open sea doth flow with pomp of waters unwithstood"—a spirit characteristic of those days which later came to seem so remote—but which is still manifesting itself in new ways, such as the third conference on the Cause and Cure of War held in Washington last January, attended by six hundred delegates from nine national women's organizations. A clubwoman there ventured the statement that while "the culture club is still with us, discussions of international relations are more popular than papers on the poets of the seventeenth century." She added to this the opinion that "the most interesting and unexpected turn in the tide of feminine affairs is woman's intelligent and almost impassioned interest in world affairs."

Ratification of the Nineteenth Amendment in 1920 brought the suffrage campaign to a triumphant conclusion in the United States. The three great women connected with the earliest stages of the campaign—Elizabeth Cady Stanton, Lucretia Mott, and Susan B. Anthony—were now dead, and Carrie Chapman Catt headed the drive to victory. Jane Addams rejoiced, not only because equality was vindicated, but also because of the lofty consequences that she anticipated in the life of the nation. In her philosophy, women possessed specifically feminine virtues, and would surely alter public policies by forcing

Carrie Chapman Catt did not always see eye-to-eye with Jane Addams but the two did cooperate in the suffrage movement, of which Mrs. Catt remained the leader nationally (1900–1904, 1915–1920) and internationally (1904–1923). Agreeing on the horror of war, they joined forces to found the National Peace Party in 1915. But Mrs. Catt parted from Miss Addams on the question of absolute pacifism. In 1917, feeling that the time had come to use force to defend right, she urged the suffrage association to back President Wilson. Certain pacifists (not including Jane Addams) attacked her so bitterly that Mrs. Catt resigned from the National Peace Party, served on the Women's Committee in Washington, and loyally did her bit to help win the war. After the war, she helped to found the League of Women Voters. She and Miss Addams resumed their old friendship, and in 1927 Mrs. Catt wrote an open letter to the DAR in which she defended her friend with some shrewd hits: "Do you really think Miss Addams is a Communist? All realize that your convictions must be intense, or your officers careless, since the attack upon Miss Addams is upon one who . . . has been a DAR herself. . . . Newton D. Baker [our wartime Secretary of War, has said]: 'Miss Jane Addams . . . lends dignity and greatness to any list in which her name appears.' . . . Miss Addams is one of the greatest women this republic of ours has produced. . . . Think it over."

Maude Royden was an energetic activist for suffrage and peace, first in her native England, and later, as a member of the WILPF, on the international scene. The first woman to occupy a pulpit regularly in a British church, she joined Emmeline Pankhurst in demanding voting rights for British women, and saw triumph in 1918 when Parliament finally allowed women to vote. Taking a strong pacifist line, in World War I, she planned to attend the women's conference at The Hague; the entire delegation, because of official opposition, was never allowed to leave England. She was among those annoyed that Nicholas Murray Butler shared with her good friend Jane Addams the Nobel Peace Prize in 1931. Her telegram to Jane read: "Joyful congratulations stop vexed at divided prize stop you are unique."

men to behave more like human beings. Thus, she thought that the ladies, peaceloving by nature, would dilute masculine belligerence. It did not turn out precisely that way, as Jane ruefully observed in 1930, capping her account with an apt quotation from G. K. Chesterton, her versatile British contemporary, who—in his poetry, social comment, and mystery tales, as well as in his writings on religion—loved the use of paradox.

■ The French have a proverb which has always seemed to me very charming: "Men make the roads but it is women who teach children how to walk." It was during a meeting of women from those countries which border upon the Pacific Ocean, held in Honolulu in the summer of 1928, that the truth of this seemed to me absolutely verified. In the first place, women had always had to deal with the nurture of living and growing things. Primitive women became the first food producers in contradistinction to the activities of men who had been merely food gatherers, and as the most important food plants flourish in climates which permit a relatively long growing season, the bulk of the world's population is therefore found in the tropics where woman's special contribution to agriculture has been given most lavishly. The Pacific area is nearer to this basic culture of woman's founding than are the Occidental countries where the culture taken over from Europe has become so highly mechanized in the lives of women as well as men. Certainly one felt that these women from China, Korea, Japan, Samoa, Fiji, the Philippines, and the Hawaiian Islands themselves, had been less mechanized than those of us who stood nearer to Western culture. . . . As the congress at Honolulu proceeded, we felt that women—especially those of the Orient—have unique opportunities to stand free from the tyranny of mechanization and to act upon the assumption that civilization is an idea, a method of living, an attitude of respect to all men. . . . There was about this conference a sense of reality, a consciousness of woman's ancient role of food producer versus the primitive one of food gatherer of men which restored us, at least to my mind, the confidence which I had lost during the war, that the work of women is nurture and production and must in the end prevail over the mechanistic tendencies of society which make for destruction. One could at least claim that women who dealt with living creatures, as over against industrial machines or commercial abstractions, had the best opportunity to acquire and to retain a direct approach to life itself. And at the present moment women in the Oriental countries are making a surprising advance. Although they received the vote in India less than ten years ago, eighty women are now members of city councils, fifty are magistrates, and a Hindu woman is deputy president of the Legislative Council of Madras, a political body representing forty-five million people. A woman is vice-chancellor of the Mohammedan University at Bhopal, and hundreds of them are lawyers, doctors, and teachers. . . .

Votes for women came at last, not only in the United States but in other countries as well, the result, it seemed, of war psychology. It is difficult to realize how very suddenly the change in status took place. I was in Vienna in 1913 when the venerable Madame Hainisch, representing the suffrage movement in Austria, invited me to attend a suffrage meeting. Because women in Austria were forbidden to belong to any political organization, the suffrage group always pretended that it was a literary society and began each meeting with a paper on some well-worn literary theme. I returned to Vienna eight years later to find, in 1921, more than twenty women sitting in the municipal council, twelve in the lower house of the national Parliament, and five in the upper house. Madame Hainisch, the mother of the president of the new republic, because she had always stood for an extension of the franchise, was eagerly honored as the leading citizen by these newly enfranchised men and women.

There was significance in the fact that the Victory Conventions of the National American Women's Suffrage Association and the First National Congress of the League of Women Voters were held simultaneously in Chicago, in 1920. The latter organization, with its analogous societies in all the countries in which women are voting, represents an effort to make an intelligent and effective use of the franchise which had been at last secured. The league demonstrates that no newly enfranchised class, from the barons to the workingmen, has ever prepared itself more conscientiously for the exercise of its new power. . . .

During the decade of suffrage, women have learned that ideas change less rapidly than events, with the result that much political thought is always out of date and inappropriate to changed conditions. Perhaps their most important duty is making this adjustment of the popular mind, and because they envisage the political situation afresh, they may enable the average citizen to escape from the deadening effects of wornout conventional phrases which so largely dominate political life. When Jeannette Rankin interrupted the roll call in the House of Representatives on April 5, 1917, to say: "I want to stand by my country—but I cannot vote for war," the feminist movement was supposed to have received a knockout blow. The patriots cried aloud that women would infect politics with pacifism—an alarm, however, which the situation in Congress twelve years later unfortunately proved unfounded. There were then eight women who were members of the lower house. They were said to "disagree on the tariff, prohibition, and farm relief, but to be united on the issue of national defense," which is interpreted into more cruisers and higher appropriations for military purposes.

I am quite sure that women in politics thus far have been too conventional, too afraid to differ with the men, too unused to trust to their own judgment, too skeptical of the wisdom of the humble to release the concern of simple women into the ordering of political life, too inclined to narrow their historic perspective to the experience of the formal women's movement—and thus unwittingly have restricted women's role in the racial development. On the whole I am quite inclined to agree with Chesterton when he wrote, "Many people have imagined that feminine politics would be merely pacifist or humanitarian or sentimental. The real danger of feminine politics is too much of a masculine policy."

Jeannette Rankin came out of Montana's Bitterroot Mountains to lead her state's suffrage movement to victory in 1914. Three years later, as the first woman to be elected to Congress, she cast the anti-war vote that Miss Addams mentions at the left. Between the wars, back in private life, Miss Rankin took up peace and labor causes, and used Hull-House for her headquarters during the period she represented the National Consumers League in the Midwest. Elected to Congress again in 1940, she adopted an isolationist position regarding World War II, and after Pearl Harbor cast the single "nay" when the House of Representatives voted for war with 388 "yeas." A severe critic of President Franklin Roosevelt, Miss Rankin maintained afterward that he had goaded the Japanese into the Pearl Harbor attack.

Ida M. (for Minerva) Tarbell (1857–1944) became acquainted with Jane Addams in the days when both were beginning to have a tangible impact on the manners and morals of American business. Miss Tarbell's important contribution was a two-volume history of Standard Oil (1904), in the best muckraking tradition; the exposé led many people to say that the trusts ought to be controlled. Using a talent for writing biography she had cultivated at the Sorbonne, she drew a lifelike —and quietly damning—portrait of John D. Rockefeller; it was so well documented that it made her readers feel such robber barons were being allowed far too much freedom for destroying others. In later life she taught classes in biography. Jane was in Arizona in 1931 when Ida was holding a class, and reported her modest reaction: "It seems that biography is an Art. I certainly discovered that autobiography was an Art that I did not possess."

CRUSADING FOR PEACE

During the first decade of the twentieth century, while Americans and Europeans were talking about the danger of war, pacifists like Jane Addams were talking about the necessity of peace. But pacifism was not a simple creed covered by a single definition. The United States had its religious pacifists, who rejected violence on principle; philosophical pacifists, who, allowing the right of self-defense, denied that any such clear-cut issue could be found in European propaganda; and isolationist pacifists, who demanded that the nation remain free of foreign entanglements. Jane found all these positions essentially negative, and therefore no answer to the dreadful monstrosity of nations contending in arms for power or territory. She had positive ideas concerning the "better alternative," the "moral equivalent," that would channel warlike passions into humane projects, and she expressed them in her lectures published under the title Newer Ideals of Peace *(1907), as well as in various speeches of the decade. Her address before a peace congress of outstanding Americans in Boston in 1904, here excerpted, allowed her to cite Tolstoyan activism in her analysis of the war issue:*

■ We now come to a new point, and we ask ourselves if there is not something more in accord with our present line of thinking, which may be said of this cause of peace, something a little more active and practical, less theoretical and sentimental than some of the old preachings of peace necessarily had to be. I am very fond of Tolstoy, but I always wince when I hear people call him a nonresistant. The word is too feeble. Tolstoy yearns to see a great display of moral energy in the resistance of evil. It is only brute force which he discards. . . . Tolstoy is trying to create new springs of energy, because he tells us that through the paths of righteousness are called forth the very best powers of mankind. . . .

As I look through the audience I see . . . people who had much to do with bringing the Doukhobors into Canada. The Doukhobors, as you know, are a nonresisting sect. They were arrested in Russia for refusing to go into the army. One young man was brought before a Russian judge who reasoned with him and said, "Why do you not submit and join the army?" In return the young man gave him a long commentary upon the teachings of Jesus, and the Russian judge said, "That is very true; we all believe that; but the time has not yet come to put that into practice." The young man replied, "The time may not have come for you, your honor, but the time has come for us." Let us hope that in a few years we may all be able to stand up and say what [Booker T.] Washington was able to say for his race a few moments ago, that the time has come for us to accept at least passive resistance if we cannot accept dynamic and creative peace.

The war that so many had feared erupted in 1914. Now the problem of the pacifists was to keep it from spreading, and to labor for a speedy end to hostilities. Jane Addams describes World War I and its aftermath, from her point of view, in Peace and Bread in Time of War *(1922), a work so relevant to the century's continuing violence that it was reissued in 1945 with a laudatory foreword by John Dewey. The Henry Street Settlement she mentions was founded by Lillian Wald, like Jane herself a famous social worker who joined the pacifist movement.*

■ It was in the early fall of 1914 that a small group of social workers held the first of a series of meetings at the Henry Street Settlement in New York, trying to formulate the reaction to war on the part of those who for many years had devoted their energies to the reduction of devastating poverty. We believed that the endeavor to nurture human life even in its most humble and least promising forms had crossed national boundaries; that those who had given years to its service had become convinced that nothing of social value can be obtained save through widespread public opinion and the cooperation of all civilized nations. Many members of this group meeting in the Henry Street Settlement had lived in the cosmopolitan districts of American cities. All of us, through long experience among the immigrants from many nations, were convinced that a friendly and cooperative relationship was constantly becoming more possible between all peoples. We believed that war, seeking its end through coercion, not only interrupted but fatally reversed this process of cooperating goodwill which, if it had a chance, would eventually include the human family itself.

The European war was already dividing our immigrant neighbors from each other. We could not imagine asking ourselves whether the parents of a child who needed help were Italians, and therefore on the side of the

The lady pacifists who marched before and during World War I often seemed a formidable group in their big hats, heavy coats, and sweeping skirts. Those in the picture below show they mean business as—firm, determined, unsmiling—they flank their placard urging a popular vote on the issue of American belligerence. Actually, they did not want merely to find out how the people felt—they wanted a powerful vote against belligerence. Their hopes for such a ballot collapsed when Congress declared war against the Kaiser's Germany on April 6, 1917, by a joint resolution.

Allies, or Dalmatians, and therefore on the side of the Central Powers. Such a question was as remote as if during the Balkan Wars we had anxiously inquired whether the parents were Macedonians or Montenegrins, although at one time that distinction had been of paramount importance to many of our neighbors. . . .

Several organizations were formed during the next few months, with which we became identified; Miss Wald was the first president of the Union Against Militarism, and I became chairman of what was called the Women's Peace Party. . . . The Women's Peace Party itself was the outcome of a two days' convention held in Washington concluding a series of meetings in different cities. . . . The "call" to the convention was issued by Mrs. Carrie Chapman Catt and myself, and on January 10, 1915, the new organization was launched at a mass meeting of three thousand people. A ringing preamble . . . was adopted with the following platform:

(1) The immediate calling of a convention of neutral nations in the interest of early peace; (2) Limitation of armaments and the nationalization of their manufacture; (3) Organized opposition to militarism in our own country; (4) Education of youth in the ideals of peace; (5) Democratic control of foreign policies; (6) The further humanizing of governments by the extension of the suffrage to women; (7) "Concert of Nations" to supersede "Balance of Power"; (8) Action towards the gradual reorganization of the world to substitute Law for War; (9) The substitution of economic pressure and of nonintercourse for rival armies and navies; (10)

Lillian Wald (above) received Jane's letter (right) dated November 12, 1915, when both were deeply concerned with the pacifist movement. Like Jane, Lillian was a well-bred young lady who left a comfortable home to labor in the slums, but she chose New York rather than Chicago. With Mary Brewster, she founded a visiting nurse service on the Lower East Side that became the nucleus of the Henry Street Settlement—second only to Hull-House in fame and influence. Her activities paralleled those of Jane: campaigns for better housing, attacks on sweatshops, and demands for welfare agencies. Lillian suggested the establishment of the federal Children's Bureau, which began in 1912. In their correspondence, Jane called Lillian "Dear Lady," and Lillian called Jane "Beloved Lady." After Jane's death, Lillian wrote: "She was the finest expression of the American spirit of democracy." That line appears in Jane's collected autobiographical works.

We have a meeting of the
Woman's Peace Party at the
McAlpin Hotel in New York,
the 19th & 20th of this month
I shall hope to see you then,
perhaps we could have a few
of the Henry St groups to talk
about the neutral conference
which has had some real

Removal of the economic causes of war; (11) The appointment by our government of a commission of men and women with an adequate appropriation to promote international peace.

The year 1915 was an important one for Jane Addams. After helping to found the Women's Peace Party (January), she traveled to The Hague to attend the first congress of the Women's International League for Peace and Freedom (April), and then came her connection with Henry Ford's peace ship (November). When Jane agreed to join the Ford mission to Europe, all she knew was that a prominent American citizen intended to get a neutral conference started, possessed the means to finance his scheme, and numbered well-known pacifists like Rosika Schwimmer of Hungary among his advisers. Nothing had been said about the peace ship itself, the news of which came to her as something of a shock.

■ At this time an unexpected development gave the conference of neutrals only too much publicity and produced a season of great hilarity for the newspapermen of two continents. Madame Rosika Schwimmer . . . had lectured in Detroit where she had been introduced to Mr. Henry Ford. For many months Mr. Ford had maintained a personal representative in Washington to keep him informed of possible openings for making peace, with the understanding that such efforts "should not be mere talk nor education." During a long interview which Madame Schwimmer held with Mr. Ford and his wife, he expressed his willingness to finance the plan of a neutral conference and promised to meet her in New York in regard to it. He arrived in New York the very day the conference of the Women's Peace Party adjourned and he met with a small committee the same evening. Up to that moment all our efforts had been bent towards securing a conference supported by neutral governments who should send representatives to the body; but as it gradually became clear that the governments would not act, we hoped that a sum large enough to defray all the general expenses of such a conference might initiate it as a private enterprise. . . .

Rosika Schwimmer had a rich Hungarian accent, a fervent desire to organize other people, and the great good luck to meet Henry Ford just when that multimillionaire was about to finance a private peace initiative. Not long before, she had been compelled to pawn her jewels; now she could plan her pacifist campaign without counting the cost: "All I have to do is wave my hand for what I think is necessary . . . and lo! it appears." Moreover, as Ford's "expert adviser" for the project, she had a voice, along with Jane Addams, in selecting passengers for the *Oscar II*. Louis Lochner, Ford's secretary, later reported: "Many names . . . suggested by Miss Addams . . . were emphatically rejected." Terming Rosika "the unquestioned field marshal," Lochner added: "My job was the combined one of a Friday to our modern Robinson Crusoe, Henry Ford, and of a Colonel House to our peace ship's Woodrow Wilson, namely Rosika Schwimmer."

Our hopes were high that evening in New York as we talked over the possible men and a few women from the Scandinavian countries, from Holland and Switzerland, who possessed the international mind and might lend themselves to the plan of a neutral conference. We were quite worldly enough to see that we should have to begin with some well-known Americans, but we were confident that at least a half dozen of them, with whom we had already discussed the plan, would be ready to go. Mr. Ford took a night train to Washington to meet an appointment with President Wilson, perhaps still hoping that the plan might receive some governmental sanction and at least wishing to be assured that, as a private enterprise, it would not embarrass the government.

During the day, as I went about New York in the interest of other affairs and as yet saying nothing of the new plan, it seemed to me that perhaps it was in character that the effort from the United States should be initiated not by the government but by a self-made businessman who approached the situation from a purely human point of view, almost as a workingman would have done. On the evening after his return from Washington, Mr. Ford reported that the President had declared him quite within his rights in financing a neutral conference and had wished all success to the enterprise.

The difficulties, however, began that very evening when Mr. Ford asked his business agent to show us the papers which chartered the Norwegian boat *Oscar II* for her next transatlantic voyage. Some of the people attending the committee meeting evidently knew of this plan, but I was at once alarmed, insisting that it would be easy enough for the members of the conference to travel to Stockholm or The Hague by various steamship lines, paying their own expenses; that we needed Mr. Ford's help primarily in organizing a conference but not in transporting of the people. Mr. Ford's response was to the effect that the more publicity the better and that the sailing of the ship itself would make known the conference more effectively than any other method could possibly do.

With her philosophy of "half a loaf is better than none," Jane regretted that she could not join a project about which she felt serious misgivings. She

This contemporary cartoon, "The Tug of Peace," portrays the peace ship as an exhibitionist extravaganza of wide-eyed idealists and interested parties along for the ride (and the free lunch). Henry Ford is at the wheel, Rosika Schwimmer lectures her dove of peace, and in the background a German U-boat skipper shouts his welcome after torpedoing an American vessel. The squirrel on the bow, the dove towed behind, the parrot endlessly squawking "Peace," the new name of the ship, *Barnum II*—all add to the air of buffoonery. The sign "Have you seen our 1916 model" refers to Ford's automobile-making, and John O'Keefe used the same theme for "The Flivvership" in the New York *World:*

"I saw a little fordship
Go chugging out to sea,
And for a flag
It bore a tag
Marked 70 h.p.
And all the folk aboardship
Cried 'Hail to Hennery!'"

must have realized in retrospect that the Ford peace ship needed her common sense to counteract the Magyar flamboyance of Rosika Schwimmer, who enjoyed meeting the press and expounding her ideas with gusto.

■ What my interpretation of the enterprise would have been, had I become part of it, is of course impossible to state, for on the eve of leaving home, a serious malady which had pursued me from childhood reappeared, and I was lying in a hospital bed in Chicago not only during the voyage on the *Oscar II*, but during the following weeks when the Neutral Conference was actually established in Stockholm. . . . Madame Schwimmer, who, as a journalist and suffrage organizer, had had wide experience in many European countries outside of Hungary, was convinced that the neutral conference would not succeed unless it had back of it the imaginative interest of the common people throughout Europe. She therefore arranged that formal receptions should be accorded to the party in the four neutral countries of Norway, Sweden, Denmark, and Holland. The entire expedition, so far as she conducted it, was in the grand manner, for she believed, rightly or wrongly, that the drooping peace movement needed the prestige and reassurance that such a policy would bring to it. Unfortunately the policy exposed her both to the charge of extravagance and of having manufactured a claque. Difficulties developed during the journey; Mr. Ford left a few days after the group arrived in Norway, in the midst of journalistic misrepresentations, and Madame Schwimmer resigned from the conference during the early months of its existence. But in spite of disasters the Neutral Conference was finally set up at Stockholm.

Emily Greene Balch (1867–1961) described herself as "the plainest of New England spinsters and ex-teachers." She was also a poet, artist, pacifist, and social worker. After graduating from Bryn Mawr, she headed a settlement in Boston before joining the faculty of Wellesley, where she taught sociology until dropped by the college for her pacifist campaign with Jane Addams during World War I. Both attended the 1915 peace congress, contributed chapters to *Women at The Hague*, and toured Europe in quest of peace. When Jane could not attend the 1916 conference of neutrals, Emily took her place. Both were prominent in the WILPF. Emily became a Quaker, but backed American belligerence in World War II as the lesser of evils. She was awarded the Nobel Peace Prize in 1946, sharing it with John R. Mott, a Methodist layman active in the YMCA and the ecumenical movement. As a sociologist, she specialized in the Slavic peoples of both Europe and America, who found her an effective spokesman. Emily observed of Jane Addams: "She was full of the love of life . . . as it is, not only as it might be."

At this time, American pacifists had to live with the disheartening knowledge that the United States, although officially neutral, would not endorse them. President Wilson—despite being pressured from the opposite side by those who wanted America to join the Allies against Germany and despite his desire for a "peace without victory"—refused to commit himself in any manner.

■ In the fall of 1915, after we had written our so-called "Manifesto," a meeting of the Women's Peace Party was called in New York City, at which we were obliged to make the discouraging report that, in spite of the fact that the accredited officials of the leading belligerent nations—namely, Great Britain, France, Russia, Belgium, Italy, Germany, Austria, and Hungary—had expressed a willingness to cooperate in a Neutral Conference, and while the neutral nations—Norway, Sweden, Denmark, and Holland—had been eager to participate in the proposed conference if it could be called by the United States, our own country was most reluctant. There seemed to us then to be two reasons for this reluctance: first, that the United States could not call a neutral conference and ignore the South American countries, although to include even the largest of them would make too large a body; and secondly, that as the Central Powers had at the moment the technical military advantage, such a conference, if convened at all, should not be summoned until the military situation was more balanced. We thought that we had adequately replied to both of these objections, but because of them or for other reasons President Wilson would not consider the proposition, nor was his attitude in the least changed later when one of our members came from a small European neutral country with the accredited proposition that her nation would call such a conference if it could be assured of the participation of the United States.

Agnes Repplier appointed herself critic-in-chief of Jane Addams, and satirized her repeatedly in tart essays, one of which speaks of "the ruthless sentimentality of Jane Addams," while another describes "a Boston gentleman... who told me he was sick to death of the three words, efficiency, reform, and Jane Addams." The essayist considered Jane "early Victorian" in her attitude toward women, and misguided on the subject of World War I—Miss Repplier's opinion being: "France knew that peace in 1915 would mean for her the uttermost defeat." A niece wrote: "In more than one of her wartime essays, Miss Repplier had quoted Miss Addams [who] finally protested to [Ellery] Sedgwick against the essayist using her as a whipping-boy. The editor of the *Atlantic* was sufficiently moved by this plea to ask Miss Repplier's permission to allude to Miss Addams . . . not by name but merely as a 'searcher after peace.' " Jane was the first woman to receive Yale's honorary degree, and Agnes was the second. Sitting on the platform beside massive former President Taft, Agnes whispered: "May I push my galoshes under your chair?" Taft looked down at their feet, and replied: "You may, Miss Repplier, but it will deceive nobody."

During the years 1916–1917, Jane Addams went through a process of disillusionment with Woodrow Wilson. He was one of her heroes at the start; she was one of his critics at the end. Looking back in 1922, she confessed an inability to comprehend the motives behind his switch from peace to war.

■ Up to the moment of his nomination for a second term our hopes had gradually shifted to the belief that the President would finally act, not so much from his own preferences or convictions, but from the impact upon him of public opinion, from the momentum of the pressure for peace, which we were sure the campaign itself would make clear to him. I was too ill at that time for much campaigning but knew quite well that my vote could but go to the man who had been so essentially right in international affairs. I held to this position through many spirited talks with Progressive friends who felt that our mutual hopes could be best secured through other parties, and as I grew better, and was able to undertake a minimum of speaking and writing, it was all for President Wilson's reelection and for an organization of a League of Nations. My feeble efforts were recognized beyond their desert when, after the successful issue in November, I was invited to a White House dinner tendered to a few people who had been the President's steadfast friends.

The results of the campaign had been very gratifying to the members of our group. It seemed at last as if peace were assured and the future safe in the hands of a chief executive who had received an unequivocal mandate from the people "to keep us out of war." We were, to be sure, at moments a little uneasy in regard to his theory of self-government, a theory which had reappeared in his campaign speeches and was so similar to that found in his earlier books. It seemed at those times as if he were not so eager for a mandate to carry out the will of the people as for an opportunity to lead the people whither in his judgment their best interest lay. Did he place too much stress on leadership?

But moments of uneasiness were forgotten, and the pacifists in every part of the world were not only enormously reassured but were sent up into the very heaven of internationalism, as it were, when President Wilson delivered his famous speech to the Senate in January, 1917, which forecast his fourteen points. . . .President Wilson. . . not only gathered together the best liberal statements yet made, formulated them in his incomparable English and added others of his own, but he was the first responsible statesman to enunciate them as an actual program for guidance in a troubled world. Among the thousands of congratulatory telegrams received by the President at that time, none could have been more enthusiastic than those sent officially and personally by the members of our little group. We considered that the United States was committed not only to using its vast neutral power to extend democracy throughout the world, but also to the conviction that democratic ends could not be attained through the technique of war. In short, we believed that rational thinking and reasonable human relationships were once more publicly recognized as valid in international affairs.

If, after the declaration of his foreign policy, it seemed to our group that desire and achievement were united in one able protagonist—the philosopher become king, so to speak—this state of mind was destined to be short-lived, for almost immediately the persistent tendency of the President to divorce his theory from the actual conduct of state affairs threw us into . . . absolute bewilderment. During a speaking tour in January 1917, he called attention to the need of a greater army, and in St. Louis openly declared that the United States should have the biggest navy in the world.

We were in despair a few weeks later when in Washington the President himself led the Preparedness parade and thus publicly seized the leadership of the movement which had been started and pushed by his opponents. It was an able political move if he believed that the United States should enter the European conflict through orthodox warfare, but he had given his friends every right to suppose that he meant to treat the situa-

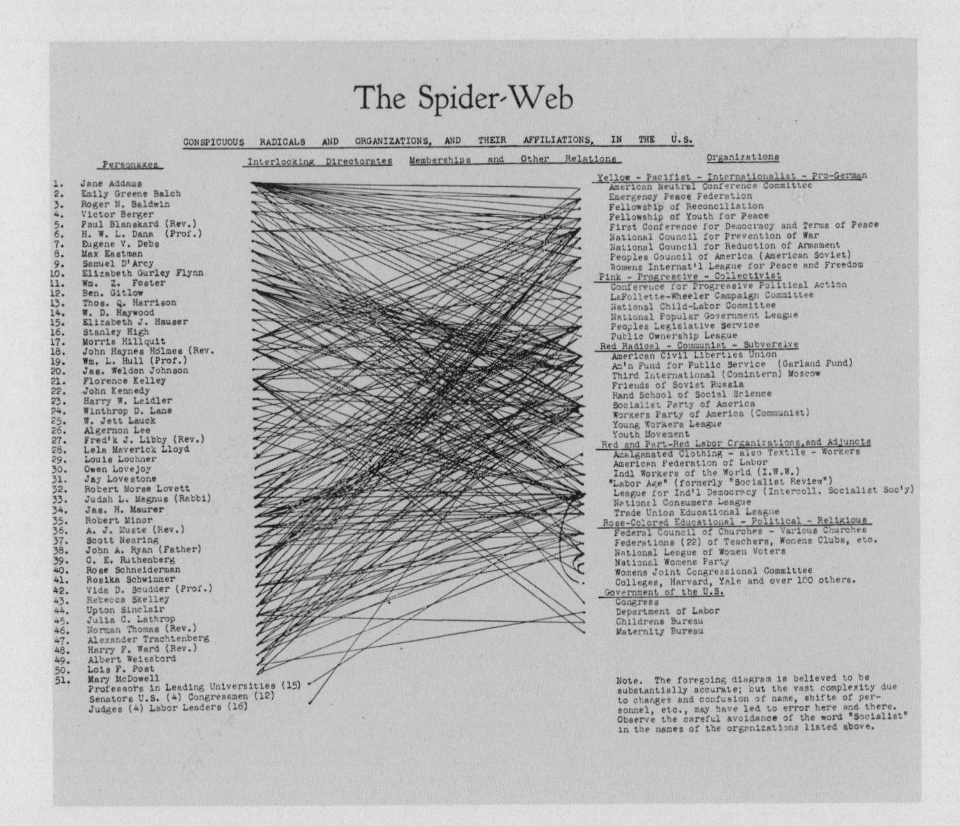

When the DAR listed Jane Addams as a "subversive," they used a diagram from Charles N. Fay's *Social Justice.* According to Jane: "The DAR with a beautiful building in Washington, and with a certain prestige in governmental circles, persistently published blacklists for the information of their members, and they also made use of the famous 'Spider-web Chart.' This was a chart giving the names of about fifty persons which were connected by fine black lines—although in a disorder no spider would tolerate—with organizations described variously as 'yellow,' 'pink,' 'red,' and 'part red' and 'rose-colored'—although they were obliged to add a sixth group, marked Congress, to accommodate the four Senators and twelve Congressmen who were on the list." To Carrie Chapman Catt, Jane added: "The assumption of the DAR's that they are public censors is comparatively recent but very widespread. . . . They have never enough to do and this is giving them activity."

tion through a much bolder, and at the same time more subtle, method. The question with us was not one of national isolation, although we were constantly told that this was the alternative to war; it was purely a question of the method the United States should take to enter into a world situation. The crisis, it seemed to us, offered a test of the vigor and originality of a nation whose very foundations were laid upon a willingness to experiment . . . .

Through the delivery of the second inaugural address the President continued to stress the reconstruction of the world after the war as the aim of American diplomacy and endeavor. Certainly his pacifist friends had every right to believe that he meant to attain this by newer and finer methods than those possible in warfare, but it is only fair to say that his words were open to both constructions. It will always be difficult to explain the change in the President's intention (if indeed it was a change) occurring between his inaugural address on March 4th and his recommendation for a declaration of war presented to Congress on April 2nd. . . .

As pacifists were in a certain sense outlaws during the war, our group was no longer in direct communication with the White House, which was of course to be expected, although curiously enough we only slowly detached ourselves from the assumption that the President really shared our convictions. He himself at last left no room for doubt, when in November he declared before the American Federation of Labor that he had a contempt for pacifists because "I, too, want peace, but I know how to get it, and they do not." We quite agreed with him that he knew how if he meant to secure peace through a League of Nations, but we could not understand how he hoped to do it through war.

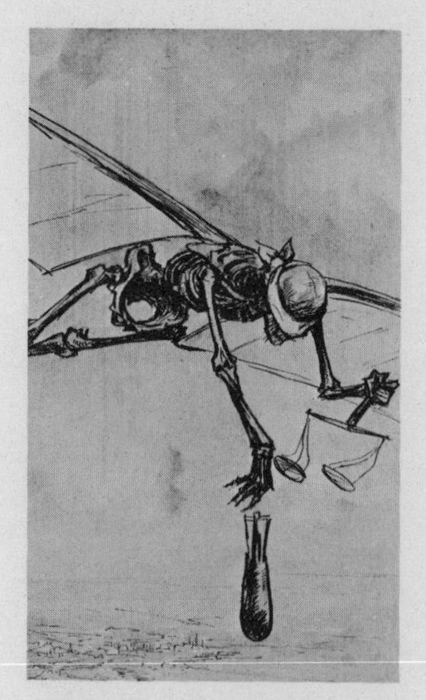

These two illustrations concern horrors perpetrated by both sides during World War I, but the artists do not imply the two sides were equally guilty. The French drawing (right) is a study in brutality: A German officer in his Prussian-style helmet, carrying a list, gestures toward the bodies of massacred French civilians as he gives the sentry orders for their disposal. The Dutch cartoon (above) presents the Allied air forces in the guise of a grisly skeleton dropping bombs with one hand, but also carrying a pair of balanced scales in the other to indicate that the Germans had sowed the wind and were now reaping the whirlwind. Many horror stories told of the Kaiser's legions during the war proved to be false when investigated afterward. Still, enough were true to leave a lingering hatred of Germany in the areas they had overrun. The conquered peoples welcomed the Allies as liberators.

THE HAVOC OF WAR

Working for European relief under Herbert Hoover during 1917–1918 gave Jane Addams an outlet for her humanitarian sentiment and practical ability. The capitulation of Germany in 1918 did not remove the necessity for this type of labor, for Europe was in a state of shock after four years of carnage, destruction, and famine. Jane saw the desolation when she attended another WILPF conference—and took the time to locate the grave of a nephew killed in the war.

■ The group of American delegates arriving in Paris at Easter, 1919, found that the English passports had been delayed and that the brilliant president of our French section and her fellow officers had been refused theirs. After various meetings in Paris, at which the French, English, and American sections were well represented, the Congress was finally arranged for May 12, at Zurich. Curiously enough, after our many delays, we at last met in the very week when the Peace Conference in Paris had become enlarged beyond the membership of the Allied and neutral nations by receiving the delegates from the Central Powers, and when in a sense the official Peace Conference as such had formally begun. Our fortnight of delay in Paris was spent in conference with our French colleagues, in interviews with various persons connected with the Peace Conference and the Food Administration, and by some of us in a five days' visit to the devastated regions.

Day after day, as rain, snow, and sleet fell steadily from a leaden sky, we drove through lands laid waste and still encumbered by mounds of munitions, exploded shells, broken-down tanks, and incredibly huge tangles of rusty barbed wire. The ground was furrowed in all directions by trenches and shell holes; we passed through ruined towns and villages in which no house had been left standing, although at times a grey head would emerge from a cellar which had been rudely roofed with bits of corrugated iron. It was always the old people who had come back first, for they least of all could brook the life of refugees. There had not yet been time to gather the dead into cemeteries, but at Vimy Ridge colored troops from the United States were digging rows of graves for the bodies being drawn toward them in huge trucks. In the Argonne we still saw clusters of wooden crosses surmounting the heaps of clay, each cross with its metal tag for inscription. I had a personal interest in these graves, for my oldest nephew had fallen in the Argonne. We searched for his grave through one long afternoon but, owing to the incompleteness of our map and the fact that there was no living soul to consult in the village nearest the farm on which the battle had been fought, we failed to find it. We met other people on the same errand, one a French curé who knew the ground with a sad intimacy.

We spent the following night at the headquarters of the reconstruction work of the Friends Service Committee in devastated France, where the work of both the English and American units was being supervised by Edward Harvey, who had been Canon Barnett's successor as warden of Toynbee Hall. After an evening of talk to which the young men had come

Herbert Hoover was already famous when Jane Addams began her assistance to him in 1917. Three years before, Belgian relief had required an American with international experience and high-level connections. Hoover qualified, accepted "the biggest wholesale grocery job in history" —and did so well that his name is still revered in Belgium. Jane recognized his ability when she saw him achieve similar success with the Food Administration in Washington. Later he was Secretary of Commerce under Harding and Coolidge, and became President himself in 1929. "The test of our whole economic and social system," he said, "is its capacity to cure its own abuses." But he was slow to understand the Great Depression. By the time he authorized government measures, it was too late to restore either prosperity or his original reputation among the American people as "the Great Engineer."

in from all the outlying villages where they were constructing temporary houses for the refugees who had returned, or plowing the fields for those who had not yet arrived, or supplying necessities to those who had come back too ill to begin their regular course of living, four of us who had long been identified with settlements sat by a small open fire and tried to disentangle the moral situation into which the war had thrown those who could not consider it legitimate, yet felt acutely the call to service on behalf of its victims and the full measure of pity for the colossal devastation and helpless misery. In the morning one of the Friends went with us to the region we had searched the day before, and although we early abandoned the motor in the shell-wrecked road, he finally found the farm and grave we sought, the third in one of three long rows.

Jane's faith in Woodrow Wilson revived during the aftermath of the war because he was struggling to convince his colleagues in Paris—Clemenceau of France, Lloyd George of Britain, and Orlando of Italy—that the times were too perilous for anything less than a just and lasting peace. Wilson's plan did not prevail, but the women in Zurich appreciated the efforts of the American President.

■ After the formal opening of the Congress had been disposed of, the first resolution proposed was on the famine and blockade. It . . . went through without a dissenting vote: "This International Congress of Women regards the famine, pestilence and unemployment extending throughout the great tracts of Central and Eastern Europe and into Asia as a disgrace to civilization. It therefore urges the Governments of all the Powers assembled at

This cartoon on the Paris Peace Conference of 1919 arose from President Wilson's call for "open covenants of peace, openly arrived at." Nonetheless, the Big Four decided to hold confidential sessions in which they could struggle with the terms of a European settlement. They barred newsmen from the proceedings. The cartoon satirizes the resulting air of secrecy, from the heavy padlocks on the doors to the conspiratorial attitudes of the Big Four. Wilson emphasizes a point with an intimate gesture of his hand, Britain's Lloyd George regards him with a knowing smirk, Italy's Vittorio Orlando bends forward to catch his words, and France's Georges Clemenceau (on Wilson's right) listens with interest, if not agreement. Some historians believe that the secret sessions were a wise precaution, since no participating individual could use them as a personal propaganda sounding board.

the Peace Conference immediately to develop the interallied organizations formed for purposes of war into an international organization for purposes of peace, so that the resources of the world—food, raw materials, finance, transport—shall be made available for the relief of the peoples of all countries from famine and pestilence.

"To this end it urges that immediate action be taken: (1) To raise the blockade; and (2) If there is insufficiency of food or transport, (a) to prohibit the use of transport from one country to another for the conveyance of luxuries until the necessaries of life are supplied to all peoples; (b) to ration the people of every country so that the starving may be fed.

"The Congress believes that only immediate international action on these lines can save humanity and bring about the permanent reconciliation and union of the peoples."

The resolution in full was telegraphed to Paris and we received a prompt reply from President Wilson. The public reception of this telegram was one of the most striking moments of the Congress and revealed once more the reverence with which all Europe regarded the President of the United States. As the university hall was too small for the increasing attendance, we held our last evening meetings in the largest church in the city. As I stood in the old-fashioned high pulpit to announce the fact that a telegram had been received from President Wilson, there fell a hush, a sense of tension on the great audience that is difficult to describe. It was as if out of the confusion and misery of Europe one authoritative voice was about to be heard. Although the telegram itself but expressed sympathy with our famine resolution, and regret that the Paris Conference could not act upon its suggestions, there arose from the audience a sigh of religious resignation, as if a good man were doing his best and in the end must succeed.

Alice Hamilton, after studying medicine at the University of Michigan and in Germany, joined Chicago's Rush laboratories in 1898. Proximity and her interest in public health brought her to Hull-House, where she soon became a resident specializing in communicable diseases. Like several of her colleagues, she had a tart sense of humor. A proper Bostonian once inquired in a condescending tone: "Are any bathing facilities provided for those who reside here?" Alice answered with feline delicacy: "Yes, indeed. You must come round some Saturday morning and help me with the Italian babies in the basement." Whenever she could, Dr. Hamilton worked at Hull-House or traveled with Jane Addams, but her great ability often brought her high appointments elsewhere. The federal government commissioned her to make a scientific study of industrial poisoning (1911–1921), and she also served as a professor at the Harvard Medical School (1919–1934).

The most heartrending victims of war and blockade were the children whose little bodies were shriveled by hunger. Jane Addams and Alice Hamilton, two ladies from Hull-House on a fact-finding tour, were horrified by the dreadful scenes they saw in Europe. Alice, looking with the trained eye of a practicing physician, realized that this was malnutrition of a deadly type, and Jane recorded the threat to the future of the nations. Both pressed for immediate shipments of food to the Continent.

■ On our return to Paris after the Zurich Congress, Dr. Hamilton and I accepted an invitation from the American Friends Service Committee to go into Germany. . . . We were received everywhere in a fine spirit of courtesy. Doctors, nurses, and city officials, who were [trying to control] tuberculosis, to keep children healthy, to prevent youthful crime, and [to] foster education, had long passed the mood of bitterness. What they were facing was the shipwreck of a nation and they had no time for resentments. They realized that if help did not come quickly and abundantly, the coming generation in Germany was largely doomed to early death or, at best, to a handicapped life.

We had, of course, seen something of the widespread European starvation before we went into Germany; our first view in Europe of starved children was in the city of Lille in northern France, where the schoolchildren were being examined for tuberculosis. We had already been told that 40 percent of the children of school age in Lille had open tuberculosis and that the remaining 60 percent were practically all suspects. As we entered the door of a large schoolroom, we saw at the other end of the room a row of little boys, from six to ten years of age, passing slowly in front of the examining physician. The children were stripped to the waist, and our first impression was of a line of moving skeletons: their little shoulder blades stuck straight out, the vertebrae were all perfectly distinct as were their ribs, and their bony arms hung limply at their sides. To add to the gruesome effect, not a sound was to be heard, for the French physician had lost his voice as a result of shell shock during the first bombardment of Lille. He therefore whispered his instructions to the children as he applied his stethoscope, and the children, thinking it was some sort of game, all whispered back to him. It was incredibly pathetic and unreal, and we could but accept the doctor's grave statement that only by a system of careful superfeeding could any of these boys grow into normal men. We had also seen starved children in Switzerland: six hundred Viennese children arriving in Zurich to be guests in private households. As they stood upon the station platforms without any of the bustle and chatter naturally associated with a large number of children, we had again that painful impression of listlessness as of a mortal illness; we saw the winged shoulder blades standing out through their meagre clothing, the little thin legs which scarcely supported the emaciated bodies. The committee of Swiss women was offering them cakes and chocolates, telling them of the children at home who were waiting for them, but there was little response because there was no vitality with which to make it.

We were reminded of these children week after week as we visited Berlin, or Frankfurt am Main, or the cities of Saxony and the villages throughout the Erzgebirge in which the children had been starved throughout the long period of the war and of the armistice. Perhaps an experience in Leipzig was typical when we visited a public playground in which several hundred children were having a noonday meal consisting for each of a pint of "war soup," composed of war meal stirred into a pint of hot water. The war meal was, as always, made with a foundation of rye or wheat flour to which had been added ground vegetables or sawdust in order to increase its bulk. The children would have nothing more to eat until supper, for which many of the mothers had saved the entire daily ration of bread because, as they sometimes told us, they hoped thus to avert the hardest thing they had to bear: hearing the children whimper and moan for hours after they were put to bed because they were too hungry to go to sleep.

These Leipzig children were quite as listless as all the others we had seen; when the playground director announced prizes for the best gardens, they were utterly indifferent; only when he said he hoped by day after tomorrow to give them milk in their soup did they break out into the most ridiculous, feeble little cheer ever heard.

The plight of the refugees reminded Jane of similar iniquities in the past history of Europe. She lamented the fact that a contemporary form of the old fanaticism had developed—nationalism—which seemed fated to remain a fruitful parent of international crimes. She was right. Nationalism was largely responsible for the outbreak of World War II four years after her death, and has kept humanity on the edge of disaster ever since.

■ We saw arriving in Rotterdam, from the German colonies in Africa and the Pacific, hundreds of German families who had been driven from their pioneer homes and their colonial business undertakings, primarily because they belonged to the outlaw nation; in many of the railroad stations in Germany there were posted directions for the fugitives coming from Posen, from Alsace, from the new Czechoslovakia, and from the Danzig corridor. . . . They told of prohibition of language, of the forced sale of real estate, of the confiscation of business, of the expulsion from university faculties, and [of] the alienation of old friends. There was something about it all that was curiously anachronistic, like the expulsion of the Jews from Spain, or Cromwell's drive through Ireland when the Catholics took refuge in the barren west country, or of the action by which France had made herself poorer for generations when she banished her Huguenots. It is as if nationalism, through the terms of the Peace Conference itself, had fallen back into an earlier psychology, exhibiting a blind intolerance which does not properly belong to these later centuries.

Woodrow Wilson came home from Paris hoping that the League of Nations, of which he was a principal architect, would blunt the worst effects of the Versailles Treaty by acting as a forum where disputes between nations could be settled peacefully. Jane Addams shared that hope in Peace and Bread:

■ One turned instinctively to the newly created League of Nations. Could it have considered this multitude of starving children as its concrete problem, feeding them might have been the quickest way to restore the divided European nations to human and kindly relationship. Was all this devastation the result of hypernationalism, and might not the very recognition of a human obligation irrespective of national boundaries form the natural beginning of better international relationships? My entire experience in Europe in 1919 was in marked contrast to my impressions received thirty-four years earlier, in 1885. Nationalism was also the great word then, but with quite another content. At that moment, in all political matters the great popular word had been "unity": a coming together into new national systems of little states which had long been separated. The words of Mazzini, who had died scarcely a decade before, were constantly on the lips of ardent young orators; the desire to unite, to overcome differences, to accentuate likenesses, was everywhere a ruling influence in

This woodcut, "Man of Peace," by the American artist Leonard Baskin, symbolizes the thesis that man is obligated to accept life as meaningful despite the relatively brief span of life that is accorded to any individual human being. Peace, represented by the dead bird, must not be destroyed —and man must not be confined by the barbed wire that represents the brutality of war.

political affairs. Italy had become united under Victor Emanuel; the first Kaiser and Bismarck ruled over a German Empire made of many minor states. It rather smacked of learning, in those days, to use the words Slavophile and Panslavic, but we knew that the movement stood for unity in the remoter parts of Europe where Bohemia was the most vocal, although she talked less of a republic of her own than of her desire to unite with her fellow Slavs. The most striking characteristic of all these nationalistic movements had been their burning humanitarianism, a sense that the new groupings were but a preparation for a wider synthesis, that a federation of at least the European states was a possibility in the near future.

In 1885 I had seen nationalistic fervor pulling scattered people together, but in 1919 it seemed equally effective in pushing those apart who had once been combined—a whole ring of states was pulling out of Mother Russia, Bavaria was threatening to leave Germany, and Italy, in the name of nationalism, was separating a line of coast, with its hinterland of Slavs, from their newly found brethren. Whereas nationalism years earlier had seemed generous and inclusive, stressing likenesses, it now appeared dogmatic and ruthless, insisting upon historic prerogatives quite independent of the popular will. Had the nationalistic fervor become overgrown and overreached itself, or was it merely for the moment so self-assertive that the creative impulse was submerged into the possessive instinct? Had nationalism become dogmatic and hardened in thirty-five years? It was as if I had left a group of early Christians and come back into a flourishing medieval church holding great possessions and equipped with well-tried methods of propaganda. The early spontaneity had changed into an authoritative imposition of power. One received the impression everywhere, in that moment when nationalism was so tremendously stressed, that the nation was demanding worship and devotion for its own sake similar to that of the medieval church, as if it existed for its own ends of growth and power irrespective of the tests of reality. It demanded unqualified obedience, denounced as heretics all who differed, insisted that it alone had the truth, and exhibited all the well-known signs of dogmatism, including a habit of considering ordinary standards inapplicable to a certain line of conduct if it were inspired by motives beyond reproach.

Wilson failed, his opponents in the Senate prevailed, and the United States never did become a member of the League of Nations. Jane Addams continued to defend the League, although she realized that it was not working very satisfactorily. (She might not have been surprised at the fate of the League after her death—its virtual paralysis by the walkout of Italy in 1937, and its ruin by World War II. She would doubtless have transferred her hopes to the United Nations when that successor to the League was established in 1946.) Here she analyzes the problems:

■ During the first year of the League, the popular enthusiasm seemed turned into suspicion; the common man distrusted the League because it was so indifferent to the widespread misery and starvation of the world, because in point of fact it did not end war and was so slow to repair its ravages and to return its remote prisoners [and] because it so cautiously refused to become the tentative instrument of the longed-for new age. Certainly its constitution and early pronouncements were disappointing. During the first months of its existence the League of Nations, apparently ignoring the social conditions of Europe, and lacking the incentives which arise from developing economic resources, had fallen back upon the political concepts of the eighteenth century—more abstractly noble than our own perhaps, but frankly borrowed and therefore failing both in fidelity and endurance.

It may be necessary, as has been said, to turn the State and its purposes into an idealistic abstraction before men are willing to fight to the death for it, but it was all the more necessary after the war to come back as quickly as possible to normal motives, to the satisfaction of simple human needs. It was imperative that there should be a restored balance in human relationships, an avoidance of all the dangers which an overstrained idealism fosters.

This return should have been all the easier because during the World War, literally millions of people had stumbled into a situation where "those great cloud banks of ancestral blindness weighing down upon

When the WILPF held its fourth international congress in the United States in 1924, the theme was: "A New International Order." The French delegates issued a memorandum interpreting this to mean that, in the modern world, all nations are interdependent, all possess equal rights, and all should be represented in a new League of Peoples (apart from the League of Nations, which was not working too well). The "New International Order" would have possessed a government with authority to supervise such mutual problems as tariffs and currencies. But there would have been no army because there would have been no war—as the delegates from many lands posing in the photograph below indicate with their placards. Although some ideas advanced at this 1924 congress remained alive, even helping to shape the United Nations in the 1940's, the "New International Order" of the WILPF never came into being.

This excerpt is from a letter of 1923 to Henrietta Barnett, who became, the following year, a Dame Commander of the British Empire, a feminine equivalent to knighthood. The lines leading into the excerpt read: "My very dear friend, we are still in Japan because we were detained by a horrid operation in Tokyo, to which I submitted about six weeks ago. Alice Hamilton—a doctor—joined us here where I am. . . ." Jane Addams and Mary Rozet Smith were on their trip around the world, and Jane, as usual, took the time to communicate the latest regarding herself to her old friend in London.

I am convalescing and so all sail across the Pacific on August-23d for the U.S.A. We have been greatly interested in Japan, their hospitality is boundless and the Japanese

human nature" seemed to have lifted for a moment and they became conscious of an unexpected sense of relief, as if they had returned to a state of primitive well-being. The old tribal sense of solidarity, of belonging to the whole, was enormously revived by the war when the strain of a common danger brought the members, not only of one nation but of many nations, into a new realization of solidarity and of a primitive interdependence. In the various armies and later among the civilian populations, two of men's earliest instincts which had existed in age-long companionship became widely operative: the first might be called security from attack; the second, security from starvation. . . .

Throughout the war the first instinct was utilized to its fullest possibility by every device of propaganda when one nation after another was mobilizing for a "purely defensive war." The second . . . became the foundation of the great organizations for feeding the armies and for conserving and distributing food supplies among civilian populations. The suggestion was inevitable that if the first could so dominate the world that ten million young men were ready to spend their lives in its assertion, surely something might be done with the second, also on an international scale, to remake destroyed civilization. . . .

Certain it is that for two years after the war the League of Nations was in dire need of an overmastering motive forcing it to function and to justify itself to an expectant world, even to endear itself to its own adherents. As the war had demonstrated how much stronger is the instinct of self-defense than any motives for a purely private good, so one dreamed that the period of commercial depression following the war might make clear the necessity for an appeal to the much wider and profounder instinct responsible for conserving human life. In the first years after the cessation of the great war there was all over the world a sense of loss in motive power, the consciousness that there was no driving force equal to that furnished by the heroism and self-sacrifice so lately demanded. The great principles embodied in the League of Nations, rational and even appealing though they were, grew vague in men's minds because it was difficult to make them objective. There seemed no motive for their immediate utilization. But what could have afforded a more primitive, genuine, and abiding motive than feeding the peoples of the earth on an international scale, utilizing all the courage and self-sacrifice evolved by the war?

PROBLEMS OF JUSTICE

The debris left by World War I included a national malaise, caused by many things, but most of all by the news from the Soviet Union. Many Americans who applauded the overthrow of the Czar early in 1917, and the establishment of a democratic regime, reacted with consternation when a second revolution late in 1917 put Russia in the hands of fanatical Communists led by Lenin and Trotsky. Reform here at home too often became identified with radicalism. Even authentic American movements were attacked by those who considered them part of an international conspiracy with headquarters in Moscow. The immigrants fell under suspicion more than ever, and a drive to curtail the flow from abroad into the United States produced the quota laws of 1921 and 1924, which singled out the peoples of southern and eastern Europe as undesirables—and thus affected the Hull-House area.

Justice in the more strictly legal sense became an agitated question during the twenties because of the Sacco-Vanzetti case (*see pages 114–115*) *and the "Monkey Trial" of 1925, when schoolteacher John Scopes stood accused of teaching evolution to his biology class. William Jennings Bryan appeared for the prosecution, Clarence Darrow conducted the defense, H. L. Mencken*

The three principal figures of the "Monkey Trial" are pictured here. John Scopes (above) was the defendant, charged with describing to his pupils the Darwinian theory of the origin of species, and thereby violating state laws protecting the fundamentalism of the Bible belt. Clarence Darrow (far left) was the defense attorney who clashed with the star for the prosecution, William Jennings Bryan (left). Darrow and Bryan are in their shirt-sleeves because the trial was held during a steaming Tennessee July, long before air conditioning. The climax came when Bryan was called to the witness stand and Darrow humiliated him with searching questions on fundamentalism. Bryan died a few days after the trial. The conviction of Scopes was later set aside by a higher state court.

lampooned the proceedings in brilliant prose, and the jury found the defendant guilty. Jane Addams was a confirmed Darwinist, yet she perceived a naïve kind of democracy at work in the "Monkey Trial." Hence, she had no apologies when she encountered amused or argumentative Europeans.

■ As an example of sudden interest, resulting in widespread education upon a given theme, the trial at Dayton, Tennessee, upon the general subject of the theory of evolution, forms a striking example. I had been in England the summer of the trial and had been so often challenged as to our situation in contrast to theirs, because [Thomas] Huxley and Dean Wace, presided over by Bishop Wilberforce, had publicly discussed the so-called conflict between science and religion in an atmosphere of scholarly tolerance. I had tried to point out that the United States could doubtless at any moment stage a debate between a polished churchman and a kindly scientist, but that such a debate would leave the situation very much where it was before; that what made the Tennessee incident so significant was the fact that legislative action had been taken against the teaching of the theory of evolution in tax-supported schools, by people who had a chance to express their actual desires through their government representatives. I was quite sure that Englishmen could be found in remote quarters of the British Isles who believed exactly what these Tennessee mountaineers believed in regard to the acts of creation; thousands of them had received their education, as had these Americans, through those who had expounded the "Book" as a sole and abiding authority. Such men in England were as totally untouched by scholarly debates as were the Tennessee mountaineers; there was this difference, however, that the latter found self-expression through the processes of local government and eagerly determined what their children should be taught upon the subject that they regarded as the most important in the world. . . .

The repercussions of the trial were the more interesting because the incident brought into the circle of their discussion a large number of people who had hitherto been quite outside their zone of interest. These remote farmers were isolated, save on the occasional Sundays when a circuit rider came to preach, by their discouraging occupation of extracting a living from a rockbound soil. Nothing could have been further from the experiences and mental processes of the intelligentsia of a cosmopolitan city than these mountaineers, nothing more diverse than the two methods of approach to the time-old question of the origin of man. Only a molten current event could have accomplished a simultaneous discussion upon the same theme by these two bodies of people.

In 1924, Jane Addams made another foray into the political arena in behalf of the Progressive party. By then, Robert La Follette had replaced Theodore Roosevelt as the party standard-bearer, and Jane's New Republic *article is called "Why I Shall Vote for La Follette." She knew "Fighting Bob" as the great Wisconsin governor and senator who stood for dynamic liberalism.*

Hon. Alvan Fuller – Governor of Mass-
The State House – Boston Mass.

Those of us long devoted to the
Americanization of foreign-born
citizens believe that clemency in
the Sacco-Vanzetti case would
afford a great opportunity for
the healing of wounds and for
a real reconciliation between
the Anglo-Saxon and Latin
Peoples. Stop –
I beg you to commute the
death sentence because I

This is the handwritten draft of the telegram Miss Addams sent to Governor Alvan Fuller of Massachusetts urging commutation of the death sentences given Sacco and Vanzetti. She continues: "... realize that thousands of our humbler fellow citizens feel as the French felt concerning Dreyfus and ardently long that these men should also have their chance for a possible vindication —stop—Although you yourself are convinced of the justice of the verdict can you not consider the earnest and conscientious convictions of many of your fellow countrymen who implore you to refrain from making the situation absolutely irrevocable." After the executions, Jane wrote: "Some of us felt that the outcome of the Sacco and Vanzetti case threw away an opportunity unique in the history of the United States for demonstrating that we are here attaining a conception of justice broad and fundamental enough to span the reach of our population and their kinsfolk throughout the world."

He had put Progressive measures into a coordinated system called the Wisconsin Idea, covering the benefits mentioned in Jane's article, and many more as well; and it was as a battle-scarred fighter for social justice that he held the allegiance of the director of Hull-House when he ran against Calvin Coolidge.

■ The first time I saw Senator La Follette was on a gala occasion, when the University of Wisconsin was celebrating her fiftieth birthday; it was on a June day in the most beautiful capital city in America. He was participating not only as Governor of the State of Wisconsin, but as an alumnus in his own right—as was Mrs. La Follette, who was a member of the same class with President Van Hise of the University. They were all very much at home, they "belonged" to the campus. . . . It was, of course, an occasion for honorary degrees and for felicitation from other universities, including mother Oxford herself—"who was so old she couldn't remember how old she was," as her red-gowned son told us. But the occasion was more than that. Many of us saw unrolling before our eyes, as never before, the underlying aim of public education itself, of that purpose to which state universities had been dedicated by Abraham Lincoln when he authorized their first federal land subsidy in the very midst of the preoccupations and privations of the Civil War.

Robert La Follette rose in politics, as Jane Addams indicates, by going directly to the people. He became district attorney, congressman, and governor of his state for three terms (1901–1907). His Wisconsin Idea made him a national figure. As a senator, he belonged to the "little group of willful men" castigated by President Wilson for being isolationists. Exposure of the scandals of Harding's Administration provoked La Follette into introducing the Teapot Dome resolution that led to the disclosure of malpractices in the handling of federal oil properties, involving many millions of dollars. With his Progressive movement prospering, he eagerly accepted its presidential nomination in 1924 and received nearly 5,000,000 votes. He died in 1925, leaving a legacy of enlightened liberalism long cherished by his devoted followers. He was followed in the Senate by his son Robert, Jr., who served there even longer than he did.

In the extraordinary group gathered there, no one personified so unequivocally and so nobly as did Governor La Follette himself, that which was meant by the continuing experiment of self-government and the necessity of securing in its behalf the most advanced type of public education. At that moment Wisconsin was a banner state in the reciprocal tasks of universal education and democratic government; the Wisconsin Idea had been promulgated. There were many new devices by which the resources of the University were brought to the masses of the people, and the state was in the midst of that splendid legislative campaign which was founded upon the assumption that law is part of the social process—part of a self-developing human experience. There was a definite connection between state and university although not always obvious: The University gave exceptional opportunities for the study and development of dairy farming, and Wisconsin was not only a pioneer in standardizing butter and cheese through the use of a state label, but it made feasible cooperative marketing through the control of freight rates on the railroads. The University had developed one of the earliest departments of economics to make firsthand studies in the conditions of industry. The program of industrial legislation fostered by Governor La Follette contained not only protection for the workers, but an industrial commission to consider their growing and changing needs, and promoted an astounding number of part-time continuation schools for the young workers. It also included a careful regulation of privately owned public utilities, and many another farsighted provision.

At that moment the Governor of Wisconsin was bending his magnificent energies to the establishment of direct primaries, and incidentally clearing the ground of the boss system. He recognized the importance of the mechanism of voting and of representation, but he did not stop there. He was stimulating many minds to think vigorously together, he was securing political action which was founded upon collective experience and widespread discussion and conviction.

Jane discreetly skips over one rather black mark on La Follette's political escutcheon; with Senators Hiram Johnson of California and William Borah of Idaho, he had been a leader of the implacable opposition to Woodrow Wilson and the League of Nations. She hoped that La Follette would change his mind about the League when he reached the White House. He never got there; Coolidge won the election of 1924.

■ I had been living for more than a decade in the Nineteenth Ward of Chicago, represented by corrupt aldermen in a city council, which was at times itself bought with the money of the seekers and holders of public franchises. The political air of Wisconsin filled my lungs like a breath from the mountaintops of the finest American tradition. I came away from my brief sojourn at its capital with a renewed faith in the possibility of enlightened self-government, and with an unwavering admiration for the man who not only "represented" the people, but under whose direction the very processes of government itself educated, stimulated and enlarged the collective capacity.

All America is familiar with Senator La Follette's career since then. It was quite logical that the voters of Wisconsin should by an overwhelming majority send their governor to the United States Senate, if only because so many of his policies required federal action for their consummation. Personally, I believe in time he will find the same necessity for action through an international body, both because of his sound political philosophy and because of his understanding of the far-flung problems of modern life. I once attended the meetings of a commission held in Geneva under the auspices of the International Labor Bureau connected with the League of Nations, when the matter under prolonged discussion was the protection of the seamen, who for many weeks every year find themselves remote from consular offices and courts of justice. The most successful protection ever offered to these men, the one achievement constantly quoted, was embodied in the La Follette Seamen's Act, which because of its intrinsic worth, and because of the eloquent speeches made by its author when urging its passage on the floor of the United States Senate, has made the name of Robert La Follette beloved literally around the world.

Some of us who recall, almost with a lump in the throat, the precious planks so enthusiastically put into a Progressive platform in 1912—many of these propositions are actually operative as laws at the present moment—rejoice in an opportunity to work for "progressive political action" under a leader who has, since 1898, successfully led a progressive movement inevitably expanding through a quarter of a century. At this moment, under his trained leadership, is taking place for the first time in the United States that which has already been achieved in other countries of Anglo-Saxon tradition—a welding together of the forward-looking voters, whether they have called themselves Socialists or liberals, proletarians or agriculturists. They all have many experiences to report, with reasons for success or failure. They hope, under the leadership of this wise man—who combines so remarkably the abilities of the expert with those of the statesman—to integrate their cooperating experiences into a progressively efficient political activity.

Hiram Johnson had a career in many ways similar to that of Robert La Follette (opposite page). A California lawyer who prosecuted grafters, he became prominent in reform circles, and was elected governor in 1910. He bettered his state through a series of reforms resembling the Wisconsin Idea—abolition of child labor, introduction of workmen's compensation, regulation of the railroads, among others. In 1912 he ran for Vice President on T.R.'s Progressive ticket. Elected to the Senate in 1916, he emerged as a champion of independence and isolation, and took the lead in repudiating the League of Nations after World War I, when he said: "The League of Nations . . . is tainted and poisoned at its source with exactly the same duplicity and wrong which have ever characterized Old World diplomacy." A diehard isolationist, he lived to cast his vote against American membership in the United Nations in 1945.

Coolidge did not "choose to run" in 1928; Hoover followed him into the White House. Late in 1929 the nation entered the Great Depression. When Jane Addams turned her thoughts to this new crisis, and to unemployment, its most agonizing aspect, she cautioned her countrymen against the old

The New York *Times* termed Nicholas Murray Butler "a member of the Parliament of Man" when the Nobel committee chose him to share its Peace Prize with Jane Addams in 1931. Of this "double recognition," the paper editorialized: "The prize may be divided but the glory is multiplied." Butler enjoyed a plenitude of glory during forty-three years (1902–1945) as president of Columbia University. His success in expanding the size, faculty, enrollment, and endowment made his administration the most creative in Columbia's history, and he was known as "Nicholas Miraculous" to generations of undergraduates. He preached public duty as well as personal scholarship, took part in community affairs, became a leading Republican, and in 1912 received meaningless electoral votes for Vice President (the losing GOP candidate had died suddenly). Partly responsible for Andrew Carnegie's decision to endow a peace foundation, Butler directed it for twenty years. Since he lectured and wrote in behalf of internationalism, and became a forceful advocate of arbitration, he had strong credentials for the Nobel Peace Prize. But Jane's friends never forgot his support of American belligerence against Germany, or his attempt to make the Columbia faculty fully "patriotic" in 1917–1918.

American assumption, still held by many, that the individual citizen could and should solve his own problems. The time had come, she argued, to marshal federal funds on a massive scale in order to meet social needs. The last article she published was about this subject: "Old Age Security," which appeared in The Booklist *(March 1935) only two months before her death. At that time, the aged had little to rely on after retirement except whatever private resources they had been able to accumulate earlier in life. Their precarious position brought them out in droves to back radicals like Huey Long of Louisiana, who proposed to "soak the rich," and Francis Townsend of California, who thought that everyone over sixty years of age should be given $200 a month by the government. To fend off the radicals and yet meet the humanitarian need, President Franklin Roosevelt proposed new legislation to Congress, and, despite heated opposition from diehard individualists, the Social Security Act was passed on August 14, 1935. Jane Addams did not live to see this happy consummation of her own philosophy, but she had already made her point:*

■ There are no experiences in an industrial neighborhood more poignant and heartbreaking than those connected with old age when it is surrounded by poverty and indifference and thus given over to neglect and loneliness. Many of these old men and women have long ago accepted their life's portion of hard work, but they have at last reached the limit of their endurance. One is sometimes reminded of those dark unknown forces by which the Greeks, when hard put to it, explained the wanton destruction of men of good intent. Many of these old people in such neighborhoods, who might have continued for many years at an occupation to which they were accustomed, were displaced by inventions, others of them were permanently thrown out by working long hours under harassing conditions before there was any legal control of industry. And yet in spite of a world-wide compunction in regard to the care for the aged, which is registered in the fact that old age insurance or some form of pension legislation for the aged has been enacted in one country after another during the past generation, we are forced to ask ourselves why the United States has been so slow in this beneficent and economically important undertaking.

Certainly we share with the rest of the world two distinct social tendencies: one is the prolongation of life so that the number of people over sixty-five years of age within the whole population has relatively increased; the other is the tendency of machine industry continually to use younger people, thus shortening the earning period of a man's life. The fact that both of these tendencies are more strikingly developed in the United States than elsewhere makes our indifference still more startling, for scarcely more than half of the states in the Union have adopted legislation for the protection of the needy aged. May we not hope that the general discussion of social security carried on throughout the country, accelerated by the appointment of the President's Commission, may stimulate state legislation by the allocation of federal funds? Would it not be a natural method of reducing the number of the unemployed to care adequately for the aged at one end [and] to prohibit the work of children at the other?

THE SUMMING UP

Her activities during the thirties prove that Jane Addams remained mentally alert after her seventieth birthday in 1930. Now she could look back over a long life and a remarkable career, and memory provided her with a host of personal experiences with which to illustrate the ideas put forward in her latest writings. When she published "Tolstoy and Gandhi" in The Christian Century *in 1931, she could draw on her personal knowledge of the two men who seemed to her to be the best representatives of the ideal of nonviolence in human affairs.*

■ Thousands of people in every nation are eagerly watching Gandhi's great experiment in India. . . . I have been much interested in this reaction, and find myself continually comparing it to certain experiences during the decade of 1890 when we first read Tolstoy's masterly exposition of the doctrine of nonresistance. Tolstoy came to the doctrine . . . as a political method fifty years ago when, during the 1870's, he was often urged to join the movement of revolt against the oppressive government of the czar. . . . What Tolstoy wished to do was to substitute moral forces for all those forces which are at present aroused in warfare. . . . Tolstoy, who collected examples of nonresistance as an enthusiastic numismatist amasses rare coins, wrote before his death that he regarded Gandhi's activities in the Transvaal as the most important of all the work being done in the world.

Curiously enough, Gandhi's first public activity . . . had taken place in South Africa. For twenty years in the Transvaal he had devoted his splendid capacities to the tireless task of protecting his countrymen from a long series of discriminatory enactments designed to prevent serious competition from the free Indian workers who had been brought into the country as indentured laborers. . . . It was during the armistice that his attitude towards the British rule in India underwent a drastic change. . . . But instead of an armed uprising . . . Gandhi eloquently advocated the use of nonviolent noncooperation as the strategy to be adopted. . . . Gandhi often acknowledges his indebtedness to the teachings of Tolstoy . . . although the doctrine and the gospel of returning good for evil had also been reinforced by his reading of the Hindu scriptures and his study of the Sermon on the Mount. . . . Gandhi's attitude toward the established government of India was not unlike Tolstoy's attitude toward the czar's government. . . .

The message of Gandhi is similar to Tolstoy's in its indictment of Western civilization and equally insistent in its call to labor and simple living. . . . This is at the base of the home industry movement, and quite naturally the spinning wheel has become the emblem of the nationalists. Gandhi himself uses it daily and when I visited his *ashram* . . . his followers showed me the long-fibered cotton which they are raising. . . .

Gandhi has embraced poverty as Tolstoy had done—neither of them, however, as St. Francis did, in response to the counsel of perfection, but through the desire to use no force . . . for the protection of their persons

When Charles A. Beard was an undergraduate at DePauw University in Indiana, according to his daughter: "He went . . . to Hull-House during the time of Jane Addams, where he was impressed by the class divisions between aristocrats and laborers; it made a deep and lasting imprint on his mind and influenced his future activities." Hull-House strengthened his inclination to look for social and economic influences behind historical events. Like Jane Addams an admirer of Ruskin, he joined the Columbia faculty in 1904, and by 1915 was a full professor. Two years later he resigned in protest over President Butler's dismissal of three faculty members considered unpatriotic. Beard, the experimental thinker, disliked Butler's conservatism. In turn, Butler, asked if he had read Beard's last book, answered: "I hope so!" Many other Americans felt the same way. Former President Taft was pained by Beard's analysis of the economic motives of the Founding Fathers. Professional historians disliked his reference to the effect of the present on their views of the past. Beard refused to recant, retract, or cease writing because of the furious criticism he provoked. He told his class at Columbia: "As long as there is corn in Indiana and hogs to eat the corn, Charlie Beard will bow to no man."

This photograph illustrates many of the points about Mahatma Gandhi that Jane Addams makes in these pages; he sits near his famous spinning wheel in his humble dwelling. Mohandas K. Gandhi ("Mahatma" means "Great Souled") caught the imagination of humanity between the two world wars when he used the "fast unto death" in behalf of his moral principles, which included civil rights for India's untouchables no less than home rule for India. Often imprisoned, he refused to call off his nonviolence campaigns against British rule except when his followers resorted to violence. In 1930 he led an immense crowd on the dramatic "salt march" to the sea. His purpose was to violate nonviolently the British laws by making illegal salt from seawater. He was imprisoned for this, but the Indian independence movement went on, interrupted by World War II, yet triumphing shortly thereafter. One of the greatest ironies of the century is that Gandhi, the apostle of nonviolence, died violently at the hands of a Hindu fanatic during a 1948 prayer meeting.

or property. . . . It was . . . in a spirit of challenge to the entire revenue system that Gandhi, in August 1930, inaugurated the civil disobedience campaign by marching to the sea with a group of his followers and conspicuously making salt from its waters, in defiance of the salt tax. . . . The British government itself . . . is also changing as a result of the situation he has in part created.

In 1932, Jane wrote what might be called her "philosophical testament" to her country—her diagnosis of what was wrong with America, and her prescription for a better future. Prone to use the anniversaries of historic events for philosophical reflections about the past and the present, she seized on the 250th anniversary of William Penn's arrival in Pennsylvania to expound the meaning of his example for contemporary Americans. To set the mood, she gave her article an old-fashioned title recalling the usage of Penn himself: "The Social Deterrent of Our National Self-Righteousness, with Correctives Suggested by the Courageous Life of William Penn." It appeared in Survey Graphic *in 1933, and is excerpted on the pages following:*

■ Our national self-righteousness, often honestly disguised as patriotism, in one aspect is part of that adolescent self-assertion sometimes crudely expressed, both by individuals and nations, in sheer boasting, which the United States has never quite outgrown. In another aspect it is that complacency which we associate with the elderly who, feeling justified

by their own successes, have completely lost the faculty of self-criticism. Innocent as such a combination may be, it is unfortunate that it should have been intensified at this particular moment when humility of spirit and a willingness to reconsider existing institutions are so necessary to world salvation.

To illustrate, with perhaps the most handsome offer concerning the war debts which has issued from Washington, the one recently made by Senator Borah: He suggests that the cancellation of war debts owed by the Allied European nations to the United States be considered with the provision that the nations taking advantage of the offer shall consent to reduce their armaments. Nothing could be fairer except that the United States makes no proposition to disarm itself. This is doubtless due to the fact that we are so sure that our own intentions are beneficent, that our army is small, and that no one could suspect us of unworthy ambitions. We really are confident of our own righteousness, but that very fact may make the offer unacceptable. . . .

It is not difficult to trace the historic beginning of such a national self-righteousness. The persecuted religious sects which first settled so much of the Atlantic Coast were naturally convinced that they bore witness to the highest truth and were therefore chosen people. William Penn himself, in his journeys to Holland and the Palatinate, said that he visited the various communities "who were of a separating and seeking turn of mind," and in spite of his insistence upon religious freedom, he was from first to last surrounded by a good many "come-outers." These very separatists, from Plymouth to Philadelphia, who ultimately federated into the thirteen colonies, probably achieved it as much through a similarity of temperament as through a common devotion to political doctrines. They undoubtedly bequeathed both to their successors, and certainly the former made a very good foundation for this national trait.

Another historic manifestation of the spirit of superiority so easily turned into self-righteousness may be discovered as early as 1830 in a national attitude toward the European immigrants who came over in ever increasing numbers, until by 1913 the annual arrivals were more than a million. A consciousness of superiority constantly tended to exalt the earlier Americans and to put the immigrants into a class by themselves, until it became an obvious deterrent and was responsible for several social maladjustments.

First, for our tardiness in protective legislation compared with other civilized nations. Naturally every approach to labor problems in the United States had to do with immigrants who formed the bulk of the wage-earning population, and it is quite likely that Americans were less concerned for the well-being of aliens than they would have been for their own kinfolk. By a curious twist, in the course of time it came to be considered patriotic to oppose governmental measures for workmen's compensation, for unemployment insurance, or for old-age security, because such legislation was not needed by the successful self-made American. As our cities developed overcrowded tenements, sweating systems, a high

William E. Borah (1865–1940) was an outspoken individualist interested in peace and good international relations, as Jane Addams notes on this page. But he rejected the idea of American participation in any world organization where disputes could be settled. William Allen White, most celebrated of Kansas journalists, spoke of Borah's "obvious indifference to the opinions of others," a trait he kept throughout his career, from Idaho lawyer to United States senator. In 1912 he tried to get the Republican nomination for Theodore Roosevelt, but refused to follow T.R. into the Progressive party. He became the highly influential chairman of the Senate Foreign Relations Committee in 1924, but never left the United States. Although a nationalist, he called for recognition of the Soviet Union by the United States. His opposition to American membership—not only in the League of Nations but also on the World Court—followed the isolationist logic of Hiram Johnson and Robert La Follette: he feared that the United States would simply surrender a dependable sovereignty for the right to belong to undependable international organizations.

infant death rate—and many another familiar aspect of hastily organized and unregulated industry—all such social disorders became associated in the public mind with the immigrant.

Jane notes that the Quaker proprietor who came to Pennsylvania in 1682 took a different attitude, not only toward Europeans on the land allotted to him by the Crown, but also toward Indians and Negroes:

William Penn (1644–1718) was a hero to Jane Addams for many reasons, as these pages indicate. She does not mention those of his attributes that did not appeal to her—his penchant for bitter religious disputation, for instance, or his desire to bring the assembly of his colony to heel. Pennsylvania (which he founded in 1681 as a refuge for minority religious groups that were being ill-treated in the Old World) became too restive for his taste when its rebellious members took his democratic utterances too literally. But Penn was, essentially, the man Jane here describes as an apostle of peace, human rights, and understanding in an age of war, despotism, and bigotry. She makes the most of the fact that Penn enunciated splendid principles that would be adopted long after his time and serve as guideposts for a nation he never heard of—the United States of America, which would be born in a city Penn had named Philadelphia ("brotherly love").

■ William Penn affords an illustration of the antithesis of all this if we are able to envisage ever so poorly the environment in which he tried out his "Holy Experiment." For our first corrective, what could have presented a more direct method of avoiding the difficulties of self-righteousness than his relation to the aliens squarely confronting him—the North American Indians—who for more than a century the New England Colonies had regarded as untamed savages. His 1682 treaty with them was made as between equals and was mutually binding. It was impressively consummated by two self-respecting political entities. When he established his government he assured the non-English settlers in his colony—the Dutch, the Swedes, and the Germans—"You shall be governed by laws of your own making and live a free and, if you will, sober and industrious people." All the nationalistic groups at once received the franchise, although in his very first assembly the Dutch and Swedes had a majority of one over the English. He was quite unperturbed by the fact that England had just been fighting the Dutch, and he welcomed the French Huguenots at the very moment when England was at war with France.

The laborers brought to the early Penn colony represented many European nationalities, but each—when his term of service expired—was to have fifty acres of ground granted to him for a shilling a year, or a ha'penny for an acre. William Penn also made provision for the despised Negro; he was to be free after fourteen years, and provided with land, tools, and stock. William Penn himself manumitted his slaves in 1701, apparently convinced that they could take care of themselves, thereby avoiding that most alluring pitfall for the self-righteous who habitually feel that they alone can care for "inferiors." His confidence in his fellowmen was exhibited in the constitution he gave to the early settlers in his growing and conglomerate colony, which was the first constitution in the world to provide for its own amendment.

National self-righteousness, a detriment to labor legislation, has the second bad effect of provoking violence between men. Too many Americans are suspicious of foreigners. They should learn from William Penn the absurdity of such suspicion, says Jane:

■ As part of the national attitude it was gradually assumed that European immigrants held all sorts of subversive doctrines which were responsible for strikes and other industrial disorders. Immigrant strikers were easily charged with heresy against basic American doctrines. On this ground, scattering the strikers by the police, and if necessary by the militia and the regulars, came to be considered a patriotic duty. Yet William Penn had reached a conclusion when he was imprisoned in the Tower as a young man, which might be very useful to us. He pointed out the irrelevance of force in all matters that pertain to human relationship, and he stood for this conviction when, in the vast wilderness stretching for miles around him in every direction, groups of white settlers were being attacked and sometimes massacred by the Indians; protection, he insisted, lay in mutual understanding and confidence; "love and persuasion have more force than weapons of war." Instead of making much of the differences in religious belief between the sophisticated Europeans and the untutored Indians, he stressed the fact that the latter also believed in God and immortality and that their social customs and traditions were well fitted to their needs. His tolerance and understanding bridged a wider chasm than any presented later to America by European immigrants.

Prohibition was nearing its end as Jane discussed Penn in 1933, but the crime it engendered remained rampant, nowhere more so than in Chicago. Condemning the easy American acceptance of gangland murders, she traces this attitude directly to anti-immigrant animosity:

■ The third result of our national attitude towards the immigrant is that through our contempt for certain of our fellow citizens we have become indifferent to the protection of human life, sapping the very foundations upon which even primitive governments were built. Our indifference to the killing of foreign gangsters has resulted in a preferential treatment of crime. It was unfortunate that the earliest outbreaks of gang violence in Chicago—more or less typical of those throughout the country—should have been associated with colonies of immigrants. Although we all knew that the men who were bootlegging, racketeering, conducting gambling houses, or systematically stealing automobiles could not have continued unless they had been able to secure political protection, the community was slow to act because, so long as the Sicilians who composed the first powerful bootlegging gang killed only each other, it was considered of little consequence.

Connivance at murder is a grave charge not to be lightly entered into, and yet during four years, from January 1928 to January 1932, we had in Chicago 232 gang killings in which the law-enforcing agencies failed to bring even one to trial. If rival gangs attempt to exterminate each other, apparently not only the good citizens but the officials responsible for the prosecution of the crime of murder virtually say, "Let them inflict their own punishments." This American attitude towards murdered gangsters of foreign birth may illustrate that hard saying of a wise man, "The essence of immorality is to make an exception of oneself." We cannot rid ourselves of the habit of blaming someone else for our troubles, holding ourselves innocent.

A vivid symbol of the Prohibition era was the cartoon figure originated by Rollin Kirby of the New York *World*. Kirby often drew Prohibition in the form of a sour-faced Puritan dressed as though for a funeral, carrying an umbrella for protection against the "Wets," and often using a baton (as here) to lead a chorus of "Drys" bellowing for enforcement of the anti-liquor laws. Jane Addams presumably disliked this characterization of the side she favored, but she is not known to have criticized Kirby's well-honed satire, which delighted so many of his fans and won him three Pulitzer Prizes for cartooning.

Frank Kellogg, U.S. Secretary of State (top); Aristide Briand, French Foreign Minister (center); and America's Francis B. Sayre all worked on peace plans. Sayre, at the urging of the WILPF, produced a model arbitration treaty in 1927. Briand sent his own proposal to Washington; Kellogg negotiated with Briand the document ultimately signed by some sixty nations after its unveiling in 1928. The Kellogg-Briand Pact led Jane Addams to hope war was outmoded. But undeclared wars soon nullified the pact—they grew more fierce until the outbreak of World War II. The peace she dreamed of remains as elusive as ever.

Preferential indifference to crime, an obvious symptom of a breakdown in democratic government, may be an indirect result of an unjustifiable habit which allows us to consider one human being of less consequence than another. Never was William Penn's ideal of religion, founded upon fraternity and righteousness, so sorely needed. Perhaps religion alone can deal successfully with such an immoral situation imbedded in complacency.

Jane calls for more independence of mind among her countrymen in the midst of their uneasiness over the Communist menace. There is a mild vein of humor in her passage on Penn's tolerance of Muscovites, or, as we would say today, Russians:

■ There is still another aspect of our self-righteousness which is much more sinister. The current manifestation of this curious national trait is due probably to excessive war propaganda which registered its effect upon our minds long after its supposed usefulness was over. It has resulted in a spirit of conformity which has been demanded from all of us in the postwar years on pain of being denounced as a "Red" or a "Traitor." Perhaps never before in our history has there been within the framework of orderly government such impatience with differing opinion. The result has been a great temptation to the timid, to the personally ambitious, and to the immature to declare adherence to the opinions considered highly respectable, and to carefully avoid and even to denounce those identified with despised radicals. Such a stultifying situation is more than ever dangerous just now because the nation needs all the free and vigorous thinking which is available in this period of worldwide maladjustment. . . .

It is easy to make a long list of William Penn's advances beyond his contemporaries. In education he came up against a stiff scholasticism, and he was expelled from Oxford at the age of eighteen primarily because the universities saw plainly that the inspirational preacher might quite easily interfere with their craft of producing dull and learned clergy and they utterly failed to see that William Penn was combining both learning and inspiration. In an age when schoolmasters were worshiping the written and printed word, he wrote on the education of children: "We press their memory too soon and puzzle and strain and load them with words and rules" and again, "Children had rather be making Tools and Instruments of Play; shaping, drawing, planning and building, than getting some Rules of propriety of speech by Heart." With slight change in phraseology, these words might have been written by John Dewey or Bertrand Russell. We may well ask ourselves, how did he achieve it? Certainly not by timidity nor by following beaten paths nor by fear of public opinion nor by devotion to precedent. In fact he avoided the latter, and once warned his colonists not to live upon the traditions of their founders, "Thereby encompassing yourselves with the sparks of your own fire."

In international affairs we have hardly caught up to him yet. When we recall the long difficulty with which the Thirteen Colonies finally federated, it is all the more remarkable that one hundred years before this was attempted, William Penn had worked out a plan for a "Dyet or Parliament of Europe to settle trouble between nations without war." In the International Assembly he proposed in 1693 for preserving the peace of Europe, he included the adherents of all religions and mentions carefully "the Turks and Muscovites, as seems but fit and just." If tolerance of religion was a test of seventeenth-century liberalism, as nationalism has become ours, he certainly "goes us one better" in regard to the Muscovite. Among other details for his International Assembly he advocated "a round room with divers doors to come in and go out at, to avoid quarrels for precedency."

Perhaps what the League of Nations needs now is such a round room with a central ventilating system which shall blow upon all alike and upon none too much. I once met an English friend as he came from an international conference in the Glass Room of the Secretariat. Affairs evidently had not gone smoothly, for he exclaimed with a worried look: "We got a bad start this morning as we often do. The English got there early, and naturally, as the room was stuffy, opened the windows, and when the French arrived with their invincible dread of a *courant d'air*, they promptly closed them—and there we were, two national delegations well irritated before we started the day's work!"

Penn provides an answer to so many problems of American life because he was an idealist who learned from actual experience. So thought Jane Addams,

A month before her death, Jane Addams (left) was photographed with one of the world's celebrated singers, Austrian-born contralto Ernestine Schumann-Heink. Both ladies had been listed four years earlier among the dozen greatest women in America; the all-male jury of selection included novelist Booth Tarkington and former Secretary of War Newton D. Baker. In April 1935, Madame Schumann-Heink—then seventy-four—came to Chicago to perform at a benefit concert for the Hull-House Music School, and captured her audience at the start by declaring in her thick German accent: "It iss too badt to be oldt!" Jane was also "oldt," but she sat happily through the concert, thrilled by her friend's rendition of classical German lieder, and proud of the fact that many of the other musicians featured in the concert were alumni of Hull-House music courses.

and she could have said the same thing about herself. She too remains a guide for all Americans—and will remain so for generation after generation:

■ Because William Penn appealed from tradition to experience, from authority to life, his most remarkable examples were in Pennsylvania where, in his absorbed devotion to his colony, he probably did not realize and certainly did not care how far he was departing from the customs of contemporary Europe. He calmly followed his own rule, "Though there is a regard due to education and the tradition of our fathers, Truth will ever deserve, as well as claim, the preference." He suppressed the excitement of hunting for witches when the chase was carried on in America as well as in Europe; he declared the spiritual quality of men and women; although two hundred offenses were punishable by death in England, William Penn reduced them to two in his colony; he insisted that all prisons should be workshops, and Pennsylvania had for a hundred years one of the best penal codes then in the world; every owner of a slave was required to pay so high a tax that slavery was finally taxed out of existence.

Such right thinking and courageous action in the life of one man has an enormous liberating power and taps new sources of human energy. It is doubtless what we need at this moment more than anything else, a generous and fearless desire to see life as it is, irrespective of the limitations and traditions which so needlessly divide us.

Jane Addams, already aged and growing feeble, roused herself with indomitable courage to attend the WILPF meeting in Washington on May 2, 1935. Those in charge of the festivities would naturally have deferred to her as the founder and honorary president of the organization. But the sentiment in the national capital went far beyond mere respect, because her admirers

Much of Jane Addams' most interesting correspondence was with Lillian Wald, to whom she wrote as early as 1899: "Will you mind a typewritten letter? I have lately learned to manage the machine myself and seem to like it better than my uncertain penmanship." After that she turned with greater frequency to the typewriter, often adding an afterthought in longhand, as in the case of this example dated March 8, 1935. On April 18 of that year Jane sent Lillian the most poignant of all these missives. One line reads: "How are you really, and how glad I shall be to see you early in June." Jane was unable to keep this appointment; she died in May. Miss Wald survived her old friend and colleague of settlement work by five years.

My health continues to improve and expect to surprise all my friends when I come back to Chicago on April 1st. I hope all goes well with you.

Always devotedly yours,

Jane Addams

Miss Lillian Wald,
House-on-the-Pond,
Westport, Conn.

P.S. Miss Cummins letter about the N.J. hospital has just come – I hope that you are safely home again by this time [illegible] *knew that she held a unique place in American life and surmised that she would not be there to occupy it much longer. Feeling that this was their last chance to pay homage to her, they besieged the Willard Hotel where twelve hundred guests gathered at the dinner in her honor, the occasion of many emotional eulogies to the grand old lady whose name had been linked to that of Hull-House for nearly half a century. Secretary of the Interior Harold Ickes spoke for them all when he declared: "Parents who want to develop the finest in their children will bring them up in the Jane Addams tradition." After the formal speeches by the prestigious men and women on the dais, Jane rose, set aside the text she had prepared, faced her audience, and delivered some extemporaneous remarks—simple, sincere, eloquent, and moving. These, the last words she publicly addressed to her fellow Americans, were cheered to the echo, and acclaimed in print. Less than three weeks later, on May 21, 1935, Jane Addams died.*

■ I do not know any such person as is described here this evening. I think I have never met her. We all know much worse things about ourselves than anyone has ever said or printed about us. I have never been sure I was right. I have often been doubtful about the next step. We can only feel our way as we go on from day to day. But I thank you all.

We may not be able to "change human nature" but we do hope to modify human behavior. . . . Today we cannot get internationalism across. We are too near the last war to get it over and to act together. But when the time does come when men will accept internationalism in the place of separate nationalism, we must be ready with the League of Nations, with the World Court, with an instructed public opinion. . . .

The source of our difficulties lies in the lack of moral enterprise. . . . At least we can seek to remove the difficulties which arise from each nation seeking to get the most for itself. It would be a splendid thing if the United States could lead the world in a new type of international relationship. . . . We move slowly, and yet much has occurred in twenty years. If we had said twenty years ago at The Hague that it would be possible to hold a disarmament conference, we would have been called idealistic visionaries. . . . Public opinion must come to realize how futile war is. It is so disastrous, not only in poison gas used to destroy lives, but in the poison injected into the public mind. We are suffering still from the war psychology. We can find many things which are the result of war, and one war is really the result of past war. . . . If it became fixed in the human mind that killing was not justified, it would be done away with along definite lines. It is a prerequisite to the lives of its citizens for a nation to build up a community relationship which destroys the feelings of distrust and inoculates goodwill and international accord.

We may be a long way from permanent peace. We need education of ourselves, of others, development of public opinion, moral enterprise. . . . Woodrow Wilson said: "No issue is dead in the world so long as men have courage." It would be a great glory if the United States could lead in this new type of statesmanship.

Harold Ickes (1874–1952) graduated from the University of Chicago in 1897, worked as a journalist, studied law, and was admitted to the bar in 1907 just in time to answer an appeal from Jane Addams, who needed a lawyer bold enough to defend the civil rights of anarchists again under suspicion in Chicago. A Russian Marxist had been shot at a police station, and a roundup of foreign-born radicals was underway when Jane phoned Ickes, whom a friend had recommended, and asked him to represent the accused. He helped ensure that justice would be done. Jane remained his strong admirer thereafter. They were in the Progressive party together, and he says in his autobiography: "I held the permanent proxy of Jane Addams as a member of the national executive committee, which was the top boss of the party." He later went back to the Republican party, but in 1932 supported F.D.R., who promptly appointed him Secretary of the Interior. A blunt man who termed himself "a curmudgeon," Ickes often riled people. To Jane Addams, however, he was the soul of chivalry—while to him, she was "the truest American that I have ever known, and there has been none braver. She actually believes that the guarantees of free speech, free press, and free assemblage were not written in a dead language."

CHRONOLOGY

PERSONAL LIFE | PUBLIC LIFE

1860–1894

Cedarville to Chicago

Personal Life

1860 Born on September 6 in the Illinois town of Cedarville.
1863 Mother dies.
1868 Father marries second wife.
1877–81 Attends Rockford Female Seminary (later Rockford College).
1881 Suffers severe mental depression on father's death.
1882 Undergoes operation to correct spinal defect.
1883–85 First European tour.
1885 Joins Presbyterian Church.
1887–88 Second European tour.

Public Life

1881 Debates with William Jennings Bryan in intercollegiate contest.
1889 Opens Hull-House.
1891 Founds Jane Club for women.
1892 Speaks at summer school in Plymouth, Massachusetts.
1893 Attends Congress of Representative Women at Chicago World's Fair; continues expansion of Hull-House.
1894 Defends Pullman strike, and criticizes Pullman in *A Modern Lear*.

1895–1910

National Acclaim

Personal Life

1895 Convalesces after attack of typhoid fever.
1896 Visits Tolstoy in Russia.
1900 Honorary member of DAR.
1902 First book, *Democracy and Social Ethics.*
1907 Publishes *Newer Ideals of Peace.*
1909 Writes *The Spirit of Youth and the City Streets.*
1910 Receives Yale honorary degree; publishes *Twenty Years at Hull-House.*

Public Life

1895 Becomes ward garbage inspector.
1898 Opposes American imperialism.
1900 Juror at Paris Exposition, gains prize for DAR exhibit.
1902 Speaks at funeral of former Governor John Peter Altgeld.
1905–09 On Chicago School Board.
1907 Attends national peace conference; joins woman suffrage committee.
1909 Heads National Conference of Social Work.
1910 Helps settle garment strike.

1911–1920

Progressivism and War

Personal Life

1912 Publishes *A New Conscience and an Ancient Evil.*
1915 Pneumonia prevents her from sailing with Ford peace ship.
1916 Supports Democrat Woodrow Wilson; publishes *The Long Road of Woman's Memory.*
1917 Saddened by accusations of being pro-German in her pacifism.
1920 Votes for Socialist Debs.

Public Life

1912 Campaigns for Theodore Roosevelt in presidential election.
1913 Attends International Suffrage Alliance in Budapest.
1915 Presides at The Hague over organization later called Woman's International League for Peace and Freedom; becomes embroiled in "bayonet controversy"; supports Ford peace ship.
1917 Opposes American entry into war.
1917–18 Works for Food Administration under Herbert Hoover.
1919 Sees misery of German people.

1921–1935

Testing and Triumph

Personal Life

1922 Records her relief work in *Peace and Bread in Time of War.*
1923 Takes trip around the world.
1924 Votes for Progressive La Follette.
1930 Publishes *The Second Twenty Years at Hull-House.*
1931 Attends fiftieth class reunion at Rockford College.
1932 Votes for Republican Hoover; publishes *The Excellent Becomes the Permanent.*
1934 Writes *My Friend, Julia Lathrop.*
1935 Dies in Chicago on May 21.

Public Life

1921 Presides over WILPF in Vienna.
1927 Blacklisted by DAR.
1929 Presides over WILPF in Prague, and is elected honorary president for life; presides over Hull-House fortieth anniversary celebration.
1931 Wins Nobel Peace Prize.
1932 Addresses both party conventions, urging international amity.
1935 Wins American Education Award; attends Washington celebrations in her honor, and addresses world by radio.

POLITICAL-MILITARY EVENTS IN AMERICA	CULTURAL-ECONOMIC EVENTS IN AMERICA	WORLD EVENTS
1860 Lincoln elected President. **1861–65** Civil War. **1863** Emancipation Proclamation. **1865** Lincoln assassinated; Thirteenth Amendment ends slavery. **1868** President Andrew Johnson is impeached but acquitted; Grant elected. **1876** Centennial of the Revolution. **1881** Garfield assassinated. **1892** Populists demand free silver; Ellis Island opened for immigrants.	**1868–70** Susan B. Anthony edits *The Revolution*, suffrage newspaper. **1869** Jay Gould causes Black Friday. **1873** First public kindergarten. **1879** George's *Progress and Poverty.* **1885** "New immigration" begins. **1886** Haymarket riot in Chicago. **1890** Census Bureau proclaims end of Western frontier; census: 62,947,714. **1893** Chicago World's Fair. **1894** Pullman strike; Howells' *A Traveler from Altruria;* Stead's *If Christ Came to Chicago.*	**1860** Garibaldi's men invade Sicily. **1866** Tolstoy's *War and Peace.* **1869** Suez Canal opened. **1870–71** Franco-Prussian War; Third Republic proclaimed in Paris. **1878** Leo XIII becomes pope. **1884** Fabian Society founded by socialists in London. **1888** Wilhelm II Emperor of Germany. **1893** Dvořák's *New World Symphony.* **1894** Nicholas II Czar of Russia. **1894–1906** Dreyfus affair in France.
1896 Supreme Court approves "separate but equal" doctrine. **1898** Spanish-American War. **1901** McKinley assassinated; Theodore Roosevelt becomes President. **1902** T.R. introduces "Square Deal." **1906** Pure Food and Drug Act. **1907** Financial panic; U.S. flotilla begins international courtesy calls. **1908** Taft elected President. **1910** T.R. breaks with Taft; Mann Act curtails organized prostitution.	**1896** F. P. Dunne creates "Mr. Dooley." **1899** Dewey's *School and Society*; Veblen's *Theory of the Leisure Class*; first use of spinal anesthesia. **1900** Susan B. Anthony retires; Carrie Nation raids saloons. **1902–12** Muckraker journalism. **1904** Steffens' *Shame of the Cities.* **1906** T.R. wins Nobel Peace Prize. **1910** National Association for the Advancement of Colored People founded.	**1895** Germany opens Kiel Canal; Marconi invents radio. **1897** Queen Victoria's Diamond Jubilee; Greco-Turkish War. **1898** The Curies discover radium. **1899** First Hague Peace Conference; Boer War begins. **1900–01** Boxer Rebellion in China. **1904** Franco-British Entente. **1905** Revolt in Russia suppressed. **1907** Kipling wins Nobel Prize. **1909** Blériot flies the English Channel. **1910** George V King of England.
1911 La Follette leads Progressives. **1912** Wilson defeats T.R. and Taft. **1913** Federal Reserve Act on banking. **1914** Wilson proclaims U.S. neutrality as World War I erupts in Europe. **1916** Wilson reelected, using slogan: "He kept us out of war." **1917** U.S. declares war on Germany. **1919** Senate rebuffs Wilson on League of Nations; Eighteenth Amendment provides for Prohibition. **1920** Nineteenth Amendment establishes woman suffrage.	**1911** Triangle Shirtwaist fire in New York leads to safety legislation. **1912** Harriet Monroe founds *Poetry*; Dreiser's *The Financier.* **1913** Woman suffrage in Illinois. **1914** First American patent for multistage rockets. **1914–20** Wartime boom. **1915** Carrie Chapman Catt heads suffrage movement. **1916** Repplier's *Counter-Currents.* **1919** Anderson's *Winesburg, Ohio.*	**1912** Anglo-German naval discussions fail; Franco-Russian naval agreement. **1912–13** Balkan Wars. **1914–18** World War I. **1915** Germans use poison gas. **1917** Germans proclaim unrestricted submarine warfare; Bolsheviks seize power in Russia. **1918** Germany capitulates. **1919** Treaty of Versailles. **1920** League of Nations established.
1921 Harding takes office surrounded by "the Ohio gang." **1923** Harding dies; Coolidge becomes President. **1924** Harding scandals exposed. **1926** Army Air Corps established. **1928** Hoover elected President. **1929** Great Depression begins. **1932** Franklin D. Roosevelt elected. **1933** F.D.R. rejects "fear itself"; New Deal begins; Twenty-first Amendment repeals Prohibition. **1934** Federal Housing Administration. **1935** Social Security Act.	**1921** Tomb of the Unknown Soldier dedicated at Arlington. **1924** Immigration quotas set. **1925** Tennessee "Monkey Trial." **1927** First full-length talking movie; first long transmission of TV signals. **1927–28** Model A Ford replaces the long-popular Model T. **1928** Justice Holmes hits wiretapping. **1929** Hemingway's *A Farewell to Arms.* **1931** Urey isolates heavy hydrogen. **1933** Unemployment reaches 13 million. **1935** Gershwin opera *Porgy and Bess.*	**1922** Mussolini's march on Rome. **1923** Hitler jailed after abortive "beer-hall putsch" in Munich. **1924** Lenin's death triggers struggle for power in Moscow. **1929** Stalin consolidates power as dictator and Trotsky goes into exile. **1930** Gandhi's "salt march" to sea challenges British authority in India. **1931** Alfonso XIII of Spain abdicates. **1933** Hitler takes power in Germany. **1935** Italy invades Ethiopia; Moscow purge trials begin.

ANNOTATED BIBLIOGRAPHY

Any bibliographer of Jane Addams faces an embarrassment of riches—she wrote so much herself, and so much has been written about her. Thus, M. Helen Perkins covered more than forty pages before finishing A Preliminary Checklist for a Bibliography on Jane Addams *(Rockford, Illinois, 1960). The following list of Jane's writings is confined to her books and important manuscripts; her articles have been mentioned and excerpted in HER OWN WORDS, where her major contributions to such magazines as* The Survey *and* Survey Graphic *can be found. The list of secondary works helpful in studying aspects of Jane Addams' career is, similarly, limited to the most useful and pertinent.*

WORKS ABOUT JANE ADDAMS' LIFE

Linn, James Weber. *Jane Addams: A Biography.* Appleton, 1935.

Miss Addams' nephew—to whom she bequeathed all her voluminous archives—wrote this memoir as a labor of love. Laudatory but reasonably objective, reliable, and comprehensive, it remains the single best source of information about her life, thought, and specific achievements. In his preface, Linn states: "My aunt read over and annotated the first draft of the first eight [of twenty-two] chapters, talked over the next three, and agreed upon the proportion of the remainder."

Tims, Margaret. *Jane Addams of Hull-House.* Allen and Unwin, 1961.

The author leans too heavily on Linn, but she does "place" Jane Addams in a broad international perspective.

Bowen, Louise de Koven. "The Jane Addams I Knew," from *Open Windows: Stories of People and Places.* Seymour, 1946.

Mrs. Bowen, although too uncritical in these pages, provides revealing and valuable glimpses into the human side of her close friend and confidante.

Maude, Aylmer. "A Talk with Miss Jane Addams and Leo Tolstoy." *The Humane Review,* Vol. III, No. 1, June 1902.

The Russian humanitarian's English translator describes the dramatic scene at Yasnaya Polyana, giving a slightly different version than that of Jane herself (see pages 165–169). She thought, but Maude did not, that Tolstoy was "scathing" in some of his remarks to her.

Taylor, Graham. "Jane Addams: The Great Neighbor." *Survey Graphic,* Vol. XXIV, No. 7, July 1935.

This is the final and considered tribute paid by one renowned Chicago social worker to another. It was published two months after the death of Jane Addams.

Conway, Jill. "Jane Addams: American Heroine." *Daedalus,* Vol. XCIII, No. 2, Spring 1964.

Despite its title, this article is not adulatory, but rather perceptive and judicial. It ranks as one of the best recent interpretations. Miss Conway sees Miss Addams as "an intellectual captured by the activism of American life."

Wagenknecht, Edward. "The Greatest Chicagoan of All," from *Chicago.* University of Oklahoma Press, 1964.

The author of this brief history of the nation's second city devotes a chapter to Jane Addams. Its title sums up his opinion of her—an opinion widely held by her fellow Chicagoans.

Scott, Anne Firor. "Saint Jane and the Ward Boss." *American Heritage,* Vol. XII, No. 1, December 1960.

This well-illustrated article analyzes the relationship between Jane Addams and Alderman John Powers at the time of their political conflict in the Nineteenth Ward.

Hackett, Francis. "Hull-House—A Souvenir." *The Survey,* Vol. LIV, No. 5, June 1925.

A well-known Irish writer describes his period of residence at the settlement, and shows that Miss Addams was indeed its guiding spirit—the one on whom everybody else relied.

Balch, Emily Greene. "Jane Addams, In Memoriam." *Unity,* Vol. CXV, Jane Addams Memorial Issue, July 15, 1935.

Miss Balch sees clearly that, toward the end of Jane Addams' life, her struggle and achievement were buried under pious platitudes of close friends and family: "I think that her greatness has been veiled by her goodness. Men have a curious tendency to turn those of eminent stature into plaster images."

Wilson, Edmund. "Hull-House in 1932," from *The American Earthquake.* Doubleday Anchor Books, 1958.

A perspicacious American literary and social critic presents an impressionistic view of Jane Addams and her institution. There are some graphic descriptions of the sufferings of the people around Halsted Street during the Great Depression.

Repplier, Agnes. "Modern Sentimentality," from *Counter-Currents.* Houghton Mifflin, 1916.

In this essay, an acidulous critic pours scorn on a fellow spinster's opinions of women and war.

The following specialized studies are useful for advanced reading or research on Jane Addams:

Farrell, John C. *Beloved Lady: A History of Jane Addams' Ideas on Reform and Peace.* Johns Hopkins Press, 1967.

This monograph—the result of graduate work at Johns Hopkins University—is the most complete study in its field, and is especially valuable for its forty-five-page bibliographical essay and its searching exposition of her social philosophy.

Dewey, John. "The Future of Pacifism," from *Characters and Events: Popular Essays in Social and Political Philosophy.* Holt, 1929.

The moral of this profound philosophical analysis is that pacifism remains a viable concept—if pacifists accept Jane Addams' definition of the word.

Curti, Merle. "Jane Addams on Human Nature." *Journal of the History of Ideas,* Vol. XXII, No. 1. April–June 1961.

An intellectual historian analyzes the logic of Jane Addams' thinking, which he considers mainly humanistic and scientific rather than religious or metaphysical.

Woods, Robert A., and Albert J. Kennedy. *The Settlement Horizon: A National Estimate.* Russell Sage Foundation, 1922.

Two sociologists describe the social movement that produced Hull-House—and in the process they devote a good share of their attention to that institution.

JANE ADDAMS' WRITINGS, PUBLISHED AND UNPUBLISHED

Addams, Jane. *Notebooks.* Swarthmore College Peace Collection: The Jane Addams Papers.
These unpublished manuscripts are basic for insight into Jane's early life, providing information that she did not put into her autobiographical publications. Swarthmore has the best collection of Addams documents—including most of those Linn inherited—and a helpful introductory "Checklist of the Jane Addams Papers," available to researchers. Swarthmore also has the official records of the Women's International League for Peace and Freedom, which contain many items by and about Miss Addams.

Addams, Jane. *Twenty Years at Hull-House.* Macmillan, 1910.
In one of the finest American autobiographies, Jane describes her life from her earliest years through two decades of her social work in the Chicago ghetto. The New American Library edition of 1961 (available in paperback) has a perceptive and important foreword by historian Henry Steele Commager.

Addams, Jane. *The Second Twenty Years at Hull-House.* Macmillan, 1930.
Continuing her autobiography, Jane deals with wider themes than her life in Chicago. But she is still very much present as a person, and her chapter on the "Devil Baby" is an enthralling triumph of her sensitivity and her pen.

Addams, Jane. *Forty Years at Hull-House.* Macmillan, 1935.
This combined publication of Jane's two autobiographical books in one volume allows the reader to follow her life story from the beginning almost to the end. Lillian Wald, head of New York's famous Henry Street Settlement, offers her own high-minded verdict on Jane in a gracious afterword.

Addams, Jane, and the Residents of Hull-House. *Hull-House Maps and Papers.* Crowell, 1895.
The other contributors included Ellen Starr, Julia Lathrop, Florence Kelley, and Alzina P. Stevens. The volume gives a statistical picture of the ghetto, and reproduces the map of nationalities that hung on the wall of Jane's Octagon Room.

Addams, Jane. *Democracy and Social Ethics.* Macmillan, 1902; Harvard University Press, 1964.
Jane, publishing her first complete book at the age of forty-two, reveals how far her thought on human problems had matured, from social work to political reform. The Harvard edition has a lengthy and useful introduction by Anne Firor Scott.

Addams, Jane. *Newer Ideals of Peace.* Macmillan, 1907.
Jane sets forth her philosophy of pacifism in her first book devoted to the subject.

Addams, Jane. *The Spirit of Youth and the City Streets.* Macmillan, 1909.
The director of Hull-House delivers a powerful indictment of the society that permitted its children too few alternatives to roaming the streets, sleeping in doorways, and pilfering food from pushcarts.

Addams, Jane. *A New Conscience and An Ancient Evil.* Macmillan, 1912.
The "ancient evil" of this volume is prostitution; the author gives many examples, based directly on her Hull-House experience, of young girls who had been victimized.

Addams, Jane, Emily G. Balch, and Alice Hamilton. *Women at The Hague: The International Congress of Women and Its Results.* Macmillan, 1915.
The three contributors to this book were American delegates to the congress. Jane Addams contributed "The Revolt against War," "Factors in Continuing the War," and "Women and Internationalism."

Addams, Jane. *The Long Road of Woman's Memory.* Macmillan, 1916.
During the havoc of the most widespread and terrible war the world had known up to that time, Jane Addams looks at the shining record of her sex as the chief contributor to the development of a peaceful, humane society. Slightly sentimental, but deeply sincere.

Addams, Jane. *Peace and Bread in Time of War.* Macmillan, 1922.
Without dramatics, Miss Adams tells the heroic story of the struggle to save the lives of stricken Europeans during and after World War I. A reprint now available carries the significant introductory essay that John Dewey wrote for this book in 1945.

Addams, Jane. *The Excellent Becomes the Permanent.* Macmillan, 1932.
This beautiful little book is composed of memorial addresses that Jane Addams delivered after the deaths of persons she knew and loved. The most poignant (see pages 175–176) is devoted to a young boy, Gordon Dewey, John Dewey's son.

Addams, Jane. *My Friend, Julia Lathrop.* Macmillan, 1935.
Dr. Alice Hamilton prepared this, the last book written by Jane Addams, for the press. It is a touching tribute to one of the author's closest colleagues.

Johnson, Emily Cooper (ed.). *Jane Addams: A Centennial Reader.* Macmillan, 1960.
The best general anthology of Jane's writings, this one presents her thoughts on the major subjects with which she concerned herself. Each section is introduced by a specialist in that particular field.

Lasch, Christopher (ed.). *The Social Thought of Jane Addams.* Bobbs-Merrill, 1965.
The editor has produced a more restricted anthology than the one just cited, but the limitations he has thus placed on his excerpts give him room to argue with some plausibility that Jane was more radical than is commonly supposed. It is a good corrective to earlier collections, which tend to depict her as the universal maiden aunt who founded Hull-House.

BOOKS ABOUT EVENTS AND PEOPLE CONTEMPORARY WITH JANE ADDAMS

Barnett, Henrietta. *Canon Barnett: His Life, Work and Friends.* Houghton Mifflin, 1919.
The widow of the first head of Toynbee Hall—the pioneering English precedent for all later settlement houses—wrote this memoir about him. Some eulogistic pages refer to Jane Addams, whom the Barnetts knew well.

Lloyd, Henry Demarest. *Wealth Against Commonwealth.* Harper, 1894.
Lloyd had known Jane Addams for several years before he wrote this, his most important book, and the two shared the same basic philosophy about capitalism and social reform. They both knew that a person's shifts of opinion matter little until a person actually does something concrete. "Change of heart," as Lloyd wrote here in this connection, is of itself "no more redemption than hunger is dinner."

Steffens, Lincoln. *The Shame of the Cities.* McClure, 1904.
Of all the "muckraker" books, none captures the immediate and brutal problems of American cities in the late nineteenth and early twentieth century better than this. Reading the section on Chicago, one's admiration for what Jane Addams did there is tinged by disbelief: one frail woman against all those bullies?

Gabriel, Ralph H. *American Democratic Thought.* Ronald Press, 1940.
A masterpiece of synthesis and clarity, this volume defines the main stream in which Jane Addams immersed herself and to which she devoted her life. Professor Gabriel stresses the natural law and the innate American faith in individualism—excellent vantage points from which to view the era Jane's career covered. Gabriel's views on how human beings can be used as symbols are illuminating when applied to Miss Addams.

Maude, Aylmer. *The Life of Tolstoy.* Oxford University Press, 1930.
This authorized biography gives a full account of the most extraordinary man Jane Addams ever met. Maude describes his train ride with Jane (and Mary Rozet Smith) from Moscow to Yasnaya Polyana, and confesses he found her social philosophy more practical than Tolstoy's.

Ginger, Raymond C. "The Women at Hull-House," from *Altgeld's America: The Lincoln Ideal versus Changing Realities.* Funk and Wagnalls, 1958.
The subject of this book is the transformation of the United States during the post-Civil War period. John Peter Altgeld is its hero; its heroines are Jane Addams and the other residents of Hull-House.

Davis, Allen F. "The Social Workers and the Progressive Party, 1912–1916." *American Historical Review,* Vol. LXIX, No. 3, April 1964.
A professional historian assays the role of Jane Addams, among others, in the effort to get Theodore Roosevelt elected, and examines the attitude of the settlement volunteers after T.R.'s defeat in 1912.

Gale, Zona. "Great Ladies of Chicago." *The Survey,* Vol. LXVII, No. 2, February 1932.
This brief article takes a look at Jane Addams and the rest of the women who made Hull-House a beacon in the field of social work.

Hamilton, Alice. *Exploring the Dangerous Trades.* Little, Brown, 1943.
The physician of Hull-House gives a technical account of the residents' campaigns to improve the hygiene of the ghetto and the city.

Kelley, Florence. *Some Ethical Gains through Legislation.* Macmillan, 1905.
Another resident of Hull-House traces the impact of humanitarianism on the laws of the land, describing changes that range from pure food to child labor, and noting the efficacy of the settlement in promoting this progress. The book is a good example of the Progressive-era outlook.

Abbott, Edith. "Grace Abbott and Hull-House." *Social Service Review,* Vol. XXIV, No. 3, September 1950.
The Abbott sisters were both residents, and Edith here supplies some interesting sidelights on what it was like to work under the supervision of Jane Addams, who called them "my two good 'Abits.' "

Davis, Philip. *And Crown Thy Good.* Philosophical Library, 1952.
An immigrant from Russia tells his personal story of how Jane Addams and Hull-House helped him to find a secure and constructive place for himself in American society.

Webb, Beatrice. *American Diary: 1898.* David A. Shannon (ed.). University of Wisconsin Press, 1963.
Beatrice and Sidney Webb were a husband-and-wife team prominent in the British labor movement. Mrs. Webb wrote this short account of their American tour, including a description of their stay at Hull-House, where various procedures left them somewhat disconcerted.

Wade, Louise C. *Graham Taylor: Pioneer for Social Justice, 1851–1938.* University of Chicago Press, 1964.
Taylor receives a much-needed scholarly treatment in this volume, which presents Jane Addams as his good friend and colleague.

Wilson, Howard E. *Mary McDowell, Neighbor.* University of Chicago Press, 1928.
The author signifies by his title that Mary McDowell—another Chicago social worker who supplemented Miss Addams' trailblazing efforts—considered herself one of the community when she guided her settlement, which was adjacent to the stockyards.

Duffus, R. L. *Lillian Wald: Neighbor and Crusader.* Macmillan, 1938.
Miss Wald assisted the author of this biography, but Duffus' friendship for her did not keep him from writing a balanced and penetrating study of New York City's venerated social worker. Parallels between the careers of Miss Wald and Miss Addams are evident.

Lutz, Alma. *Susan B. Anthony: Rebel, Crusader, Humanitarian.* Beacon, 1959.
The numerous illustrations in this volume give added vitality to the life story of the greatest figure of the suffrage movement in America.

Peck, Mary Gray. *Carrie Chapman Catt: A Biography.* Wilson, 1944.
The triumph of the suffrage movement forms the setting for the personal triumph of its leader, Mrs. Catt, in this detailed work—which also includes enough original material to rank as a virtual source book.

Bussey, Gertrude, and Margaret Tims. *Women's International League for Peace and Freedom, 1915–1965: A Record of Fifty Years' Work.* Allen and Unwin, 1965.
The authors provide a general history of an organization that Jane Addams was instrumental in founding, long headed, and deeply cherished. They are informative on the programs backed by the WILPF since her death, which are logical extensions of the ideals Miss Addams so eloquently proclaimed.

INDEX

(indicates an illustration; pages 7-88 are in the Biography; pages 89-120 are in the Picture Portfolio; pages 121-229 are in Her Own Words.)*

Abbott, Edith, 57
Abbott, Grace, 57
Adams, Henry, 59
Addams, Alice (sister of Jane), 19
  Sarah W. Addams described by, 13
Addams, Anna Haldeman (stepmother of Jane), 15, 16-17, *19, 31, 38, *91, 123
  attitude of, toward Jane's work, 50
  conflict between Jane and, 35
  description of, by Linn, 18-19
  Jane's relationship with, 19
Addams, Jane, *15, *30, *80, *87, *91, *103, *123, *227
  "America's uncrowned queen," 81
  ancestors of, 9
  articles by, 137-164, 169-175, 178-184, 187-190, 192-194, 216-228
  attitude of:
    toward capitalism, 56
    toward clothes, 38
    toward Socialist movement, 56
  autobiography of, 79, 122
  awards to, 86, 87
  "bayonet" speech by, 72
  birth of, 9, 12
  birthplace of, 90, *123
  books by, 58, 61, 64, 68, 75, 79, 86, 122, 178, 198, 211
  called "Saint Jane," 49
  campaigner for Theodore Roosevelt, 65, 69, 185-187, 188
  capacity of, to judge people, 60
  Carnegie Hall address by, 72
  characterizations of, 24, 27, 35, 38, 45, 48, 54, 60, 68, 79, 82-83, 85-86, 100-101, 105, 165, 195, 200, 203
  childhood of, 12-15, 90-91
  church affiliations of, 39
  college address by, 63
  comment by:
    on cigarettes, 54
    on expulsion from DAR, 85
  criticisms of, 45, 54, 59, 60, 65, 69, 72-73, 75, 78, 113, 166, 173, 195, 204, 205
  death of, 88, 228, 229
  death of mother of, 13, 90
  descriptions of, 23, 24, 27, 45, 49, 78, 82, 90, 173
  disposition of, 35
  education of, 15, 21, 91, 92
  elevator anecdote concerning, 38
  epitaph for, 88
  epithets applied to, 60
  European trips of, 33-37, 39-40, 53, 67, 75, 92-97, 130-136
  fashionable tastes of, 38
  father of. *See* Addams, John Huy
  first encounter with death, 20
  friendships of, 27
  as "garbage inspector," 51, 100-101
  generosity of, 38
  handwriting of, *121, *128, *136, *168, *172, *182, *200, *214, *217, *228
  health of, 32, 35, 53, 80, 81, 86, 92, 129-130, 165
  honorary degrees awarded to, *64, 86, 87, 204
  humor of, 85
  labor legislation achieved by, 101
  last speech by, 229
  lectures by, 68, 198
  loneliness of, 85
  Luther admired by, 39
  marriage proposal rejected by, 27-28
  mother of. *See* Addams, Sarah Weber
  muckrakers approved by, 56
  newspaper attacks on, 60-61
  Nobel Peace Prize awarded to, 80
  a nonsmoker, 85
  optimism of, 57
  pacifism of, 66-67, 68-69, 71, 72-73, 74, 77, 79, 80, 110, 198
  parents of, 9
    See also Addams: John; Sarah
  at peace demonstration, *112
  "philosophical testament" of, 222-228
  philosophy of, 58-59
  platform manner of, 57
  Plymouth addresses by, 136-145, 145-152
  political activities of, 64, 65, 79, 81, 185-190, 216-219
  post-World War I activities of, 76-77, 209-211
  Powers' criticism of, 173
  prose style of, 64
  psychic interests of, 19
  qualities of, 79
  radio address by, on international linkup, 87-88
  religious belief of, 39, 86
  round-the-world trip of, 77, 115, 214
  school board, work on, 60-61, 140, 177
  search by, for nephew's grave, 207
  self-characterization revealed in diary, 12
  sense of justice a characteristic of, 60, 64, 67
  sentimentality attributed to, 75
  sisters of. *See* Addams: Alice; Mary
  social reforms brought about by, 108
  speech by, on Toynbee, 150
  speech by, on George Washington, 125-127
  stepbrothers of. *See* Haldeman: Dr. Harry; George
  stepmother of. *See* Addams, Anna
  as a student, 15
  in suffrage parade, *109
  a teetotaler, 85
  temper of, 35, 45, 132
  tolerance shown by, 45
  tombstone inscription for, 88
  verses by, 184-185
  White House visit of, 38
  at WILPF dinner, *87
Addams, John Huy (father of Jane), 12-13, *30
  anti-slavery sentiments of, 12, 120
  birth of, 9
  death of, 31, 92, 129
  feminist movement approved by, 62
  influence of, on Jane's beliefs, 63
  Jane's reaction to death of, 32
  Jane's reminiscences of, 122-124
  Lincoln's friendship for, 15-16
  marriage of, 9
  photo of, compared with Jane's, *30
  Quaker beliefs of, 14, 66
  reaction of, to Lincoln's assassination, 124
  second marriage of, 15, 18
  state senate nomination refused by, 19
Addams, Laura Jane. *See* Addams, Jane
Addams, Mary (sister of Jane), 18
  marriage of, 19
  Sarah W. Addams described by, 13
Addams, Sarah Weber (mother of Jane), 9, 13
  death of, 13, 90
Addams, Weber (brother of Jane), 13
Afton River, Ayrshire, Scotland, *92
Altgeld, John Peter, 174, *183
  a Hull-House advocate, 53
  Jane a speaker at funeral of, 59, 60
America, ills of, diagnosed by Jane, 222-228
American Education Award to Jane (1935), 87
American Federation of Labor, 206
American Friends Service Committee, 209
  Jane's work for, 113
  See also Friends Service Committee
American industry (1881), *44
American Legion, Jane attacked by, 78
American Relief Association, 113
anarchist scares in the United States, 59-60, 169, 174, 229
Anderson, Marian, WILPF sponsor, 116
Anthony, Susan B., 62, 131, 132, *193, 195
Armenian child victims of Allied blockade, *76
Arnold, Matthew, *28, 30, 33
Astor, J. J., 68
Attlee, Clement, 41

Baker, Newton D., 227
  Jane praised by, 195
Balch, Emily Greene, *203
  garment workers described by, 107
band, Hull-House, *61, 151
Barnett, Canon and Mrs. Samuel Augustus (Henrietta), 41, *42, 168, 207, 214
Baskin, Leonard, woodcut by, 212
bayonet fighting in World War I, *111
Beard, Charles A., 53, *221
Bellamy, Edward, 44
Bellows, George, painting of slums by, 107
Beloit College, 19, 25, 27, 29
Bennett, Helen, Jane characterized by, 68
Bessemer process, *17, 18
Big Four, 208
"Black Friday" (1869), 20
Blake, Mrs. Tiffany, 68-69
Blarney Castle, *36, 130
Boardman, Mabel, criticism of Jane by, 65
Booth, Edwin, 133
Borah, William E., 218, *223
Bowen, Louise de Koven, 51, 88, *104, 105
  Jane characterized by, 38, 60
  Jane's friendship with, 85
Bowen Country Club, *77, *104, *105
Bowen Hall, 51, 52
Brewster, Mary, 200
Briand, Aristide, *226
British writers, Jane influenced by, 28-29
Brown, John, steward of Queen Victoria, *34

Browning, Robert, 28, *29
Bryan, William Jennings, 30, 55, 72, 183, *215
bullfight, Spanish
Jane's attendance at, 40
illustration of, *40
Burns, John, 60, *165
Burns, Robert, 132, 133, *134
Butler, Edward, 51
Butler, Nicholas Murray, *220, 221
Nobel Peace Prize (1931) shared by Jane and, 80, 196, 198, 220
Butler Gallery, 29, 51

California, University of, 87
capitalism, American (1900), 56
capital punishment, Jane's opposition to, 115, 116, 117
Capone, Al, 84
Carlyle, Thomas, 28, *29, 30, 129, 188
Carnegie, Andrew, 56, 69, 85, *171, 220
Carnegie Endowment for International Peace, 80, 171
Carpenter, Francis B., Lincoln family portrait by, 124
Carr, Charlotte, *151
Jane's successor at Hull-House, 151
Carter, Orrin N., Jane's pacifism criticized by, 73
Catt, Carrie Chapman, 62, 192, *195, 200, 205
suffrage parade led by, *63
Cedarville, Illinois, 13, 16-17, 31-32, 80, *90
Addams home in, 19, 20, 21
birthplace of Jane, 12, 90, *123
Jane's burial at, 88
charity, giving and receiving, 178-185
charity visitor. *See* welfare worker
Chessman, Caryl, protest against execution of, *117
Chesterton, G. K., 196, 197
Chicago, 9, 10, 11, *98, *99
"Century of Progress" celebration, 86
challenge of, 42-43, 47
First Ward ball, *53
Jane's arrival in (1889), 45
typhoid epidemic in, 59
See also slums, Chicago
Chicago, University of, 141, 176
Hull-House relationship with, 140
Settlement, 38
Chicago *Chronicle*, Jane maligned by, 45
Chicago Commons Social Settlement, 59
Chicago Museum of Science and Industry, 175
Chicago River, engraving of, from *Harper's Weekly* (1884), *43
Chicago Trades Council, 56
child laborers, *58, 138, *155, 162
child labor laws, 163
Jane's influence on, 108, 155
children, first White House conference on, 62
children, hungry German, 209-210
Jane's aid in raising funds for, 113
Kollwitz poster sketch of, *113
Children's Bureau, United States, 200
Grace Abbott head of, 57
Julia Lathrop first chief of, 102, 136, 138
Christianity, Jane's ideas on, 23, 39, 67-68, 145, 148-150, 156, 167-168
cities
Jane's belief in, 80, 152
problems of, 145-147
young people in, 146-147, 148
civil rights movement, 78
Civil War, 56, 69, 85, 124, 218
Cleveland, Grover, 53, 98, 109, *161, 183
Climbing Boys Act, 146
Cobden, Richard, quoted on war, 75
Coit, Stanton, 42
collective bargaining, 153
Hull-House role in, 145
Jane's belief in, 64
college women, Jane's opinion of, 94, 97
Commager, Henry Steele, 100-101
Committee for Municipal Suffrage for Women, Jane chairman of, 63
Communists, 215, 226
Conference for a New Peace, at The Hague, 77
Congress of Representative Women, 63
Conway, Jill, 85
Cook County Commissioners Meeting, Jane's last public appearance at, 88
Coolidge, Calvin, 217, 218, 219
Coughlin, "Bathhouse John," ball run by, 53
Covent Garden, London, *135
Craig, Edith, 132
crime, American indifference to, 225-226
Culver, Helen, 151
Hull's home given to Jane by, 46

DAR. *See* Daughters of the American Revolution
Darrow, Clarence, 53, *215
Darwin, Charles, 25-26, 45, *147, 149
Jane's reading of, 66, 128
Daughters of the American Revolution (DAR)
Grant Wood's satirization of, *112
Jane considered subversive by, 78, 195, 205
Jane's membership in, revoked, 85, 112, 205
See also "Spiderweb Chart"
Davidson, Thomas, 41
Davis, Allen F.
description of Jane by, 173
Jane's Progressive party activities assessed by, 65
Davis, Philip, 48
Davis, Richard Harding, *73
"bayonet" speech rebuttal by, 72
Debs, Eugene V., 53, *159
Hardie's meeting with, 167
Jane's vote for, as President, 76, 159
presidential candidate, 55-56
Democracy and Social Ethics (Jane's first book), 58, 178, 179
Democratic National Committee, 65
Depression, the Great, 79, 80-81, 82, *83, 84, 86, 141, 207, 219
De Quincey, Thomas, 30, *127
Devil Baby, The, 190-192
Dewey, John, 49, 61, *176, 226
birthday toast to, by Jane, 176-178
elegy by Jane for son of, 175-176
influence of, on Jane, 22
Jane's pacifism praised by, 73, 199
relations of, with Hull-House, 27, 51, 52, 176
diaries, comparison of Jane's with her father's, 12
Dickens, Charles, 33, 146, 172
Dickinson, Emily, comparison of Jane with, 35
disarmament, WILPF favors, 116
disarmament conference, possibility of, 229
Disraeli, Benjamin, 35, 41
Dolls Club members, Hull-House, *61
Doré, Gustave, 36
Douglas, Corinne Williams, 23
Drew, Daniel, 20
cartoon depicting Gould and, *20
Du Bois, William Edward Burghardt, *190
Dunne, Edward F., 60, 61, *177
Dürer, Albrecht, 46

Edison, Thomas A., 72
education, 15, 21-22, 60-61, 101, 139, 144-145, 189-190, 226
Edward VII, funeral of, *67
Eighteenth Amendment, 84, 85
See also Prohibition
election scene, Chicago (1892), *98
Eliot, Charles W., 21
emancipation, 125, 127, 188
Europe. *See* Addams, Jane: European trips
evolution, *25-26 58, 128, 147-148, 215-216
Excellent Becomes the Permanent, The (Jane Addams), 86

Fabian Society, 41, 142, 164
Federal Farm Board, 81
Federal Home Loan Act, 81
Fellowship of the New Life, 41
Field, Marshall, 174
Fisk, James, 20
flower girls, Covent Garden, London, *135
Food Administration, U.S., 74, 207
Jane's work for, 75, 113
See also Hoover, Herbert
Ford, Henry, 201
Hague Peace Conference supported by, 71
See also peace ship
Ford, Thomas, 11
Fort Dearborn, 10, *11
Fourteen Points, 76, 204
Fox, George, 14
Friends Service Committee, 207
See also American Friends Service Committee
Fuller, Governor A. T., *114, 115, 217

Gale, Zona, 51
Galsworthy, John, 52, *187
Galt, Edith Bolling, 191
Gandhi, Mahatma, *222
Jane impressed by, 77
See also "Tolstoy and Gandhi"
gangland murders, American acceptance of, 225
Garfield, James A., 31, *32
Garibaldi, Giuseppe, *13
garment workers, 138, 153-*155
description of, by Emily Balch, 107
exploitation of, *154
unionization of, aided by Jane, 108
garment workers strike, 64, *153
gas attack, Wilfred Owen's description of, 111
gas masks, French soldiers wearing, *110
George, Henry ("Single Tax"), 44, 45
Germany's poor, in Kollwitz etching, *97
Gibbon, Edward, *131
Gielgud, John, 132
Gladstone, William Ewart, 41
Goodman, Benny, 102, *151
Gorki, Maxim, 60
Gould, Jay, *20
stock exchange panic provoked by, 20
Granata, William, *52
Grant, General, 16, 20

gratitude, Jane's idea of, 60
Grey, Sir Edward, quoted on World War I, 66
gristmill, play spot of Jane's childhood, 14-15, *90
Guild of St. George, 41
Guiteau, Charles J., shooting of Garfield by, 31, *32
Guiteau, Flora, 31

Hackett, Francis, Jane's Hull-House activities evaluated by, 68
Hague, The, 201
  Conference for a New Peace at, 77
  International Committee, at, 72
  Peace Palace at, 69
Hague Peace Conference, 70, 71
Hainisch, Madame, 197
Haldeman, Anna (Mrs. William), stepmother of Jane. *See* Addams, Anna
Haldeman, George (stepbrother of Jane), 16, 18, 25, 31, 32, 38, *91, 136
  Jane's friendship with, 19
  Jane's unwillingness to marry, 35
Haldeman, Dr. Harry (stepbrother of Jane), 19, 26, 32
  European trip recommended for Jane by, 92
  operates on Jane, 33
Haldeman, William, 18
Hamilton, Dr. Alice, 27, 45, 51, *209, 214
  "bayonet" speech interpreted by, 72-73
  Health Department reorganization instigated by, 59
Hamilton, Norah, 102
Hanna, Mark, comment by, on Pullman strike, 160
Hardie, Keir, *167
Harding, Warren G., 76, 159, 207, 218
Harper, William Rainey, *140
Harper's Weekly, illustrations from, *17, *40, *43, *69, *145, *154
Hart, Harry, 153
Harvard University, 21, *22, 66, 209
Harvey, Edward, 207
Hatch Act of 1887, 22
Hauptmann, Gerhart, 97
Haworth, Eleanor Frothingham, 24, 27
Haymarket riot, 43, 53, 144, *145, 183
H-bomb test, first, *116
Henry Street Settlement, 179, 199, 200
  See also Wald, Lillian
Hicks, Elias, 14, *122
Hicksite Quakers, 14, 193
Hillman, Sidney, 153
Hitler, Adolf, 84
Hoover, Herbert, 87, 113, *207, 219
  Jane's vote for (1932), 81
  as President, 81, 207
  World War I work of, 74-75
  See also Food Administration
Horner, Governor Henry, epitaph for Jane by, 88
Howe, Julia Ward, 64
Howells, William Dean, 44
Hughes, Charles Evans, 82
Hull, Charles J., 45, 99
Hull, Mrs. Cordell, *87
Hull-House, *89, *99
  activities at, *61, 100-101, 138-139, 140-141, *163
  adult education, program of, 52
  aim of, 50
  amateur actor at, *52, *118
  art gallery for, 51
  art school for children at, *101, 102
  art show (1891), 42
  arts encouraged by, 61-62
  beneficiaries of, 102, 140
  bus company tours to, 86
  "a cathedral of humanity," 51-53
  charitable work by, 142
  Christmas at, 108, 172
  classes at, 141, 144
  clubs and services at, 100-105, 141-144
  cooking class at, 119, *143
  cooperation of, with public agencies, 142
  day nursery at, 143
  Depression times at, 82
  descriptions of, 48, 54, 78
  diet kitchen, 143
  Dolls Club at, *61
  effect of Jane's pacifism on, 77
  establishment of, 9, 137
  financial contributions to, 51
  first decade of, 98
  guests of, 52, 54
  gymnasium at, *118, 141
  human problems brought to, 50
  income of (1917-29), 77
  incorporation of, 51, 150
  influence of, 52
  as an information bureau, 142
  integration at, 48, 119
  kindergarten at, 142, 143
  Labor Museum at, *100, *185
  lectures at, 141
  local opinions of, 48
  music school at, 227
  Negroes welcome at, 63, 119-120
  neighborhood surrounding, 46-48, 58, *107, 137-138
  newspaper criticism of, 52
  Octagon Room of, 57-58
  open-air market near, *49
  opening of, 46, 48
  playground a project of, 52
  poem on, by Jane, 184-185
  principles governing, 49, 51
  radicalism charged against, 52
  reading class at, 18
  refurbished interior of, *100
  relationship of, with University of Chicago, 140
  residents of, 27, 35, 45, 50-51, 68, 138, 150, 155-156, 209
  restoration of, *89
  social life at, 140, 141
  tenth anniversary of, 55
  theater in, 52
  tourist guide's *faux pas* at, 86
  twentieth anniversary of, 62
  visitors to, 42, 60, 86, 142, 169, 187, 221, 227
  volunteers at, 50, 51, 102
  workers, 57
Hull-House Association
  ball game sponsored by, *120
  work of, 118, 120
Hull-House Maps and Papers, 101-102, 138
  excerpt from, 153-157
  Nineteenth Ward map prepared for, *102
Hull-House Players, 52
humanitarians, 39, 42, 52, 74, 81, 101, 116, 139, 143-144, 149-150, 197, 207, 212
Hunter, Robert, 55
Huxley, Thomas Henry, 147, *149, 216

Ickes, Harold, *229
Illinois, 9, 10, 11, 12, 15, 90, 123
Illinois Commission on Occupational Diseases, set up by Dr. Hamilton, 59
Illinois Equal Suffrage Association, 65
Illinois, University of
  Hull-House memorials at, 118
  restored Hull-House on campus of, *89
immigrant labor, *Judge* magazine cover, *109
immigrants, *47, 69
  American animosity toward, 215, 223, 225-226
  in Chicago, 46-48, 50, 98, 139-140
  in Hull-House area, 58, 137-138
  plight of, during Depression, 82
imperialism, Jane's opposition to, 68, 182
Infant Welfare Society nurses, *58, *180
"inner light," 14, 15, 28, 122
internationalism, 75, 84, 229
international peace. *See* Carnegie Endowment for; League of Nations; United Nations; World Court
International Suffrage Alliance, 69, 193
Interstate Oratorical Contest, 30
Ireland, *92, 129-132
Irving, Sir Henry, 132, *133
Irving, Washington, 15, *128
Isaak, Abraham, 59-60
Italy, *93

James, Henry, 34-35, 188
James, William, 110, *188
  a Hull-House lecturer, 52
  ideas of, on armed conflict, 66
  Jane described by, 49
Jane Club, the, 52
Japanese schoolgirls and officials, *114
Johns Hopkins University, 21-22, 32, 176
  George Haldeman a student at, 19, 38, 136
Johnson, Amanda, 51
Johnson, Hiram, 218, *219, 223
Judge cover on immigrant labor, *109
juvenile courts, 101, 177
juvenile crime, 184

Kelley, Florence, 51, 62, 86, 191
Kelley, Nicholas, 35
Kellogg, Frank, *226
Kenna, "Hinky-Dink," ball run by, 53
Kerensky, Premier Alexander, 194
Keyser, Mary, housekeeper at Hull-House, 46
King, William Lyon Mackenzie, 102, *150
King Lear, *158
  Jane's application of, to Pullman strike, 157-161
Kirby, Rollin, Prohibition cartoon by, 225
Kirkland, Wallace, 102, 105
Kirkland School, 29
Koht, Halvan, 81
Kollwitz, Kaethe
  etchings by, 37, 97
  poster sketch by, 113
Kropotkin, Prince Peter, *169
Ku Klux Klan, 78

Labor conditions (1900), 55
labor movement, 153-157, 160, 162, 168
La Follette, Robert, 176, *218-219, 223
  Jane's article on, 216-219
Lathrop, Julia, 51, 86, 87, 102, 136, *138, 176
League of Nations, 76, 138, 191, 204, 206, 211, 218-219, 223, 227, 229
  failure of, 212-215
League of Women Voters, 195, 197
Lincoln, Abraham, 10, 17, 48, 188-189, 218
  assassination of, 124

friendship of John Huy Addams and, 15-16
Lincoln family, *124
Lindsay, Vachel, tribute to Altgeld by, 183
Lindsey, Judge Ben, 102
Linn, James Weber
biographer and nephew of Jane, 12
comment by, on Jane's religious affiliations, 39
description of Anna Haldeman Addams by, 18-19
evaluation of Galsworthy by, 187
Jane's pride in, 83
reactions to Jane's death noted by, 88
Lippmann, Walter, 85-86
Lloyd, Henry D., 27, 52
Lloyd George, David, 66
Lochner, Louis, 201
Lodginghouse Act, 146
London, *36, *93, *135
Jane's reaction to, 36-37, 94, 133-136
slums of, *36, 41, *94, *95, 134-136
London Charity Organization Society, 41
Long, Huey, 220
Lowell, Lawrence, *115
Luther, Martin, *39

Macbeth, Jane's analysis of, 127-129
McCormick harvester plant, 43, 145
McCulloch, Catherine Waugh, suffragette, 63
MacDonald, Ramsay, 41
McDowell, Mary, 38, 195
at peace demonstration, *112
McKinley's assassination, 65, 169
anarchist scare following, 59-60, 169, 174
"Man of Peace," woodcut by Baskin, *212
"Man With the Muckrake," etching by Strang, *56
"Marching Weavers," etching by Kollwitz, *37
Marxists, Russian, Jane's attitude toward, 56
Masters, Edgar Lee, 161
Maude, Mr. and Mrs. Aylmer, 165, 166
Jane's letter on Tolstoy published by, 167-169
Mazzini, Giuseppe, *13, 157, 161, 211
Middle Hall, Rockford Seminary, *26
Mile End Road. *See* London, slums of
missionary in Ceylon, *24
"Monkey Trial," 215-216
Moore, Dorothea, Hull-House problems described by, 50
Moore, Thomas, 18, *130
Moral Equivalent of War (William James), 66
Morgan, J. P., 161
Morrill Act (1862), 22
Morris, William, 41
Motley, John Lothrop, *129
Mott, John R., 203
Mott, Lucretia, 62, 195
muckrakers, 56, 170
Muggeridge, Malcolm, 142
Municipal Order League, 141, 142
Mussolini, Benito, 84

NAACP. *See* National Association for the Advancement of Colored People
Nast, Thomas, cartoon of Carl Schurz by, 126
National American Women's Suffrage Association, 193, 197
National Association for the Advancement of Colored People (NAACP), 187, 190
Jane's part in founding of, 63-64, 119
National Conference of Social Work, 62
National Consumers League, 197
nationalism, 211, 212
Jane's ideas on, 67, 68, 75-76, 222-228
National Peace Party, 195
Negro cook, Hull-House union membership sought for, 57
Negroes, 48-49, 56, 83, 98, *179, 189-190, 224
citizenship rights of, 62, 63-64
Hull-House open to, 63, 119-120
Progressive party and, 187-188
and slavery, 120, 125, 127, 188-189, 224, 228
Negro revolt (1956), 64
Neighborhood Guild, 42
New Conscience and an Ancient Evil, A (Jane Addams), 75
New Deal, 82
Newer Ideals of Peace (Jane Addams), 68, 198
New York City, 9, *33, 70, 71, 74
Nightingale, Florence, 146
Nineteenth Amendment, 63, 193, 194, 195
Nineteenth Ward (Chicago) map, *102, 107
Nobel citation, Jane's, 81
Nobel Peace Prize (1931), 80, 115, 186, 220
nonresistance, 168-169, 221
nonviolence, 64, 66-67, 80, 221-222

Oglesby, Richard J., *125
"Old Abe," famous bald eagle, *16, 17
"Old Age Security," Jane's article on, 220
opium, Jane's Rockford experiment with, 127
Ordway, Edward, 182
Oscar II. See peace ship
Owen, Wilfred, quoted, 111

Pacifism, 198-206
Jane's belief in, 66-67, 68-71, 75, 77, 79, 110-112, 195, 197
Theodore Roosevelt's reaction to Jane's, 68-69
World War I attitudes toward, 73, 75
pacifists, 74, 196, 198, *199
Page, Walter Hines, 136, *137
Hoover praised by, 74
Palmer, Mrs. Potter, 38, *174
Pankhurst, Emmeline, 196
Paris Peace Conference, 207, 209
cartoon, *208
Pasquale, Eleanore, 102-*103, 105
peace, crusading for, 198-206
Peace and Bread in Time of War (Jane Addams), 75
quotes from, 199-201, 211-212
peace cartoon, *202
peace demonstration led by Jane and Mary McDowell, *112
peace movement, women's, Theodore Roosevelt's opposition to, 70
Peace Palace, 69, 171
peace ship, 71-72, *74, 201-203
cartoon of, *202
Peattie, Mrs. Elia W., Jane characterized by, 45, 82-83
Penn, William, 9, *224
article by Jane based on life of, 222-228
Penny Provident Fund Savings Bank, 142
Perkins, Frances, 82, 87
Philadelphia, 9, 14, 32, 224
Philippines, Jane's interest in, 68, 182
Plato Club, at Hull-House, 176
playgrounds, Jane's efforts to establish, 101
Poe, Edgar Allan, 128
Polly (Addams family nurse), 20
Pond, Allen, 45
Poverty (Robert Hunter), quote from, 55
Powers, John, 52, 169-175, *173
pragmatism, Jane's belief in, 22, 49, 58, 188
prejudice, discussion of, by Jane, 188-190
Progressive party, 63
Jane's support of, 64, 65, 185-190, 216-219
and the Negro, 187-188
See also Roosevelt, Theodore
Prohibition, 84-*85, 225
Prohibition cartoon by Kirby, *225
Public School Art Society, 29
Pullman, George, 53, 158, 159, *160
Pullman strike, 53, *108, 127, 158-161, 183

Quaker beliefs, 62, 122
See also Hicksite Quakers; "inner light"
Quaker meeting, *14
Quakers, Indiana, *8

Racial bigotry, Hull-House episode concerning, 57
racial problem, discussion of, by Jane, 188-190
Rankin, Jeannette, *197
Reconstruction Finance Corporation, 81
reform movement, 55, 107-109
British, 146
Repplier, Agnes, *204
Jane criticized by, 75, 204
Rockefeller, John D., 52, 140, 198
Rockford College, 32
assistance to Hull-House by, 140, 141
Prohibition address by Jane at, quoted, 84-85
Rockford Female Seminary, 21, 22-30, 38
Addams girls' attendance at, 19
Jane a student at, 28, 63, 91, 127
Jane's graduation from, 30, 92
Roosevelt, Eleanor, *87
Jane admired by, 82, 84, 87
Roosevelt, Franklin Delano, 220
campaigning (1932), *84
criticism of, by Jeannette Rankin, 197
election of (1932), 81
inauguration of (1933), 81, 82
qualities shared by Jane and, 86-87
Roosevelt, Theodore, 62, *186, 187, 223
cartoon of, *69
Jane's political support of, 65, 69, 185-187, 188
Jane's visit to, 38
muckrakers named by, 56
reaction of, to Jane's pacifism, 68-69
women's peace movement opposed by, 70
Rosenwald, Julius, *175
Ross, Edward A., 56
Royden, Maude, *196
comments by, on Jane, 62, 77-78
Ruskin, John, *28, 30, 41, 136, 221
Russia
revolution in, 215
role of, in World War I, 194
suffragettes' message to, *194
Russians, famished, *113

Sacco-Vanzetti case, 115, 215
montage by Shahn on, *114-*115
sentence, telegram by Jane urging clemency, *217
"Sacredness of Human Life, The," WILPF resolution on, 116
Salisbury, Rollin, marriage proposal of, rejected by Jane, 27-28
Sayre, Francis B., *226
School and Society, The (John Dewey), 61, 177
Schumann-Heink, Ernestine, *227
Schurz, Carl, cartoon of, by Thomas Nast, *126
Schwimmer, Rosika, 71, *201, 203
role of, in Ford peace ship, 200
Scopes, John, *215
Scotland, quotes from Jane's notebook on visit to, 132-133
Scott, Walter, 132, 133, *134
sculptor, youthful Hull-House, *61
Second Twenty Years at Hull-House, The (Jane Addams), 79
excerpts from, 190-192, 195
Sedgwick, Ellery, 204
segregation, 63, *119, 189-190
Jane's attitude toward, 49, 120
Seneca, *96
settlement
definition of, 41, 152
first American, 42
ideal, Jane's view of, 152-153, 157
settlement houses
criticism of, 59
reason for, 51, 139, 150-151
See also Chicago Commons; Chicago, University of; Henry Street Settlement; Neighborhood Guild; Toynbee Hall
sewing trades. *See* garment workers
Shaftesbury, Earl of, *146
Shahn, Ben
Prohibition painting by, 85
Sacco-Vanzetti montage by, 114-115
Shakespeare, William, 16, 18, 127-129, 133, 157-161
Shaw, Anna, 193
Shaw, George Bernard, 41, 135, *164
Sill, Anna P., 23, 24, 27
Sill Hall, Rockford Seminary, *91
Silver Purchase Act, 161
Sin and Society (Edward A. Ross), quote from, 56
slavery, 12, 120, 125, 127
slums
Chicago, 42, 43, 46, 48, 82, *106, 107, *139
London, *36, 41, *94, *95
Smith, Mary Rozet, 27, 51, *101
death of, 86
Jane's companion on round-the-world trip, 77, 190, 214
Jane's companion on visit to Tolstoy, 54, 165, 166, 168
Jane's friendship with, 27, 85
Smith College, 21, 64
Social Darwinism, 26, 45
Socialist movement, 55-56
Socialist party, 29, 76
social justice movements, encouragement of, 37
social reforms, Jane's battles for various, 108
Social Security Act, 220
social work, speeches by Jane on reasons for, 136–152
See also National Conference of Social Work
Spencer, Herbert, 26, *29, 66, 128
"Spiderweb Chart," 78, *205
Spirit of Youth and the City Streets, The (Jane Addams), 61
Stalin, Joseph, 84, 176
Stang, Professor, 81
Stanton, Elizabeth Cady, 62, 193, 195
Starr, Ellen Gates, 45, 51
co-founder of Hull-House with Jane, 25, 29, 40
comment by, on Jane's optimism, 57
conversion of, to Catholicism, 29
Jane's second trip to Europe with, 39-40
Jane's theological discussions with, 28
letters to, from Jane, 32, 39, 136
Socialist party membership of, 29
tea served by, at Hull-House, *50
Stead, William T., 43, 68
Steffens, Lincoln, 43, *170
stock market collapse (1929), 79
Strang, William, etching by, 56
suffrage, woman, 24, 27, 62, 63, 108, 167, 192-197
suffrage cartoon, *192
suffrage parade
Jane a participant in, *109
led by Carrie Chapman Catt, *63
suffragettes, Boston, 65
White House picket, *194
Sumner, William Graham, 26, 45
"survival of the fittest," 26, 42, 45, 128
Swope, Gerard, 102

Taft, William Howard, 65, 204, 221
Tarbell, Ida M., *198
Tarkington, Booth, 227
Taylor, Graham, 27
accusations against, 59
Jane characterized by, 45
Jane's political activities criticized by, 65
Teachers' Federation, dispute of, with Chicago school board, 60
Terry, Ellen, *132, 133
Theory of the Leisure Class, The (Thorstein Veblen), quote from, 55
Thoreau, Henry David, 77, 80
Titanic, Jane's reaction to sinking of, 68
Tolstoy, Count Leo, 57, 149, *166, 198
comment by, on *King Lear*, 158
Jane's meeting with, 53-54, 165-169
quoted by Jane on urban life, 164-165
"Tolstoy and Gandhi," article by Jane, 221-222
Townsend, Francis, 220
Toynbee, Arnold, 41, 96
Jane's speech on, 150
Toynbee Hall, 41, *96, 207
Jane inspired by, 97
Jane's visit to, 42
Triumphant Democracy (Andrew Carnegie), 56
Tuchman, Barbara, 66
Twain, Mark, 20, 34, 188
Twenty Years at Hull-House (Jane Addams), 64
excerpts from, 122-124, 134-136
Tyler, Alice Kellogg, portrait of Mary Rozet Smith by, 101
typhoid, in Chicago, 59, 98

Ulm Cathedral, *96, 97
Jane inspired by, 39-40, 52
Union Against Militarism, 200
Jane's interest in, 69
unions
article by Jane on, 161-164
bigotry in, 57
at Hull-House, 57, 155
Jane's backing of, 154
United Nations, 116, 190, 212
United States. *See* Children's Bureau; Food Administration
University Settlement Association, 41
urban problems, Jane's ideas on, 80-81, 164-165

Van Vorst, Bessie and Marie, wage scale (1900) reported by, 55
Veblen, Thorstein, *141
on American wealth, 55
Versailles Treaty, 75, 112, 211
Victoria, Queen, 33, *34, 133
Vietnam, wounded Americans in, *117
Visiting Nurses' Association, 142
worker of, *179

Wace, Dean Henry, 216
wages, laborers' (1900), 55
Wald, Lillian, 62, 65, 199, *200
letter to, from Jane, *228
See also Henry Street Settlement
Walpole, Sir Robert, 150
Walsh, John J., 59
Ward, Lester, 45
ward boss. *See* Powers, John
Washington, Booker T., 22, *189, 190, 198
Jane's comment to, on "suffrage," 62
Washington, George, Jane's admiration of, 125-127
Watterson, Henry, 189
Waugh, Catherine. *See* McCulloch, Catherine Waugh
Weavers, The (Gerhart Hauptmann), 97
Webb, Beatrice
comment on, by Muggeridge, 142
Jane and Hull-House characterized by, 54
Webb, Sidney, *142
Weber, Colonel George, 9
Weber, Sarah. *See* Addams, Sarah Weber
welfare money, spending of, 183-184
welfare worker, 179, 180-183
Weybright, Victor, Jane and Hull-House described by, 78
White, William Allen, 223
Wilberforce, Bishop Samuel, Huxley's debate with, 149, 216
WILPF. *See* Women's International League for Peace and Freedom
Wilson, Edmund, 83
on Chicago slums, 82
Wilson, Harold, 41
Wilson, Woodrow, 21, 65, 70, 76, 137, 188, *191, 194, 201, 203, 204-206, 208, 209, 211, 212, 218, 229
Fourteen Points of, 76, 204
letter to Jane from, *191
reelection campaign truck of (1916), *71
Wisconsin Idea, The, 217, 219
Wisconsin, University of, 68
woman suffrage. *See* suffrage
Woman Who Toils, The, (Marie and Bessie Van Vorst), 55
Woman's Club, Hull-House, 51
Women's International League congress, Jane's address to, 78
Women's International League for Peace and Freedom (WILPF), 75, 77, 87-88, 112, 116, 196, 201, 203, 207, *213, 226, 228
disarmament favored by, 116
fourth international congress of, *213
Jane the founder and president of, 78, 112

Jane's Nobel Prize money given to, 81, 115
Marian Anderson and, 116
Maude Royden a member of, 196
resolution by, on killing, 116
twentieth anniversary of, 87-88
Women's Peace Party, 69, *70, *110, *111, 200, 201
women's rights, Jane's belief in, 62-63
See also suffrage
Wood, Grant, satirization of DAR by, 112
workers, Europe's ill-treated, *37
Working People's Social Science Club, 144-145
World Court, 76, 223, 229
Jane's belief in, 81
World War I, 66, 67, 69, 70, 71-75, 80, *111, 176, 190, 198-199, 206, 215
description of, by Jane, 198-200
Jane's activities during, 66-75, 110

Yale University confers degree on Jane, 64
Yasnaya Polyana, 54, 165
See also Tolstoy
young people, problems of, 146-148

Zero, Mr., at Ford peace ship, 72
"Zulu car," immigrants traveling by, *47
Zurich Congress, 209

PICTURE CREDITS

The sources for the illustrations are listed below. Some have been abbreviated as follows: Acme—*Acme Photo;* AP—*Associated Press;* BA—*Bettmann Archive;* Bachrach—*Bachrach Photographers;* BB—*Brown Brothers;* CHS—*Chicago Historical Society;* CP—*Culver Pictures;* Harris—*Harris & Ewing;* Hoover—*Hoover Library on War, Revolution, and Peace;* Illinois—*University of Illinois;* INP—*International News Photo;* Keystone—*Keystone View Co., Inc.;* Kirkland—*Wallace Kirkland;* Life—*Life Picture Collection;* MCNY—*Museum of the City of New York;* N-YHS—*New-York Historical Society;* NYPL—*New York Public Library;* Rockford—*Rockford College;* Swarthmore—*Swarthmore College Peace Collection;* WW—*Wide World Photo.*

The drawings on page 230 are by Bette J. Davis. Photographers are credited after source and —.

Cover: Rockford—Kirkland. 2 Jane Addams Peace Association, drawing by Violet Oakley. 4-5 (left to right) Rockford—Kirkland; Robert Crandall Associates for Life; Swarthmore—Frank Lerner.

BIOGRAPHY: 7 Rockford—Kirkland, painting by Lydia Purdy Hess Lowry. 8, 11 CHS. 13 Museo del Risorgimento, Turin, Italy—David Lees. 14 Friends Historical Collection, Haverford College—Alfred Eisenstaedt. 15 Illinois—Kirkland. 16 State Historical Society of Wisconsin. 17 NYPL. 19 Illinois—Kirkland. 20 Life. 22 Harvard University—Gary Gladstone. 24, 25 CP. 26 CHS. 28-29 (left to right) Pictures, Inc.; CP; Pictures, Inc.; The March of Time Ltd. (2). 30 (both) Kirkland. 32 WW. 33 John Jay Pierrepont. 34 James Reid. 36 (top) Mark Kauffman; (bottom) Radio Times. 37 Galerie St. Etienne, New York—Frank Lerner. 39 Staatsbibliothek, Berlin. 40 CP. 42 Kirkland. 43 CHS. 44 CP. 46 Brooklyn Museum Collection. 47 CP. 49 CHS. 50, 52, Kirkland. 53, 56 NYPL. 58 (left) National Child Labor Committee—Lewis W. Hine; (right) CHS. 61 (all) Kirkland. 63 WW. 64 BB. 67 W. and D. Downey, London, courtesy of Mr. Albert W. Kerr. 69 NYPL. 70 BB. 71 INP. 73 WW. 74 European Picture Service—Paul Thompson. 76 INP. 77 Kirkland. 80 AP. 83 Acme. 84 Press Association, Inc. 85 MCNY. 87 WW. 88 Kirkland.

PICTURE PORTFOLIO: 89, 90, 91 Kirkland. 92-93 (top left) B. Seed; (top right) Larry Burrows for Life; (lower left) William Sumits for Life; (lower right) Eliot Elisofon for Life. 94 (both) Radio Times. 95 Pictures, Inc. 96 (top and lower left) Dmitri Kessel for Life; (lower right) London Borough of Tower Hamlets, London. 97 Galerie St. Etienne, New York—Frank Lerner. 98-99 (top left and right) CHS; (lower left) CHS—Arthur Siegel; (lower right) Illinois—Kirkland. 100-101 Illinois—Kirkland. 102 NYPL. 103 Kirkland. 104 Robert Crandall Associates for Life, painting by Alton S. Tobey. 105 Kirkland. 106 Los Angeles County Museum of Art—J. R. Eyerman. 107 CHS. 108-109 (left and lower right) CHS; (top right) CP. 110-111 (top) European Picture Service; (lower left) Musée des Deux Guerres Mondiales, Vincennes, Université de Paris, painting by Henri de Groux, courtesy of American Heritage Publishing Co., Inc.; (lower right) Smithsonian Institution—Henry Beville, sketch by George Harding. 112-113 (top left) Edwin and Virginia Irwin Memorial, Cincinnati Art Museum—F. Bourges for Life; (top right) Galerie St. Etienne, New York; (lower left) Illinois—Kirkland; (lower right) Hoover—H. Baskerville for Life, painting by Ivan Wladimiroff. 114-115 (top left) Swarthmore—Frank Lerner; (lower left) Ben Shahn—Eric Schaal; (lower right) Illinois—Kirkland. 116-117 (top left) U.S. Air Force; (top right) Bill Ray for Life; (lower right) Larry Burrows for Life. 118-119 (left) Bill Eppridge for Life; (top right) Gordon Parks for Life; (lower right) Hull-House Association, Moore Services, Inc., Chicago—Arthur Siegel. 120 Hull-House Association, Moore Services, Inc.—Chicago Photographers.

HER OWN WORDS: 121 Swarthmore—Frank Lerner. 122 CP. 123 (both) Kirkland. 124 N-YHS. 125, 126, 127 NYPL. 128 (top) N-YHS; (bottom) Swarthmore—Frank Lerner. 129 BB. 130 NYPL. 131 CP. 132, 133 The March of Time Ltd., London. 134 (top) Life; (bottom) NYPL. 135 Radio Times. 136 Illinois. 137 Life. 138 Kirkland. 139 CHS. 140 University of Chicago. 141 Keystone. 142 Barrett's Photo Press Ltd., London. 143 Illinois—Kirkland. 145 Library of Congress. 146 Pix Inc. 147 Larry Burrows for Life. 149 BA. 150 Life. 151 Kirkland. 153 CHS. 154 NYPL. 155 George Eastman House, Rochester—Lewis Hine. 158 NYPL. 159 CP. 160, 161 BA. 163 (both) Kirkland. 164 INP. 165 CP. 166 BB. 167 Lafayette Ltd., London. 168 Illinois. 169 Life. 170 WW. 171 Pach Brothers. 172 Swarthmore—Frank Lerner. 173 CHS. 174 Chicago *American.* 175 Harris. 176 CP. 177 BB. 179, 180 CHS. 182 Ordway Papers, Manuscript Division, NYPL. 183 CHS. 185 Kirkland. 186 Keystone. 187 Acme. 188 Life. 189 Harris. 190 Pix Inc. 191 (top) Bachrach; (bottom) Swarthmore—Frank Lerner. 192 Life. 193 BA. 194 INP. 195 The New York *Times* Studio. 196 Acme. 197 INP. 198 Keystone. 199 Harris. 200 (top) Pix Inc.; (bottom) Lillian Wald Papers, Manuscript Division, NYPL. 201 WW. 202 NYPL. 203 Women's International League for Peace and Freedom. 204 Life. 205 Courtesy of The Cosmos Press Inc. 206 (top) Museum of Fine Arts, Boston; (bottom) Elizabeth Timberman for Life. 207 Hoover. 208 Life. 209 Bachrach. 212 Brooklyn Museum Collection. 213 Swarthmore—Frank Lerner. 214 Illinois. 215 (top) INP; (bottom) WW. 217 Swarthmore—Frank Lerner. 218, 219 Harris. 220 Kosti Ruohomaa for Life. 221 Globe Photos. 222 Margaret Bourke-White. 223 BB. 224. NYPL. 225 BA. 226 (top) Harris; (middle) WW; (bottom) Acme. 227 WW. 228 Lillian Wald Papers, Manuscript Division, NYPL. 229 WW.

1 2 3 4 5 6 7 8 9 10 11 12 13 14 15—U—72 71 70 69 68